National Economic Impact Analysis of Terrorist Attacks and Natural Disasters

National Economic Impact Analysis of Terrorist Attacks and Natural Disasters

Edited by

Harry W. Richardson

Honorary Doctorate, Universidad Autonoma del Estado de Mexico (UAEM), Mexico

JiYoung Park

Associate Professor, University of Buffalo, USA and Associate Professor, Sungkyunkwan University, Korea

James E. Moore II

Professor, University of Southern California, USA

Qisheng Pan

Professor, Texas Southern University, USA

Edward Elgar

Cheltenham, UK • Northampton, MA, USA

Published by
Edward Elgar Publishing Limited
The Lypiatts
15 Lansdown Road
Cheltenham
Glos GL50 2JA
UK

Edward Elgar Publishing, Inc.
William Pratt House
9 Dewey Court
Northampton
Massachusetts 01060
USA

A catalogue record for this book
is available from the British Library

Library of Congress Control Number: 2014947031

This book is available electronically in the ElgarOnline.com Social and Political Science Subject Collection, E-ISBN 978 1 78347 586 5

MIX
Paper from
responsible sources
FSC® C013056

ISBN 978 1 78347 585 8

Typeset by Servis Filmsetting Ltd, Stockport, Cheshire
Printed and bound in Great Britain by T.J. International Ltd, Padstow

In Memory of Wassily Leontief and Walter Isard

Contents

Contributors

Joongkoo Cho, Research Analyst, Division of Land Use and Environmental Planning, Southern California Association of Governments, Los Angeles, CA, USA.

Peter Gordon, Emeritus Professor, Price School of Public Policy, University of Southern California, Los Angeles, CA, USA.

Bumsoo Lee, Associate Professor of Urban and Regional Planning, University of Illinois, Urbana–Champaign, IL, USA.

James E. Moore II, Professor of Systems and Design Engineering and Vice-Dean of Academic Affairs, Viterbi School of Engineering, University of Southern California, Los Angeles, CA, USA.

Qisheng Pan, Professor and Chair of the Department of Urban Planning and Environmental Development, Texas Southern University, Houston, TX, USA.

ChangKeun Park, PhD in Agricultural and Applied Economics, University of Georgia, Athens, GA, USA.

JiYoung Park, Associate Professor, University of Buffalo, NY, USA and Sungkyunkwan University, Seoul, Korea.

Harry W. Richardson, Honorary Doctorate, Autonomous University of the State of Mexico, Toluca, Mexico and formerly the James Irvine Chair of Urban and Regional Planning, University of Southern California, Los Angeles, CA, USA.

Minsu Son, BK Assistant Professor, Seoul National University, Seoul, Korea.

1. Introduction

Harry W. Richardson and JiYoung Park

The National Interstate Economic Model (NIEMO) used in this book was developed less than a decade ago but built upon a longer heritage of trying to implement a Multi-Regional Input-Output (MRIO) model. This book is dedicated to the memory of Wassily Leontief and Walter Isard who laid out what appeared to be an impossible but intriguing dream. Because of vastly improved databases and an amazing expansion of computer capacity, we believe that we have come close to recognizing their vision. Of course, conceptually we could go further. Rather than NIEMO's 47 sectors x 52 regions, we could proceed to try and model 500+ sectors and 3,000 counties. This is nice to talk about, but of course impossible to do. The matrix would have 2.25 trillion cells, and even with ideal data structures in place would take years for one run. Also, there are no trade flow data at the county level, although the IMPLAN Group is experimenting with the idea. We rely on the Commodity Flow Survey for interstate flows (ORNL, 2000). In other words, our view is that we have achieved the maximum degree of spatial disaggregation available at this time. A next step might be to create a national metropolitan area model involving about 350 metropolitan areas rather than 3,000 counties, but even this step lies in the future.

In addition, we are not going to present an overview of input-output analysis; the second edition of Miller and Blair (2009) gives you everything that you need to know. A book by one of the editors (Richardson, 1972), written over 40 years ago, spells out the spatial disaggregation and remains relatively up to date. Our approach is standard input-output analysis: direct impacts (that is, final demand), indirect impacts (that is, backward linkages) and induced impacts (that is, secondary consumption effects). However, most of our NIEMO studies exclude induced impacts on the grounds that services rarely cross state borders: the one major exception is the Gulf oil spill described in Chapter 9, where intrastate-induced impacts were important and there were also important induced effects among states because of seafood supply substitutions. The major contribution of this book, in our opinion, is the high level of spatial disaggregation.

There are four editors of this book. Richardson, Gordon and Moore have been here from the beginning (Gordon played a major role in the design, interpretation and explanation of almost all the research studies, as mentioned in the individual chapters but declined to be a co-editor). Pan and Park, initially PhD research assistants but now well-established tenured professors, are the technical experts capable of dealing with multi-million cell matrices.

The NIEMO model is described in Chapter 2. Non-technical readers will find the case studies comprehensible and do not need to analyse Chapter 2 in great detail if they are willing to take a leap of faith and trust that the models have sufficient validity.

The early chapters in the book (Chapters 3–6) are about terrorism, typically simulations of exogenous attacks to estimate the business interruption effects. These are much easier to analyse than a real life event, when the shock and endogenous forces become entangled. For example, consider 9/11, which is not in this book (although some of the consequences of an airplane attack are discussed in Chapter 5). How do you separate out the shock from a mild recession that was going on at the time? The recovery was relatively strong and quick, but we do not have a sufficiently spatial disaggregated model of New York and New Jersey to unravel the direct and indirect effects.

Chapters 7 and 8 (which deal with international border closures, as the result of a global pandemic, and foot-and-mouth disease) could be about either terrorist attacks or natural disasters, more likely but not necessarily the latter.

The next chapters of the book (Chapters 9–12) focus on natural disasters (hurricanes, the Gulf oil spill and tornadoes), all of them real ones. This complicates the estimation of direct impacts because of the commingling of exogenous shocks and endogenous events. However, like many counter-terrorist researchers, we began as specialists in natural disasters, and we have grappled with this problem over the years.

Two chapters in the book (Chapters 5 and 6) deal with two non-spatial applications: a man-portable air-defense systems (MANPADS) attack against the US airline fleet and a hypothetical attack on a baseball stadium. Although these chapters are somewhat outside an application of the main model of the book, they illustrate the point that some important policy issues can be analysed non-spatially. The baseball stadium study was in response to a request from the Department of Homeland Security, but it could easily have been an attack on the Los Angeles Coliseum during a University of Southern California football game with a capacity crowd occasionally larger than 100,000; we did not have time to analyse that. As for the major airlines, they have offices and facilities in many cities in addition to their hubs, so apportioning the direct impacts by state is very difficult, perhaps impossible.

Two penultimate chapters (Chapter 13 on the West Coast ports shutdown of 2002 and Chapter 14 on the extension of the Panama Canal planned for 2015) fall outside the focus of terrorist attacks and natural disasters that dominate the book. However, they are included because their economic impacts are so easily analysed by NIEMO. They illustrate that the model's applications can be so much wider than their terrorism and natural disaster scope. Of course, both are man-made events but neither can be defined as disasters even though some but not all of their economic impacts are negative. In particular, the extension of the Panama Canal is not a zero-sum game.

As our dedication implies, Wassily Leontief and Walter Isard have been inspirational in our research for decades. However, there have been several others who have been influential, and directly helpful. A few of their names include Ben Stevens, Leon Moses, Geoff Hewings, Bill Miernyk, Charlie Tiebout, Bill Beyers, Ron Miller, Karen Polenske, Jean Paelinck, Michael Lahr, Randy Jackson and Jan Oosterhaven.

REFERENCES

Miller, R.E. and P.D. Blair (2009), *Input-Output Analysis: Foundations and Extensions*, 2nd edn. Englewood Cliffs, NJ: Prentice Hall.

ORNL (Oak Ridge National Laboratory) (2000), *Freight USA: Highlights from the 1997 Commodity Flow Survey and Other Sources*. Washington, DC: Bureau of Transportation Statistics, US Department of Transportation.

Richardson, H.W. (1972), *Input-Output and Regional Economics*. London: Weidenfeld and Nicolson.

2. National Interstate Economic Model (NIEMO)

JiYoung Park and Harry W. Richardson

2.1 BACKGROUND TO MULTIREGIONAL IO CONSTRUCTION

Many economists and planners are interested in evaluating the socioeconomic impacts of various disruptions. Occasionally, they use geographically detailed input-output (IO) models. Isard demonstrated as early as 1951 that traditional (national) IO models are inadequate because they cannot capture the effects of linkages and interactions among regions. To examine the full (short-term) impacts of unexpected events, such as terrorist attacks or natural disasters on the US economy, the economic links among states should be considered. Multiregional input-output models (MRIOs) include interregional trade tables and avoid some of the problems associated with excessive aggregation. Building an operational MRIO for all the states of the United States, however, requires highly detailed interstate shipments data.

Although Chenery (1953) and Moses (1955) had formulated relatively simplified MRIO frameworks in response to the earlier discussions by Isard (1951), data problems persisted and have stymied most applications. The non-existence or rarity of useful interregional trade data is the most problematic issue. Intraregional and interregional data must be comparable and compatible, yet the currently available shipments data between states are only sporadically available and difficult to use.

It is not surprising, then, that few MRIO models have been constructed or widely used in the United States. The best known are the 1963 US data sets for 51 regions and 79 sectors published in Polenske (1980) and the 1977 US data sets for 51 regions and 120 sectors released by Jack Faucett Associates (1983), then updated by various Boston College researchers and reported in 1988 (Miller and Shao, 1990).

More recently, there have been some attempts to estimate interregional trade flows using Commodity Flow Survey (CFS) data (Jackson et al., 2006; Liu and Vilain, 2004; Park et al., 2009; USDOT, Federal Highways

Admistration, 2002). The US Commodity Transportation Survey Data on inter-regional trade flows have been available since 1977 but reporting was discontinued for some years. For the years since 1993, this data deficit can be met to some extent with the recent (CFS) data from the Bureau of Transportation Statistics (BTS), but these data are incomplete with respect to interstate flows. Based on the currently available CFS data, Jackson et al. (2006) used IMPLAN data (from the Minnesota IMPLAN Group) to adjust the incomplete CFS reports by adopting gravity models constrained via distance and by making other adjustments. Along similar lines and using the same basic data sources, we elaborate Park et al. (2009), who suggested a different estimation approach that relied on an adjusted flow model (AFM) and a doubly constrained Fratar model (DFM). To proceed in this way, it was first necessary to create conversion tables to reconcile the CFS and IMPLAN sectors. The detailed procedure bridging the CFS and IMPLAN sectors are explained in the study of Park et al. (2009).

This chapter focuses on four versions of a National Interstate Economic Model (NIEMO): NIEMO itself, which is a standard but operational multiregional input-output model (MRIO); TransNIEMO, which adds on a national highway network to handle interregional freight flows; FlexNIEMO, which constructs a supply-side MRIO that permits relaxation of the fixed production coefficients assumption; and a version that analyses both intrastate and interstate induced impacts.

NIEMO revives an approach adopted in the late 1970s and the early 1980s (Jack Faucett Associates, 1983; Polenske, 1980), the development of a MRIO. We combine state-level data from the IMPLAN IO models with the estimated interregional trade flows based on the CFS using an approach developed in Park et al. (2009). NIEMO is aggregated to 47 economic sectors over 52 regions (50 States, Washington, DC and the Rest of the world). This results in a MRIO matrix with almost 6 million cells. Construction of the model involves substantial data assembly and considerable data manipulation.

NIEMO is a MRIO that is fully operational. The idea for such a model has a long history stretching back to Isard's suggestion of the 'ideal interregional model' (Isard, 1951, 1960) and Leontief's valiant but failed attempt to operationalize a variant of the model in the 1960s. The importance of sub-national models has long been recognized. Aggregation accounts for the loss of information, especially when positive effects in one area cancel negative impacts in another. It is also clear that most politicians have a keen interest in local constituencies. To say that NIEMO has succeeded where Leontief failed is not an immodest statement, but rather a reflection of the improvements in databases and computing capacity over the past

30 years. However, building bridges among the various data sources have been a substantial task.

NIEMO is not an exact replica of the original design as conceived by Isard and Leontief. Rather, NIEMO rests on the successful integration of state-level IO information with data from the CFS. The NIEMO approach is valuable because it uses only secondary data sources yet represents an innovative regional science procedure. Since 1993 the CFS has been the largest single nationwide data source for freight movement flows. The BTS and the Census Bureau collect CFS data from a sample survey of industries through the Economic Census. Although the CFS provides a wide range of commodity shipments and multimodal movement data with five-year cycle updates, some user groups have not been satisfied with its content details (USDOT, RITA and BTS, 2005). The most commonly addressed weaknesses of the CFS are its incomplete coverage by commodity sectors and regional detail, and its inability to fully capture imports and exports (Giuliano et al., 2010; Park et al., 2009; Southworth and Peterson, 2000, 2005). ORNL (2000) showed that the CFS estimates cover less than 75 percent of all the freight tons moved annually in the United States, because the survey drops many establishments classified as farms, forestry, fisheries, construction, transportation, governments, foreign establishments, services and most retail activities.

Nevertheless, Park et al. (2009) managed to estimate interstate trade flows, applying an AFM and a DFM. The systematic approach relies on 1997 CFS and 2001 IMPLAN data, but it could be updated. To reconcile different definitions and classifications of the commodities among multiple data sources, we created a new commodity sector scheme of 47 sectors (29 commodity, 18 service), referred to as the USC sectors. Several applications of the initial version of NIEMO (excluding interstate services trade) show that the state-to-state trade flows and the flows between the states and the rest of world for the 29 USC commodity sectors are all readily computable.

We use NIEMO to estimate total economic impacts including indirect impacts. As the case studies show, we have developed and applied NIEMO to estimate the impacts of various natural and man-made disasters. While many types of economic approaches including benefit-cost analysis, single-region IO modeling, social accounting models, partial equilibrium models, and computable general equilibrium (CGE) models, are available for estimating economic impacts (Rich et al., 2005a; Rich et al., 2005b), none of these tools provide national economic impacts at the level of individual states. For example, our studies, estimating the indirect and induced effects of impacts associated with capacity losses at the twin ports of Los Angeles-Long Beach (see Chapter 13), showed that two-thirds of the impacts leaked outside the Southern California region. Without an interstate model such as NIEMO, we would have had no idea where these leakage effects might occur.

While a mathematical method to estimate interregional trade flows by Canning and Wang (2005) permits an empirical performance test, our foundation of estimating interregional trade flows is an approach based on secondary data sources. It uses CFS and IMPLAN, but adopts a different approach to estimating missing CFS data, a DFM to update the MRIO matrix to a base year.

Constructing NIEMO requires two basic kinds of tables: industrial trade coefficients tables and regional interindustry coefficients tables. While trade tables by industry are difficult to construct because of incomplete information in the CFS data, the interindustry tables present fewer problems because reliable data are available from IMPLAN at the state and industry levels. For details of the procedure used to estimate values for the empty cells in the trade flow matrix, see Park et al. (2009). Once initial trade flow matrices are estimated for sectors based on a reconciliation of CFS and IMPLAN data, these can then be iteratively refined via a Fratar model. However, the conventional Fratar model cannot estimate the diagonal (intrastate flow) values, so NIEMO incorporates a DFM to supplement the off-diagonal flow estimates from the standard Fratar model, providing consistent estimates for both on- and off-diagonal values.

Usually, IO models measure the direct (final demand), indirect (intermediate input flows) and induced (secondary consumption associated with direct and indirect employment) effects of changes in economic activity. In applying NIEMO we chose, in most cases, to measure the direct and indirect impacts only, for two reasons. First, it is a convention in MRIO to ignore induced effects (Miller and Blair, 1985), presumably because induced consumption is less likely to cross interregional, for example, interstate, boundaries (see Chapter 10 for a deviation from this position). Second, although there are local induced impacts associated with local indirect effects, the local and the imported indirect impacts are typically allocated in a MRIO model via some assumption that falls short of the accurate allocations of the 'ideal' interregional IO model (Isard, 1951). For example, imported inputs of an origin sector are allocated to a particular destination sector in the same proportion as local inputs.

In pursuing our research goals, the choice of approaches involved difficult trade-offs. The use of linear economic models is justified by various factors, including the richness of the detailed results made possible at relatively low cost; NIEMO, for example, has approximately 6 million multipliers. The principal insight that drives our research is that, with some effort, it is possible to integrate data from IMPLAN's state-level

IO models with the CFS data and other sources for all individual States, making it possible to build an operational MRIO model.

The drive behind the development of NIEMO was two-fold: to assess the interstate impacts of events analysed with our regional model (Richardson et al., 2015); and to allow us to extend the range of problems that may be studied at the interstate level.

2.2   BUILDING NIEMO

The CFS on interregional trade flows have been available since 1977 but reporting was discontinued for some years. For the years since 1993, this data deficit can be met to some extent with the recent (CFS) data from the BTS, but these data are incomplete with respect to interstate flows. A key step was to create conversion tables to reconcile the CFS and IMPLAN sectors.

The primary requirements for building an interstate model for the United States of the Chenery-Moses type are two sets of data, regional coefficients tables and trade coefficients tables (Miller and Blair, 1985). Models of this type can be used to estimate interstate industrial effects as well as interindustry impacts on each state, based mainly on the two data sources: regional IO tables that provide intraregional industry coefficients for each state and interregional trade tables to provide comparable trade coefficients. This implies the creation of three types of matrices: an intraregional interindustry matrix; the interregional trade matrix; and the combined interregional, interindustry matrix (in other words, the NIEMO matrix). Before creating the matrices, however, the data reconciliation problem has to be addressed.

The main steps involved in building and testing NIEMO are shown in Figure 2.1. We developed the 47 USC sectors into which many of the other classification systems can be converted. Figure 2.2 shows the industrial code conversion matrix among the many data sources used in this study.

The detailed conversion processes occasionally involved case-by-case reconciliations. Inevitably, some conversions involved mapping one sector into more than one. The light-gray cells of Figure 2.2 represent one-to-one allocations. The dark-gray cells denote bridge allocations with plausible weights specified on a case-by-case basis.

A major problem in developing an interstate interindustrial model stems from the fact that it is difficult to obtain data describing trade flows among states in the United States. Since 1993, however, CFS data have been used, in spite of the fact that there are still problems such as high sampling variability and disclosure rules limiting the use of individual company data.

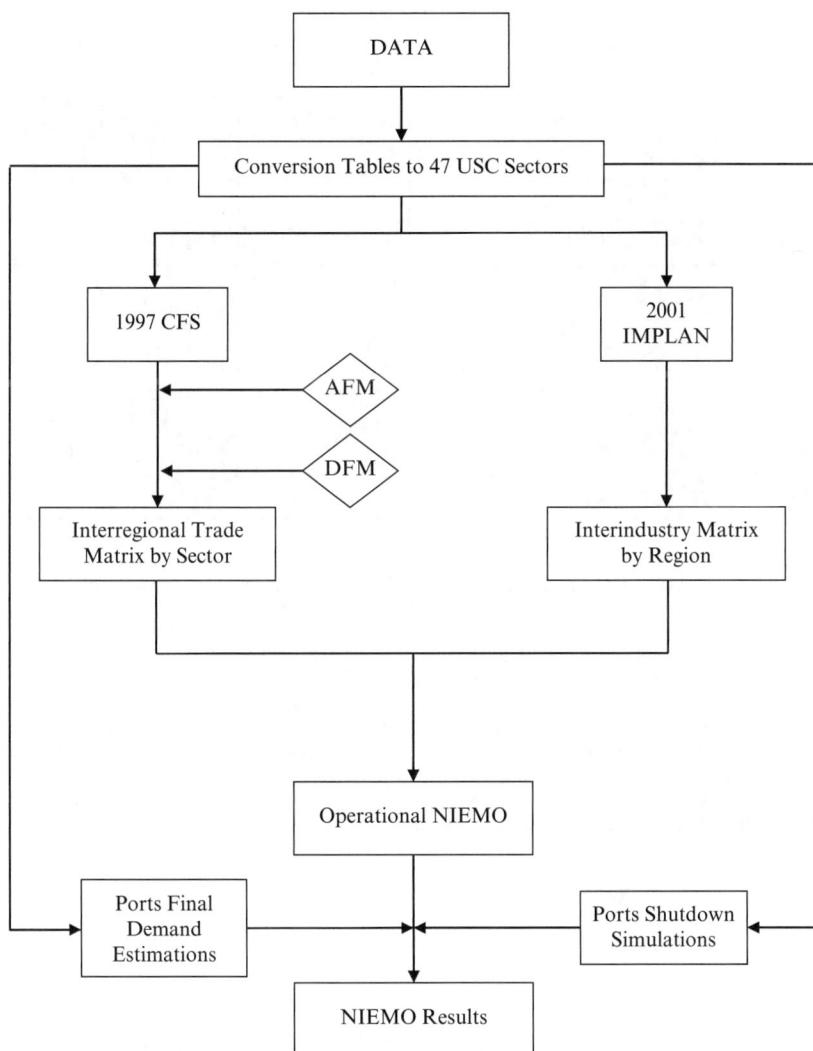

Source: Richardson et al. (2008).

Figure 2.1 NIEMO modeling steps

The existence of many unreported values requires relying on other data sources to approximate completeness. It is not surprising, therefore, that since the work by Polenske (1980) and Jack Faucett Associates (1983), there has been no comprehensive inventory of MRIO flows in the US.

CODE	USC	SCTG	BEA	NAICS	IMPLAN (2001)	SIC	HS	SITC	WCUS
USC		C, E	C, E	C, E	C, E	C, W	C, E	C, W	C, W
SCTG	C, E		C, E	C, E	C, E	P	C, E	C, W	C, W
BEA	C, E	C, E		A	A	P	A	P	P
NAICS	C, E	C, E	A		A	C, W	C, E	P	P
IMPLAN (2001)	C, E	C, E	A	A		P	C, E	P	P
SIC	C, W	P	P	C, W	P		P	P	P
HS	C, E	C, E	A	C, E	C, E	P		C, W	C, W
SITC	C, W	C, W	P	P	P	P	C, W		C, E
WCUS	C, W	C, W	P	P	P	P	C, W	C, E	

Notes:
C: Created, *A*: Available from other sources, *P*: Possible to create, *E*: Bridge allocations evenly made, where necessary, without any weights, *W*: Bridge allocations made with plausible weights.
USC: USC Sectors Newly Created, SCTG: Standard Classification of Transported Goods (http://www.bts.gov/cfs/sctg/welcome.htm), BEA: Bureau of Economic Analysis (http://www.bea.doc.gov), NAICS: North American Industry Classification System (http://www.census.gov/epcd/www/naics.html), IMPLAN: IMPLAN 509 sector codes, SIC: Standard Industrial Classification (http://www.osha.gov/oshstats/sicser.html), HS: Harmonized System (http://www.statcan.ca/trade/htdocs/hsinfo.html), SITC: Standard International Trade Classification available from WISERTrade (http://www.wisertrade.org/home/index.jsp), WCUS: Waterborne Commerce of the United States (http://www.iwr.usace.army.mil/ndc/data/datacomm.htm).

Source: Park et al. (2007).

Figure 2.2   Industrial code conversions

The 1997 CFS reports trade flows between US states for 43 Standard Classification of Transported Goods (SCTG) sectors while the industry and commodity sectors (the data file of IMPLAN Version 2) include 509 sector estimates, available for all states. The CFS trade flows data include both foreign and domestic trade. This means that all commodities coming into a US port are listed as outbound from that port and inbound to the next destination; likewise, all commodities going to a port from anywhere in the United States are outbound from the origin and inbound to the port. For these reasons, foreign imports in 2001 IMPLAN are added to the IMPLAN Total Commodity Output tally. In the current application, the 1997 CFS data were used as a baseline and updated to 2001 using 2001

IMPLAN data. The years will be updated to a more recent period in the near future.

Differences among alternative industry classification systems from different data sources make data reconciliation especially difficult in the absence of standardized and tested conversion bridges. The estimation of 2001 trade flows from 1997 CFS, therefore, required intermediate conversion steps between the SCTG code system used in the 1997 CFS and the IMPLAN system of sectors, not always one-to-one matched pairs. Figure 2.3 shows the data reconciliation steps when creating a SCTG-IMPLAN conversion bridge enabling the aggregation of 509 IMPLAN sectors to 43 SCTG sectors.

The following paragraphs and equations summarize NIEMO. The traditional Leontief demand-side model is expressed as

$$X = (I - A)^{-1} \cdot Y, \tag{2.1}$$

where X is the $m \times 1$ total output vector for m sectors,
Y is the $m \times 1$ vector of final demand from private consumers, government, investment, and net exports of outputs from m sectors and
A is the $m \times m$ matrix of technical coefficients that captures interindustry relationships in terms of backward linkages between m sectors.

The inverse matrix in Equation (2.1) is referred to as the demand-driven IO model.

The demand-driven version of NIEMO can be expressed similarly as

$$X_{NIEMO} = (I - W)^{-1} \cdot Y_{NIEMO}, \tag{2.2}$$

where X_{NIEMO} is the $nm \times 1$ total output vector for USC sectors $m(= 1, \ldots, 47)$ in each region $n(= 1, \ldots, 52)$,
Y_{NIEMO} is the $nm \times 1$ vector of region-specific final demand and foreign exports and
W is a $nm \times nm$ matrix that combines technical coefficients with coefficients describing interregional trade flows.

The matrix W is defined as

$$W = C_{NIEMO} \cdot A_{NIEMO}, \tag{2.3}$$

where A_{NIEMO} is a block diagonal matrix of technical coefficients linking input commodities to output industries within each region $n(= 1, \ldots, 52)$ and

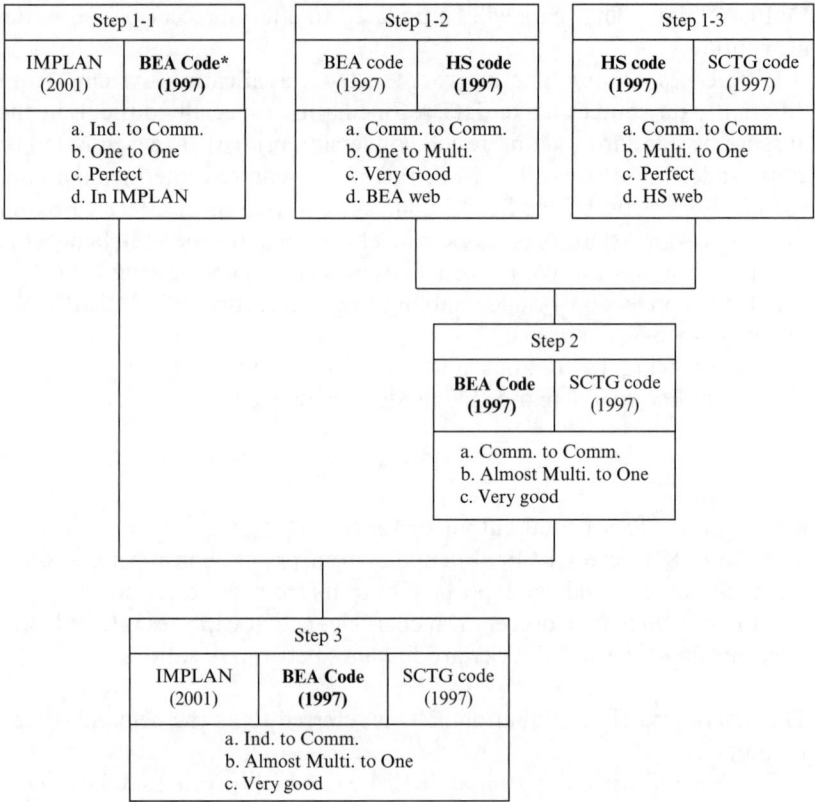

Step 1-1	
IMPLAN (2001)	**BEA Code*** **(1997)**
a. Ind. to Comm. b. One to One c. Perfect d. In IMPLAN	

Step 1-2	
BEA code (1997)	**HS code** **(1997)**
a. Comm. to Comm. b. One to Multi. c. Very Good d. BEA web	

Step 1-3	
HS code **(1997)**	SCTG code (1997)
a. Comm. to Comm. b. Multi. to One c. Perfect d. HS web	

Step 2	
BEA Code **(1997)**	SCTG code (1997)
a. Comm. to Comm. b. Almost Multi. to One c. Very good	

Step 3		
IMPLAN (2001)	**BEA Code** **(1997)**	SCTG code (1997)
a. Ind. to Comm. b. Almost Multi. to One c. Very good		

Notes:
*Bold: Used as bridge code.
a: Ind. = Industry, Comm. = Commodity.
b: One = one sector, Multi. = sectors more than one.
c: (Merged) Data status.
d: Source and abbreviations.
BEA: Bureau of Economic Analysis (http://www.bea.doc.gov); SCTG: Standard Classification of Transported Goods (http://www.bts.gov/cfs/sctg/welcome.htm).

Source: Park et al. (2007).

Figure 2.3   Data reconciliation steps between SCTG and IMPLAN

C_{NIEMO} is a $nm \times nm$ collection of diagonal matrices describing inter-regional trade flows.

The matrix C_{NIEMO} is defined as

$$C_{NIEMO} = C \cdot (\hat{C}_R)^{-1},   \tag{2.4}$$

where C is a *nm* × *nm* matrix of trade flows and
$\hat{C}_R$ is a *nm* × *nm* matrix formed by diagonalizing the 1 × *nm* row vector
C_R, consisting of the column sums of C.

Note that we identify losses of foreign exports and final demand losses
or gains as different types of direct impacts, and that these vary across
scenarios. Foreign exports losses and government expenditures define
a region-specific vector of direct impacts. Final demand losses or gains
define vectors of regionally distributed direct impacts. Our scenarios
involve two mechanisms for distributing impacts across regions. First, we
use the standard MRIO procedure to distribute calculated region-specific
final demand impacts across states

$$Y'_{NIEMO} = C_{NIEMO} \cdot Y_{NIEMO}. \tag{2.5}$$

Distributing final demand losses resulting from the complete elimination of activity in a given sector is more complicated. This requires modifying the commodity trade coefficients matrix C_{NIEMO} to delete domestic
exports from the quarantine area, for example, California in one of our
case studies (see Chapter 8). We set the entries for the California row
vector, for example, describing USC Sector 1 Live animals and fish, meat,
seafood in the matrix C_{NIEMO} to zero. In addition, outbound state flows
from this sector are redistributed to origins in other states based on existing flow proportions. This defines a modified matrix $C_{MOD\cdot NIEMO}$ that is
used to allocate final demand losses

$$Y'_{MOD\cdot NIEMO} = C_{MOD\cdot NIEMO} \cdot Y_{NIEMO}. \tag{2.6}$$

This provides three types of direct impacts: region-specific direct
impacts ΔY_{NIEMO}; and, via Equations (2.5) and (2.6), regionally distributed impacts $\Delta Y'_{NIEMO}$ and $\Delta Y'_{MOD\cdot NIEMO}$. Total economic impacts may be
estimated as

$$\Delta X_{NIEMO} = (I-W)^{-1}\Delta Y_{NIEMO}+(I-W)^{-1}\Delta Y'_{NIEMO}+(I-W)^{-1}\Delta Y'_{MOD\cdot NIEMO}$$
$$= (I-W)^{-1}[\Delta Y_{NIEMO} + \Delta Y'_{NIEMO} + \Delta Y'_{MOD\cdot NIEMO}]. \tag{2.7}$$

2.3 TRANSNIEMO

TransNIEMO involves three sub-models (Figure 2.4), a national highway
network model, a transportation cost impact model and NIEMO (a
demand-driven MRIO model as described above). Applications of

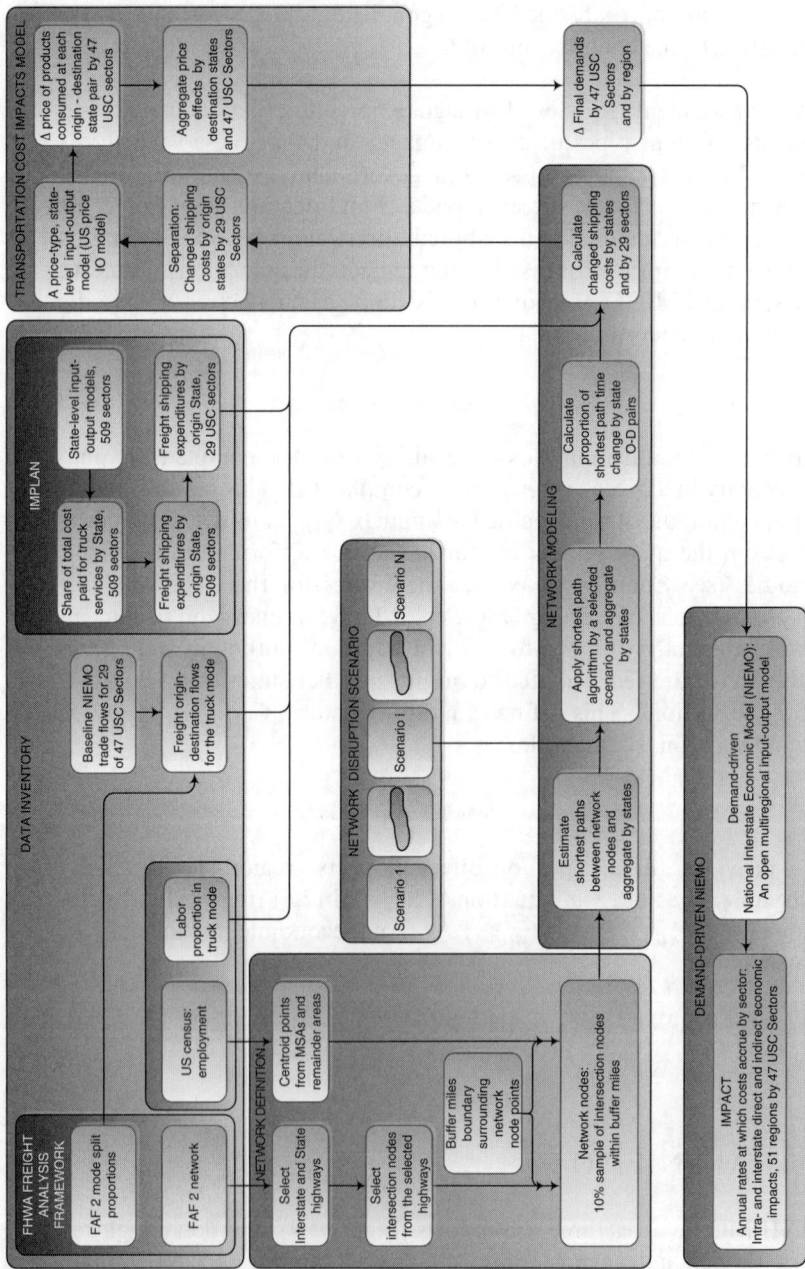

Source: Gordon et al. (2010).

Figure 2.4   Framework of TransNIEMO

TransNIEMO also require appropriate substantial data preparation. The model is applied to generate one-year results, but because NIEMO is linear it is a simple matter to down-scale the results to shorter periods. The three major research steps associated with the three sub-models are discussed below.

The highway network model can be applied to problems such as combining the highway networks with bridge or tunnel disruption scenarios. A user equilibrium (UE) model is applied twice for each test: first to develop a baseline and second by applying the scenario. The UE approach is appropriate when there is significant congestion on the network. When dealing with freight flows on highway networks among metropolitan regions, applying the UE algorithm is reasonable. The results from applying the UE algorithm include the times and the distances from origin regions to destination regions. We assume that trip durations are related to truckers' labor costs and distance is associated with the other variable costs besides labor. The results from the network model simulations are used as inputs into the transportation cost impact model. The first empirical application of TransNIEMO, in which geography boundaries are limited to California and Arizona, is found in Park et al. (2011a).

While NIEMO and its related models are spatially disaggregated only to the state level, the transportation nodes for freight modes are the major metropolitan areas, which are the dominant centers of economic activity. Furthermore, in most states there is one or more major metropolitan area. Hence, the interstate freight flows had to be expanded to the flows among 114 nodes (specifically 'economic centroids') to make them comprehensible. The non-metropolitan regions in selected cases also account for a significant proportion of state gross domestic product and freight origin-destination (O-D) movements. Although local governments are mostly responsible for transportation infrastructure planning within their jurisdictions, most highways serve areas beyond their boundaries.

The Freight Analysis Framework (FAF) provides a comprehensive data set but not all of the data are directly applicable to our research problems, because services are also included in the annual flows among NIEMO sectors. Service values need to be excluded from the model.

Therefore NIEMO freight flows are used as freight flow input values. However, NIEMO does not account for transportation mode. Consequently, truck proportions from FAF are used to apportion NIEMO-estimated trade flows to obtain truck shipments. These are then loaded onto the highway network.

We also require data on the shipping costs associated with all flows. Total shipping costs between states are estimated using data from NIEMO, IMPLAN and FAF as follows

$$ShipCost_{ij}^k = TTradeValue_{ij} \times TruckP_{ij} \times TruckCostValue_i^k, \quad (2.8)$$

where

$ShipCost_{ij}^k$ are aggregated shipping costs from state i to j by commodity sector k.

$TTradeValue_{ij}$ are total trade values obtained from NIEMO for 49×49 states (Hawaii is omitted for obvious reasons).

$TruckP_{ij}$ are truck proportions of total trade calculated by applying truck output values divided by total output values obtained from FAF data. Data for 114 Metropolitan Statistical Areas (MSAs) by 114 MSAs are aggregated to 49 states by 49 states.

$TruckCostVaule_i^k = \frac{PurTruckSer_i^k}{TIndValue_i^k}$ are truck costs per value. These are the truck cost proportions in origin states obtained from IMPLAN. IMPLAN's sectors are aggregated to 29 USC commodity sectors. $PurTruckSer_i^k$ are the total value of purchased services by the trucking sector and $TIndValue_i^k$ are the total output of industry sectors.

Increased time and distance proportions are estimated by applying the UE model. Time changes and distance changes are separately modeled in Equations (2.6) and (2.7).

$$\Delta T_{ij}^k = ShipCost_{ij}^k \times (PTimeCost_{ij} \times PLaborCost), \quad (2.9)$$

where

ΔT_{ij}^k are increased costs caused by the increased time of travel.

$PTimeCost_{ij}$ are the proportions of time changes calculated as total increased time divided by total baseline time. Data for 114 MSAs by 114 MSAs flows are aggregated to 49 states by 49 states.

$PLaborCost$ is the proportion of labor costs in the operations of the transportation industry (0.65).

$$\Delta D_{ij}^k = ShipCost_{ij}^k \times (PDistCost_{ij} \times PVarCost), \quad (2.10)$$

where

ΔD_{ij}^k are increased costs associated with increased shipping distance.

$PDistCost_{ij}$ are proportions of distance change calculated as total increased distance divided by total baseline distance. Data for 114 MSAs by 114 MSAs are aggregated to 49 states by 49 states.

$PVarCost$ is the assumed proportion of variable costs in operation of the transportation industry (0.35).

Total increased shipping costs are estimated by adding the two increased costs, time and distance. Equation (2.11) shows the procedure for estimating increased shipping costs.

$$\Delta ShipCost_{ij}^k = \Delta D_{ij}^k + \Delta T_{ij}^k, \tag{2.11}$$

where
$\Delta ShipCost_{ij}^k$ are increased shipping costs from origin state i to destination state j for industry sector k resulting from an event. In the short run, shipping costs are assumed to be non-decreasing. In the event of an emergency, sellers can pass on higher costs. They may cut prices because of competitive pressures, but probably only in the longer run.

The increased shipping costs, $\Delta ShipCost_{ij}^k$, are passed forward and lead to increased prices at destinations resulting in lower consumer expenditures. Dietzenbacher (1997) has shown that the supply-driven IO model is more meaningful for estimating price increases than the Leontief price IO model when absolute costs in value-added sectors are available. An application of a supply-driven IO model is summarized in Equation (2.12).

$$\Delta CS_j^k = \sum_{j=1}^{51} (\Delta ShipCost_{ij}^k \times InvMtrxO_i) , \tag{2.12}$$

where
ΔCS_j^k are decreased consumer expenditures at destination j and industry sector k.
$\sum_{k=1}^{47} \Delta CS_j^k$ are direct impacts by states and $\sum_{j=1}^{51} \Delta CS_j^k$ are direct impacts by sector.
$InvMtrxO_i = (I - B)_i^{-1}$ is a 47 × 47 supply-driven inverse matrix and B is the direct output coefficients matrix in destination state i.

The reduced consumer expenditures associated with increased shipping costs drive reductions in household final demand. We assume that there are no substitution effects and final demand is directly affected by the reduced consumer expenditures. Equation (2.13) applies the demand-driven NIEMO to estimate the state-by-state economic impacts resulting from these reductions in household final demand.

$$\Delta X_j^k = InvMtrxD \times (-\Delta CS_j^k) , \tag{2.13}$$

where
ΔX_j^k are decreased final outputs in destination states j and industry sector k.
$\sum_{k=1}^{47} \Delta X_j^k$ are total impacts by states and $\sum_{j=1}^{51} \Delta X_j^k$ are total impacts by sector.
$InvMtrxD$ is an inverse matrix of NIEMO which is (47 × 52) × (47 × 52) demand-driven inverse matrix.

We applied the equation found in Berwick and Farooq (2003, Appendix A) to calculate truckers' labor cost per mile

$$LRPM + \frac{(TD/S + WT)*LRPH}{TD}, \qquad (2.14)$$

where
$LRPM$ = Labor (Wage) Rate Per Mile, given as 0.493 ($/mile),
TD = Trip Distance = 100 miles,
S = Speed = 65 MPH,
WT = Wait Time = 1 hour and
$LRPH$ = Labor (Wage) Rate per Hour = $17/hour.

The equation given in the literature assumes $LRPH$ = $10/hour. We believe the current $LRPH$ is close to $17, and we modified the numerical terms $LRPM$ and $LRPH$ in Equation (2.14), and obtained $0.9 per mile. In the literature, other variable costs are given as $0.48 per mile, and we estimated labor cost to be 65 percent of total variable cost, or

$$0.65 = 0.9/(0.9 + 0.48). \qquad (2.15)$$

A full nationwide TransNIEMO was applied to study the economic impacts of three hypothetical road closure scenarios: two bridge service disruptions on the Mississippi River and one tunnel service disruption in the Rocky Mountains (see Chapter 3 for the results of the analysis).

2.4   FLEXNIEMO

FlexNIEMO is used to construct period-to-period versions of NIEMO. The approach, developed recently by Park et al. (2011b), allows the fixed coefficients in the IO world to be continuously modified, reflecting previous economic events and changes in interindustry relations. For example, a problem using the supply-side model is how to reflect demand-side adjustments during the recovery. With the supply-side FlexNIEMO, some of the major shortcomings inherent in the IO model can be overcome. Based on supply- and demand-driven economic IO models suggested by Park et al. (2011b) and Gordon et al. (2009), where the entire detailed modeling approaches are found, we summarize the procedure here.

The FlexNIEMO approach begins with estimating total impacts. Let $^{N}X^{s}$ be the total input row vector for the various commodity and service sectors, m = economic sectors and n = regions. Also, let $^{N}X^{d}$ be the total output column vector for the same economic sectors and regions. If ^{N}Z is a $nm \times nm$ block diagonal matrix of direct technical flows between industries within a region, and C is a $nm \times nm$ block diagonal matrix of interregional trade flows, then the total output for a demand-driven version of the spatially disaggregated model is

$$^{N}X^{d} = (I - C^{d}\,{}^{N}A_0)^{-1N}F, \qquad (2.16)$$

where $^{N}A_0 = {}^{N}Z({}^{N}\hat{X}^{s})^{-1}$,
$C^{d} = C(\hat{C}_i^{m})^{-1}$,
$C_j^{m} = \sum_i c_{ij}^{m}$ and
^{N}F is a column vector of region specific final demand losses.

Based on the same set of matrices, similar to Equation (2.16), the total output for the supply-driven version of NIEMO is

$$^{N}X^{s} = {}^{N}V(I - {}^{N}B_0 C^{s})^{-1}, \qquad (2.17)$$

where $^{N}B_0 = ({}^{N}\hat{X}^{d})^{-1N}Z$,
$C^{s} = (\hat{C}_i^{m})^{-1}C$,
$C_i^{m} = \sum_j c_{ij}^{m}$ and
^{N}V is a row vector of region specific reductions in value added factors.

Given the vectors $_{t_1}^{N}F$ and $_{t_1}^{N}V$ for period t_1, via the calculation process suggested in Gordon et al. (2009) and Park et al. (2011b), new vectors of total output, $_{t_1}^{N}X^{s}(=_{t_1}^{N}X^{d})$, are derived. The same process can be applied for the target periods k, that is, t_k.

2.5 LOCAL AND DOMESTIC TRADE-INDUCED IMPACTS

As pointed out earlier, most applications of NIEMO focus solely on direct and indirect impacts, primarily because the secondary consumption associated with induced impacts rarely crosses State borders. However, in Chapter 10 where we analyse the impacts of the Gulf oil spill we expand the model to measure two types of induced impacts: local (that is, intrastate) and those associated with domestic interstate trade.

This required the following manipulations of the data:

$$D^{\text{IMPLAN}} = (\text{INDU\_R}^{\text{IMPLAN}}) \times (\text{Dom\_Trade})^{\text{IMPLAN}}, \qquad (2.18)$$

where
D^{IMPLAN} = domestic trade effects ascribed to the induced effects that occurred in a state that experienced direct impacts; this is defined as the product of INDU_R^{IMPLAN} and (Dom_Trade)^{IMPLAN},
INDU_R^{IMPLAN} = ratio of induced effects to direct and indirect effects via IMPLAN in a state that experienced the impact and
(Dom_Trade)^{IMPLAN} = total domestic trade effects for that state via IMPLAN.

Note that if $D^{IMPLAN} > (Dom\_Trade)^{IMPLAN}$, then we treat $D^{IMPLAN} = (Dom\_Trade)^{IMPLAN}$.

We translate the 509 IMPLAN sector system to the 47 USC Sector system used as an input for the second NIEMO run, and redefine

$$EX^{NIEMO} = D^{IMPLAN} \text{ if the domestic trade is exports and}$$
$$IM^{NIEMO} = D^{IMPLAN} \text{ if the domestic trade is imports.}$$

Hence, the total impact prompted by local induced effects within the directly impacted state is defined as Tr_IP; Tr_IP^{exp} represents induced domestic exports effects and Tr_IP^{imp} represents induced domestic imports effects. These were calculated as

$$Tr\_IP^{exp} = DIVS \times DTC \times EX^{NIEMO}, \qquad (2.19\text{-}1)$$

where
$DIVS = (I-DNIEMO)^{-1}$,
DNIEMO = the technical and trade coefficients in the demand-driven NIEMO and
DTC = the trade coefficients in the demand-driven NIEMO.

$$Tr\_IP^{imp} = IM^{NIEMO} \times STC \times SIVS \qquad (2.19\text{-}2)$$

where
$SIVS = (I-SNIEMO)^{-1}$,
SNIEMO = the technical and trade coefficients in the supply-driven NIEMO and
STC = the trade coefficients in the supply-driven NIEMO.

In the final step we estimate net induced impacts, which equal total induced impacts from the application of IMPLAN in the impacted Gulf States but via subtracting the induced trade impacts. This is also a part of Type II's induced effects to be added to the original NIEMO results. The net induced impacts resulting from the IMPLAN sector system are again aggregated to the USC sector system.

2.6   CONCLUSIONS

This chapter has presented a methodological review of one of the two key models on which the case studies analysed in this book are based. This model is the National Interstate Economic Model (NIEMO) that is used for nationwide economic studies, as opposed to the Southern California

Planning Model (SCPM) that is used for applications in Southern California. NIEMO is the most detailed and most comprehensive attempt to implement Isard and Leontief's dream of an operational multiregional input-output (MRIO) model, although there have been other contributions along the way by Chenery, Moses, Polenske, Jackson (Jackson et al., 2006) and others.

However, we have also attempted to go beyond the standard concept of the MRIO by extending it in three important directions. First, by developing TransNIEMO we added a highway network that enabled us to explore the transportation as well as the spatially disaggregated economic impacts of any exogenous shock, such as a terrorist or a natural disaster. Second, we attempted to deal with one of the major criticisms of MRIO, the fixed production coefficients assumption, by developing FlexNIEMO with a capacity for changing interindustry coefficients by introducing a supply-side component. Third, we devised a method of tackling a familiar critique of MRIOs, their inability to measure induced as well as indirect impacts. Although there is still a need for further progress on these approaches, a more refined conceptualization of MRIO is moving in the right direction.

REFERENCES

Berwick, M. and M. Farooq (2003), *Truck Costing Model for Transportation Managers.* Fargo, ND: Upper Great Plains Transportation Institute, North Dakota State University, available at http://www.mountain-plains.org/pubs/html/mpc-03-152/index.php.
Canning, P. and Z. Wang (2005), 'A flexible mathematical programming model to estimate interregional input-output accounts', *Journal of Regional Science,* **45**, 539–63.
Chenery, H.B. (1953), 'Regional analysis', in H.B. Chenery, P.G. Clark and V.C. Pinna (eds.), *The Structure and Growth of the Italian Economy.* Rome; US Mutual Security Agency, pp. 98–139.
Dietzenbacher, E. (1997), 'In Vindication of the Ghosh Model: A Reinterpretation as a Price Model', *Journal of Regional Science,* **37**, 629–51.
Giuliano, G., P. Gordon, Q. Pan, J.Y. Park and L. Wang (2010), 'Estimating freight flows for metropolitan area highway networks using secondary data sources', *Networks and Spatial Economics,* **10** (1), 73–91.
Gordon, P., J.Y. Park and H.W. Richardson (2009), 'Modeling input-output impacts with substitutions in the household sector: a numerical example', *Economic Modeling,* **26** (3), 696–701.
Gordon, P., H.W. Richardson and J.E. Moore II et al. (2010), *TransNIEMO: Economic Impact Analysis using a Model of Consistent Interregional Economic and Highway Network Equilibria,* Los Angeles, CA: Center for Risk and Economic Analysis of Terrorism Events (CREATE), University of Southern California.

Isard, W. (1951), 'Interregional and regional input-output analysis: a model of a space economy', *Review of Economics and Statistics*, **33**, 318–28.

Isard, W. (1960), *Methods of Regional Science*. New York: Wiley.

Jack Faucett Associates, Inc. (1983), *The Multiregional Input-Output Accounts, 1977: Introduction and Summary, Vol. I (Final Report)*. Washington, DC: US Department of Health and Human Services.

Jackson, R.W., W.R. Schwarm, Y. Okuyama and S. Islam (2006), 'A method for constructing commodity by industry flow matrices', *Annals of Regional Science*, **40**, 909–20.

Liu, L.N. and P. Vilain (2004), 'Estimating commodity inflows to a substate region: using input-output data: commodity flow survey accuracy tests', *Journal of Transportation and Statistics*, **7** (1), 23–37.

Miller, R.E. and P.D. Blair (1985), *Input-Output Analysis: Foundations and Extensions*, 2nd edn. Englewood Cliffs: NJ: Prentice-Hall.

Miller, R.E. and G. Shao (1990), 'Spatial and sectoral aggregation in the commodity-industry multiregional input-output model,' *Environment and Planning A*, **22**, 1637–56.

Moses, L.N. (1955), 'The stability of interregional trading patterns and input-output analysis', *American Economic Review*, **45**, 803–32.

ORNL (Oak Ridge National Laboratory) (2000), *Freight USA. Highlights from the 1997 Commodity Flow Survey and Other Sources*. Washington, DC: Bureau of Transportation Statistics, US Department of Transportation.

Park, J.Y. and P. Gordon (2010), 'An evaluation of input-output aggregation error using a new MRIO model', Paper presented at the North American Meeting of the Regional Science Association International 52nd Annual Conference, Las Vegas, Nevada, 10–12 November.

Park, J.Y., P. Gordon, J.E. Moore II, H.W. Richardson and L. Wang (2007), 'Simulating the state-by-state effects of terrorist attacks on three major US ports: applying NIEMO (National Interstate Economic Model)', in H.W. Richardson, P. Gordon and J.E. Moore II (eds), *The Economic Costs and Consequences of Terrorism*. Cheltenham, UK and Northampton, MA, USA: Edward Elgar, pp. 208–34.

Park, J.Y., P. Gordon, J.E. Moore II and H.W. Richardson (2009), 'A two-step approach to estimating state-by-state commodity trade flows', *Annals of Regional Science*, **43** (4), 1033–72.

Park, J.Y., J. Cho, P. Gordon, J.E. Moore II, H.W. Richardson and S. Yoon (2011a), 'Adding a freight network to a national interstate input-output model: a TransNIEMO application for California', *Journal of Transport Geography*, **19** (6), 1410–22.

Park, J.Y., P. Gordon, J.E. Moore II and H.W. Richardson (2011b), 'Constructing a flexible National Interstate Economic Model', Paper presented at the 19th International Input-Output Conference, Alexandria, Virginia, 13–17 July.

Polenske, K.R. (1980), *The U.S. Multiregional Input-Output Accounts and Model*. Lexington, MA: DC Heath.

Rich, K.M., A. Winter-Nelson and G.Y. Miller (2005a), 'Enhancing economic models for the analysis of animal disease', *Revue Scientifique et Technique – Office International Des Epizooties*, **24**, 847–56.

Rich, K.M., G.Y. Miller and A. Winter-Nelson (2005b), 'A review of economic tools for the assessment of animal disease outbreaks', *Revue Scientifique et Technique – Office International Des Epizooties*, **24**, 833–45.

Richardson, H.W., P. Gordon, J.E. Moore, II, J.Y. Park and Q. Pan (2008), 'The economic impacts of terrorist attacks on the twin ports of Los Angeles-Long Beach', in J.M Quigley and L.A Rosenthal (eds.), *Risking House and Home: Disasters, Cities, Public Policy*, Berkeley, CA: Berkeley Public Policy Press, pp. 173–96.

Richardson, H.W., Q. Pan, J.Y. Park and J.E. Moore II (2015), *Regional Economic Impacts of Terrorist Attacks, Natural Disasters and Metropolitan Policies*. Heidelberg: Springer.

Southworth, F. and B.E. Peterson (2000), 'Intermodal and international freight network modeling', *Transportation Research C*, **8**, 147–66.

USDOT (US Department of Transportation), Federal Highway Administration (2002), *Freight Analysis Framework (FAF) Overview*. Washington, DC, available at http://www.ops.fhwa.dot.gov/freight/freight_ analysis/faf/index.htm.

USDOT, RITA and BTS (US Department of Transportation, Research and Innovative Technology Administration and Bureau of Transportation Statistics) (2005), *Transportation Statistics Annual Report*. Washington, DC, available at http://www.bts.gov/publications/transportation_statistics_annual_report/2005/pdf/entire.pdf.

3. Bridge and tunnel closures (TransNIEMO)*

JiYoung Park, Harry W. Richardson, Peter Gordon, James E. Moore II, Qisheng Pan and JoongKoo Cho

3.1 INTRODUCTION

In this chapter, we present an application of TransNIEMO, a model developed to address the neglect of infrastructure in Multiregional Input-Output (MRIO) models. This builds on the National Interstate Economic Model (NIEMO) that features in other chapters. TransNIEMO adds the nation's highway network to accommodate intra- and interindustry trade. This new model achieves consistent highway network and economic equilibria.

The US economy is vulnerable to terrorist attacks, and modeling how disruptions at major choke points on the nation's highways might impact the US economy on a state-by-state and industry-by-industry basis is a topic of particular interest. In our view, TransNIEMO is the only operational model that can be used for this type of analysis. While this chapter focuses on simulated attacks on three major choke points, disruptions from natural or man-made events on any other vulnerable highway link can easily be modeled. Perhaps surprisingly, as a proportion of the nation's total output, the losses experienced in the three scenarios are relatively small. This reflects high levels of redundancy in the highway network. However, there are significant differences in both state-by-state and industry-by-industry impacts, and highway infrastructure (especially bridges and tunnels) are vulnerable to disruption or structural failure from neglect, natural or man-made disasters and the possibility of terrorist attacks, a major national concern. Even absent the terrorist threat, the aging of key infrastructure links has been widely noted. According to the National Bridge Inventory, 12.1 percent of bridges were rated structurally deficient, and 13.3 percent rated functionally obsolete in 2007 (USDOT-FHWA, 2008a). Although a bridge rated either structurally deficient or functionally obsolete is not unsafe for all vehicles under normal conditions, it is more vulnerable in emergency situations and especially so in cases of old designs that lack modern safety features.

The failures of the I-10 Twin Span Bridge during Hurricane Katrina in 2005 and the I-35W highway bridges during rush hour in Minneapolis in 2007 have brought home to planners and policy makers concerns about the safety of highway bridges and the possible effects of bridge collapse on highway performance and the economy at both local and national levels. Xie and Levinson (2009) evaluated the effects of the I-35W bridge collapse on regional traffic patterns and estimated the economic losses imposed on travelers in terms of travel time delay using a regional travel demand and investment model. However, their research focused on regional effects of the bridge collapse and did not examine any ripple effects on traffic with respect to the national highway network. In addition, freight trips were not modeled directly.

According to the Federal Highway Administration (FHWA), there are 50 tunnels over 500 meters in length along the 4 million miles of US roadways. Most tunnels are constructed to improve highway system performance. For example, planners have proposed a longer than 16-mile tunnel, the world's longest highway tunnel, under Long Island Sound to reduce the traffic congestion in the New York metropolitan area. In comparison to bridges, tunnels have received less attention even though they are also vulnerable to natural and man-made disasters.

Turning to the demand side, because of rapid population growth and brisk economic development, freight transportation has grown dramatically in recent years. Total US freight ton-miles increased from 2,420 to 3,137 billion between 1993 and 2002, an annual growth rate of 2.9 percent. As the dominant freight mode, trucks moved about 40 percent of total revenue ton-miles of freight, accounting for almost 74.3 percent of the total dollars and 67.2 percent of the total tons of all freight shipments in 2002 (USDOT, 2004). The total Vehicle Miles Traveled (VMT) on public roads increased by 39.4 percent (from 2.1 to 3.0 trillion) between 1990 and 2005 while truck VMT grew at a much faster rate by 52.2 percent during the same period. Freight moved by the US transportation system reached 21.0 billion tons in 2006, and was worth about $14.9 billion. Trucks on highways moved about 60.4 percent in tonnage and 65.4 percent of dollar value (USDOT-FHWA, 2008a). The FHWA (2003) projected that freight volume will nearly double between 1998 and 2020, increasing from 9 billion tons to about 17 billion tons (USDOT-FHWA, 2003). The US Department of Transportation (USDOT) also estimated that truck volumes on the National Highway System (NHS) will increase 230 percent from 2002 and reach 10,000 trucks per day by 2035 (USDOT-FHWA, 2008b).

This chapter cites the relevant preceding literature, describes how a computable highway network and its constituent parts were assembled, explains the minimum path algorithm that was used, describes network flow results of various simulated disruptions and wraps up with conclusions and reflections.

Hillestad et al. (2009) noted that an important element of an adaptable and resilient freight transportation system includes identification and analysis of key vulnerabilities in the freight system, and simulations of possible responses to the disruption. This research extends the regional freight transportation models discussed in Gordon and Pan (2001), Pan (2006), Giuliano et al. (2007) and Park et al. (2011) to analyse interregional and interstate freight flows and simulates the response of highway freight flows to disruptions. It uses data from the USDOT's Freight Analysis Framework (FAF2) to establish a baseline of freight flows on the national highway network. It also creates highway bridge and tunnel disruption scenarios in specified regions to estimate state-level costs of highway infrastructure failure, measured in terms of increased time and distance.

3.2   IDENTIFYING NETWORK LINKS, CENTROIDS, BRIDGES AND TUNNELS

3.2.1   Identifying Network Links and Centroids

The first steps in the development of TransNIEMO involved the representation of a computable version of the nation's highway network. This task involved three challenges: to identify major economic and network centroids; to describe and connect the important highway links; and to include the tunnels and bridges that might be choke points if disrupted. Centroid identification was the most complex of these tasks.

At the metropolitan scale, defining centroids to represent sources of aggregate demand in a relatively small traffic analysis zone and connecting this demand to physical facilities at the boundary of the zone is a relatively straightforward exercise. At the national level, the same step is much more challenging. Analysis zones must define a much larger region. An economic centroid characterizing this region aggregates a much larger volume of demand than in a metropolitan-level model, and there is a multitude of ways the demand in this region might be incident to the physical facilities that make up the transportation network.

Two definitions of centroid were used. The major metropolitan areas were designated as the 'economic' centroids, while a representative sample of nearby highway nodal points were designated as 'network' centroids.

The economic centroids are defined to represent an economic center of gravity for the region, and as a result are most often near metropolitan areas that include considerable infrastructure. The transportation demand at each of the economic centroids is connected via virtual (dimensionless, costless) links to many network centroids in the vicinity of the economic centroid. The Freight Analysis Framework (FAF2) highway provides link and node geographic reference data for the base network. The FAF origin-destination (O-D) database employs 114 domestic regions defined in the 2002 Commodity Flow Survey (CFS) plus 17 international gateways and seven international regions (US Census Bureau, 2004; USDOT, 2004). Because the goal of this study is to examine commodity or truck flows on the national highway network, we use the 114 domestic origin and destination regions in the FAF network to represent the economic centroids (Park et al., 2009). There are 12,204 O-D pairs representing total flows between economic centroids.

However, it is unrealistic to load trucks onto the regional highway network connecting major metropolitan areas via a single network node at each location. We use econometric and spatial analysis to identify multiple network nodes (network centroids) at many highway interchanges via which to connect each regional economic centroid to the highway network. The total number of network centroids in our system is 1,877. We add two virtual centroid connectors to each network centroid and incorporate these centroid connectors into the network comprised of the FAF 2002 data set. This places the total number of network links, both physical and virtual, at 275,176.

Most of the highway network links were available from the FAF network. The total number of arcs in the original FAF network is 170,773. Restricting attention to the three major highway facility classes (the Interstate system, US Routes and State Routes) reduces this to 131,068 arcs. When we add county roads, off-interstate business routes, and reconcile a variety of mathematical discontinuities resulting from (1) apparent state-level coding errors in the FAF data and (2) apparent changes in route names, the number of arcs increases to 135,116.

The main steps followed in assembling and processing the data are as follows.

Step 1: Select Interstate highways, US Routes and State routes.
Step 2: Add county roads and off-interstate business routes because these facilities connect highways to local areas.
Step 3: Scan border areas between states because the names of roads often change at state boundaries. Add connecting arcs in such cases.

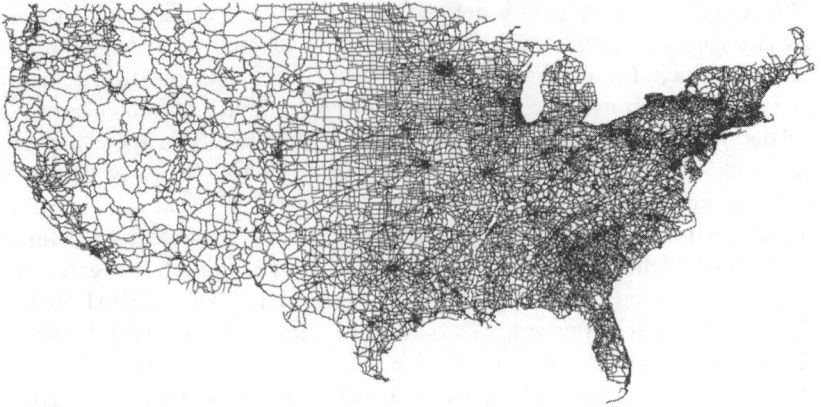

Figure 3.1   Modified US highway network

Step 4:   Scan for any remaining, mathematically disconnected arcs on any highway. Where it is apparent that these highway facilities should be connected, add arcs between the disconnected.

Finally, we assembled the reconciled system highways represented in Figure 3.1.

3.3   IDENTIFYING BRIDGES, TUNNELS AND SCENARIOS

We were interested in scenarios identifying the nature and dimensions of losses from disruptions along potentially major highway choke points. Two criteria were considered for selecting critical bridges or tunnels in the Interstate Highway Program. First, there should be high volumes of truck traffic on the bridge or tunnel. Second, there should be limited alternatives available for detour in cases of emergency. For these reasons, we focused on the bridges over the Mississippi River and tunnels under mountain ranges. Figure 3.2 shows major bridges crossing the Mississippi River. The locations of tunnels are shown in Figure 3.3.

According to the National Bridge Inventory (NBI) database, there were 599,766 bridges in the USA in December 2007 (USDOT-FHWA, 2008a). Based on the information gathered from a variety of sources, including the American Association of State Highway and Transportation Officials (AASHTO), Historic Bridges of the US and the FHWA FAF, there are

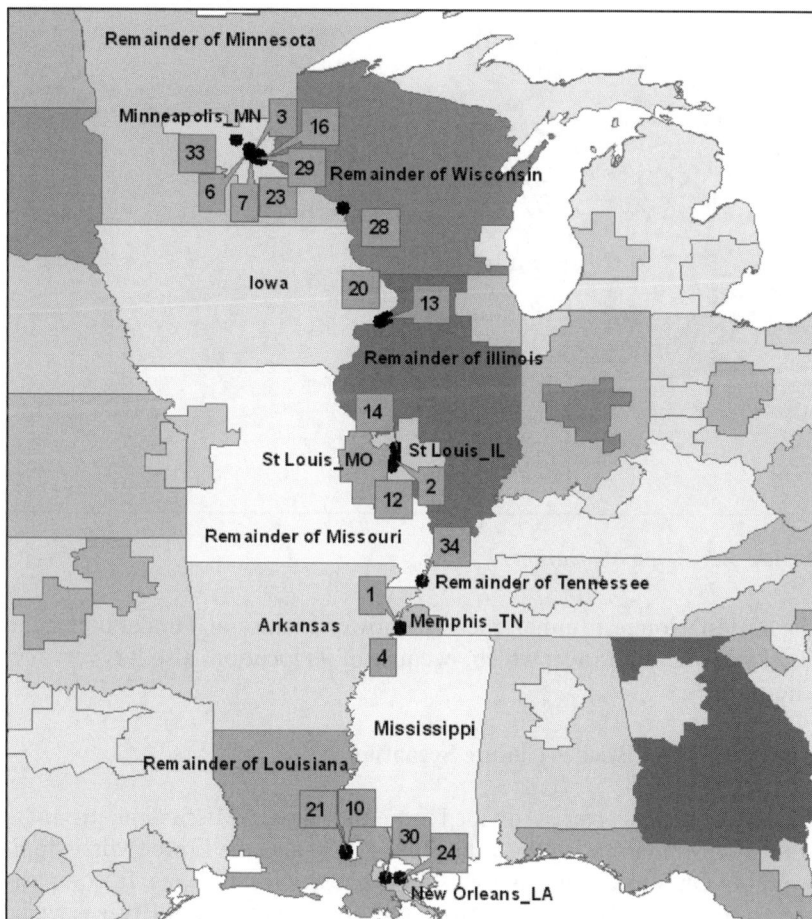

Figure 3.2   Bridge locations on the Mississippi River

about 28 bridges over the Mississippi River with Annual Average Daily Traffic (AADT) counts greater than 10,000.

Three scenarios were selected for this study. Tables 3.1 and 3.2 summarize relevant information for the selected bridges. The Memphis–Arkansas Memorial Bridge and Hernando de Soto Bridge accommodated 30,000 average daily truck trips in 2002 and these two bridges are relatively far away from alternative bridges. These two bridges were selected for the first scenario. Four other bridges over the Mississippi River, selected via the same criteria, were chosen for the second scenario. Table 3.3 shows our third case, a tunnel disruption scenario involving

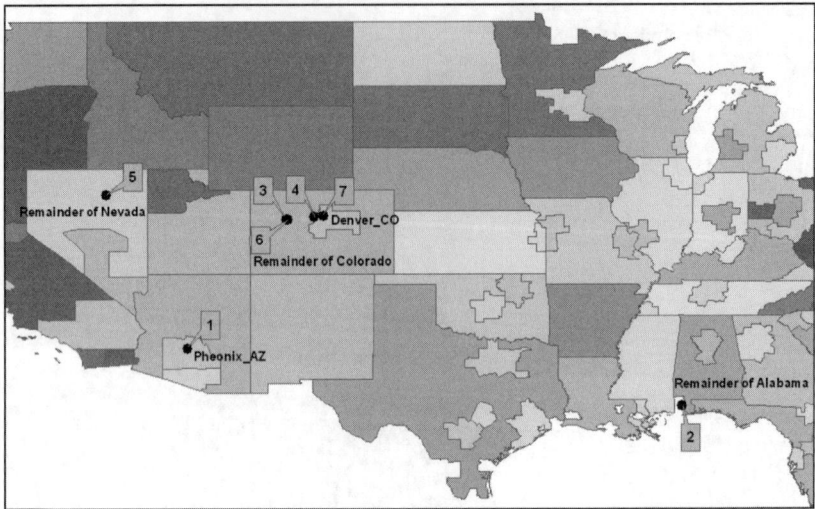

Figure 3.3   Tunnel locations

the nation's longest tunnel, the Eisenhower Memorial Tunnel under the Rocky Mountain range; which, because of its location, also has very few alternatives.

3.3.1   The Two Bridges Closure Scenario

The Mississippi River is divided into the Upper Mississippi, from its source in Minnesota south to the Ohio River, and the Lower Mississippi, from the Ohio to the Mississippi's mouth near New Orleans. In comparison to the Upper Mississippi River, the Lower Mississippi River is wider and has fewer bridges. For example, there are only two bridges across the borders of Tennessee, Arkansas and Mississippi: the Memphis–Arkansas Memorial Bridge and the Hernando de Soto Bridge (see Table 3.1). These accommodate some of the highest truck traffic flows across all the bridges over the Mississippi River.

The collapse of these two bridges could be expected to impose significant impacts on the level of service provided by the transportation networks because of limited alternatives in the immediate region for re-routing flows over the Mississippi River. Our first scenario assumes bridge failures for the Memphis–Arkansas Memorial Bridge and the Hernando de Soto Bridge. We seek to estimate all consequent re-routings of freight flows on the 275,168 links in the restricted national highway network.

Table 3.1   Two bridges disruption scenario

Bridge no.[a]	Link ID	Bridge name	Highways (carries)	AADT02[b]	AADTT02[c]	FAF02[d]	CAP02[e]
1	168373	Memphis–	I-55/US-61/	51,500	19,021	3,261	3,584
	36349	Arkansas Memorial Bridge	US-64/US-70	49,990	11,418	3,261	3,615
4	36180	Hernando de	I-40	49,380	11,660	9,750	5,441
	36239	Soto Bridge		44,430	10,719	9,750	5,428

Notes:
a. Bridge numbers are matched with locations in Figure 3.2.
b. AADT02 is the annual average daily traffic in FAF 2002 data.
c. AADTT02 is the annual average daily truck traffic in FAF 2002 data.
d. FAF02 is the average truck traffic based on freight demand model and FAF 2.2 O-D data.
e. CAP02 is the estimated capacity in FAF 2002 data.

Table 3.2   Four bridges disruption scenario

Bridge no.[a]	Link ID	Bridge name	Highways (carries)	AADT02[b]	AADTT02[c]	FAF02[d]	CAP02[e]
10	52030	Horace Wilkinson Bridge	I-10	85,000	7,268	7,268	5,704
20	90865	I-74 Bridge/ Iowa–Illinois Memorial Bridge	I-74/US 6	75,390	5,260	1085	4,109
43	90800	Rock Island Centennial Bridge	US 67	20,707	615	6	2,921
86	90781	I-280 Bridge	I-280	22,334	2,240	315	3,836

Notes:
a. Bridge numbers are matched with locations in Figure 3.2.
b. AADT02 is the annual average daily traffic in FAF 2002 data.
c. AADTT02 is the annual average daily truck traffic in FAF 2002 data.
d. FAF02 is the average truck traffic based on freight demand model and FAF 2.2 O-D data.
e. CAP02 is the estimated capacity in FAF 2002 data.

3.3.2   The Four Bridges Closure Scenario

In addition, we identified four bridges with the highest Annual Average Daily Truck Traffic (AADTT). These are the Horace Wilkinson Bridge on I-10 in Louisiana, the Iowa–Illinois Memorial Bridge on I-74, Rock Island Centennial Bridge on US 67 and the Interstate Highway I-280 Bridge

Table 3.3   Tunnel scenario

Tunnel no.[a]	Link ID	Tunnel name	Highways (carries)	AADTT02[b]	CAP02[c]
4	150797	Eisenhower Memorial	I-70	3,571	4,201
	149432	Tunnel		3,571	4,020

Notes:
a. Tunnel number is matched with locations in Figure 3.3.
b. AADTT02 is the annual average daily truck traffic in FAF 2002 data.
c. CAP02 is the estimated capacity in FAF 2002 data.

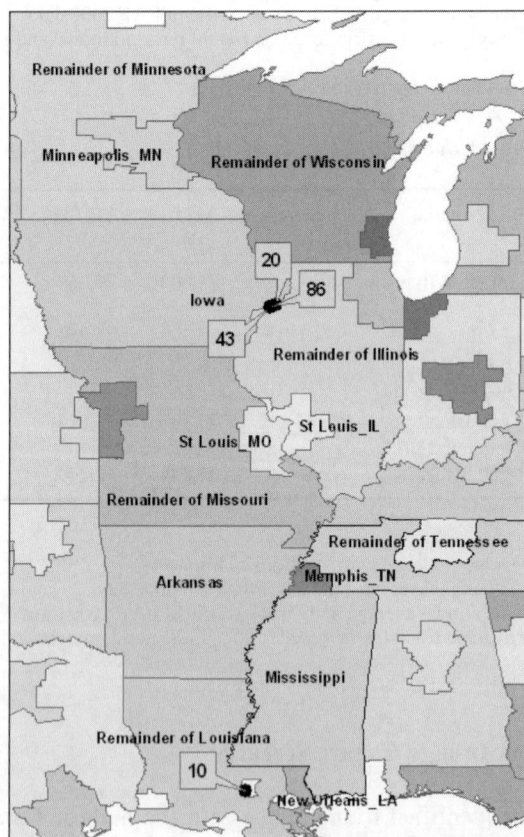

Figure 3.4   Locations of the four selected bridges over the Mississippi River

(see Table 3.2). The I-74, US 67 and I-280 bridges are located at the border between Iowa and Illinois. Our second scenario assumes that these four bridges over the Mississippi River collapse at about the same time because of a terrorist attack.

3.3.3 Tunnel Closure Scenario

Located west of Denver, Colorado on I-70, the Eisenhower Memorial Tunnel is a two-bore tunnel, 2.7 miles in length. It is one of the highway system's highest elevation tunnels and among the longest mountain tunnels built in the Interstate Highway Program. Table 3.3 shows the traffic of the Eisenhower Memorial Tunnel recorded in the FAF 2002 data set. This third scenario assumes closure of this tunnel from either a terrorist attack or a natural disaster.

3.4 MODELING PROCEDURES

The equilibrium model and the iterative processes are applied to estimate freight flows in the baseline and for the bridge and tunnel collapse scenarios. The model ran 20 iterations in the freight trip assignment. The freight tonnage data in the FAF 2002 O-D database were converted to passenger-car equivalent (PCE) values based on the ton per PCE ratios estimated by Giuliano et al. (2007). The baseline link volumes in PCEs per hour estimated by the user equilibrium assignment with link capacity constraints split the national highway network into approximately two halves, a very dense network to the east of the Rocky Mountains and a much sparser network to the west.

3.4.1 Economic Impacts of Disruptions: NIEMO and TransNIEMO

The tests described here are for a one-year disruption of selected highway links. NIEMO is linear, making it a simple matter to down-scale the results to shorter periods. The three major research steps associated with the three sub-models are discussed in the Appendix to this chapter.

Highway network model
The FAF2 2002 data were used to assemble and construct highway network links as described in Section 3.2. The network and baseline flows were used to define bridge and tunnel collapse scenarios, and were also employed in the freight network model to estimate the changes in freight flows under different shut-down scenarios.

The highway network model is applied by combining the highway networks with the bridge or tunnel disruption scenarios. A user equilibrium (UE) model was applied twice for each test: first to develop a baseline and second by applying the scenario. The UE approach is appropriate when there is significant congestion on the network. As we are dealing with freight flows on highway networks among metropolitan regions, applying the algorithm is reasonable. The results from applying a UE algorithm include the times and the distances from origin regions to destination regions. We assume that trip durations are related to truckers' labor costs and distance is associated with the other variable costs besides labor. The results from the network model simulations are used as inputs into the transportation cost impact model.

Transportation cost impact model (supply-side MRIO model) and NIEMO (demand-driven MRIO model)
FAF provides a comprehensive data set but not all of the data are directly applicable to our research problem because services are also included in the annual flows among NIEMO's industrial sectors. These service values are excluded from the model (but see Chapter 10 for how to include them). NIEMO freight flows are used as freight flow input values. However, NIEMO does not account for transportation modes. Consequently, truck proportions from FAF are used to apportion NIEMO-estimated trade flows to obtain truck shipments. These are then loaded onto the highway network. Increases in shipping costs will increase commodity prices (Berwick and Farooq, 2003). This, in turn, suppresses consumer expenditures. Consequently, we also require data on the shipping costs associated with all the flows. Total shipping costs between states are estimated using data from NIEMO, IMPLAN and FAF effects of scenario disruptions.

3.4.2   Network Effects

Calculations proceed at a maximally disaggregate level. Each economic centroid is connected to multiple network centroids in the vicinity of the economic centroid, and each network centroid serves as an origin for an equal share of the freight transportation requirements associated with the economic centroid. Each serves as a destination for an equal share of the demand imposed on the network at network centroids in the vicinity of other economic centroids. Once network equilibrium flows are achieved, travel times and changes in travel times between economic centroids are computed as averages across the pairs of network centroids corresponding to each pair of economic centroids. When network capacity is removed from the system, travel times on a few links will decrease. These are links that are no longer accessible as a result of removing a link or links. However, alternative routes see an increase in flows and a decrease in level of service as freight flows divert away from routes that are no longer feasible.

Table 3.4 lists the top 20 O-D pairs with the highest percentage of time difference between the baseline and four bridges collapse scenario, estimated from the equilibrium assignment model with capacity constraints. Based on the model's results, the increased freight shipping time in the bridge collapse scenario was 674 million PCE*hours across all 12,204 O-D pairs of economic centroids. The net increase in route travel times is 373,836 hours system-wide. Because the economic centroids area is associated with large, sub-state regions that are constrained by state boundaries, these results can be further aggregated to state-level results using standard geographic information systems (GIS) tools.

Similarly, Table 3.5 lists the top 20 O-D pairs with the highest percentage of time difference between the baseline and two bridges collapse scenario, also calculated via the equilibrium assignment model with capacity constraints. The model estimated that freight shipping time increased 3,061 million PCE*hours across all 12,204 economic centroid O-D pairs. The net increase in route travel times is considerably lower than in the case of the previous scenario, only 5,633 hours system-wide. As before, these results can reasonably easily be aggregated to state-level values. Some numerical fidelity is lost because freight shipping times for state-to-state O-D pairs are calculated from the times for corresponding economic centroids.

Table 3.6 reports the top 20 O-D pairs with the highest percentage of time difference between the tunnel baseline and closure scenarios. Based on the model calculations, the total increase in freight shipping time in the tunnel closure scenario was 576 million PCE*hours for the flows between the economic centroid O-D pairs. Total route travel time increase between centroid pairs was 293,252 hours. It is clear that the bridge collapse scenarios are more costly than the tunnel closure scenario in terms of total shipping costs in PCE*hours. Further, the two bridges collapse scenario has significantly greater freight transportation impacts on the national highway network than did the alternative scenarios. This is undoubtedly the result of the limited number of alternative routes across the Lower Mississippi, and the considerable diversion of flows produced from the loss of these links. The aggregate impact on route travel times is reduced as a result of the reduced freight transportation demands the loss of these bridges delivers to many links

Table 3.4 Top 20 O-D pairs with highest percentage time difference between baseline and four bridges collapse scenario measured by user equilibrium assignment with capacity constraints

Origin	Destination	Path no.	O-D value (KPCE)	Original network		Impacted network		Difference		% Difference	
				Average time (hours)	Average distance (miles)	Average time (hours)	Average distance (miles)	ΔTime (hours)	ΔDistance (miles)	Time	Distance
Washington	Washington	25	2,412.65	0.0774	2.5718	0.0832	2.5718	0.0058	0.0000	7.49	0.00
East St Louis	Kansas City	143	3,741.16	9.3160	265.1774	9.9774	306.6700	0.6614	41.4926	7.10	15.65
East St Louis	Kansas City	117	2,507.16	9.5857	283.3957	10.2616	310.0446	0.6759	26.6489	7.05	9.40
St Louis	Kansas City	99	4,212.47	9.0395	268.3507	9.6479	288.2723	0.6084	19.9216	6.73	7.42
St Louis	Kansas City	121	5,576.23	8.7973	253.8011	9.3875	281.3807	0.5902	27.5796	6.71	10.87
Remainder of New Jersey	Virginia Beach	65	5,175.00	9.7019	262.4011	10.2464	295.6473	0.5445	33.2462	5.61	12.67
Louisville	Cincinnati	169	6,029.04	4.0133	126.4906	4.2239	126.6708	0.2106	0.1802	5.25	0.14
Washington	Silver Spring	65	3,591.79	0.5582	20.8432	0.5848	21.2479	0.0266	0.4047	4.77	1.94
Washington	Richmond	65	2,197.48	4.4437	124.0159	4.6536	124.9630	0.2099	0.9471	4.72	0.76
Delaware	Virginia Beach	169	5,030.60	8.5889	257.2477	8.9713	277.8631	0.3824	20.6154	4.45	8.01
Louisville	Dayton	143	4,877.08	4.9912	171.2554	5.2044	172.5271	0.2132	1.2717	4.27	0.74
East St Louis	Remainder of Missouri	208	4,791.78	6.4026	199.8073	6.6576	211.3535	0.2550	11.5462	3.98	5.78
East Chicago	Chicago	231	7,831.15	3.2123	72.2430	3.3392	73.6664	0.1269	1.4234	3.95	1.97
Baltimore	Columbus	169	1,679.37	15.5931	445.8562	16.2044	436.8825	0.6113	−8.9737	3.92	−2.01
East St Louis	Denver	169	608.71	24.5111	870.7580	25.4584	904.0775	0.9473	33.3195	3.86	3.83
Louisville	Kansas City	143	1,425.34	17.4836	544.6757	18.1573	609.5848	0.6737	64.9091	3.85	11.92
Delaware	Richmond	169	4,857.46	8.0157	235.1792	8.3229	243.4783	0.3072	8.2991	3.83	3.53
Louisville	Kansas City	117	776.48	17.7187	563.3867	18.3969	620.0807	0.6782	56.6940	3.83	10.06
St Louis	Denver	143	1,358.99	23.9899	859.9821	24.8828	881.3679	0.8929	21.3858	3.72	2.49
Remainder of New Jersey	Raleigh	65	381.47	13.4500	421.0213	13.9480	436.9897	0.4980	15.9684	3.70	3.79

Note: KPCE = kilometers of passenger car equivalents.

36

Table 3.5 *Top 20 O-D pairs with highest percentage time difference in the two bridges scenario in the FAF network measured by authors' user equilibrium assignment with capacity constraints*

Origin	Destination	Path no.	O-D value (KPCE)	Original network		Impacted network		Difference		% Difference	
				Average time (hours)	Average distance (miles)	Average time (hours)	Average distance (miles)	ΔTime (hours)	ΔDistance (miles)	Time	Distance
Memphis	Arkansas	216	4,942.52	6.077	200.0925	8.8559	232.1458	2.7789	32.0533	45.73	16.02
Arkansas	Memphis	216	2,898.35	5.4773	197.1962	7.601	229.9408	2.1237	32.7446	38.77	16.61
Memphis	Remainder of Missouri	144	3,380.14	9.2256	337.2369	11.9935	364.4715	2.7679	27.2346	30.00	8.08
Remainder of Missouri	Memphis	144	2,629.59	8.76	339.8415	11.0556	378.9636	2.2956	39.1221	26.21	11.51
Memphis	St Louis	99	2,736.74	6.7725	287.6912	8.4565	287.8123	1.684	0.1211	24.87	0.04
Memphis	Tulsa	81	855.79	12.3741	447.5175	15.4327	491.103	3.0586	43.5855	24.72	9.74
Memphis	East St Louis	117	1,131.81	7.1028	294.6997	8.6806	312.5435	1.5778	17.8438	22.21	6.05
Memphis	Oklahoma City	81	1,144.63	13.9647	492.7952	16.9553	549.5469	2.9906	56.7517	21.42	11.52
Tulsa	Memphis	81	859.58	11.5858	440.5571	13.958	495.1701	2.3722	54.613	20.48	12.40
Memphis	Kansas City	99	701.54	13.7844	507.1309	16.5921	548.2106	2.8077	41.0797	20.37	8.10
Mississippi	St Louis	264	1,215.35	10.4096	486.1331	12.5198	496.123	2.1102	9.9899	20.27	2.05
Memphis	Kansas City	81	790.95	13.8688	512.8989	16.6625	552.8285	2.7937	39.9296	20.14	7.79
Memphis	Lawton	117	923.72	14.5516	539.5989	17.3091	579.7381	2.7575	40.1392	18.95	7.44
Memphis	Remainder of Kansas	432	791.84	15.7737	597.221	18.7524	648.3663	2.9787	51.1453	18.88	8.56
Mississippi	East St Louis	312	622.94	10.7345	492.7173	12.6682	519.0557	1.9337	26.3384	18.01	5.35
Mississippi	Arkansas	576	2,298.91	7.173	267.8714	8.4606	275.7856	1.2876	7.9142	17.95	2.95
Kansas City	Memphis	81	740.43	13.1589	527.6307	15.5112	548.2904	2.3523	20.6597	17.88	3.92
New Orleans	St Louis	121	348.62	13.35	665.6185	15.7326	676.0811	2.3826	10.4626	17.85	1.57
Kansas City	Memphis	99	640.86	13.0884	520.1453	15.4227	538.6018	2.3343	18.4565	17.83	3.55
Oklahoma City	Memphis	81	614.02	12.9968	485.3012	15.3035	542.0572	2.3067	56.756	17.75	11.70

Note: KPCE = kilometers of passenger car equivalents.

Table 3.6   Top 20 O-D pairs with highest percentage time difference in the tunnel scenario in the FAF network measured by authors' user equilibrium assignment with capacity constraints

Origin	Destination	Path no.	O-D value (KPCE)	Original network		Impacted network		Difference		% Difference	
				Average time (hours)	Average distance (miles)	Average time (hours)	Average distance (miles)	ΔTime (hours)	ΔDistance (miles)	Time	Distance
Denver	Colorado Springs	286	5,250.24	4.4701	147.2388	4.8573	163.2640	0.3872	16.0252	8.66	10.88
Colorado Springs	Denver	286	6,978.55	3.9356	148.9149	4.2747	154.4561	0.3391	5.5412	8.62	3.72
Virginia Beach	Washington	65	1,820.90	5.2506	185.4439	5.6120	194.1242	0.3614	8.6803	6.88	4.68
Remainder of Arizona	Tucson	48	547.62	8.1142	283.2915	8.6025	319.9456	0.4883	36.6541	6.02	12.94
Detroit	Cleveland	247	3,250.51	8.1479	212.1253	8.6044	201.3256	0.4565	-10.7997	5.60	-5.09
Colorado Springs	Colorado Springs	484	18,919.65	5.6769	195.7112	5.9879	200.9215	0.3110	5.2103	5.48	2.66
Richmond	Washington	65	1,966.75	4.4716	124.8251	4.7018	122.7343	0.2302	-2.0908	5.15	-1.67
Virginia Beach	Arlington	169	3,910.82	5.1743	186.3768	5.4103	191.9705	0.2360	5.5937	4.56	3.00
Washington	Washington	25	1,169.30	0.0774	2.5718	0.0809	2.5718	0.0035	0.0000	4.52	0.00
Phoenix	Denver	65	203.89	23.3198	894.1576	24.3305	898.9331	1.0107	4.7755	4.33	0.53
Detroit	Pittsburgh	221	2,536.94	11.4584	327.9988	11.9395	329.6250	0.4811	1.6262	4.20	0.50
St Louis	Indianapolis city (balance)	121	1,936.33	7.9232	266.7490	8.2536	294.8386	0.3304	28.0896	4.17	10.53
Louisville	Cincinnati	169	2,387.55	4.0133	126.4906	4.1779	135.1950	0.1646	8.7044	4.10	6.88
East St Louis	Indianapolis city (balance)	143	1,364.92	7.2922	239.3810	7.5903	263.7704	0.2981	24.3894	4.09	10.19
Delaware	Camden	143	2,285.84	1.3459	53.4612	1.4006	53.3452	0.0547	-0.1160	4.06	-0.22
New Mexico	Denver	286	1,510.40	10.0302	432.7385	10.4286	451.6375	0.3984	18.8990	3.97	4.37
Oklahoma City	New Mexico	198	799.78	19.2989	632.3813	20.0600	659.2125	0.7611	26.8312	3.94	4.24
Grand Rapids	Cleveland	171	2,194.21	10.6561	342.0840	11.0668	328.3309	0.4107	-13.7531	3.85	-4.02
Remainder of Michigan	Cleveland	399	2,981.19	10.2120	307.2122	10.6012	298.3683	0.3892	-8.8439	3.81	-2.88
Minneapolis	Wyoming	208	648.18	19.9055	777.6148	20.6623	803.8577	0.7568	26.2429	3.80	3.37

Note: KPCE = kilometers of passenger car equivalents.

in the network. The economic consequences of all these re-routings are discussed below.

3.4.3   Economic Consequences

The national output loss is similar in all three cases (about $17.8 billion), but the spatial distribution of impacts varies among scenarios. Ohio (9.87 percent of US output losses), Missouri (7.10 percent), California (6.74 percent) and Texas (5.94 percent) are the most impacted states in the two bridges disruption scenario. Missouri and Ohio are near the Mississippi River, California's ports handle most of the nation's trans-Pacific trade and Texas is a large state. In terms of sectors, USC Sectors 1 (live animals, live fish, meat, seafood and so on; 4.73 percent), 5 (other prepared foodstuffs, fats, oils; 4.66 percent), 31 (construction; 5.84 percent) and 32 (wholesale trade; 5.04 percent) are most heavily impacted by this event, primarily because these goods feature prominently in interstate trade. In the four bridges disruption scenario, Missouri (11.20 percent), California (6.35 percent), Ohio (6.05 percent) and Indiana (5.97 percent) are the most affected states. The same four USC sectors experience the maximum decline. As for the tunnel disruption simulation, Colorado (21.91 percent), Ohio (8.14 percent) and California (7.83 percent) and the same four USC sectors are again the most impacted.

Interestingly, several states distant from the target bridges are seriously impacted. Possible reasons for these results could be explained by the network algorithm that we applied. The UE algorithm considers traffic congestion; when there is congestion in any region, truck flows are diverted to other routes. So even though the state is not proximate to the closed bridges, that state can be affected. Second, freight volumes in the state may explain the phenomenon. For example, California is severely affected in all three scenarios although it is not near the various target bridges or the tunnel. California's two major ports of Los Angeles and Long Beach handle about 60 percent of container imports to the USA. Large portions of these imported cargos are delivered by truck to the rest of the USA. Third, network connections may be another factor explaining the results. If major highways are connected to the disrupted bridges and if a state uses that highway for significant freight movements, then that state can also be affected by the closure.

The unexpected result is that the total output losses are relatively small in both absolute and relative terms, despite the obvious importance of the facilities identified in these scenarios. There is apparently sufficient redundancy in the US highway network that re-routings can be found that impose relatively small costs on truckers and on the economy as a whole.

3.5   CONCLUSIONS

This study has described the methodology for estimating the sector-by-sector and state-by-state economic impacts of highway bridge collapse and tunnel closure on freight transportation costs measured by time and by distance. A regional freight transportation model developed in our previous studies has been extended to analyse interregional and interstate freight flows. It is a UE model with capacity constraints. We incorporated a UE algorithm into the model (Frank and Wolfe, 1956) to compute UE flows on the national highway network. We also organized network link data developed from the FAF 2002 data set to achieve an efficient computation process.

Three scenarios were designed for the implementation of the equilibrium model. One scenario hypothesized the collapse of four highway bridges in Louisiana and at the border of Iowa and Illinois. The second scenario assumed the collapse of two bridges with the highest traffic volume over the Lower Mississippi River in the Memphis area. The third scenario hypothesized the closure of the Eisenhower Memorial Tunnel at Denver, Colorado. The effects of bridge collapse and tunnel closure on highway freight flows were examined. The simulation results showed that bridge collapse scenarios were worse than the tunnel closure scenario in terms of total shipping costs in PCE*hours of travel measured at either the regional or state level. The collapse of two bridges in the Memphis area triggered the highest increase in freight shipping costs. The results from the equilibrium model clearly show the ripple effects of the bridge collapse and tunnel closure on the national highway network while the somewhat unrealistic all-or-nothing assignment model limits the effects to the directly impacted highways.

There are some limitations in this study, especially in the capacity constraints on freight movement. The representation of congestion cost follows a metropolitan-level perspective that relies on an assumption of steady-state flows. This is only a first order approximation for flows in a national network. Still, there is empirical evidence of freight sensitivity to congestion costs (Winston and Langer, 2006), and the UE model provides much more realistic results relative to an all-or-nothing assignment approach, especially for freight re-routing on the highways closer to the collapsed bridges. Unfortunately, passenger flows have not yet been incorporated into the equilibrium model with capacity constraints because the passenger flow data are unavailable for the FAF 2002-based highway network. Consequently, the results do not reflect any interactions between passenger flows and freight flows on the national highway network.

This study has only considered the re-routing of freight flows on a single mode, that is, highway network. It does not incorporate other modes, especially the rail network. In future research, the rail and air networks will be combined with the highway network to build up an integrated freight transportation network and a multimodal freight model will be developed to estimate the change of freight flows in the bridge collapse and tunnel closure scenarios. However, we suspect that short-run mode substitution options are limited.

Infrastructure planning in light of the terrorist threat as well as the possibility of natural disasters and degradation from wear and tear begins with an assessment of the economic value of alternative investments. One way to assess economic value is to estimate the economic losses that would result were any element of the infrastructure degraded. A modeling approach to this problem involves extensive disaggregation. All states and many economic sectors are engaged in continuous trade at substantial levels. Most of this trade takes place via trucks on the NHS (including Interstate highways and major roads).

Representing all of this complexity in an operational model has been our primary task. In this study, we have described the steps involved in assembling the data and testing the model.

From a policy perspective, one unexpected result is the small adjustments needed even when high traffic-volume bridges and tunnels are destroyed. Re-routing involves modest increases in freight costs. In the short run, for trucks already en route, the additional time and distance costs could be substantial. However, once the disruptions are known, the extensive redundancy in the national highway and major roads system permits long-distance trucking companies to choose alternative routes that add little, if anything, to freight costs. Sometimes, negative results can be as important as positive results. We were surprised by these findings. However, the policy implications for homeland security are profound. This study suggests that the negative economic impacts from bridge and tunnel destruction (at least in terms of additional freight costs) are less than from other types of terrorist attacks. Fiscal resources are scarce, and the Department of Homeland Security must prioritize its allocation of funds (GAO, 2009).

NOTE

*   Acknowledgments: research contributions by SooHyun Cho, Eunha (Eileen) Jun, Christine Ngyuen, SungHo Ryu and SungSu (Stephen) Yoon.

REFERENCES

Berwick, M. and M. Farooq (2003), *Truck Costing Model for Transportation Managers*. Upper Great Plains Transportation Institute, North Dakota State University, available at http://www.mountain-plains.org/pubs/html/mpc-03-152/index.php.

Frank, M. and P. Wolfe (1956), 'An algorithm for quadratic programming', *Naval Research Logistics Quarterly*, **3** (1), 95–110.

GAO (Government Accounting Office) (2009), *Highway Infrastructure: Federal Efforts to Strengthen Security Should be Better Coordinated and Targeted on the Nation's Most Critical Highway Infrastructure*, Report GAO-09-57. Washington, DC: Government Accounting Office.

Giuliano, G., P. Gordon, Q. Pan, J.Y. Park and L. Wang (2007), 'Estimating freight flows for metropolitan area highway networks using secondary data sources', *Networks and Spatial Economics*, **10** (1), 73–91.

Gordon, P. and Q. Pan (2001), *Assembling and Processing Freight Shipment Data: Developing a GIS-based Origin-Destination Matrix for Southern California Freight Flows*, Report No. FHWA/CA/OR-2001–15. Sacramento, CA: California Department of Transportation.

Hillestad, R., B.D. Van Roo and K.D. Yoho (2009), *Key Issues in Modernizing the U.S. Freight-Transportation System for Future Economic Growth*. Santa Monica, CA: Rand Corporation.

Pan, Q. (2006), 'Freight data assembling and modeling: methodologies and practice', *Journal of Transportation Planning and Technology*, **29** (1), 43–74.

Park, J.Y., P. Gordon, J.E. Moore II and H.W. Richardson (2009), 'A two-step approach to estimating state-to-state commodity trade flows', *Annals of Regional Science*, **43**, 1033–72.

Park, J.Y., J. Cho, P. Gordon, J.E. Moore II, H.W. Richardson and S.S. Yoon (2011), 'Adding a freight network to a National Interstate Input-Output model: a TransNIEMO application for California', *Journal of Transportation Geography*, **19** (6), 1410–22.

US Census Bureau (2004), *2002 Commodity Flow Survey*, available at http://www.census.gov/prod/eco 02tcf.

USDOT (US Department of Transportation) (2004), *2002 Commodity Survey: United States*. Washington, DC: Bureau of Transportation Statistics and US Census Bureau.

USDOT-FHWA (US Department of Transportation-Federal Highway Administration) (2003), *2002 Status of the Nation's Highways, Bridges, and Transit: Conditions & Performance*, FHWA-PL-03-004. Washington, DC.

USDOT-FHWA (US Department of Transportation-Federal Highway Administration) (2008a), *Our Nation's Highways 2008*, FHWA-PL-08-021. Washington, DC.

USDOT-FHWA (US Department of Transportation-Federal Highway

Administration) (2008b), *Freight Facts and Figures 2008*, FHWA-PL-08-052. Washington, DC.

Winston, C. and A. Langer (2006), 'The effect of government highway spending on road user's congestion costs', *Journal of Urban Economics*, **60**, 463–83.

Xie, F. and D. Levinson (2009), 'Evaluating the effects of I-35W bridge collapse on road-users in the twin cities metropolitan region', Transportation Research Board Meeting 2009, Paper No. 09-1138, Washington, DC.

4. Theme parks*

Harry W. Richardson, JiYoung Park, Peter Gordon, James E. Moore II and Qisheng Pan

4.1 INTRODUCTION

> After September 11, many of us came to realize how little Bin Laden and al Qaeda understood the United States. In striking major targets in New York and Washington, they made us nationally resolute. But if they had any sense of how to tear out the heart of America, they would have targeted six Midwest shopping malls simultaneously or *five Southern amusement parks*, or a random selection of elementary schools. (Podhoretz, 2010, emphasis added)

The motive for this chapter was to address this very serious question. No theme park has been attacked. Many of the terrorists are technically incompetent with respect to bomb and explosives technology. Far worse is that they do not understand what binds us.

This chapter is not intended as a road map for terrorists. Rather, it is one of a series of studies by our group on the economic impact of a variety of hypothetical terrorist attacks in the United States. This research suggests that even a single attack on a theme park may have widespread national economic not to mention human repercussions. The results imply that significant prevention strategies may be justified.

Our research studies use either or both of two economic impact models, the Southern California Planning Model (SCPM) and the National Interstate Economic Model (NIEMO). This research uses only the latter model and traces the interregional economic effects of attack scenarios on major theme parks (13, including two clusters) located in a modest number of states (eight). The theme parks are identified by state but not by metropolitan area to mask specific identity. It is important to note that our results are underestimates because our analysis, by focusing on the major theme parks, ignores some of the smaller parks. We have also omitted one park that would have passed the scale threshold. We left it out because the theme park was a relatively minor component of economic activities at the site.

4.2 NIEMO

The details of the model used in this analysis (NIEMO) are explained in Chapter 2 so only a brief description is offered here, just enough for the chapter to stand independently. The model revives an approach adopted in the late 1970s and the early 1980s (Jack Faucett Associates, 1983; Polenske, 1980), the development of a multiregional input-output model (MRIO). Our version combines state-level data from the IMPLAN input-output models with interregional trade flows based on the Commodity Flow Survey (CFS; see ORNL, 2000) aggregated to 47 economic sectors over 52 regions (50 states, Washington, DC and the 'Rest of the World'). This results in a MRIO matrix with almost 6 million cells. Construction of the model involved substantial data assembly and considerable data manipulation.

There have been two attempts to estimate interregional trade flows using data from the 1997 CFS. Jackson et al. (2006) used IMPLAN data to adjust incomplete CFS information primarily by adopting gravity models constrained via distance. The second attempt (Park et al., 2005) is the foundation of this study. It uses the same basic data sources but adopts a different estimation approach to update missing CFS data and a doubly constrained Fratar model (DFM) to estimate the MRIO matrix (Chapter 2 gives more details).

Constructing NIEMO requires two basic kinds of tables: industrial trade coefficients tables and regional interindustry coefficients tables. While trade tables by industry are difficult to construct because of incomplete information in the CFS data, the interindustry tables present fewer problems because reliable data are available from IMPLAN at the state and industry levels. For details of the procedure used to estimate values for the empty cells in the trade flow matrix, see Park et al. (2005). Once initial trade flow matrices are estimated for sectors based on a reconciliation of CFS, IMPLAN and SCPM data, these can then be iteratively refined.

4.2.1 Direct and Indirect but Not Induced Impacts

Usually, input-output models measure the direct (final demand), indirect (intermediate input flows) and induced (secondary consumption associated with direct and indirect employment) effects of changes in economic activity. In applying NIEMO, we have chosen in most of our research to estimate the direct and indirect impacts only, for several reasons. First, it is a convention in MRIO to ignore induced effects (Miller and Blair, 2009; Miller and Shao, 1990) because induced consumption is less likely to cross interregional, for example, interstate, boundaries. Second, although there are local induced impacts associated with local indirect effects, the local and the imported indirect impacts are typically allocated in a MRIO model via some assumption that falls short of the accurate allocations of the 'ideal' interregional input-output model. For example, imported inputs of an origin sector are allocated to a particular destination sector in the same proportion as local inputs. Third, in the specifics of the theme park application, there may be positive induced effects in origin states associated with negative direct effects in theme park states. In other words, if would-be visitors to the theme parks stay home they may spend some of their tourist money on additional consumption. This is not a conventional induced impact of the kind measured in input-output models because it is not a secondary consumption effect resulting from employment change. For these reasons, we chose not to measure induced impacts, even if the net effect is to generate under-bounded estimates.

The direct impacts in this research are not limited to theme park expenditures. Overnight visitors to theme parks spend money on accommodation and often on transportation (such as rental cars), and all visitors buy food and often shop. Our estimates include these expenditures. However, we do not include air transportation because of the difficulty of assigning impacts to individual states as most have major operations in several states, not merely the headquarters state. However, the maximum impact would be sizeable, about $11.85 billion over the 18-month recovery period assumed in our base scenario.

4.2.2   Terrorism and Tourism

Because there has never been a major terrorist attack on any tourist site in the United States, the attack of domestic origin by Eric Rudolph in Centennial Park, Atlanta, during the 1996 Olympic Games is the closest approximation. Consequently, we have no history on which to construct feasible scenarios. We have chosen to analyse a relatively simple type of attack: a large conventional bomb attack at a major theme park. Our focus is on economic impacts, so we do not explore the potential deaths and injuries and damage to tourist facilities and infrastructure. The scale of attack that we have in mind might kill about 20 people, injure ten times as many and destroy sufficient tourist attractions and facilities to close at least part of a theme park for a few months during reconstruction, and the park overall for perhaps the first month. Our best estimate is that in terms of human and infrastructure impacts, this would be a $250 million event, and thus relatively small in terms of potential terrorist events. In any event, our analysis is restricted to conventional economic impacts, specifically business interruption. We leave it to others to estimate the human and physical infrastructure costs of terrorist events. In our view, the human and infrastructure dollar costs would be swamped by the long-term blow to the theme park component of the tourist sector as visitors stayed away in droves out of fear. A major research task is to estimate the recovery period. We discuss this important but difficult task below.

Another key point is that the economic losses we report in our main findings would be gross not net losses. However, this may be based on an unreasonable assumption because tourists would not necessarily stay at home but would substitute other, presumably safer, destinations, or alternatively (not examined here) spend vacation savings on other expenditures. To capture the possibility of diversion, we explore one scenario that is not meant to be more illustrative than realistic. We assume that all the daily visitors to the theme parks stay home while the overnighters substitute visits to national parks, broadly defined to include some national monuments, national historical parks and national resort areas. In this scenario, then, there are net losses but also some redistribution of tourist revenues from some locations and sites to others, often in different states.

Drakos and Kutan (2003) hypothesize a 'zero sum game' in which total tourist revenues remain the same but tourists switch from destinations affected by terrorism to others that are currently considered safe. Their study looked at tourism in Greece, Turkey and Israel, with Italy included as a control destination not affected by terrorism in recent years. A terrorist incident in Greece was estimated to reduce the country's market share among the four destinations by 1 percent. Specifically, in our substitution scenario, we assume that 55 percent of total visitors who are day trippers to the theme parks stay home while 45 percent of overnight visitors to theme parks are allocated to a fairly comprehensive group of national parks and similar nationally designated destinations. These shifts are allocated in proportion to the national parks' most recent visitor rolls.

We explore a range of alternative attacks, not simultaneous attacks. In this chapter, we are not identifying specific theme parks but are looking at some of the major theme parks distributed across eight states. Also, in a few cases, several theme parks are located in the same metropolitan region; we refer to these as 'clusters.' We hypothesize that an attack at one theme park in a cluster will have more of an impact on other theme parks in the cluster than on theme parks outside the cluster, for example, in other states. Our rationale for studying several attacks in several states is to illustrate the capacity of our national interstate model (NIEMO) to trace multiregional economic impacts from any source of changes in final demand.

Our expectation is that the theme park sector of US tourism would take a long time to recover from a terrorist attack on a single theme park, and that the economic impacts would be nationwide in scope. There are several reasons for this view. One is the role played by theme parks in shaping the American psyche. Another is our focus on protecting children who form a sizeable share, perhaps the majority, of theme park visitors. A third is the concept of 'probability neglect.' This concept means that for psychological reasons we may suffer from fear that exaggerates risk and discounted harm because this fear fails to take sufficient account of the low probability of being a victim. The same phenomenon explained some of the downward trend in air travel after 9/11. A fourth reason is the power of the 'displacement effect.' There are so many tourist substitutions available that it is easy to cancel (or postpone) a theme park trip and go somewhere else. We explore the national parks case that we justify in terms of the argument that lower densities reduce risk, but there is a wide range of alternatives to theme park visits such as a beach holiday, a motoring holiday, a foreign trip and many others.

4.2.3   International Evidence

In the absence of prior episodes in the United States, we decided to look at the evidence from international terrorist attacks on tourist sites. However, the previous literature on tourism recovery from terrorism is relatively thin (Aly and Strazicich, 2000; Pizam and Smith, 2000). Drakos and Kutan (2003) present evidence for a relatively short time period (1996–99) on the recoveries from tourist attacks in three countries: seven months in Greece and Turkey and four months in Israel. The shorter time period in Israel probably reflects a degree of immunity and reduced sensitivity for residents, and even for tourists, associated with the greater frequency of terrorist events. This raises a more general point: infrequency combined with a larger attack in the United States might make for a longer recovery period.

A related point to the scale issue is that what seems to count most in terms of impact is not the number of incidents but the number of fatalities. Moreover, the negative relationship between tourist revenues and the number of fatalities appears to be non-linear. Another approach, adopted by Enders and Sandler (1991) is to calculate the number of international terrorists deterred by each terrorist incident. In their study of Spain, they calculated that 140,000 tourists were deterred by each Basque incident. This resulted in a second calculation that in 1988, with 5.392 million foreign tourists visiting Spain and 18 terrorist incidents, there would have been 50 percent more tourists without them. Finally, Frey et al. (2004) surveyed a range of studies with divergent results, with recovery periods as short as 2–3 months or as long as 18–21 months.

We decided to use the extreme attacks in Luxor (Egypt) in 1997 and in Bali (Indonesia) in 2002 as the best predictors of the recovery phase of a theme park attack in the United States. We have not studied in detail the attacks in Egypt in Taba in October 2004 and Sharma el Sheikh in July 2005, but we believe that the recovery periods have been broadly similar. The principal reasons for our choices are the scale of the attacks and the quality of the data. A monthly data series for international visitors is available in both cases. Moreover, the results of the two cases are broadly consistent with each other. In both cases, the number of visitors declined precipitously immediately after the attacks and then recovered very slowly over the next six months. The somewhat different example of the post-tsunami recovery of Phuket in Thailand after December 2004 is also consistent with this finding. This was the short-term impact. In the Bali case, annual tourism did not return to the pre-attack levels until 2004, and monthly data did not consistently (month after month) exceed the pre-attack levels until 18 months after the attack.

Of course, in the absence of a historical record, any scenario is little better than a hypothetical guess. Nevertheless, it is useful as an illustration, and the scenario we chose is consistent with the international evidence. The other key assumption is that if one theme park is attacked attendance will suffer at all US theme parks.

Our working assumptions are as follows:

1. A cluster consisting of several theme parks in the same Consolidated Metropolitan Statistical Area (CMSA) or Primary Metropolitan Statistical Area (PMSA) and an individual (isolated) theme park are treated as equivalents.
2. A theme park (or cluster) attacked would be closed for one month, would then operate at 30 percent capacity for the next six months and approach normal (pre-attack) levels linearly through to the 18th month.[1]
3. The major theme parks (our sample) in the country would operate at 50 percent of normal capacity for six months and then recover to normal (pre-attack) levels linearly through to the 18th month.[2]

Of course, theme park visits are subject to seasonal fluctuations, for example, opening hours change during the year, as is international tourism. For example, the peak months in Bali are May and June. We chose to ignore this complication. However, any deviation from our assumptions is easily accommodated within the model.

4.2.4 Results

We analysed attacks on 13 theme park complexes in eight states. Two of the complexes were clusters of several parks within the same metropolitan region in Florida and California. We designate them Cluster A (FL) and Cluster B (CA), respectively. Table 4.1 presents a summary of the results. Recall our assumption about the spillover effects on other theme parks not under direct attack, namely that other theme parks in a cluster would suffer the same fate in terms of impacts as if they were directly attacked. A cluster attack would result in an economic impact of $23.62–24.92 billion, certainly less costly than the 9/11 attack. Outside the clusters in Florida and California, the impacts would be smaller, in the $20.75–20.94 billion range, but still sizeable. Of course, this result is a consequence of our specific assumptions that an attack on any major theme park would have nationwide repercussions on all major theme parks. We also report below on the most conservative of assumptions, that is, no spillover effects.

The foreign indirect impacts are in the $415–419 million range except for Florida and California, and $499 million and $472 million in these two states. Note that there are no foreign direct impacts because the direct impacts measure the effects on the theme park states. The term 'foreign' measures leakages to the rest of the world outside the United States, and these impacts are all indirect. Despite the importance of international tourism, the foreign impacts are quite small but consistent with the 2 percent estimate of international visitors at the theme parks.

The direct impacts are in the $11.82–14.19 billion range and the indirect impacts fall within a range of $8.93–9.01 billion. The Florida and California clusters have somewhat larger impacts, whereas the impacts of attacks in other states are of similar magnitude.

4.2.5 The No Spillovers Case

These results are very sensitive to the spillover effect assumptions. We do not believe that other theme parks in the country would be immune from the effects of an attack on a theme park in another state, but we can combine some of the data in Table 4.1 into another table (Table 4.2) to demonstrate the implications if this belief was incorrect. The data here show the results if the economic impacts are confined to the theme park(s) in the state subject to attack. This is the limiting case of minimal impacts, and is useful from that perspective even if not very realistic. As shown in Table 4.2, the differences are dramatic, with impacts varying from less than half a billion dollars in Virginia to up to more than $11.61 billion in the Florida cluster. The economic multipliers are more or less similar, in the 1.48–1.85 range. Remember that these may be underestimates because of the exclusion of induced impacts.

Table 4.1 Summary of theme park impacts, $ million

Cluster	Direct			Indirect				Total
	Intrastate	Other theme park states	Total	Intrastate	All other states	Foreign	Total	
Cluster A (FL)	7,622.3	6,562.7	14,185.0	3,983.0	6,253.8	499.1	10,735.9	24,920.9
Cluster B (CA)	5,971.0	7,499.1	13,470.1	3,312.3	6,361.6	472.0	10,146.0	23,616.1
NV	681.2	11,263.2	11,944.4	326.8	8,246.1	417.7	8,990.7	20,935.1
OH	815.6	11,070.2	11,885.8	551.9	8,018.3	417.7	8,987.9	20,873.7
NJ	719.1	11,147.0	11,866.1	398.9	8,134.3	416.2	8,949.4	20,815.5
PA	361.6	11,474.4	11,836.0	286.9	8,238.1	415.5	8,940.5	20,776.5
VA	308.9	11,509.3	11,818.1	204.0	8,310.1	415.0	8,929.1	20,747.2
IL	371.5	11,467.8	11,839.4	315.8	8,210.9	415.7	8,942.4	20,781.8

Table 4.2   Theme park impacts: limiting case, no spillovers, $ million

Cluster	Direct	Indirect	Total	Multiplier
Cluster A (FL)	7,622.3	3,983.0	11,605.3	1.523
Cluster B (CA)	5,971.0	3,312.3	9,283.3	1.555
NV	681.2	326.8	1,008.0	1.480
OH	815.6	551.9	1,367.5	1.677
NJ	719.1	398.9	1,117.9	1.555
PA	361.6	286.9	648.6	1.793
VA	308.9	204.0	512.9	1.661
IL	371.5	315.8	687.3	1.850

The overall conclusion is that if there are no spillovers, the terrorist payoff is maximized by attacking a large theme park or a park in a major metropolitan area with many theme parks, such as in Florida or California. On the other hand, if there are significant spillovers, an attack on any known theme park, even one of modest size with presumably less protection because the expense risks are lower, will result in similar nationwide economic impacts. Unfortunately, we do not and will not know which is the more likely scenario unless it happens.

It is a reasonable argument, however, that the spillover scenarios are more plausible. It is our belief that a successful attack on any theme park in the country would have national repercussions. The reason is based on public perception of risks and behavioral adjustments. Given that a theme park visit is a deferrable event and has many attractive alternative vacation trip substitutes, why would a rational person not postpone such a visit by either going elsewhere or staying at home? This behavior is consistent with the hypothesis of 'probability neglect' mentioned above. If valid, any theme park attack would result in nationwide fear, if not panic, and a widespread if temporary shunning of all theme parks. Perception also influences the recovery period. In this research, we have used the 2002 Bali and the 1997 Luxor attacks as a template for the decline and recovery trajectory. This is probably conservative given that an American family with children considering a visit to a theme park after an attack might react more cautiously than, say, Australian singles to a holiday in Bali after a bar attack.

4.2.6   The Distribution of Geographical Impacts

One question is the sensitivity of the spatial distribution of indirect impacts to the location(s) of the direct impact. To test this, we assumed a $100 million decline in theme park revenues in each of the nine major theme park states. Note that for this simple test, we did not include the ripple effects of revenue losses at theme parks in states other than in the state attacked, so this analysis is somewhat distinct from the other scenarios discussed in this chapter. The results are displayed in Table 4.3. They are not surprising. More than 90 percent of the impacts are intrastate, and the interstate impacts reflect a significant distance decay effect. In other words, the proportionate indirect impacts tend to be larger in states that are nearby to the state where the direct impacts occur.

4.3 A DIVERSION SCENARIO: THE NATIONAL PARKS

A standard objection to models of the kind used in this research is that, as noted above, declines in final demand are not necessarily net losses. For example, the business interruptions and structural damage associated with a natural disaster, such as an earthquake or a hurricane, are usually offset later by a revival of pent-up demand and an injection of reconstruction funds. There are losses involved, such as the opportunity costs of resources diverted to reconstruction, but there are offsets to many losses.

So it may be in this case. A decline in visitors to theme parks after a terrorist attack is likely to be partially offset by an increase in other, presumably considered safer, types of tourist activities. It is not reasonable to expect everyone to stay home. Thus, part of the change in the tourist scene will be a redistribution of tourist expenditures rather than a total loss. To illustrate this effect, we consider a single substitution scenario to measure the potential offset. Theme park visitors are divided into two categories: day trippers (55 percent) and overnighters (45 percent). We assume that the day trippers stay home. An alternative would be for them to spend the money saved on other items of consumer expenditure. We divert the overnighters to other tourist activities. In the example explored here, we assume – somewhat unrealistically – that they all go to national parks and similar nationally designated destinations. The results of this scenario are reported in Table 4.4.

We consider the maximum impact case, an attack on a theme park in Cluster A (Florida), and reallocate all the lost overnight visitors at all theme parks in the country over the 18-month recovery period to the designated set of national parks and resort areas in proportion to their current visitor levels. We excluded all parks with less than 0.5 million annual visitors, national highways and monuments in New York City and

Table 4.3   Interstate impacts of a $100 million direct loss in theme park states, $ million

							Total impacts								
State	CA	%	FL	%	IL	%	NV	%	NJ	%	OH	%	PA	%	VA	%
AL	0.26	0.1	1.00	0.6	0.31	0.2	0.11	0.1	0.29	0.2	0.58	0.3	0.18	0.1	0.25	0.1
AK	0.08	0.0	0.02	0.0	0.02	0.0	0.02	0.0	0.01	0.0	0.05	0.0	0.01	0.0	0.06	0.0
AZ	0.44	0.3	0.10	0.1	0.08	0.0	0.21	0.1	0.05	0.0	0.07	0.0	0.07	0.0	0.08	0.0
AR	0.44	0.3	0.46	0.3	0.43	0.2	0.13	0.1	0.16	0.1	0.50	0.3	0.40	0.2	0.21	0.1
CA	153.51	88.2	1.28	0.7	1.51	0.8	5.27	3.2	1.18	0.7	1.25	0.7	1.17	0.7	0.91	0.5
CO	0.34	0.2	0.18	0.1	0.60	0.3	0.11	0.1	0.14	0.1	0.28	0.2	0.14	0.1	0.22	0.1
CT	0.09	0.0	0.15	0.1	0.10	0.1	0.09	0.1	0.21	0.1	0.11	0.1	0.18	0.1	0.15	0.1
DE	0.04	0.0	0.04	0.0	0.03	0.0	0.01	0.0	0.18	0.1	0.04	0.0	0.14	0.1	0.62	0.3
DC	0.01	0.0	0.01	0.0	0.01	0.0	0.01	0.0	0.01	0.0	0.01	0.0	0.01	0.0	0.05	0.0
FL	0.24	0.1	152.00	86.2	0.24	0.1	0.16	0.1	0.34	0.2	0.49	0.3	0.36	0.2	0.35	0.2
GA	0.24	0.1	2.46	1.4	0.40	0.2	0.14	0.1	0.61	0.4	0.67	0.4	0.56	0.3	0.79	0.4
HI	0.11	0.1	0.03	0.0	0.04	0.0	0.02	0.0	0.02	0.0	0.03	0.0	0.02	0.0	0.04	0.0
ID	0.29	0.2	0.09	0.1	0.16	0.1	0.06	0.0	0.09	0.1	0.17	0.1	0.08	0.0	0.06	0.0
IL	0.87	0.5	1.02	0.6	155.75	87.2	0.30	0.2	0.64	0.4	1.48	0.8	0.87	0.5	0.73	0.4
IN	0.35	0.2	0.39	0.2	0.99	0.6	0.19	0.1	0.30	0.2	1.03	0.6	0.36	0.2	0.69	0.4
IA	0.78	0.5	0.41	0.2	1.42	0.8	0.14	0.1	0.37	0.2	0.63	0.3	0.38	0.2	0.31	0.2
KS	0.56	0.3	0.18	0.1	0.51	0.3	0.15	0.1	0.80	0.5	0.52	0.3	0.15	0.1	0.60	0.3
KY	0.20	0.1	0.35	0.2	0.46	0.3	0.11	0.1	0.18	0.1	0.96	0.5	0.31	0.2	0.65	0.4
LA	0.55	0.3	0.71	0.4	0.47	0.3	0.19	0.1	0.17	0.1	0.26	0.1	0.24	0.1	0.28	0.2
ME	0.08	0.0	0.06	0.0	0.08	0.0	0.02	0.0	0.06	0.0	0.05	0.0	0.12	0.1	0.07	0.0
MD	0.07	0.0	0.08	0.0	0.10	0.0	0.05	0.0	0.29	0.2	0.10	0.1	0.44	0.2	1.21	0.7
MA	0.14	0.1	0.21	0.1	0.15	0.1	0.11	0.1	0.26	0.2	0.18	0.1	0.21	0.1	0.24	0.1
MI	0.45	0.3	0.56	0.3	0.71	0.4	0.31	0.2	0.57	0.3	1.68	0.9	0.57	0.3	0.80	0.4
MN	0.55	0.3	0.32	0.2	0.90	0.5	0.17	0.1	0.32	0.2	0.72	0.4	0.39	0.2	0.28	0.2
MS	0.15	0.1	0.34	0.2	0.24	0.1	0.06	0.0	0.13	0.1	0.23	0.1	0.16	0.1	0.16	0.1
MO	0.39	0.2	0.30	0.2	0.73	0.4	0.74	0.5	0.40	0.2	0.36	0.2	0.34	0.2	0.29	0.2

MT	0.17	0.1	0.03	0.0	0.21	0.1	0.03	0.0	0.03	0.0	0.04	0.0	0.04	0.0	0.02	0.0
NE	0.68	0.4	0.53	0.3	0.55	0.3	0.09	0.1	0.27	0.2	0.55	0.3	0.54	0.3	0.27	0.1
NV	0.13	0.1	0.03	0.0	0.02	0.0	146.93	89.7	0.02	0.0	0.03	0.0	0.02	0.0	0.02	0.0
NH	0.05	0.0	0.04	0.0	0.04	0.0	0.03	0.0	0.03	0.0	0.04	0.0	0.06	0.0	0.06	0.0
NJ	0.31	0.2	0.46	0.3	0.41	0.2	0.14	0.1	149.39	88.2	0.36	0.2	0.70	0.4	0.40	0.2
NM	0.06	0.0	0.07	0.0	0.07	0.0	0.04	0.0	0.04	0.0	0.08	0.0	0.05	0.0	0.03	0.0
NY	0.42	0.2	0.50	0.3	0.49	0.3	0.20	0.1	1.54	0.9	0.79	0.4	1.57	0.9	0.65	0.4
NC	0.26	0.1	0.77	0.4	0.28	0.2	0.13	0.1	0.44	0.3	0.60	0.3	0.61	0.3	2.11	1.2
ND	0.10	0.1	0.05	0.0	0.17	0.1	0.06	0.0	0.06	0.0	0.12	0.1	0.11	0.1	0.04	0.0
OH	0.53	0.3	0.71	0.4	0.85	0.5	0.54	0.3	0.66	0.4	158.75	86.4	1.12	0.6	0.86	0.5
OK	0.31	0.2	0.22	0.1	0.21	0.1	0.13	0.1	0.16	0.1	0.19	0.1	0.14	0.1	0.15	0.1
OR	0.48	0.3	0.12	0.1	0.20	0.1	0.18	0.1	0.09	0.1	0.20	0.1	0.08	0.0	0.10	0.1
PA	0.47	0.3	0.65	0.4	0.59	0.3	0.34	0.2	1.86	1.1	1.24	0.7	157.60	87.9	1.56	0.9
RI	0.03	0.0	0.05	0.0	0.02	0.0	0.03	0.0	0.04	0.0	0.05	0.0	0.04	0.0	0.04	0.0
SC	0.11	0.1	0.37	0.2	0.14	0.1	0.07	0.1	0.12	0.1	0.28	0.2	0.20	0.1	0.37	0.2
SD	0.18	0.1	0.07	0.0	0.20	0.1	0.04	0.1	0.06	0.0	0.22	0.1	0.13	0.1	0.07	0.0
TN	0.29	0.2	0.53	0.3	0.30	0.2	0.16	0.1	0.38	0.2	0.48	0.3	0.39	0.2	0.85	0.5
TX	2.52	1.4	3.50	2.0	0.94	0.5	2.01	1.2	1.95	1.1	0.99	0.5	2.50	1.4	1.21	0.7
UT	0.29	0.2	0.11	0.1	0.08	0.0	0.19	0.1	0.04	0.0	0.09	0.1	0.07	0.0	0.06	0.0
VM	0.03	0.0	0.04	0.0	0.05	0.0	0.01	0.0	0.04	0.0	0.03	0.0	0.06	0.0	0.03	0.0
VA	0.13	0.1	0.27	0.2	0.30	0.2	0.09	0.1	0.27	0.2	0.36	0.2	0.47	0.3	157.67	86.7
WA	0.93	0.5	0.25	0.1	0.25	0.1	0.27	0.2	0.15	0.1	0.22	0.1	0.18	0.1	0.16	0.1
WV	0.05	0.0	0.05	0.0	0.06	0.0	0.03	0.0	0.06	0.0	0.73	0.4	0.26	0.1	0.80	0.4
WI	0.70	0.4	0.63	0.4	1.97	1.1	0.26	0.2	0.58	0.3	1.00	0.5	0.85	0.5	0.50	0.3
WY	0.06	0.0	0.02	0.0	0.17	0.1	0.07	0.0	0.02	0.0	0.06	0.0	0.03	0.0	0.02	0.0
US subtotal	170.51	98.0	172.85	98.0	174.99	98.0	160.97	98.3	166.09	98.0	179.95	97.9	175.67	98.0	178.20	98.0
Foreign	3.45	2.0	3.54	2.0	3.63	2.0	2.87	1.7	3.33	2.0	3.78	2.1	3.59	2.0	3.67	2.0
Total	173.96	100.0	176.39	100.0	178.61	100.0	163.84	100.0	169.42	100.0	183.73	100.0	179.26	100.0	181.87	100.0

Note: $100 million are distributed according to sector proportions, which are adopted from the proportions in Cluster B.

55

Table 4.4 Diversion of theme park overnight visitors to national parks, by state and USC sectors, $ million

Code	Proportion	USC 33	USC 35	USC 44	USC 45	1st_Total	USC 33	USC 35	USC 44	USC 45	2nd_Total
AK	0.012	13.74	20.85	18.28	40.46	93.33	1.68	2.56	2.24	4.96	11.44
AZ	0.055	65.00	98.64	86.44	191.37	441.46	7.97	12.09	10.60	23.46	54.12
AR	0.016	18.66	28.31	24.81	54.92	126.70	2.29	3.47	3.04	6.73	15.53
CA	0.118	137.95	209.35	183.46	406.16	936.91	16.91	25.66	22.49	49.79	114.86
CO	0.027	32.18	48.84	42.80	94.75	218.57	3.95	5.99	5.25	11.62	26.79
DC	0.015	17.73	26.91	23.58	52.21	120.43	2.17	3.30	2.89	6.40	14.81
FL	0.050	59.12	89.72	78.63	174.07	401.55	7.25	11.00	9.64	21.34	49.23
GA	0.027	31.98	48.54	42.53	94.16	217.21	3.92	5.95	5.21	11.54	26.63
HI	0.031	36.80	55.85	48.95	108.36	249.96	4.51	6.85	6.00	13.28	30.64
IN	0.011	12.94	19.64	17.21	38.10	87.89	1.59	2.41	2.11	4.67	10.77
KY	0.017	20.14	30.57	26.79	59.30	136.80	2.47	3.75	3.28	7.27	16.77
LA	0.004	4.25	6.46	5.66	12.53	28.89	0.52	0.79	0.69	1.54	3.54
ME	0.013	15.78	23.95	20.99	46.47	107.19	1.93	2.94	2.57	5.70	13.14
MD	0.012	14.32	21.73	19.04	42.16	97.24	1.76	2.66	2.33	5.17	11.92
MA	0.040	47.46	72.02	63.12	139.73	322.33	5.82	8.83	7.74	17.13	39.52
MI	0.007	8.09	12.28	10.76	23.82	54.95	0.99	1.50	1.32	2.92	6.74
MN	0.002	1.78	2.70	2.37	5.24	12.09	0.22	0.33	0.29	0.64	1.48
MS	0.012	14.43	21.90	19.19	42.48	97.99	1.77	2.68	2.35	5.21	12.01
MO	0.025	29.29	44.44	38.95	86.23	198.91	3.59	5.45	4.78	10.57	24.38
MT	0.021	25.00	37.93	33.24	73.59	169.76	3.06	4.65	4.08	9.02	20.81
NV	0.036	41.92	63.62	55.75	123.43	284.74	5.14	7.80	6.84	15.13	34.91

NJ	0.032	37.41	56.76	49.75	110.13	254.04	4.59	6.96	6.10	13.50	31.14
NM	0.003	3.00	4.55	3.99	8.83	20.37	0.37	0.56	0.49	1.08	2.50
NY	0.045	52.91	80.30	70.37	155.78	359.36	6.49	9.84	8.63	19.10	44.06
NC	0.042	49.77	75.52	66.18	146.52	337.99	6.10	9.26	8.11	17.96	41.43
OH	0.020	23.63	35.86	31.43	69.58	160.51	2.90	4.40	3.85	8.53	19.68
OK	0.008	9.12	13.84	12.13	26.85	61.93	1.12	1.70	1.49	3.29	7.59
PA	0.051	59.80	90.75	79.53	176.07	406.14	7.33	11.12	9.75	21.59	49.79
SC	0.006	6.49	9.84	8.63	19.10	44.06	0.80	1.21	1.06	2.34	5.40
SD	0.022	25.50	38.70	33.92	75.09	173.21	3.13	4.74	4.16	9.21	21.23
TN	0.031	36.70	55.69	48.80	108.04	249.23	4.50	6.83	5.98	13.25	30.56
TX	0.027	32.17	48.82	42.79	94.72	218.51	3.94	5.98	5.25	11.61	26.79
UT	0.046	53.83	81.68	71.58	158.48	365.57	6.60	10.01	8.78	19.43	44.82
VA	0.044	51.65	78.38	68.68	152.06	350.76	6.33	9.61	8.42	18.64	43.00
WA	0.034	39.94	60.61	53.12	117.59	271.26	4.90	7.43	6.51	14.42	33.25
WV	0.007	8.23	12.49	10.95	24.24	55.91	1.01	1.53	1.34	2.97	6.85
WY	0.029	34.57	52.46	45.97	101.78	234.79	4.24	6.43	5.64	12.48	28.78
Total	1.000	1173.28	1780.52	1560.34	3454.41	7968.55	143.84	218.23	191.29	423.50	976.87

Note: In the cases where one national park is located in two or more states, the number of diverted visitors is allocated to each state according to the total proportions in each state.

57

Washington, DC. The consequences, as shown in Table 4.5, are a marked geographical redistribution of tourist expenditures and their impacts because theme parks are typically located in densely populated urban settings while national parks are usually located in lower density rural settings. Other substitution scenarios, such as a shift to beach holidays, would also have marked, but very different, geographical impacts, perhaps less consequential because of the relatively high concentration of both theme parks and beaches in Florida and California.

More specifically, the big losers are Florida ($10.89 billion) and California ($4.80 billion), with Ohio a distant third ($0.76 billion). Although California, and to a lesser extent Florida, are well endowed with national park-related facilities, their potential positive economic impacts are swamped by losses associated with theme parks. The top gainers are Arizona ($0.73 billion), Utah ($0.65 billion), New York ($0.58 billion), North Carolina ($0.56 billion), Massachusetts ($0.54 billion) and Wyoming ($0.44 billion). At least one half of these are low density, sparsely populated states, which presumably would be much safer in terms of the risks of death or injuries to visitors. Overall, the impacts are well dispersed so that no gainer is anywhere near the ballpark of the two main losers. Given the assumptions, the diversion scenario still involves a net loss of $8.97 billion.

4.4   CONCLUSIONS

This study reports on an analysis of the economic impacts of hypothetical terrorist attacks on America's more prominent theme parks. A key assumption of the research is that in the public's psyche, an attack on one theme park will be perceived as an attack on all. However, we also report the results of a more conservative assumption, specifically that of a 'no spillover' effect. We also recognize that even a major terrorist attack on a theme park will not ruin American vacation habits. Vacationers will probably switch to holidays considered safer. We examine one scenario: substituting visits to national parks, and their low density environments, for theme parks.

The results can be easily summarized. In the spillover cases, even an attack on a moderately sized theme park will result in more than a $20 billion hit to the economy. An attack on a cluster could result in $25 billion of economic damages. In addition, the loss in airline revenues could run as high as almost $12 billion. These numbers combined are in the same neighborhood as the costs of the 9/11 disaster. On the other hand, if the repercussions are constrained in terms of spillovers, the impact could be as low as $513 million or as high as $11.6 billion, depending upon which theme park

Table 4.5   Net theme park impacts: Florida, Cluster A, $ million

State	Direct impacts			Indirect impacts			Total impacts		
	First year	Second year	Total	First year	Second year	Total	First year	Second year	Total
AL	0.0	0.0	0.0	-57.4	-7.1	-64.5	-57.4	-7.1	-64.5
AK	93.3	11.4	104.8	57.0	7.0	64.0	150.4	18.4	168.8
AZ	441.5	54.1	495.6	210.8	25.9	236.7	652.3	80.0	732.3
AR	126.7	15.5	142.2	54.8	6.7	61.5	181.5	22.2	203.7
CA	-2,819.3	-343.2	-3,162.5	-1,463.5	-178.1	-1,641.7	-4,282.8	-521.4	-4,804.1
CO	218.6	26.8	245.4	117.1	14.4	131.4	335.6	41.1	376.8
CT	0.0	0.0	0.0	-4.1	-0.5	-4.6	-4.1	-0.5	-4.6
DE	0.0	0.0	0.0	0.8	0.1	0.9	0.8	0.1	0.9
DC	120.4	14.8	135.2	52.9	6.5	59.4	173.3	21.2	194.6
FL	-6,384.8	-786.7	-7,171.5	-3,308.4	-407.7	-3,716.1	-9,693.2	-1,194.4	-10,887.6
GA	217.2	26.6	243.8	-28.7	-3.6	-32.3	188.6	23.0	211.6
HI	250.0	30.6	280.6	132.7	16.3	149.0	382.7	46.9	429.6
ID	0.0	0.0	0.0	-4.8	-0.6	-5.4	-4.8	-0.6	-5.4
IL	-218.9	-26.7	-245.6	-170.9	-20.9	-191.8	-389.8	-47.6	-437.3
IN	87.9	10.8	98.7	39.0	4.8	43.8	126.9	15.6	142.5
IA	0.0	0.0	0.0	-28.8	-3.5	-32.3	-28.8	-3.5	-32.3
KS	0.0	0.0	0.0	-12.8	-1.6	-14.3	-12.8	-1.6	-14.3
KY	136.8	16.8	153.6	64.3	7.9	72.2	201.1	24.7	225.8
LA	28.9	3.5	32.4	-20.7	-2.5	-23.2	8.2	1.0	9.2
ME	107.2	13.1	120.3	62.5	7.7	70.1	169.7	20.8	190.5
MD	97.2	11.9	109.2	53.2	6.5	59.7	150.4	18.4	168.9
MA	322.3	39.5	361.8	155.8	19.1	174.9	478.1	58.6	536.7
MI	55.0	6.7	61.7	4.3	0.5	4.8	59.2	7.3	66.5
MN	12.1	1.5	13.6	-6.7	-0.8	-7.5	5.4	0.7	6.1
MS	98.0	12.0	110.0	44.9	5.5	50.4	142.9	17.5	160.4
MO	198.9	24.4	223.3	101.5	12.4	114.0	300.4	36.8	337.2
MT	169.8	20.8	190.6	104.7	12.8	117.5	274.4	33.6	308.1
NE	0.0	0.0	0.0	-35.2	-4.3	-39.5	-35.2	-4.3	-39.5
NV	-116.5	-14.0	-130.6	-56.6	-6.8	-63.5	-173.2	-20.9	-194.0

Table 4.5 (continued)

State	Direct impacts			Indirect impacts			Total impacts		
	First year	Second year	Total	First year	Second year	Total	First year	Second year	Total
NH	0.0	0.0	0.0	1.4	0.2	1.5	1.4	0.2	1.5
NJ	−250.8	−30.4	−281.2	−143.3	−17.4	−160.8	−394.1	−47.8	−442.0
NM	20.4	2.5	22.9	13.0	1.6	14.6	33.4	4.1	37.5
NY	359.4	44.1	403.4	154.4	18.9	173.4	513.8	63.0	576.8
NC	338.0	41.4	379.4	159.1	19.5	178.6	497.1	60.9	558.0
ND	0.0	0.0	0.0	−0.7	−0.1	−0.7	−0.7	−0.1	−0.7
OH	−412.8	−50.2	−463.0	−262.3	−31.9	−294.2	−675.0	−82.2	−757.2
OK	61.9	7.6	69.5	33.5	4.1	37.6	95.4	11.7	107.1
OR	0.0	0.0	0.0	−7.4	−0.9	−8.3	−7.4	−0.9	−8.3
PA	193.1	23.8	216.9	84.4	10.4	94.8	277.5	34.2	311.7
RI	0.0	0.0	0.0	−0.5	−0.1	−0.6	−0.5	−0.1	−0.6
SC	44.1	5.4	49.5	11.2	1.4	12.6	55.3	6.8	62.0
SD	173.2	21.2	194.4	103.4	12.7	116.1	276.6	33.9	310.5
TN	249.2	30.6	279.8	115.3	14.1	129.4	364.5	44.7	409.1
TX	218.5	26.8	245.3	−73.7	−9.1	−82.8	144.8	17.7	162.5
UT	365.6	44.8	410.4	213.0	26.1	239.1	578.6	70.9	649.5
VM	0.0	0.0	0.0	−1.2	−0.1	−1.3	−1.2	−0.1	−1.3
VA	168.8	20.8	189.6	91.6	11.3	102.9	260.4	32.1	292.5
WA	271.3	33.3	304.5	132.1	16.2	148.3	403.4	49.5	452.8
WV	55.9	6.9	62.8	31.9	3.9	35.9	87.9	10.8	98.6
WI	0.0	0.0	0.0	−33.3	−4.1	−37.4	−33.3	−4.1	−37.4
WY	234.8	28.8	263.6	154.2	18.9	173.1	389.0	47.7	436.7
US subtotal	−4,667.2	−572.4	−5,239.6	−3,166.2	−388.4	−3,554.7	−7,833.4	−960.8	−8,794.3
Foreign	0.0	0.0	0.0	−155.1	−19.0	−174.1	−155.1	−19.0	−174.1
Total	−4,667.2	−572.4	−5,239.6	−3,321.3	−407.4	−3,728.8	−7,988.5	−979.9	−8,968.4

Note: *Unit: $ million; **final demand losses are calculated by each Metropolitan Statistical Area, but are aggregated by state to be used in NIEMO.

was attacked. In the diversion scenario, that is, substitution of national parks for theme parks, there still is an economic loss as some people will stay home, increase their savings and plan a vacation for the following year. However, there is a significant offset. Florida and California are net losers because even though they have important national parks their economic impacts are modest compared with their theme parks. The big winners, that is, in terms of net gains, are sparsely populated states with rich natural and recreational resources, such as Arizona, Utah and Wyoming.

4.4.1 Policy Implications

Because of the scarcity of both Department of Homeland Security (DHS) and private sector resources any study of the economic impact of a terrorist attack needs to consider the cost-effectiveness of the scale and scope of alternative prevention measures. It is somewhat easier to do this with economic impact analyses because they generate implicit guidelines on how much is worth spending. The economic impact estimates in this study are sizeable, yet are probably underestimates because of our exclusion of induced impacts and focus on only the largest theme parks. They certainly justify significant expenditures on prevention, probably much more than those (based on anecdotal evidence) currently in place. The problem is the distribution of those expenditures among theme parks. In the spillovers scenarios, even the smaller theme parks are attractive terrorist targets because they are less protected but may have nationwide economic impacts almost as damaging as in the case of a cluster attack. If such scenarios are considered more probable, it may pay the DHS to subsidize, or offer other incentives for, prevention measures in smaller theme parks. In no spillovers scenarios, the implication is to focus on the larger theme parks, especially in the clusters. Also, if there is a case for subsidies, the provider should be local or state entities because the externalities will be more local than national. However, we suspect that, regardless of spillovers or not, the most visible theme parks, nationally and/or internationally, are the most vulnerable because of their symbolic value as representatives of American culture.

NOTES

* Acknowledgment: research contribution by Soojung Kim.
1. The calculation is as follows:
   Let the i month be M_i and the j year be Y_j, where $i = 1, \ldots, 18$ and $j = 1$ and 2.
   $M_1 = (\text{Raw\_Data})/12$.
   $M_i = M_i - M_i *0.3 = M_i *0.7$, where $i = 2, \ldots, 7$.

Also, $M_i = M_i - M_i*0.3 - M_i*0.7*(i - 7)/(18 - 7) = M_i*0.7*(1 - (i - 7)/11)$, where $i = 8,\ldots, 18$.
Hence, $Y_1 = \sum_{i=1}^{12} M_i = M_1 [1 + 0.7*6 + 0.7*\{5 - (1 + \ldots + 5)/11\}]$ and $Y_2 = \sum_{i=13}^{18} M_i = M_1*0.7*\{6 - (6 + \ldots + 11)/11\}$.

2. Similar to note 1, by letting the j year be Y_j',
    $Y_1' = \sum_{i=1}^{12} M_i = M_1 *0.5[6 + 0.5*\{6 - (1 + \ldots + 6)/12\}]$ and $Y_2' = \sum_{i=13}^{18} M_i = M_1 *0.5*\{6 - (7 + \ldots + 12)/12\}$.

REFERENCES

Aly, H.Y. and M.C. Strazicich (2000), *Terrorism and Tourism: Is the Impact Permanent or Transitory?* Columbus, OH: Ohio State University.

Drakos, K. and A.M. Kutan (2003), 'Regional effects of terrorism and tourism in three Mediterranean countries', *Journal of Conflict Resolution*, **47** (5), 621–41.

Enders, W.K. and T. Sandler (1991), 'Causality between transnational terrorism and tourism: the case of Spain', *Terrorism*, **14** (1), 49–58.

Frey, B.S., S. Luechinger and A. Stutzer (2004), 'Calculating tragedy: assessing the costs of terrorism', Working Paper 205, Institute of Empirical Research in Economics, University of Zurich.

Jack Faucett Associates (1983), *The Multiregional Input-Output Accounts 1977: Introduction and Summary, Vol. I (Final Report)*, prepared for the US Department of Health and Human Services, Washington, DC.

Jackson, R.W., W.R. Schwarm, Y. Okuyama and S. Islam (2006), 'A method for constructing commodity by industry flow matrices', *Annals of Regional Science*, **40**, 909–20.

Miller, R.E. and P.D. Blair (2009), *Input-Output Analysis: Foundations and Extensions*, 2nd edn. New York: Cambridge University Press.

Miller, R.E. and G. Shao (1990), 'Spatial and sectoral aggregation in the commodity-industry Multiregional Input-Output Model', *Environment and Planning A*, **22**, 1637–56.

ORNL (Oak Ridge National Laboratory) (2000), *Freight USA: Highlights from the 1997 Commodity Flow Survey and Other Sources*. Washington, DC: Bureau of Transportation Statistics, US Department of Transportation.

Park, J., P. Gordon, J.E. Moore II, H.W. Richardson and Q. Pan (2005), 'Simulating the state-by-state effects of terrorist attacks on three major U.S. ports: applying NIEMO (National Interstate Economic Model)', Paper presented at the 2nd CREATE Symposium on the Economic Impacts of Terrorist Attacks, University of Southern California, 19–20 August.

Pizam, A. and G. Smith (2000), 'Tourism and terrorism: a quantitative analysis of terrorist attacks and their impact on tourist destinations', *Tourism Economics*, **6** (2), 123–38.

Podoretz, J. (2010), 'This too shall pass', *Commentary*, September.

Polenske, K.R. (1980), *The US Multiregional Input-Output Accounts and Model*. Lexington, MA: DC Heath.

5. An attack on the airline system*

JiYoung Park, Harry W. Richardson, Peter Gordon and James E. Moore II

5.1 INTRODUCTION

Apart from major changes in the nation's defense posture, we now know that the economic effects of the 9/11 terrorist attacks were relatively short-term in their impact (Park et al., 2009). This corroborates the idea that short-term impact studies of hypothetical attacks can be useful to policy makers allocating limited resources as they evaluate the benefits (costs avoided) of various defensive measures. Here we consider the short-term economic costs of an attack on the US commercial air system. Much is now known about the post-9/11 performance of the air travel industry: it took several years to recover. However, a full accounting of the economic costs has, to our knowledge, never been undertaken. Nevertheless, a careful analysis of the after-effects of the events of 9/11 is useful in estimating the economic impacts of another attack. We have a particular type of attack in mind, an attack using a shoulder-borne missile launcher to bring down a plane at close range near an airport soon after take-off or before landing. A surface-to-air missile such as the one that shot down the Malaysian airplane (MH17) on 17 July 2014 is much less likely to attack a plane within the United States although it might attack a US airliner at non-US locations. This can be protected against by installing and maintaining missile deflectors on all commercial aircraft to prevent missile attacks from MANPADS (Man-portable Air Defense Systems) or even RPGs (Rocket Propelled Grenades). Because this would be costly, the key question is whether the avoided costs of disruption to the national airline system following a successful attack would justify the expense. The aim of this chapter is to shed light on this issue.

This chapter summarizes our work on quantifying the economic impacts of a hypothetical terrorist attack on the US commercial air transport system. Wherever possible, we draw on data from the post-9/11 experience. We apply NIEMO, but in a narrower context than in most of our research studies with the IMPLAN data of the Minnesota IMPLAN

Group, Inc. Much of our work (Gordon et al., 2005) has focused on estimating spatially disaggregated economic impacts, but a national model is more relevant in this case. The state-by-state airline revenue losses are particularly difficult to estimate in light of the geographically dispersed nature of airline carriers and related infrastructure and vendors. In addition, unlike in the case of the theme parks (heavily concentrated in California and Florida; see Chapter 4) or the baseball stadiums (fairly widely dispersed although the New York Yankee Stadium would be an attractive target for terrorists; see Chapter 6), there are many locations for a simulated airliner attack and the choice would be quite arbitrary. It is a different story for the natural disaster locations (for example, New Orleans, New York and New Jersey, Joplin) that can be analysed with real world rather than simulated events.

We model a seven-day shutdown of the entire US commercial air transportation system, followed by a two-year period of recovery, using the post-9/11 experience of the system as a basis for our analysis. Our overall loss estimates for the two years range from $248 billion to $394 billion. Most of these impacts are post-shutdown losses incurred during the recovery period.

5.2   PREVIOUS STUDIES

We are aware of two other relevant precursor attempts to model substantial disruption of the commercial US air transport system. Balvanyos and Lave (2005) estimated consumer surplus losses from an air travel shutdown and reported that the estimated loss would be as much as $2 billion per day.

Santos and Haimes (2004) published results from an input-output impact simulation of a 10 percent US air transport system shutdown associated with $12 billion in direct effects. These authors derived input-output multipliers of 1.2 (Type I) and 3.6 (Type II) for the United States, and used these to estimate a range of total losses from $14.2 billion to $43 billion for the year.

5.3   APPROACH AND ASSUMPTIONS

Our approach differs from the two cited studies in several respects. Most important of these is our treatment of the after-effects of the attack. Our assumptions and procedures are listed here. These are deliberately conservative.

- As there was a complete shutdown of the US commercial air system after 9/11, we assume an initial seven-day shutdown of the entire commercial air system. The shutdown period could vary, but the precise assumption is not very important given that this proportion of the total impact is small, in the range of 5 percent.

- We only estimated demand-induced effects. There are few supply-side effects because freight shipments will probably recover quickly. In the interests of a conservative estimate of impacts, we assume that passengers may be fearful of air travel, but crates are not. Some freight pilots may have reservations about flying too early and have to be bid into service, although there is no evidence that this was the case after 9/11. Business travelers, for the most part, will find and engage in productive activities that substitute for air travel. They will remain at work and perform other tasks.
- For losses following the seven-day shutdown period, we assumed that air freight transport (20 percent of total air revenues) resumes immediately at its pre-attack levels. Passenger travel, on the other hand, takes a considerable length of time to recover because of fear, caution and other psychological effects. This is especially true for leisure travelers, whose trips are easily postponable or for which many can find ground-based substitutes. Business travelers who fly more regularly will return to flying sooner. Becker and Rubinstein (2004) argue that fear is a fixed cost so that the average fixed costs of fear will decline as the number of trips increase.

To simulate the impacts of the shutdown, we set final demand for IMPLAN Sector 391 (air transportation) to zero. This eliminates all passenger and freight traffic. We did not consider any additional ancillary costs associated with the re-routings that occur as the system is shut down.

To simulate the gradual, post-shutdown return to normal traffic, we gathered data on the monthly air passenger losses (domestic as well as international trips) for the 24 months following 9/11 (Table 5.1). We then estimated polynomial trends for each type of air travel from historical data and used these to project what the monthly passenger volumes would have been had there not been an attack on 9/11. The differences between projected and actual were assumed to be the monthly air travel losses (Table 5.1).

Next, we estimated air traveler expenses for average person-trips for domestic as well as international travel (Table 5.2). These estimates were derived from data provided by the Travel Industry Association of America (2005).

Final demand losses add up to $1,231 per domestic person-trip and are distributed over the IMPLAN expenditure sectors as shown (airline tickets, ground transportation, accommodations, food, gifts and shopping, and amusement). Corresponding losses per international person-trip are $2,325.

Table 5.1   Number of monthly air passengers, 1999–2004

Year	Type	January	February	March	April	May	June
1999	Domestic	41,036,190	40,719,445	49,893,855	48,297,891	48,166,998	50,899,806
	International	9,960,297	8,879,168	11,210,638	10,455,436	10,859,652	11,708,162
	Monthly total	50,996,487	49,598,613	61,104,493	58,753,327	59,026,650	62,607,968
2000	Domestic	41,557,193	43,729,534	52,990,192	50,354,369	52,325,210	54,724,492
	International	10,192,898	9,860,251	11,958,099	11,643,945	12,024,434	13,083,128
	Monthly total	51,750,091	53,589,785	64,948,291	61,998,314	64,349,644	67,807,620
2001	Domestic	44,109,939	43,180,235	53,058,085	50,794,947	51,122,786	53,473,441
	International	11,000,962	9,738,886	12,013,455	11,581,797	11,502,673	12,722,468
	Monthly total	55,110,901	52,919,121	65,071,540	62,376,744	62,625,459	66,195,909
2002	Domestic	38,557,639	38,644,502	48,500,814	45,437,855	47,127,122	49,277,700
	International	9,286,653	8,411,103	10,709,653	9,614,915	10,156,679	11,259,303
	Monthly total	47,844,292	47,055,605	59,210,467	55,052,770	57,283,801	60,537,003
2003	Domestic	43,342,568	41,465,828	50,387,896	47,364,610	49,413,135	52,541,303
	International	10,212,099	8,739,037	10,119,337	8,751,524	9,212,897	10,832,970
	Monthly total	53,554,667	50,204,865	60,507,233	56,116,134	58,626,032	63,374,273
2004	Domestic	44,158,311	45,660,468	54,563,833	53,653,714	53,338,190	57,289,444
	International	10,699,049	9,763,902	11,499,015	11,257,596	11,359,680	12,612,501
	Monthly total	54,857,360	55,424,370	66,062,848	64,911,310	64,697,870	69,901,945

Source: Bureau of Transportation Statistics (n.d.).

Table 5.3 shows estimates of final demand losses for the three periods (the seven-day shutdown, the remainder of year 1 and all of year 2) for both types of passenger traffic and for the major expenditure sectors. These are derived by applying the expenditures per passenger to one-half of the predicted trip losses on the assumption that most passengers took round-trips, in which case two boardings are associated with each trip expenditure. IMPLAN's multipliers were then applied to these direct effects.

These losses were offset by increases in consumption of telecommunications services, to simulate the substitution of teleconferencing for face-to-face business meetings. The question of whether telecommunications and travel are substitutes or complements is unresolved. It is reasonable to expect that some telecommunications would be used to substitute for travel in the event of a shutdown of the nation's airports. However, we found no usefully identifiable data on these effects. Instead, we assumed, perhaps conservatively, a 5 percent increase in telecommunications final demand in the seven days of the air system shutdown, followed by a slow return (that is, decline) to pre-shutdown telecommunications demand over

July	August	September	October	November	December	Total
53,705,361	52,182,372	44,613,266	49,501,618	47,908,281	46,286,717	573,211,800
12,957,704	13,127,099	10,860,605	10,924,093	10,158,967	9,869,726	130,971,547
66,663,065	65,309,471	55,473,871	60,425,711	58,067,248	56,156,443	704,183,347
55,621,547	54,515,661	46,398,645	50,958,213	49,659,124	47,075,544	599,909,724
14,231,008	13,968,466	11,709,233	11,195,364	10,554,355	10,868,254	141,289,435
69,852,555	68,484,127	58,107,878	62,153,577	60,213,479	57,943,798	741,199,159
55,805,088	56,405,712	30,546,484	40,290,718	40,691,635	40,901,001	560,380,071
13,726,350	13,728,413	8,184,100	7,455,906	7,558,632	8,915,944	128,129,586
69,531,438	70,134,125	38,730,584	47,746,624	48,250,267	49,816,945	688,509,657
51,256,869	51,315,219	40,275,540	48,378,381	45,185,895	50,021,864	553,979,400
12,171,349	12,306,136	9,739,036	9,886,525	9,312,268	10,437,949	123,291,569
63,428,218	63,621,355	50,014,576	58,264,906	54,498,163	60,459,813	677,270,969
56,144,210	54,320,947	44,575,728	50,347,404	47,456,128	50,132,111	587,491,868
12,304,750	12,532,510	9,875,102	10,059,026	9,803,950	10,882,026	123,325,228
68,448,960	66,853,457	54,450,830	60,406,430	57,260,078	61,014,137	710,817,096
59,997,823	57,726,626	47,905,667	54,476,781	51,945,573	52,770,682	633,487,112
14,065,609	13,638,885	10,860,263	11,067,822	10,382,041	11,529,836	138,736,199
74,063,432	71,365,511	58,765,930	65,544,603	62,327,614	64,300,518	772,223,311

the next 24 months. This stimulus has a small effect on the economy, and the effect would remain relatively small even if doubled or tripled, so the precise assumption is not critical to the results.

5.4 RESULTS

We also calculated values for both Type I and Type II multipliers. The latter calculation is based on the IMPLAN Social Accounting Matrix (SAM), and incorporates a minor modification of the way that household incomes are assessed relative to the procedure IMPLAN calculates other multipliers. Applying these two results makes it possible to bracket low-end and high-end impacts.

Type I effects are the direct effects from Table 5.3 and indirect effects consisting of losses by suppliers and vendors in the associated expenditure sectors. Type II multipliers add the induced effects of reduced spending by households with members employed in any of the directly or indirectly affected industries. Both sets of results are shown in Table 5.4.

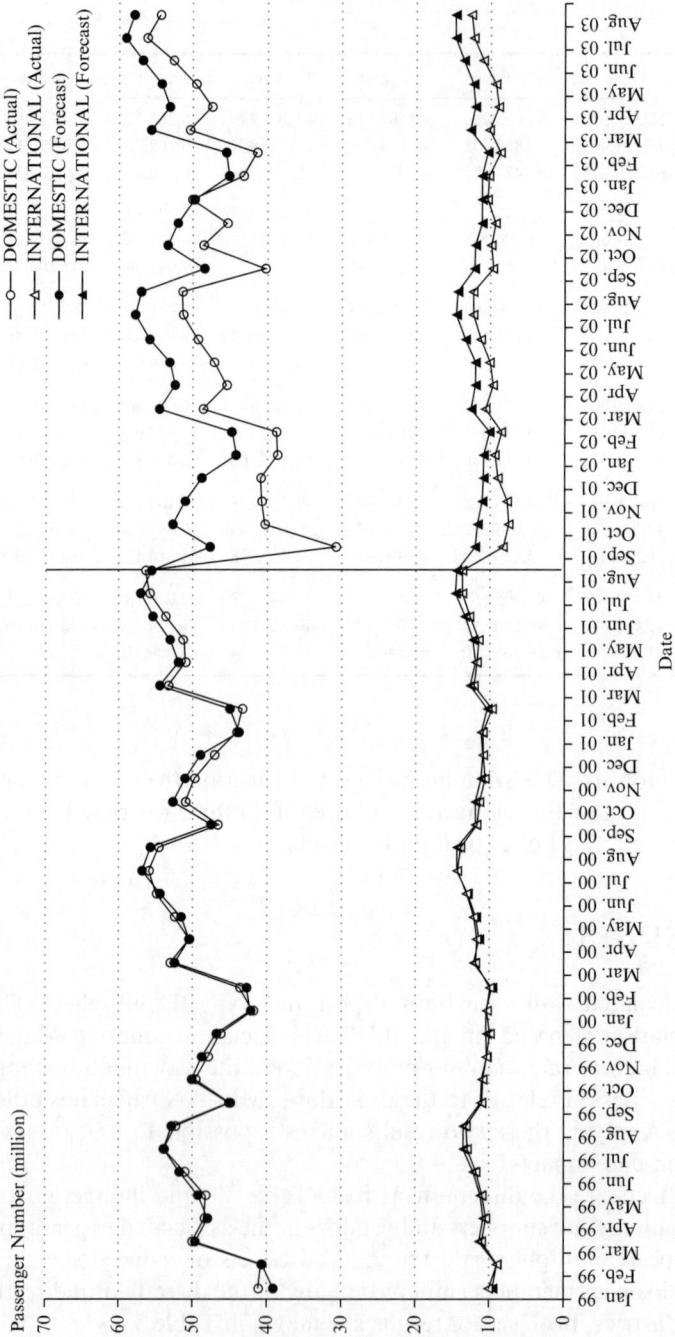

Passenger Number (million)

- DOMESTIC (Actual)
- INTERNATIONAL (Actual)
- DOMESTIC (Forecast)
- INTERNATIONAL (Forecast)

Date

Source: Calculations by the authors.

Figure 5.1 Forecasts of monthly domestic and international air passengers

Table 5.2   Passenger air travel expenditures by major sector

Domestic travel				
Economic sector	$ per party[a]	Persons per party[b]	$ per person	Percentage (%)
Airline tickets	455	1.4	325	26.39
Transportation	272		194	15.78
Accommodations	394		281	22.85
Food	243		174	14.10
Gifts/shopping	230		164	13.34
Amusement	130		93	7.54
Total	1,724		1,231	100.00
International travel				
Economic sector	$ per party[c]	Persons per party[d]	$ per person	Percentage (%)
Airline tickets[e]	–	–	667	28.67
Transportation	413	1.56	265	11.38
Accommodations	1,005	1.47	684	29.41
Food	391	1.58	247	10.63
Gifts/shopping	455	1.56	291	12.51
Amusement	290	1.69	172	7.40
Total	2,554		2,325	100.00

Notes:
a.   Aggregate Average Trip Spending on air from Maplesden et al. (2002), Table 14, p. 45, excluding N/A entries.
b.   Average Trip Party Size for business travelers from Maplesden et al. (2002), Table 3, p. 22.
c.   Aggregate Average Trip Spending on business from Maplesden et al. (2002), Table 28, p. 78, excluding N/A entries. This is for air transportation.
d.   Proportions of Average Trip Party Size for international travelers calculated from Maplesden et al. (2002), Table 25, p. 74.
e.   The average ticket price per person is assumed as $1,000 for international airline tickets. We use 66.7 percent of this value to account for the share of tickets that may have been purchased abroad. See http://www.lawa.org/lax/statistics/tcom−1201.pdf.

Source: Maplesden et al. (2002).

For the seven-day shutdown, we predict system losses ranging from $13.5 billion to $21.3 billion, depending on the choice of multipliers. The higher bound approximates Balvanyos and Lave's (2005) cost estimates of $2 billion per day. Balvanyos and Lave take a different approach to this question, estimating costs in terms of changes in consumer surplus. The principal finding in our analysis is that up to 95 percent of the total impact

Table 5.3   Final demand losses (and gains) from terrorist attacks ($ million)

Reductions: domestic passengers (million)[a]	Reductions: international passengers (million)[a]	IMPLAN sector	Sector description	$ per domestic passenger	$ per international passenger	All domestic travel ($ million)	All international travel ($ million)	Total travel ($ million)
			First seven days[b]					
4.63[d]	1.12[d]	391	Air transportation	–	–	–	–	-1,873.12
		392~395	Other transportations	194.29	264.58	-900.15	-297.53	-1,197.68
		479~480	Accommodations	281.43	683.96	-1,303.89	-769.15	-2,073.04
		405, 481	Food	173.57	247.11	-804.18	-277.88	-1,082.06
		408~412	Gifts/shopping	164.29	290.91	-761.16	-327.15	-1,088.30
		475~478	Amusement	92.86	172.04	-430.22	-193.47	-623.69
			Subtotal losses	906.43	1658.60	-4,199.59	-1,865.18	-7,937.89
		422	Telecommunications[c]	–	–	–	–	167.22
			Net losses	906.43	1,658.60	-4,199.59	-1,865.18	-7,770.67
			Remainder of the first year					
48.003[d]	14.294[d]	391	Airline tickets	325.00	666.67	-15,600.85	-9,529.11	-25,129.96
		392~395	Other transportations	194.29	264.58	-9,326.22	-3,781.79	-13,108.02
		479~480	Accommodations	281.43	683.96	-13,509.31	-9,776.27	-23,285.58
		405, 481	Food	173.57	247.11	-8,331.88	-3,532.05	-11,863.93
		408~412	Gifts/shopping	164.29	290.91	-7,886.15	-4,158.22	-12,044.36
		475~478	Amusement	92.86	172.04	-4,457.39	-2,459.15	-6,916.54
			Subtotal losses	1,231.43	2,325.27	-59,111.80	-33,236.60	-92,348.40
		422	Telecommunications[c]	–	–	–	–	15,258.83
			Net losses	1,231.43	2,325.27	-59,111.80	-33,236.60	-77,089.58

Second year

	Code					
	25.642[d]	12.469[d]				
Airline tickets	391	325.00	666.67	−8,333.73	−8,312.83	−16,646.56
Other transportations	392~395	194.29	264.58	−4,981.92	−3,299.09	−8,281.01
Accommodations	479~480	281.43	683.96	−7,216.46	−8,528.44	−15,744.90
Food	405, 481	173.57	247.11	−4,450.76	−3,081.22	−7,531.99
Gifts/shopping	408~412	164.29	290.91	−4,212.66	−3,627.47	−7,840.12
Amusement	475~478	92.86	172.04	−2,381.07	−2,145.27	−4,526.34
Subtotal losses		1,231.43	2,325.27	−31,576.60	−28,994.32	−60,570.92
Telecommunications[c]	422	–	–	–	–	4,795.63
Net losses		1,231.43	2,325.27	−31,576.60	−28,994.32	−55,775.29

Notes:
a. The reduction in passengers was calculated by multiplying 7/31 by the monthly passenger volume for August 2001.
b. Losses during a seven-day interruption in service (1.92 percent of one year) estimated based on a reduction in final demand in the IMPLAN air transportation sector (391).
c. We assume final demand for telecommunications services increases by 5 percent during the seven-day shutdown and then decreases linearly, month to month, over the next two years.
d. Because all passengers are assumed to board with round-trip tickets, we applied one-half of reported air passenger trips to the cost/trip estimates.

71

Table 5.4 Simulation results ($ million)

Economic sector	IMPACTS			Type I multipliers	IMPACTS		Type (II) SAM multipliers
	Direct	Indirect	Total		Induced	Total	
First seven days							
Air transportation[a]	−1,873	−1,685	−3,558	1.8995	−1,922	−5,480	2.9256
Other transportations	−1,198	−1,042	−2,239	1.8696	−1,162	−3,402	2.8402
Accommodations	−2,073	−1,169	−3,242	1.5639	−1,861	−5,103	2.4616
Food	−1,082	−892	−1,974	1.8246	−1,171	−3,146	2.9071
Gifts/shopping	−1,088	−694	−1,783	1.6380	−1,139	−2,921	2.6842
Amusement	−624	−344	−968	1.5513	−640	−1,608	2.5782
Telecommunications[b]	167	90	257	1.5372	126	383	2.2891
Seven-day totals	−7,771	−5,736	−13,507	1.7139	−7,770	−21,277	2.7381
Remainder of the first year							
Airline tickets	−25,130	−22,604	−47,734	1.8995	−25,785	−73,519	2.9256
Other transportations	−13,108	−11,399	−24,507	1.8696	−12,722	−37,229	2.8402
Accommodations	−23,286	−13,131	−36,417	1.5639	−20,902	−57,319	2.4616
Food	−11,864	−9,783	−21,647	1.8246	−12,843	−34,490	2.9071
Gifts/shopping	−12,044	−7,684	−19,728	1.6380	−12,601	−32,329	2.6842
Amusement	−6,917	−3,813	−10,730	1.5513	−7,102	−17,832	2.5782
Telecommunications[b]	15,259	8,198	23,456	1.5372	11,472	34,928	2.2891
First-year totals	−77,090	−60,216	−137,306	1.7592	−80,484	−217,790	2.8252

Second year							
Airline tickets	−16,647	−14,973	−31,620	1.8995	−17,081	−48,701	2.9256
Other transportations	−8,281	−7,201	−15,482	1.8696	−8,037	−23,519	2.8402
Accommodations	−15,745	−8,879	−24,624	1.5639	−14,133	−38,757	2.4616
Food	−7,532	−6,211	−13,743	1.8246	−8,154	−21,897	2.9071
Gifts/shopping	−7,840	−5,002	−12,842	1.6380	−8,202	−21,044	2.6842
Amusement	−4,526	−2,496	−7,022	1.5513	−4,648	−11,670	2.5782
Telecommunications[b]	4,796	2,576	7,372	1.5372	3,605	10,977	2.2891
Second-year totals	−55,775	−42,185	−97,960	1.7473	−56,650	−154,610	2.7720
Total two-year losses	−140,636	−108,137	−248,773	1.7525	−144,904	−393,676	2.7993

Notes:

a. Losses during a seven-day interruption in service (1.9178 percent of one year) estimated based on a reduction in final demand in the IMPLAN air transportation sector (391).

b. We assume final demand for telecommunications services increases by 5 percent during the seven-day shutdown and then decreases linearly, month to month, over the next two years.

of the attack is likely to occur in the post-shutdown period (this finding makes speculation about the length of the shutdown less important, for example, whether seven days or the four days as after 9/11). We estimate that net system losses over the entire two-year period would range from $248.8 billion to $393.7 billion. These total loss estimates capture the economic consequences that would follow an attack, but exclude the costs associated with the loss of life and the replacement cost of aircraft that would be incurred as the result of an attack.

5.5   POLICY IMPLICATIONS

The estimated cost of deploying countermeasures to the threat of shoulder-launched missiles to the US airline fleet range widely, depending on the technology and objectives involved (O'Sullivan, 2005). The initial cost of equipping the US commercial fleet of approximately 6,800 aircraft is above $10 billion; by how much depends on different cost estimates per plane. However, this is not the principal cost of countermeasures. The equipment may deteriorate quickly and may require frequent replacement. As a result, these systems include extensive logistics, refurbishment, training and maintenance requirements that might impose additional costs of more than $5 billion per year (USDHS, 2004).

As estimated in this research, the benefits of avoiding an attack in terms of its impact on the airline industry and associated economic activities would be about $394 billion (with Type II multipliers) in the first two years (Table 5.4). The cost-benefit results of implementing this defense system would be immense. Although these findings never elicited an official positive response from the Department of Homeland Security, there were many favorable informal reactions. Nevertheless, the scheme was never adopted. The explanation was the objection of the major US airlines on cost grounds. If our results were reasonably acceptable, the only rational interpretation of this reaction was a belief that the likelihood of an attack, whether by MANPADS, RPGs or surface-to-air missiles, was very low.

Although the scope of this study was limited to the US commercial airline sector within the boundaries of the US economy, the destruction of MH17 on 17 July 2014 makes clear that this is a global issue. The only major airline in the world to adopt this type of defense system (to our knowledge) is the Israel airline, El Al.[1] Worldwide implementation would raise the costs although the benefits in terms of reduced world air travel are unclear at the time of writing because some travelers may perceive that the risks of future attacks might be moderate, as the conditions of the airspace above Ukraine might be considered a rarity. However, although surface-to-air missile launchers such as used in this case require resources and preparation, attacks at lower heights with MANPADS or RPGs could be more or less ubiquitous (the world MANPADS/RPG stock is between 500,000 and 750,000, and about 1 percent of the stock is non-governmental, that is, on the black market). A reasonable estimate of the size of the world commercial airline fleet (passenger and cargo) of jet planes (with seating capacity for passenger planes above 90 seats) was 20,910 in 2013, approximately three times the size of the US fleet. By 2033 the world fleet might be more than 42,000 planes (the growth of 21,000 planes, replacement of 15,000 and retention of 6,000); Boeing Corporation, 2014. A MANPADS countermeasure (C-MANPADS) system for the current world fleet would cost at least $100 billion for the purchase of equipment and its maintenance over a five-year period.

Israel began technological countermeasures in 2003 (Flight Guard developed by the Elbit Company). The method was controversial because some critics raised the issue of a potential fire hazard as a result of the use of flares. A replacement technology, Multi-Spectral Infrared Countermeasure (MUSIC) was first developed in 2009.

Military planes in many countries have been fitted with MANPADS countermeasures. This has not been the case with civil aircraft with the exception of Israel. There have been about 40 attacks on civil aircraft since 1978, not all of them successful. Most of them took place in the past 20 years, and were primarily limited to Africa and Asia.

Returning to the domestic case, there are large loss estimates associated with a shutdown of US airports, primarily because of long-term reductions in air travel demand similar to those observed following the nationwide airport shutdown prompted by the events of 9/11. We expect that this drop in demand would be repeated following any subsequent shutdown, such as a successful MANPADS or RPG attack. Given the estimated costs of MANPADS countermeasures, deployment may be justified for a wide range of attack probabilities, even low ones. Of course, our analysis does not accommodate other possible types of ground-based attacks such as bombing an airport terminal.

Estimating the full costs of a major disruption in any large industry is a challenging task. Where we have needed to make assumptions, our choices have erred on the conservative side. However, the input-output methodology we use to estimate economic impacts does not accommodate many of the substitutions that economic agents might find when they have time to investigate the adjustments available to them. Our conservative modeling assumptions help to counter this limitation.

The costs of installing missile deflectors on planes both in the United

States and around the world would not have been cheap, but if the decline in air travel and associated sectors (especially the tourist industry) after a successful attack replicated what happened after 9/11 these preventive actions would have been justified. More convincing than the technical analysis in this chapter is that it is highly probable that the horrific tragedy of 17 July 2014 would not have occurred.

On the other hand, the event has a downside. Although there are major obstacles to more surface-to-air missile attacks 33,000 feet in the air, the proliferation of MANPADS or RPG attacks on airplanes close to take-off or landings is a high risk. The most common and one of the least expensive RPGs (not a guided missile launcher such as the MANPADS), the Russian-made RPG-7, with its major function as an anti-tank missile, has a short effective maximum range, but some more recently developed MANPADS have a longer range. It is difficult to prevent MANPADS or RPG attacks on airplanes because a lone terrorist could bring such a weapon in a van, step out for a few minutes and shoot down a plane. The peripheries around many airports are sparsely populated so that without continuous and detailed patrols it would be difficult to detect a terrorist and there is rarely any need for one to be inside the airport perimeter. Given this ease, a succession of attacks could take place at several airports within a short period of time, even simultaneously with a little terrorist coordination either within a single country or internationally. The result would be devastating to air travel, and the economic costs stretched over time (months or even years) would be immense. Considering the global aviation network, a global IO model may address the negative impacts of simultaneous global attacks.

NOTES

*   Acknowledgment: research contribution by Soojung Kim.
1.   The other smaller Israeli airlines, Arkia and Israir, also implemented countermeasures because it was a government decision.

REFERENCES

Balvanyos, T. and L.B. Lave (2005), *The Economic Implications of a Terrorist Attack on Commercial Aviation in the USA*, Report to the Center for Risk and Economic Analysis of Terrorism (CREATE), University of Southern California, Los Angeles.
Becker, G. and Y. Rubinstein (2004), 'Fear and the response to terrorism: an economic analysis', available at http://www.cornell.edu/international/events/upload/BeckerrubinsteinPaper.pdf.

Boeing Corporation (2014), *Current Market Outlook, 2014–2033*, available at http://boeing.com/commercial/cmo/.

Bureau of Transportation Statistics (n.d.), US Department of Transportation (annual), http:// www.transtats.bts.gov/Data_Elements.

Gordon, P., J.E. Moore II and H.W. Richardson (2005), 'The economic impact of a terrorist attack on the twin Ports of Los Angeles-Long Beach,' in H.W. Richardson, P. Gordon and J.E. Moore II (eds), *The Economic Impacts of Terrorist Attacks*. Cheltenham, UK and Northampton, MA, USA: Edward Elgar, pp. 262–85.

Maplesden, H.C., F.X. Wang, T.X. Tian and S.D. Cook (2002), *Expenditure Patterns of Travelers in the U.S.* Washington, DC; Travel Industry Association of America.

O'Sullivan, T. (2005), *External Terrorist Threats to Civilian Airliners: A Summary Risk Analysis of MANPADS, Other Ballistic Weapons Risks, Future Threats, and Possible Countermeasure Policies*, Center for Risk and Economic Analysis of Terrorism (CREATE), University of Southern California, Los Angeles, available at http://www.usc.edu/dept/create/reports/MANPADS_MSEditVers_v2.pdf.

Park, J.Y., P. Gordon, E. Jun, J.E. Moore II and H.W. Richardson (2009), 'Identifying the regional economic impacts of 9/11', *Peace Economics, Peace Science and Public Policy*, **15** (2), Article 6.

RAND Corporation (2005), *Protecting Commercial Aviation Against the Shoulder-fired Missile Threat*. Santa Monica, CA: RAND Corporation.

Santos, J.R. and Y.Y. Haimes (2004), 'Modeling the demand reduction input-output (I-O) inoperability due to terrorism of interconnected infrastructures', *Risk Analysis*, **24** (6), 1437–51.

Travel Industry Association of America (2005), *Expenditure Patterns of Travelers in the U.S.* Washington, DC: TIAA.

US Department of Homeland Security (2004), 'Fact sheet: countering missile threats to commercial aircraft', Press release distributed by the Bureau of International Information Programs, US Department of State, 6 January, available at http:// usinfo.state.gov/xarchives/display.html?p=washfileenglish&y=2004&m=January &x=20040106171221ikceinawza0.6426508&t=usinfo/wf-latest.html.

6. A stadium attack

Bumsoo Lee, Peter Gordon, James E. Moore II and Harry W. Richardson

6.1 INTRODUCTION

The application of standard economic impact models to the study of hypothetical terrorist attacks is not as straightforward as might be expected. The models are more powerful and user-friendly than ever. However, they are based on multipliers in search of appropriate multiplicands. Supplying the latter requires analysts to create plausible and detailed scenarios that can be fitted to the models.

This is the nature of the research reported here. The purpose of this chapter is two-fold. First, we suggest an analytical framework to study the full economic impacts of hypothetical bioterrorist attacks on targets. In particular, we emphasize the importance of estimating economic impacts that occur through systems and behavior linkages beyond direct losses. Second, we provide a case study that analyses the economic impacts of a hypothetical bioterrorist attack on a major league sports stadium. Any large sports stadium is an attractive target for (bio)terrorist attacks because it is a place of mass public gatherings on a predictable basis, often with minimal security controls (Australian Government Attorney-General's Department, 2006).

The estimated loss of a bioterrorist attack on a stadium ranges from $62 billion to $73 billion. The largest loss comes from the loss of lives, followed by the reduced demand for sports stadium visits. By comparison, analysts using different methods have found that the annual total cost of cancer in the United States is slightly more than $200 billion, including the costs of medical expenses and the costs of lost productivity because of illness and premature death (American Cancer Society, 2006). The annual cost of deaths from auto accidents has been put at $230 billion by the National Highway Traffic Safety Administration (2005). In other words, the costs associated with a stadium attack are not minimal.

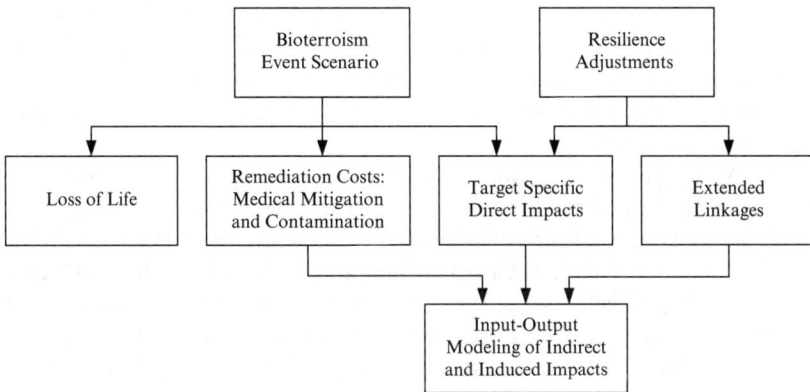

Figure 6.1   Analytical framework for impact studies of bioterrorism attacks

6.2   ANALYTICAL FRAMEWORK

Figure 6.1 presents a general framework for analysing the economic impacts of hypothetical bioterrorist attacks using input-output analysis. We developed this analytical framework by further elaborating Rose's (2006) conceptual framework for modeling total economic impacts of extreme events. For any type of bioterrorism event, the first step is to create a hypothetical event scenario that has a sufficiently high probability of occurrence to justify investigation. Each scenario should define the type of bioterrorist target, the size of the attack and the expected size and time frame of direct damage and disruption.

Major direct costs include casualties, illnesses, contamination and business interruption. Unlike natural disasters or other conventional terrorism events, property damage is expected to be minimal in the case of bioterrorism events. The size of human and physical losses would be a function of many factors such as the kind, quantity and quality of the bioagents released, climatic conditions and emergency response. These damages can be estimated through a simulation model that would incorporate a bioagent dispersion model and epidemiological curves. There is a possibility of public resistance to reoccupancy of decontaminated facilities. This fear factor would result in more prolonged business interruption and potentially some type of property loss. We are unable to model these effects and therefore, have not included them in our analysis. We expect the economic incentives to return facilities to service would dominate most decisions.

In general, the economic impacts of bioterrorism events can be estimated in three major categories: loss of life; remediation costs; and event/

target specific impacts. It is standard to apply the value of a statistical life (VSL) to estimate the economic value of lives lost. We employ input-output (IO) modeling to estimate total impacts associated with the other two types of economic costs. This approach accounts for economic linkages between activities.

The VSL is a critical component in estimating monetary costs of any fatality or health risks resulting from natural, environmental and man-made hazards or analysing the benefits of reducing these risks. The VSL can be defined as what a society is willing to pay for a marginal reduction in fatality risks (Fisher et al., 1989). The VSL is generally estimated based on either revealed or stated preference data (Kochi et al., 2006). Because estimated VSL varies across studies using different methods and data, policy analysts typically use mean values drawn from multiple estimates. We use $5.4 million, which is obtained from a relatively recent meta-analysis that used an empirical Bayesian pooling method (Kochi et al., 2006).

Besides the human costs (casualties), a bioterrorism attack would call for extensive medical services and decontamination activities. Direct costs of medical mitigation and decontamination are estimated by multiplying the average unit cost of each service by the quantity of total services required. We use unit costs of medical services from a recent cost-benefit study of countermeasures against anthrax terrorism (Braithwaite et al., 2006), adjusted to 2003 dollars using the consumer price index for all urban consumers (CPI-U). We also assume that infected patients with severe symptoms need to be hospitalized for seven days on average (Kaufmann et al., 1997), and that all potentially exposed people without severe symptoms would have one outpatient visit for medical services. Hospitalization cost per day and outpatient cost per visit used in this study are $810 and $75, respectively. Decontamination cost is assumed to be $40 per ft^2.

While most previous studies treat these remediation costs as merely direct costs, the resources (expenditures) directed to these remediation activities are expected to have other impacts on the economy. On the one hand, remediation activities draw on certain resources in the current economy that would have been used in other productive activities. This is certainly a cost to society regardless of whether it is paid for by government agencies or by private parties.

We assume that most of the remediation costs will be covered by the federal government in the case of bioterrorism events. There are three possible funding sources of such government expenditures: increased taxes; increased deficit spending; and reductions in other government expenditures. Whatever the funding source, the economic consequences would be similar: increased tax liabilities that will ultimately reduce household consumption; and increased deficit expenditures or reduced public expenditures on other programs would affect future household consumption and would have opportunity costs. Thus, we model the remediation costs as reduced overall household consumption using the expenditure pattern of households in the $35,000–$50,000 income bracket.

On the other hand, resources directed to remediation activities would also stimulate the economy. These positive impacts can offset the local economic losses to some extent when the resources come from outside the region in the form of insurance payments or financial assistance. We model these positive impacts as increased final demand in corresponding economic sectors. These sectors include hospital sectors for medical mitigation and waste management and environmental consulting services for decontamination. The net economic impacts will depend on the relative size of output multipliers associated with the relevant industrial sectors.

A related question in modeling remediation costs involves the social costs of taxation. It is widely recognized that there are considerable social costs when transferring the purchasing power of taxpayers to the government (Slemrod and Yitzhaki, 1996). Broadly stated, the costs consist of administrative, compliance and marginal welfare costs (Tran-Nam et al., 2000). The compliance costs incurred by taxpayers are estimated to range from 5 to 7 percent of the income tax collected (Slemrod and Sorum, 1984). We know of no empirical estimate for the administrative costs of US income taxes. However, studies for other countries suggest that they are usually 1 percent or less of collected revenues (Evans, 2003).

Marginal welfare costs (often referred to as deadweight losses) of the US income tax because of the distortions of resource allocation have been estimated to be around 25 cents per revenue dollar (Parry, 2002). This cost is taken into account in our modeling approach by reducing the overall consumption of taxpayers and estimating its multiplier effects. We consider only the operating (administrative and compliance) costs of taxation in reducing households' final demand, using a conservative value of 5 percent. This takes out $1.05 from overall household consumption for each extra dollar of government expenditure on remediation activities.

Finally, we need to model bioterrorism event/target specific impacts beyond remediation costs and standard multiplier effects. These event/target specific impacts occur through behavioral and system linkages, and are often much larger than the direct damages and the multiplier effects (Rose, 2007). One important aspect of risk-related behavior is that it can be socially amplified or attenuated (Pidgeon et al., 2003; Renn et al., 1992). When fears are heightened in the case of terrorism, people tend to 'neglect probability' and are likely to exhibit excessive risk aversion (Sunstein, 2003). The risk aversion of consumers directly translates into reduced demand for the goods and services involved, for example, air travel demand decline in the wake of the 9/11 events. Amplified risk perceptions and risk-related behavior may lead to additional and sizable economic impacts.

While there are many theoretical and conceptual models explaining the social basis of risk, much more research is needed to quantify behavioral changes in response to actual or hypothetical terrorism events. As a result, we rely on available information relating to the aftermath of historical events when predicting the target specific impacts of hypothetical bio-terrorist attacks. This approach is similar to benefit-transfer or value-transfer, which is the application of monetary unit values or functions obtained from one non-market valuation study to other policy decision environments (Brookshire and Neill, 1992; Spash and Vatn, 2006). This value-transfer approach is most valid when the conditions of the primary study and policy application are well defined (Luken et al., 1992). Thus, we need to draw upon historical events similar to a hypothetical terror-ist attack scenario. Because the data on terrorism are rather tenuous, however, a range of estimates makes more sense than a point estimate.

In the final step of the economic impact analysis, we apply the 2003 IMPLAN national IO model to estimate indirect and induced effects. All direct impacts combining remediation and event/target specific impacts are inputs to the IO model as final demand changes, and Type II multipli-ers are used to estimate the total economic impacts.

However, there is an important caveat to the approach. IO analysis relies upon fixed multipliers. Yet market economies are defined in terms of the ability of agents to respond to price signals. Most adjustments take place in the long run. Recovery from losses could then be made, at least to some degree.

6.3   ESTIMATES OF ECONOMIC COSTS

6.3.1   Stadium Attack Scenario

A successful terrorist attack on a stadium can potentially cause massive casualties and high-impact imagery, and hence gain terrorists high-profile publicity (Australian Government Attorney-General's Department, 2006). Our analysis is based on the scenario that terrorists release a bioagent in a stadium where a National Football league (NFL) game is playing before 75,000 spectators. A desktop analysis using Hazard Prediction and Assessment Capability (HPAC) employing notional biological agents, urban density and weather conditions predicted a range of potential consequences. This economic scenario models an attack in which 20,000 illnesses and 7,000 casualties occur among the attendees. In this scenario, the bioagent would contaminate a neighboring area of 5.5 km² and would cause an additional 11,000 illnesses and 3,600 deaths.

We expect that the entire contaminated area including the stadium would be quarantined for one month immediately after the biological attack occurs. The affected public spaces and roads would be open after this initial one-month quarantine period. However, it would take much more time to decontaminate individual buildings in the contaminated area. We assume that 50 percent of the contaminated buildings would be not be habitable until six months after the attack, and that it would take one year to complete the decontamination.

6.3.2 Remediation Costs

Direct remediation costs are listed in Table 6.1. We assessed the quantity of remediation activities required based on the scenario descriptions and applied the unit costs of each service. We assumed that all attendees at the football game and residents in the contaminated neighboring area are potentially exposed to the released biological agents and would need to have at least one outpatient examination or treatment. The number of residents in the area is calculated by using the average population density of the ten largest US urbanized areas.

As explained in the previous section, remediation activities are costs to the economy, but at the same time have some stimulating effects. We estimated total economic impacts for both positive and negative shocks using the IMPLAN 2003 national model. Although the estimated amount of these direct costs plus taxation costs (5 percent) is about $305 million, the actual reduction in final demand from the household sector is about

Table 6.1 Direct remediation costs

Remediation costs	Direct costs ($)	Calculation
Medical mitigation		
Hospitalization	175,770,000	31,000 total illnesses • $810/day • 7 days
Outpatient	4,734,600	63,128 potentially exposed[a] • $75/per visit
Decontamination	110,000,000	2,750,000 ft² • $40/ft²

Note: a. 63,128 potentially exposed = 55,000 uninfected attendees + 8,128 residents in the neighborhood; 8,128 residents = 5.5 km² • 1,478 residents/km² (average population density in the ten largest urbanized areas).

$286 million after taking into account the demand for foreign products (imports), which do not directly contribute to US regional or national production. The net effect was about $154 million because Type II multipliers for decontamination and medical sectors were larger than for overall household consumption sectors (Table 6.2).

6.3.3   Economic Impacts through Behavior and System Linkages

A successful terrorist attack would have extended economic impacts through behavior and system linkages. A biological attack on an NFL stadium would likely scare many sports fans away from most major stadium visits for some period. However, there is little research or data available on the impacts of historical stadium terrorism events. Further, the magnitude of any historical stadium terrorism events is so small that they have little bearing on estimating the impacts of our stadium scenario. Thus, we have chosen to draw upon behavior changes after two other historical terrorism events: the 9/11 attacks and the Bali nightclub bombing.

Reduced professional sports game attendance after the 9/11 attacks
Stein et al. (2004) report that a survey of the psychological consequences conducted about two months after the 9/11 events revealed that 11 percent of the respondents avoided large gathering places including sports stadiums. Figure 6.2 presents the attendance trends in two big professional sports leagues, the National Football League (NFL) and the Major League Baseball (MLB).

Most of the significant short-term disturbances in attendance were due to special incidents within each professional sport league, including the creation of new teams, the increased number of games scheduled and players' strikes. In recent NFL history, players' strikes in 1982 and 1987 resulted in large drops in attendance while small jumps in 1995, 1999 and 2002 indicate the addition of new teams to the league. Strikes also occurred in 1972, 1981, 1994 and 1995.

It is reasonable to conclude that the deviation in attendance from the normal trend during 2001 and 2002 seasons was because of the 9/11 events. However, the 9/11 terrorism events had only moderate impacts on the two stadium sports, with about a 1.4 percent drop in attendance for the NFL games in 2001 and about 6.5 percent drops in MLB attendance in 2002 and 2003. Note that the 2001 season of the MLB was almost over by the time of the 9/11 attacks. We also found that there was negligible impact on the two major arena sports, that is, the National Basketball Association (NBA) and the National Hockey League (NHL).

Because the 9/11 terrorism events were not a direct attack on a sports

Table 6.2   Direct, indirect and induced impacts of remediation costs

NAICS two-digit sectors ($ thousand)	Remediation expenditures (+)				Reduced household expenditure (−)				Net total
	Direct	Indirect	Induced	Total	Direct	Indirect	Induced	Total	
Agriculture	0	1,899	6,991	8,890	1,306	6,820	5,010	13,136	−4,247
Mining	0	2,000	4,062	6,062	173	4,384	2,911	7,468	−1,406
Utilities	0	4,396	8,934	13,330	5,907	3,985	6,403	16,295	−2,965
Construction	0	3,272	2,785	6,058	0	2,968	1,996	4,964	1,094
Manufacturing	0	43,754	77,771	121,525	43,182	45,629	55,740	144,550	−23,025
Wholesale trade	0	7,919	19,396	27,315	13,150	9,179	13,901	36,231	−8,916
Transportation and warehousing	0	11,537	13,450	24,987	4,286	10,079	9,640	24,005	981
Retail trade	0	1,986	33,560	35,546	37,185	1,863	24,053	63,102	−27,555
Information	0	13,179	24,374	37,553	12,551	14,071	17,469	44,091	−6,538
Finance and insurance	0	16,393	40,610	57,003	24,994	21,317	29,106	75,418	−18,415
Real estate and rental	0	30,753	27,723	58,475	14,442	18,440	19,869	52,752	5,724
Professional and technical services	110,000	29,932	21,300	161,232	4,210	18,986	15,266	38,462	122,770
Management of companies	0	5,964	6,234	12,198	0	6,982	4,468	11,450	748
Administration and waste services	0	27,537	10,951	38,489	975	10,675	7,849	19,499	18,990
Educational services	0	401	5,003	5,404	3,530	205	3,586	7,320	−1,917
Health and social services	180,505	141	43,037	223,683	42,591	377	30,845	73,812	149,870
Arts and recreation	0	1,134	5,932	7,066	4,315	1,400	4,252	9,967	−2,901
Accommodation and food services	0	5,898	18,680	24,578	18,487	2,801	13,388	34,676	−10,098
Other services	0	5,491	17,914	23,404	12,795	4,266	12,839	29,900	−6,495
Government and non NAICS	0	2,682	34,348	37,030	32,046	2,133	24,618	58,797	−21,767
Institutions					10,033	0	0	10,033	−10,033
Total	290,505	216,267	423,056	929,827	286,158	186,561	303,210	775,929	153,899

Note: NAICS – North American Industry Classification System.

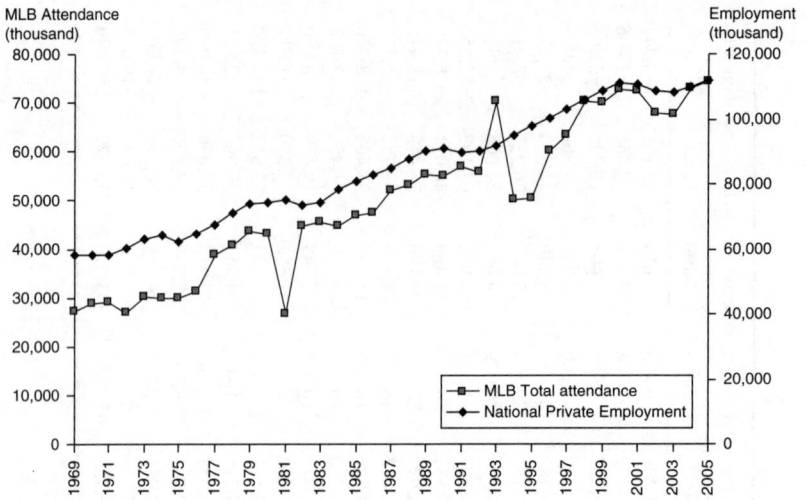

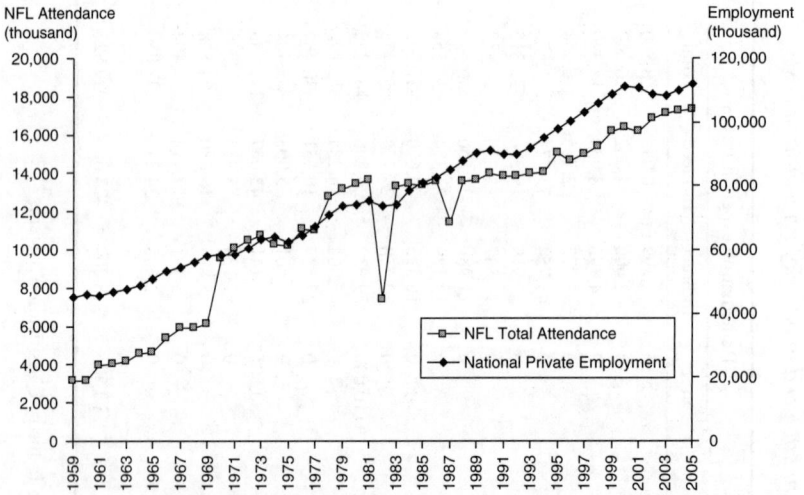

Sources: NFL data come from Team media guides, Official NFL *Record & Fact Books*, 1984–2005, ESPN.com, and NFL.com, available at http://studentwebs.coloradocollege. edu/~a_campbell/datastats.htm. MLB data for 1969–2000 come from the *Journal of Statistics Education* data archive, available at http://www.amstat.org/publications/jse/ datasets/MLBattend.dat. More recent MLB data are available at http://studentwebs. coloradocollege.edu/~a_campbell/ datastats.htm.

Figure 6.2   Trends in attendance at NFL and MLB games prior to and after the 9/11 attacks

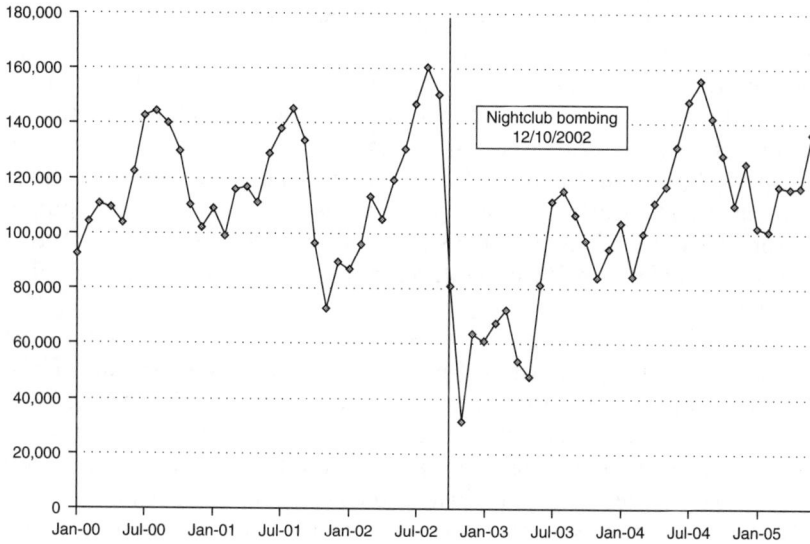

Source: Bali Tourism Board (n.d.) and Bureau of Labor Statistics (2006).

Figure 6.3   Tourist arrivals to Bali after the nightclub bomb

stadium, the effects on stadium visits reflect people's general avoidance of gathering places, not stadia in particular. However, it is reasonable to expect that a direct bioterrorism attack on a sports stadium would have much larger impacts with respect to stadium attendance.

Reduced tourist visits to Indonesia after the Bali nightclub bombing

We also studied tourist behavior in the wake of the nightclub bombing on the Indonesian island of Bali on 12 October 2002. This terrorist attack by an extremist Islamist group killed 202 tourists and injured 209. As shown in Figure 6.3, it took approximately one and a half years for tourist visits to Bali to recover to the previous levels. For the one-year period after the attack (October 2002 to September 2003), the number of tourists visiting Bali dropped by about 35 percent compared to the one-year period before the attack (October 2001 to September 2002).

It is widely reported that terrorism significantly diminishes tourism. International tourism is especially vulnerable as there are many substitutable international tourist destinations. Thus, we consider this Bali nightclub bombing case as the upper bound of the decrease in professional sports game attendance in the wake of a bioterrorism attack on an NFL stadium.

Recovery scenarios of professional sports game attendance and substitutes
We assume that any professional sports games would be cancelled for
one month after the hypothetical biological attack on an NFL stadium,
which translates to about an 8 percent reduction in annual attendance
at professional sports games. We expect that a significant proportion
of sports fans would avoid attending sports games even after the professional sports league resumes play. In the absence of actual stadium
terrorism events of comparable size, we decided to test high- and low-
impact scenarios drawing upon the cases of the 9/11 attacks and the Bali
bombing.

In the low-impact scenario, we assume a 7 percent reduction in the
demand for sports game visits after reopening professional leagues. Thus,
the total impact in the first year would be about a 15 percent decrease.
We assume the demand would recover by the end of the first year after
the attack in this low-impact scenario. In the high-impact scenario, we
assume a 40 percent reduction in attendance during the first year, including the first month shutdown. We also assume that the impact would
last into the second season at a level of 10 percent in the high-impact
scenario.

- Low-impact scenario: 15 percent decrease for the first year.
- High-impact scenario: 40 percent decrease for the first year and 10
  percent decrease for the second year.

What would be the substitute activities that people might choose instead
of attending professional sports games? Where and how much would
sports fans spend from money they had saved by avoiding stadium visits?

The first alternative could be watching sports games on home TV.
With the introduction of high-definition (HD) digital broadcasting and
HD TVs typically with a large screen, sports fans can increasingly enjoy
televized sports via relatively high-quality images. Thus, we expect that
sports fans who avoid stadium visits would spend more money on purchasing digital TV equipment and cable TV network sports packages.
Indeed, the consumption results for the 2000s show that expenditures on
TV, radio and sound equipment generally move in an opposite direction to
the expenditures on fees and admissions, which include professional sports
game visits (Bureau of Labor Statistics, 2006).

The second alternative to sports game visits can be personal exercise
activities. Some proportion of sports spectators may become consumers of
fitness and recreational sports. Finally, people may spend more time with
family at home or in community parks. There is little economic impact
in this case. However, we exclude from the list of substitutes activities

involving other entertainment sectors such as museums and amusement parks because a stadium attack would also motivate people to avoid visits to other public gatherings.

Without any substantiated information on relevant substitutions and cross-elasticities, we assume that one-half of the reduced final demand in 'spectator sports' goes to the substituting sectors. We assume that equal thirds of this budget for substitutes goes to each of the three substitution sectors: 'audio and video equipment,' 'cable networks and program distribution' and 'fitness and recreational sports centers.'

Estimation of total impacts of reduced demand for spectator sports

The indirect and induced impacts of reduced demand for spectator sports and substitution activities are estimated using 2003 IMPLAN data. The upper part in Table 6.3 (low-impact scenario) shows impacts by two-digit NAICS sectors. The lower part (high-impact scenario) suppresses details because sectoral patterns are the same as for the results from the low-impact scenario.

In the low-impact scenario, the assumed 15 percent reduction in sports attendance costs $4.9 billion in output losses including direct, indirect and induced impacts. However, substitution effects offset these costs by about $2.6 billion. The net economic loss is about $2.3 billion. In the high-impact scenario, the net effects of the first and second year are estimated as losses of $6.2 and $1.5 billion, respectively.

6.3.4 Business Interruption Costs in Surrounding Areas

In addition, businesses in neighboring communities would also be severely disrupted. Applying average employment density for the top ten largest US cities (1,471 jobs/km²) calibrated based on the 2000 Census Transportation Planning Package (CTPP) data, we estimate that 8,091 jobs would be disrupted or relocated from the contaminated area of 5.5 km².

There are two possible ways to estimate the business interruption costs. First, one can create relocation scenarios for these businesses and estimate total economic losses. Second, one can estimate aggregate metropolitan-wide employment disruptions with reference to a historical event such as the aftermath of the 9/11 attacks and translate these into economic losses. We have chosen the second method for two reasons. First, it is difficult and arbitrary to create business relocation and closure scenarios. Second, economic losses estimated via the first method do not take into account metropolitan-wide economic impacts resulting from reduced tourism and infrastructure disruptions.

Table 6.3 Direct, indirect and induced impacts of reduced stadium visits

(a) Low-impact scenario ($ million)

	Reduced sports attendance (−)				Substitutions (+)				Net total
	Direct	Indirect	Induced	Total	Direct	Indirect	Induced	Total	
Agriculture	0	2.2	46.2	48.4	0	2.5	15.2	17.7	−30.7
Mining	0	2.0	26.9	28.9	0	5.3	8.8	14.1	−14.8
Utilities	0	6.6	59.1	65.7	0	14.8	19.4	34.2	−31.4
Construction	0	6.1	18.4	24.6	0	10.0	6.1	16.0	−8.5
Manufacturing	0	32.4	514.3	546.7	272.6	184.4	169.0	626.0	79.3
Wholesale trade	0	5.8	128.3	134.0	0	44.1	42.1	86.3	−7.8
Transportation and warehousing	0	12.4	88.9	101.4	0	28.3	29.2	57.6	−43.8
Retail trade	0	2.6	221.9	224.5	0	5.0	72.9	77.9	−146.6
Information	0	29.1	161.2	190.3	272.6	201.4	53.0	526.9	336.6
Finance and insurance*	0	27.9	268.6	296.5	0	41.8	88.2	130.1	−166.4
Real estate and rental* (The two asterisked sectors usually described as FIRE)	0	37.1	183.3	220.4	0	75.4	60.2	135.7	−84.8
Professional and technical services	0	35.5	140.9	176.4	0	97.7	46.3	144.0	−32.4

Management of companies	0	6.4	41.2	47.7	0	24.1	13.5	37.7	−10.0
Administration and waste services	0	27.1	72.4	99.5	0	25.8	23.8	49.6	−49.9
Educational services	0	0.2	33.1	33.3	0	0.5	10.9	11.4	−21.8
Health and social services	0	1.8	284.6	286.4	0	0.0	93.5	93.5	−192.9
Arts and recreation	1,635.6	184.3	39.2	1,859.1	272.6	19.8	12.9	305.3	−1,553.8
Accommodation and food services	0	5.0	123.5	128.5	0	8.2	40.6	48.8	−79.7
Other services	0	5.0	118.5	123.4	0	24.1	38.9	63.0	−60.4
Government and non NAICS	0	4.0	227.1	231.2	0	7.2	74.6	81.9	−149.3
Total	1,635.6	433.5	2,797.7	4,866.8	817.8	820.6	919.3	2,557.7	−2,309.1

(b) High-impact scenario ($ million)

Season 1 total	4,361.7	1,155.9	7,460.6	12,978.3	2,180.9	2,188.2	2,451.4	6,820.5	−6,157.7
Season 2 total	1,090.4	289.0	1,865.2	3,244.6	545.2	547.1	612.9	1,705.1	−1,539.4
Total	5,452.1	1,444.9	9,325.8	16,222.8	2,726.1	2,735.3	3,064.3	8,525.7	−7,697.1

Note: 2003 final demand for spectator sports was $10,904 million.

Employment disruptions in the New York metropolitan area after the 9/11 attacks

The national economy entered a recession in early 2001 and the events of 9/11 deepened the recession in New York City and the surrounding metropolitan area. However, the employment growth rates of New York City and the metropolitan area recovered to the national level after one year.

To eliminate the influence of the economic recession and improve the estimate of the net impact of the 9/11 events, we used a vector autoregressive (VAR) model (Bram et al., 2002), in which employment growth in New York City and the metropolitan area is explained by its own lags and lagged national employment growth. Three and seven lags were used in New York City and the metropolitan models, respectively. We used seasonally adjusted employment data from the US Department of Labor's Bureau of Labor Statistics.

The predicted employment paths for New York City and for the metropolitan area reflect their own past trends as well as the national trend. Employment levels had almost recovered to the predicted level within one year after 9/11. We conclude that the difference between the actual and predicted employment levels represents the employment disruptions associated with the 9/11 attacks net of nationwide economic recession impacts. Average net employment losses for the first year were 49,600 (1.36 percent) and 64,700 (0.77 percent) in New York City and its metropolitan area, respectively.

Estimating business interruption costs

The events of 9/11 also resulted in the relocation of 138,000 jobs from among the 941,800 jobs located in New York's downtown at the time. This employment disruption includes all economic impacts net of the recession effect, for example, business disruption from infrastructure shutdowns, temporary business closure for relocation and reduced economic activities from reduced tourism.

Based on the relocation need for 8,091 jobs in our scenario, and applying the same job loss ratio as in the aftermath of the 9/11 attacks (47 percent = 64,700/138,000), we estimate that there would be about 3,793 jobs lost for one year. Then, we distributed the total employment disruption across two-digit NAICS sectors based on the average industrial composition in the top ten largest US metropolitan areas. Finally, we converted the employment losses to output losses using labor productivity (output per unit employment) by industry obtained from the IMPLAN 2003 national database (Table 6.4). In doing so, we also took into account the higher productivity of metropolitan workers compared to the national average.

Table 6.4   Business interruption costs

	Expected employment losses	Industrial composition in top ten largest metropolitan areas (%)	Output per employee ($ thousand)	Expected output losses ($ million)
Agriculture, forestry, fishing and mining	22	0.6	118.61	2.6
Construction	242	6.4	121.37	29.4
Manufacturing	513	13.5	340.18	174.4
Wholesale trade	152	4.0	153.84	23.4
Retail trade	432	11.4	61.65	26.6
Transportation and warehousing and utilities	213	5.6	164.32	34.9
Information	162	4.3	306.67	49.8
FIRE	326	8.6	193.61	63.1
Professional, administration and waste management	480	12.7	101.37	48.7
Educational, health and social services	771	20.3	76.44	59.0
Arts, recreation, accommodation and food services	282	7.4	53.90	15.2
Other services (except public adminstration)	198	5.2	59.43	11.8
Total	3,793			538.9

Hill and Lendell (2005) provide productivity differences (gross product per job) among different types of places, Manhattan, the rest of the New York Cosolidated Metropolitan Statistical Area (CMSA) and the United States for 2004. In their estimation, the productivity of Manhattan workers and New York metropolitan workers were 2.18 and 1.12 times the national average, respectively. Some portions of these productivity differences are due to differences in industrial mix. We decomposed productivity gains in the New York central business district (CBD) and metropolitan area because of industrial mix differences by comparing the total output level estimated based on the national average sectoral productivities and the value estimated based on national averages for industrial composition and productivity. These industrial mix effects account for 19 percent and 4 percent of the productivity differences for the New

York CBD and metropolitan area, respectively. Thus, we applied a productivity factor of 1.08 for metropolitan workers after controlling for industrial mix effects. That is, we estimated that the productivity of metropolitan workers in each industry is, on average, 8 percent higher than the national average.

There could be nationwide macroeconomic impacts beyond the economy of the stricken metropolitan area, but we predict that the long-term macroeconomic impacts of a single terrorist attack on a sports stadium in an individual city would be minor. Several studies support this idea, finding that the long-term economic consequence of the unprecedented 9/11 attacks, which took nearly 2,800 lives, was not economically significant although it resulted in business relocation within the New York metropolitan area (Chernick, 2005).

6.4   CONCLUSIONS

Table 6.5 summarizes the total economic costs of a hypothetical bioterrorist attack on a professional sports stadium. Obviously, the loss of lives is the largest component of the total economic costs. Economic impacts incurred by reduced demand for sports game attendance were also large, ranging from about $5 to $16 billion. The net effect is still substantial, even after accounting for substitution effects from consumers' redirected demands. The economic effects of expenditures on remediation activities and taxes to fund these activities almost cancelled each other out. Finally, communities near the stadium attack are also expected to suffer more than half a billion dollars of business interruption costs.

The formal study of the economic impacts of terrorist attacks is a relatively new field. This research explores ways to develop and apply scenarios that describe hypothetical but plausible attacks, with a focus on bioterrorist attacks. We have showed that available off-the-shelf impact models (in this case IMPLAN) can be usefully applied. We also showed that such an application requires the development of detailed, compelling and plausible scenarios grounded in available data and literature.

There are two reasons for conducting the research. First, policy makers can be guided in their mitigation allocations by improved estimates of the economic severity of various events. Second, researchers can study our approaches, elaborate them and apply them to a broader and longer list of possible terrorist attacks.

Table 6.5 Summary of total economic costs

(a) Low-impact scenario ($ thousand)

	Direct	Indirect	Induced	Total
Loss of lives				-57,240,000
Remediation expenditures (+)	290,505	216,267	423,056	929,827
Reduced household spending (−)	-286,158	-186,561	-303,210	-775,929
Reduced demand for sports attendance (−)	-1,635,638	-433,480	-2,797,730	-4,866,848
Substitutions (+)	817,818	820,591	919,293	2,557,702
Business interruption costs (−)				-538,875
Total				-61,952,949

(b) High-impact scenario ($ thousand)

	Direct	Indirect	Induced	Total
Loss of lives				-57,240,000
Remediation expenditures (+)	290,505	216,267	423,056	929,827
Reduced household spending (−)	-286,158	-186,561	-303,210	-775,929
Reduced demand for sports attendance (−)	-5,452,126	-1,444,933	-9,325,763	-16,222,822
Substitutions (+)	2,726,063	2,735,306	3,064,312	8,525,680
Business interruption costs (−)				-538,875
Total				-73,308,923

95

REFERENCES

American Cancer Society (2006), *Cancer Facts and Figures 2006*. Atlanta, GA: American Cancer Society.

Australian Government Attorney-General's Department (2006), *Stadiums Risk Context Statement*. ACT, Australia: Australian Government Attorney-General's Department.

Bali Tourism Board (n.d.), http://www.bali_tourism_board.org/en/tourism and economy statistics.

Braithwaite, R.S., D. Fridsma and M.S. Roberts (2006), 'The cost-effectiveness of strategies to reduce mortality from an intentional release of aerosolized anthrax spores', *Medical Decision Making*, **26** (2), 182–93.

Bram, J., J. Orr and C. Rapaport (2002), 'Measuring the effects of the September 11 attack on New York City', *Federal Reserve Bank of New York Economic Policy Review*, **8**, 5–20.

Brookshire, D.S. and H.R. Neill (1992), 'Benefit transfers – conceptual and empirical issues'. *Water Resources Research*, **28** (3), 651–5.

Bureau of Labor Statistics (2006), *Consumer Expenditure Surveys, 1984–2005*, Washington, DC: US Department of Labor, Bureau of Labor Statistics.

Chernick, H. (ed.) (2005), *Resilient City: The Economic Impact of 9/11*. New York: Russell Sage Foundation.

Evans, C. (2003), 'Studying the studies: an overview of recent research into taxation operating costs', *Journal of Tax Research*, **1** (1), 64–92.

Fisher, A., L.G. Chestnut and D.M. Violette (1989), 'The value of reducing risks of death – a note on new evidence', *Journal of Policy Analysis and Management*, **8** (1), 88–100.

Hill, E.W. and I. Lendell (2005), 'Did 9/11 change Manhattan and the New York region as places to conduct business?', in H. Chernick (ed.), *Resilient City: The Economic Impact of 9/11*. New York: Russell Sage Foundation, pp. 23–61.

Kaufmann, A.F., M.I. Meltzer and G.P. Schmid (1997), 'The economic impact of a bioterrorist attack: are prevention and post-attack intervention programs justifiable?', *Emerging Infectious Diseases*, **3** (2), 83–94.

Kochi, I., B. Hubbell and R. Kramer (2006), 'An empirical Bayes approach to combining and comparing estimates of the value of a statistical life for environmental policy analysis', *Environmental and Resource Economics*, **34** (3), 385–406.

Luken, R.A., F.R. Johnson and V. Kibler (1992), 'Benefits and costs of pulp and paper effluent controls under the Clean-Water-Act', *Water Resources Research*, **28** (3), 665–74.

National Highway Traffic Safety Administration (2005), *State Traffic Safety Information for Year 2005*. Washington, DC: US Department of Transportation.

Parry, I.W.H. (2002), 'Tax deductions and the marginal welfare cost of taxation', *International Tax and Public Finance*, **9** (5), 531–52.

Pidgeon, N., R.E. Kasperson and P. Slovic (eds), (2003), *The Social Amplification of Risk*. Cambridge: Cambridge University Press.

Renn, O., W.J. Burns, J.X. Kasperson, R.S. Kasperson and P. Slovic (1992), 'The social amplification of risk – theoretical foundations and empirical applications', *Journal of Social Issues*, **48** (4), 137–60.

Rose, A. (2006), 'Estimating the total economic impacts of extreme events', Paper presented at the National Academy of Sciences Meeting of the Panel of the Biological Agent Risk Analysis, Washington, DC, 28 August.

Rose, A. (2007), 'Estimating the total economic impacts of extreme events: application to a radionuclide attack on a municipal water system', Paper presented at the 46th Western Regional Science Association Annual Meeting, Newport Beach, California, February.

Slemrod, J. and N. Sorum (1984), 'The compliance cost of the United States individual income-tax system', *National Tax Journal*, **37** (4), 461–74.

Slemrod, J. and S. Yitzhaki (1996), 'The costs of taxation and the marginal efficiency cost of funds', *International Monetary Fund Staff Papers*, **43** (1), 172–98.

Spash, C.L. and A. Vatn (2006), 'Transferring environmental value estimates: issues and alternatives', *Ecological Economics*, **60** (2), 379–88.

Stein, B.D., M.N. Elliott and L.H. Jaycox et al. (2004), 'A national longitudinal study of the psychological consequences of the September 11, 2001 terrorist attacks: reactions, impairment, and help-seeking', *Psychiatry*, **67** (2), 105–17.

Sunstein, C.R. (2003), 'Terrorism and probability neglect,' *Journal of Risk and Uncertainty*, **26** (2), 121–36.

Tran-Nam, B., C. Evans, M. Walpole and K. Ritchie (2000), 'Tax compliance costs: research methodology and empirical evidence from Australia', *National Tax Journal*, **53** (2), 229–52.

7. International border closures

JiYoung Park, Peter Gordon, Harry W. Richardson and James E. Moore II

7.1 INTRODUCTION

Recurrent reminders that an international avian influenza epidemic is a real possibility have prompted a variety of public policy discussions. A recent World Bank study estimated that the global economy would lose $2 trillion from an outbreak, or 3 percent of world gross domestic product (GDP). Another report in *The Lancet* (by the Harvard Initiative for Global Health Group; Murray et al., 2006), largely based on an analogy drawn from the Spanish Flu epidemic of 1918–20, presented various estimates of possible US fatalities. These included a low threshold of 114,483, a median threshold of 297,883, a mean threshold of 383,881 and a high threshold of 744,226. Applying the US Environmental Protection Agency's (EPA) valuation of a statistical life, $5.8 million (now increased to $9.1 million by EPA, $7.9 million by the US Food and Drug Administration (FDA)), these fatalities amount to large imputed dollar amounts: $664 billion, $1.728 trillion, $2.227 trillion and $4.317 trillion, respectively. These estimates, astronomical though they are, ignore the treatment costs of those who get sick but do not die, quarantine costs and other disaster management costs. The Harvard loss estimates are also much higher than the values estimated by Meltzer et al. (1999), who estimated US losses in the range of $71–$166 billion. While *The Lancet* study argued that a future pandemic might be even worse than in 1918–20, it also accepts that fatalities might be lower because of improved medical management (although the health care system could be overwhelmed), anti-viral medicines, quarantine and vaccination. While early fears of an international pandemic have subsided, it is probably safe to say that terrorists with an admitted interest in acquiring and using weapons of mass destruction have taken note of the loss magnitudes that were discussed as well as reports that the H5N1 strain can be spread by human-to-human contact.

The closure of the United States to international trade and travel for as long as one year has been proposed as an extreme policy that might be justified by such an extreme threat. In this research, we ask whether such extreme measures can be justified in economic terms. We attempt to measure the economic impacts of a one-year border closure. The hypothetical disruptions are obviously severe, well beyond anything that the US economy has ever experienced, and raise additional analytical issues that we take up briefly at the end of this chapter.

Our modeling approach (reported in some of our previous papers; see Gordon et al., 2007b; Park et al., 2007) enables us to report most of the impacts at the level of the individual states and the District of Columbia (DC). Political decision making in a federal system requires spatially disaggregated information. We utilized the National Interstate Economic Model (NIEMO), the only operational multiregional input-output (MRIO) model of the United States, which provides estimates for 47 sectors (the USC sectors), and the 50 states plus DC. We applied demand-side and supply-side versions of NIEMO whenever direct spatial impacts could be located (stopping international air travel, trade and cross-border shopping). We also used USIO, a 47-sector aggregation of the national IMPLAN IO model for circumstances in which the spatial locations of direct impacts remain unknown. Our simulations are for 2001, the year for which we had access to the most relevant data (Minnesota IMPLAN Group, 2003). We did not address the costs or the feasibility of implementing border closures.

In round numbers, the bottom line from the summing of our most optimistic scenarios is that a one-year border closing results in a total output loss of $2.359 trillion. Dividing our low-end estimated output loss by an aggregate economic multiplier of approximately 1.655 (from our results), we get an overall GDP loss of approximately $1.425 trillion, or approximately 14 percent of 2001 GDP.

These are the aggregated impacts from five kinds of disruptions: a one-year shutdown of all international air travel, in and out of the United States; a one-year shutdown in international commodity trade (except gas and oil, which would be delivered via pipeline); a one-year shutdown of legal as well as illegal immigration; and a one-year disruption of all cross-border shopping. In each case, we tried to model and include various plausible mitigations. Also in the interests of conservatism, we restricted our reporting to Type I input-output (IO) multiplier results. Multiplier results would be approximately 50 percent greater if values for Type II multipliers are reported. Given the limited mitigations that we were able to model, the more conservative results seem the most plausible. Nevertheless, such a large event is difficult to model, and the results must be understood in light of many caveats. Also, our models are linear, so predictions for shorter duration border closings would merely consist of proportionately smaller impacts.

7.2   INVENTORIZING LOSSES

7.2.1   International Air Travel Losses

Air travel losses can be estimated for various scenarios. We report on the most optimistic, which includes the assumed diversion of 65 percent of US-based overseas travel to US travel (for domestic vacations) and a 25 percent increase in telecommunications activities as substitutions for canceled business trips. Direct losses such as hotel, food, shopping and ground transportation were located at major airports (including an average 5 percent local airport revenues from ticket sales taxes; 95 percent of ticket sales revenue losses were allocated nationally).

The various modeling steps involved are:

1. Calculating annual passenger volumes for four trip types (US-based international inbound, US-based international outbound, abroad-based international inbound, abroad-based international outbound) for each of the US international airports and aggregating each of the four volumes to the 50 states and DC (see Tables 7A.1 and 7A.2 in the Appendix).
2. Calculating per passenger spending patterns for each of the representative trip types by major USC sector (see Table 7A.3 in the Appendix).

The resulting estimated direct losses for the whole nation are shown in Table 7A.4 in the Appendix. Table 7A.5 shows the national effects of just the lost air ticket sales, specifically the 95 percent of these sales that are distributed across the nation. This creates an overall loss of nearly $84 billion.

However, the two proposed mitigations (substituting telecommunications and domestic travel) reduce losses substantially with most of the positive offsetting impacts coming from the increased use of telecommunications. In light of the mitigations, direct losses were estimated to be just over $58 billion. These prompted more than $113 billion of total losses. As expected, almost 95 percent of the losses would be felt in three of the USC sectors and almost two-thirds of that would impact the Transportation Sector (Table 7.1).

These results are in light of both kinds of assumed mitigations. Taking these one at a time, the results of the assumed telecommunications offset are shown in Table 7A.6 in the Appendix; these are results for the nation as a whole because the location of telecommunications offset impacts is unknown.

Table 7.1   Total (direct and indirect) losses for the top three impacted sectors across the 50 states and DC ($ million)

Sector	Sector code	Total sector losses	Percent of total
Transportation	USC 33	−71,231.45	62.80
Accommodations, food services	USC 45	−19,499.01	17.19
Retail trade	USC 35	−16,321.99	14.39
Subtotal: top three impacted sectors		−107,052.45	94.38
Total: 47 USC sectors		−113,428.83	100.00

We also modeled the state-level mitigations from lost international tickets sales to US travelers made up by the increased sales of domestic air travel. To the extent that there are geographic effects, these are shown in Table 7A.7, which accounts for the effects of differences in local purchases.

7.2.2   Trade Losses

The most optimistic international trade loss scenario allows for the continuation of energy imports (USC Sector 10) and it also includes the presumption of substantial economic resilience by assuming that canceled exports replace canceled imports as much as possible. To plausibly model that possibility, we had to disaggregate industries to the maximum extent possible; this analysis was conducted at the six-digit Harmonized System (HS) Commodity Code level for each state. These data by port of entry were available from WISERTrade. At this disaggregated level, we assumed that if local exports are greater than imports, then local exports are sold to local importers: exporting sectors experience only partial losses and the importing sectors are not disrupted. We applied the NIEMO demand-side model. On the other hand, if exports were less than imports, then the local importing industries purchase from local exporting industries: importing sectors experience partial losses and the exporting sectors are not disrupted. We then applied the NIEMO supply-side model.

The results of international trade losses for the most impacted states and sectors are shown in Tables 7.2a and 7.2b. Table 7A.8 in the Appendix shows the state-by-state effects of trade losses, both with and without the two assumed mitigations.

*Table 7.2a   Total (direct and indirect) impacts due to trade losses across
47 sectors for the top three impacted states ($ million)*

State	Total state losses	Percent of total
California	−220,685.56	9.93
Texas	−148,719.02	6.69
Illinois	−90,465.95	4.07
Subtotal: top three impacted states	−459,870.53	20.69
Total: 47 USC sectors	−2,223,037.28	100.00

*Table 7.2b   Total (direct and indirect) impacts due to trade losses across
51 states for the top three impacted sectors ($ million)*

Sector	Sector code	Total sector losses	Percent of total
Electronic and Other Electrical Equipment, Components, and Office Equipment	USC24	−285,665.30	12.85
Misc. Manufactured Products, Scrap, and Mixed Freight	USC29	−248,300.23	11.17
Motorized and Other Vehicles	USC25	−206,953.18	9.31
Subtotal: top three impacted sectors		−740,908.71	33.33
Total: 47 USC sectors		−2,223,037.28	100.00

7.2.3   Legal Immigration Losses

Annual legal net immigration per year is approximately 1.5 million. We assume that the labor force participation rate of immigrants is 67 percent, and that there are 1 million workers among them. There are also estimates of the occupations of this group. Our first step was to assign occupations to industries, using US Bureau of Labor Statistics (BLS) information. We then applied Borjas's labor supply elasticity (–0.3; Borjas, 2003). This raised wages in selected sectors. We then used a national IO price model to calculate sector-level price effects and used these to reduce final demands. Table 7.3 shows the major impacted sectors. The left side of Table 7A.9 in the Appendix provides the state-by-state details for price effects. The right side provides state-by-state details for reduced final demand effects.

Table 7.3 Total (direct and indirect) impacts due to legal immigration losses across 51 states for the top three impacted sectors ($ million)

Sector	Sector code	Total sector losses	Percent of total
Health Care and Social Assistance	USC43	−1,090.68	10.78
Construction	USC31	−995.60	9.84
Retail trade	USC35	−678.86	6.7
Subtotal: top three impacted sectors		−2,765.14	27.32
Total: 47 USC sectors		−10,121.90	100.00

7.2.4 Illegal Immigration Losses

This part of the analysis was similar to our treatment of legal immigration. Of course, the magnitudes involve less precision: our mid-level estimate of annual illegal immigration is 628,000 (Gordon et al., 2007a). This value is conservative. The Pew Hispanic Center (Passel, 2006) provides an estimate of 850,000 unauthorized immigrants per year. We allocate most of these people to some of the 47 USC sectors, based on proportions of illegal employment predominantly working in agriculture, construction, retail, other production and other services sectors. We then followed the same estimation procedure as in the case of legal immigrants. The results on the most impacted sectors are shown in Table 7.4. Table 7A.10 in the Appendix shows sector-level detail, including price effects in the left columns and final demand effects in the right columns.

Table 7.4 Total (direct and indirect) impacts due to illegal immigration losses across 50 states and the District of Columbia for the top three impacted sectors ($ million)

Sector	Sector code	Total sector losses	Percent of total
Construction	USC31	−479.30	23.51
Retail trade	USC35	−342.87	16.82
Real Estate and Rental and Leasing	USC38	−96.06	4.71
Subtotal: top three impacted sectors		−918.23	45.04
Total: 47 USC sectors		−2,038.91	100.00

Table 7.5a　Total (direct and indirect) impacts due to cross-border shopping losses across 47 sectors for the top three impacted states ($ million)

State	Total state losses	Percent of total
Texas	−3,553.20	35.74
Arizona	−2,533.17	25.48
California	−986.02	9.92
Subtotal: top three impacted states	−7,072.39	71.14
Total: 47 USC sectors	−9,941.23	100.00

Table 7.5b　Total (direct and indirect) impacts due to cross-border shopping losses across 50 states and the District of Columbia for the top three impacted sectors ($ million)

Sector	Sector code	Total sector losses	Percent of total
Retail trade	USC35	−6,139.92	61.76
Professional, Scientific and Technical Services	USC39	−615.75	6.19
Real Estate and Rental and Leasing	USC28	−530.84	5.34
Subtotal: top three impacted sectors		−7,286.51	73.30
Total: 47 USC sectors		−9,941.23	100.00

7.2.5　Annual Incoming Border-crossing Sales Losses

Data for annual inbound border-crossings by state are available from the US Bureau of Transportation Statistics. Based on various reports, we assumed that 60 percent of these are foreign visitors crossing over to shop in the United States and spending $100 per shopping visit. We also assumed that 40 percent of the crossings are returning US shoppers who would shop domestically instead. The results for the most impacted states and sectors are shown in Tables 7.5a and 7.5b. State-level details are shown in Table 7A.11 in the Appendix.

7.2.6　Summary of Losses ($ million)

The total projected losses mentioned in the introduction are the sum of the losses documented in the previous five subsections. As expected, the loss of commodity trade, even with the major mitigations that we included, accounts for the overwhelming share of the disruption (Table 7.6).

Table 7.6   Total (direct and indirect) impacts ($ million) of border closure

	Loss
International air travel	113,429
International trade	2,223,037
Legal immigration	10,122
Illegal immigration	2,039
Cross-border shopping	9,941
Total	2,358,568

7.3   CONCLUSIONS

Our approach is based on the premise that border closure effects vary from place to place and that local (state-level, in this case) effects are what most political decision makers consider. This motivates a modeling approach that estimates state-level effects.

Interestingly, the magnitude of estimated costs is close to the cited median dollar value of expected loss of life. Until other information becomes available, our first-order estimates suggest that the total costs of the proposed border closure policy match the magnitude of the cost of the threat. In this case, benefits are costs forgone because policies are implemented. If sealing the national border is 100 percent effective in precluding fatalities from a pandemic, then we estimate that the economic impact of a one-year closure would be approximately equal to the value of lives saved. The value of life is measured in this case in terms of federal standards. This comparison ignores the costs avoided by not needing to treat survivors, and assumes energy imports continue. Consequently, this first analysis is incomplete, but it is apparent that a border closure strategy would likely be too expensive to justify, and that the cost-effectiveness measures of more limited responses or mitigations are likely to be considerably higher.

In an event as extreme as a long-term US border closure, complex global repercussions, especially via changes in capital markets, that might further multiply economic impacts are likely to be important. These are missing from our models, and it may be impossible to meaningfully anticipate such effects given the number of simultaneous economic relationships and magnitudes involved. We are also missing enforcement costs as well as the welfare losses from reduced consumer choice (Broda and Weinstein, 2004). On the other hand, much of the natural resiliency of market economies is also left out of our approaches, and these effects would mitigate impacts.

We must acknowledge that the utility of our research, and any research focusing on extreme, nation-level events, rests on the possibility that the many positives as well as the many negatives that are beyond the scope of the models used might roughly balance.

Obviously, many methodological questions remain. How should we best model extreme events? Can we expect to ever be able to reliably model the economic impacts of extreme events? Available models, by design, highlight perturbations at the economic margin, where adjustment strategies are reasonably limited. The MRIO analysis executed here precludes many meaningful adjustments on the part of all producers and consumers. Yet the essence of meaningful economic behavior is adjustment, including strategies ranging from resource conservation to technological innovation and beyond. When policy makers are compelled by statutory responsibilities or by circumstances to make choices about events beyond the margin, it becomes unclear how to analyse and evaluate options. Beyond the margin, it may be important to resort to subjective applications of domain expertise. Work by RAND researchers on the effects of nuclear attack makes use of 'scenario analysis' and 'strategic gaming' exercises that basically rely on expert judgment (Meade and Molander, 2007; see also Carter et al., 2007 and Zimmerman et al., 2007). Analytical results provided by model structure to treat the margin might still be used to inform the initial stages of such a process.

REFERENCES

Borjas, G.J. (2003), 'The labor demand curve *is* downward sloping: reexamining the impact of immigration on the labor market', *Quarterly Journal of Economics*, **20**, 1335–74.

Broda, C. and D.E. Weinstein (2004), 'Globalization and the gains from variety', Federal Reserve Bank of New York, Staff Report No. 180.

Carter, A.B., M.M. May and W.J. Perry (2007), 'The day after: action following a nuclear blast in a U.S. city', *The Washington Quarterly*, **30** (4), 19–32.

Gordon, P., J.E. Moore II, J.Y. Park and H.W. Richardson (2007), 'The economic impacts of a terrorist attack on the U.S. commercial aviation system', *Risk Analysis*, **27** (3), 565–72.

Maplesden, H.C., F.X. Wang, T.X. Tian and S.D. Cook (2002), *Expenditure Patterns of Travelers in the U.S.: 2002 Edition*. Washington, DC: Research Department of the Travel Industry Association of America.

Meade, C. and R.C. Molander (2007), *Considering the Effects of Catastrophic Terrorist Attack*. Santa Monica, CA: RAND, Center for Terrorism Risk Management Policy.

Meltzer, M.I., N.J. Cox and K. Fukuda (1999), 'Modeling the economic impact of pandemic influence in the U.S.: implications for setting priorities for intervention', *Emerging Infectious Diseases*, **5**, 659–71.

Minnesota IMPLAN Group, Inc. (2003), *IMPLAN® Data Files 2001*. Stillwater, MN: Minnesota IMPLAN Group, Inc.

Murray, C.L., A.D. Lopez, B. Chin, D. Feehan and K.H. Hill (2006), 'Estimation of potential global pandemic influenza mortality on the basis of vital registry data from the 1918–20 pandemic: a quantitative analysis', *Lancet*, **368**, 2211–18.

Park, J.Y., P. Gordon, J.E. Moore II and H.W. Richardson (2007), 'Simulating the state-by-state effects of terrorist attacks on three major U.S. ports: applying NIEMO (National Interstate Economic Model)', in H.W. Richardson, P. Gordon and J.E. Moore II (eds), *The Economic Costs and Consequences of Terrorism*. Cheltenham, UK and Northampton, MA, USA: Edward Elgar, pp. 208–34.

Passel, J.S. (2006), *The Size and Characteristics of the Unauthorized Migrant Population in the U.S. – Estimates Based on the March 2005 Current Population Survey*. Washington, DC: Pew Hispanic Center.

US Department of Transportation (2006), *U.S. – International Travel and Transportation Trends: 2006 Update*. Washington, DC: US Department of Transportation Research and Innovative Technology Administration and Bureau of Transportation Statistics.

Zimmerman, R., C.E. Restropo, J.S. Simonoff and L.B. Lave (2007), 'Risk and economic costs of a terrorist attack on the electric system', in H.W. Richardson, P. Gordon and J.E. Moore II (eds), *The Economic Costs and Consequences of Terrorist Attacks*. Cheltenham, UK and Northampton, MA, USA: Edward Elgar, pp. 273–90.

APPENDIX

Table 7A.1   State-by-state estimates of international passenger volumes, base year 2005[d]

State	Total inbound flows from international origins	Proportions of total US arrivals from international origins[a,c]	Arrivals of International passengers (AIP) from international origins	Proportion of AIP to US total	Arrivals of US residents (IAUS) from international origins	Proportion of IAUS to US total
AL	1,475	0.021% [c]	1,227	0.004%	248	0.001%
AK	52,435	0.750% [c]	43,620	0.159%	8,815	0.020%
AZ	890,631	1.929% [a]	528,910	1.929%	361,721	0.818%
AR	509	0.007% [c]	423	0.002%	86	0.000%
CA	12,597,191	16.395% [a]	4,495,735	16.395%	8,101,456	18.327%
CO	849,231	1.039% [a]	284,798	1.039%	564,433	1.277%
CT	48,006	0.686% [c]	39,936	0.146%	8,070	0.018%
DE	–	0.000% [c]	0	0.000%	0	0.000%
DC	2,580,552	36.898% [c]	2,146,737	7.829%	433,815	0.981%
FL	10,224,178	14.985% [a]	4,109,224	14.985%	6,114,954	13.833%
GA	3,676,131	2.226% [a]	610,281	2.226%	3,065,850	6.935%
HI	2,108,498	30.148% [c]	1,754,039	6.396%	354,459	0.802%
ID	126	0.002% [c]	105	0.000%	21	0.000%
IL	5,616,636	3.932% [a]	1,078,163	3.932%	4,538,473	10.267%
IN	34,550	0.494% [c]	28,742	0.105%	5,808	0.013%
IA	524	0.007% [c]	436	0.002%	88	0.000%
KS	645	0.009% [c]	537	0.002%	108	0.000%
KY	546,907	7.820% [c]	454,967	1.659%	91,940	0.208%
LA	37,980	0.543% [c]	31,595	0.115%	6,385	0.014%
ME	6,454	0.092% [c]	5,369	0.020%	1,085	0.002%
MD	286,920	0.816% [a]	223,770	0.816%	63,150	0.143%
MA	1,983,484	2.967% [a]	813,708	2.967%	1,169,776	2.646%
MI	1,938,839	1.113% [a]	305,140	1.113%	1,633,699	3.696%
MN	1,306,762	0.371% [a]	101,713	0.371%	1,205,049	2.726%
MS	749	0.011% [c]	623	0.002%	126	0.000%
MO	167,179	0.519% [a]	142,399	0.519%	24,780	0.056%
MT	58	0.001% [c]	48	0.000%	10	0.000%
NE	2,567	0.037% [c]	2,135	0.008%	432	0.001%
NV	856,052	12.240% [c]	712,141	2.597%	143,911	0.326%
NH	10,056	0.144% [c]	8,365	0.031%	1,691	0.004%
NJ	4,598,623	3.412% [a]	935,764	3.412%	3,662,859	8.286%
NM	295	0.004% [c]	245	0.001%	50	0.000%
NY	10,131,931	20.846% [a]	5,716,297	20.846%	4,415,634	9.989%
NC	1,071,051	0.964% [a]	264,455	0.964%	806,596	1.825%

Total outbound flows to international destinations	Proportions of total US departures to international destinations[b,c]	Departures of international passengers (DIP) to international destinations	Proportion of DIP to US total	Departures of US residents to international destinations (IDUS)	Propor-tions of IDUS to US total
2,021	0.014% [c]	759	0.002%	1,262	0.003%
64,232	0.434% [c]	24,133	0.070%	40,099	0.109%
909,656	6.146% [c]	341,768	0.989%	567,888	1.537%
666	0.005% [c]	250	0.001%	416	0.001%
12,648,021	20.000% [b]	5,256,479	15.211%	7,391,542	20.000%
820,241	5.542% [c]	308,173	0.892%	512,068	1.386%
46,631	0.315% [c]	17,520	0.051%	29,111	0.079%
4	0.000% [c]	2	0.000%	2	0.000%
2,555,433	4.000% [b]	1,077,125	3.117%	1,478,308	4.000%
10,262,260	6.000% [b]	8,044,797	23.280%	2,217,463	6.000%
3,647,994	24.649% [c]	1,370,591	3.966%	2,277,403	6.162%
2,118,845	14.317% [c]	796,073	2.304%	1,322,772	3.579%
524	0.004% [c]	197	0.001%	327	0.001%
5,551,295	5.000% [b]	3,703,409	10.717%	1,847,886	5.000%
30,898	0.209% [c]	11,609	0.034%	19,289	0.052%
2,278	0.015% [c]	856	0.002%	1,422	0.004%
774	0.005% [c]	291	0.001%	483	0.001%
558,455	3.773% [c]	209,818	0.607%	348,637	0.943%
33,367	0.225% [c]	12,536	0.036%	20,831	0.056%
5,495	0.037% [c]	2,065	0.006%	3,430	0.009%
291,562	1.970% [c]	109,543	0.317%	182,019	0.493%
1,983,037	3.000% [b]	874,306	2.530%	1,108,731	3.000%
1,900,136	12.839% [c]	713,902	2.066%	1,186,234	3.210%
1,308,609	8.842% [c]	491,658	1.423%	816,951	2.211%
265	0.002% [c]	100	0.000%	165	0.000%
164,058	1.109% [c]	61,638	0.178%	102,420	0.277%
95	0.001% [c]	36	0.000%	59	0.000%
1,449	0.010% [c]	544	0.002%	905	0.002%
838,183	5.663% [c]	314,914	0.911%	523,269	1.416%
9,862	0.067% [c]	3,705	0.011%	6,157	0.017%
4,569,535	5.000% [b]	2,721,649	7.876%	1,847,886	5.000%
505	0.003% [c]	190	0.001%	315	0.001%
10,082,301	21.000% [b]	2,321,182	6.717%	7,761,119	21.000%
1,068,898	7.222% [c]	401,596	1.162%	667,302	1.806%

Table 7A.1   (continued)

State	Total inbound flows from international origins	Proportions of total US arrivals from international origins[a,c]	Arrivals of International passengers (AIP) from international origins	Proportion of AIP to US total	Arrivals of US residents (IAUS) from international origins	Proportion of IAUS to US total
ND	127	0.002% [c]	106	0.000%	21	0.000%
OH	176,570	2.525% [c]	146,887	0.536%	29,683	0.067%
OK	1,051	0.015% [c]	874	0.003%	177	0.000%
OR	256,533	0.593% [a]	162,742	0.593%	93,791	0.212%
PA	1,938,357	2.151% [a]	589,938	2.151%	1,348,419	3.050%
RI	18,027	0.258% [c]	14,996	0.055%	3,031	0.007%
SC	9,925	0.142% [c]	8,257	0.030%	1,668	0.004%
SD	711	0.010% [c]	591	0.002%	120	0.000%
TN	218,559	3.125% [c]	181,817	0.663%	36,742	0.083%
TX	5,956,051	3.264% [a]	895,079	3.264%	5,060,972	11.449%
UT	178,024	2.545% [c]	148,096	0.540%	29,928	0.068%
VT	2	0.000% [c]	2	0.000%	0	0.000%
VA	5,739	0.082% [c]	4,774	0.017%	965	0.002%
WA	1,143,749	1.261% [a]	345,826	1.261%	797,923	1.805%
WV	28	0.000% [c]	23	0.000%	5	0.000%
WI	96,515	1.380% [c]	80,290	0.293%	16,225	0.037%
WY	6	0.000% [c]	5	0.000%	1	0.000%
Total	71,627,199		27,421,952	100%	44,205,247	100%

Notes:
a.   Proportions of arrivals in the United States from overseas international locations are available from the International Trade Administration (ITA) Office of Travel and Tourism Industries (OTTI) at http://tinet.ita.doc.gov/cat/f-2005-45-541.html.
b.   Proportions of departures of US residents to overseas international locations are available from the ITA OTTI at http://tinet.ita.doc.gov/view/m-2005-O-001/index.html.
c.   Some proportions are unavailable from OTTI or are available but inconsistent. Adjusted proportions are calculated by authors based on the difference between the 'total inbound or outbound passengers' and 'the sum of preliminary fixed inbound or outbound passengers' available from the ITA OTTI at http://tinet.ita.doc.gov/. The differences between inbound passengers to all states and inbound passengers to OTTI's selected major states are used to estimate proportions not provided by OTTI. These adjusted proportions are used to calculate international arrivals unreported by OTTI. US-based outbound passengers are estimated similarly.
d.   Our approach combines two different data sources to estimate four types of passenger flows (domestic inbound from foreign origins, domestic outbound to foreign destinations, international inbound from foreign origins and international outbound to foreign destinations). Our results include modest discrepancies between inbound and outbound international and domestic passenger flows. Much of the discrepancy is due to passengers arriving or departing outside the 2005 base year. We have not attempted corrections.

Total outbound flows to international destinations	Proportions of total US departures to international destinations[b,c]	Departures of international passengers (DIP) to international destinations	Proportion of DIP to US total	Departures of US residents to international desti-nations (IDUS)	Proportions of IDUS to US total
2,176	0.015% [c]	818	0.002%	1,358	0.004%
172,409	1.165% [c]	64,776	0.187%	107,633	0.291%
4,767	0.032% [c]	1,791	0.005%	2,976	0.008%
259,889	1.756% [c]	97,643	0.283%	162,246	0.439%
1,925,884	3.000% [b]	817,153	2.365%	1,108,731	3.000%
17,763	0.120% [c]	6,674	0.019%	11,089	0.030%
10,130	0.068% [c]	3,806	0.011%	6,324	0.017%
821	0.006% [c]	308	0.001%	513	0.001%
209,548	1.416% [c]	78,729	0.228%	130,819	0.354%
6,001,647	6.000% [b]	3,784,184	10.951%	2,217,463	6.000%
193,382	1.307% [c]	72,656	0.210%	120,726	0.327%
11	0.000% [c]	4	0.000%	7	0.000%
5,431	0.037% [c]	2,040	0.006%	3,391	0.009%
1,135,398	2.000% [b]	396,244	1.147%	739,154	2.000%
132	0.001% [c]	50	0.000%	82	0.000%
97,742	0.660% [c]	36,723	0.106%	61,019	0.165%
11	0.000% [c]	4	0.000%	7	0.000%
71,514,726		34,557,016	100%	36,957,710	100%

Table 7A.2   Annual passenger volumes: international travel

Travelers based in the United States		Travelers based abroad	
Case 1: Inbound	Case 2: Outbound	Case 3: Inbound	Case 4: Outbound
44,205,247	36,957,710	27,421,952	34,557,016

Sources: US Department of Transportation, Bureau of Transportation Statistics (BTS), TranStats Table T-100, 'International market (all carriers, 2005)', http://www.transtats. bts.gov/ (Case 1: Inbound and Case 4: Outbound). Data from the International Trade Administration's Office of Travel and Tourism Industries (OTTI), http://tinet.ita.doc.gov, were used to calculate foreign arrivals and outbound trips taken by US residents.

Table 7A.3   Domestic spending patterns of international passengers

Sector code	Expenditure[a]	Based in the United States		Based abroad	
		$ per passenger inbound	$ per passenger outbound	$ per passenger inbound	$ per passenger outbound
USC33	Airline Tickets[b]	333.33	333.33	333.33	333.33
USC33	Transportation	90.67	90.67	143.50	143.50
USC45	Accommodation	0.00	0.00	686.00	0.00
USC35	Foods	0.00	0.00	267.31[c]	0.00
USC45	Grocery Stores	0.00	0.00	60.69[c]	0.00
USC35	Gifts/Shopping	0.00	0.00	406.00	0.00
USC44	Amusement	0.00	0.00	264.00	0.00
	Total	424.00	424.00	2,160.83	476.83

Notes:
a. All expenditures except Airline Tickets are based on US expenditures per round-trip from proprietary data purchased from the Travel Industry Association (http://www.tia. org). See also Table 7A.2.
b. These values are applied to all international boardings or alightings at US airports in 2005 (http://www.bts.gov). We assume that the average cost of an international round-trip is $1,000, and that two-thirds of this value accounts for the share of tickets that may have been purchased for US carriers. See http://www.lawa.org/lax/statistics/tcom-1201.pdf. We separately consider both trip types and assume that half are made by US residents and half by foreign residents.
c. Based on $328 for the Food/Beverage Sector (Maplesden et al., 2002, p. 74), which we separate across two USC sectors on the premise that Food/Beverage Sector spending is similar to the pattern shown by domestic travelers (Maplesden et al., 2002, p.73). The proportions shown are 81.5 percent for the Foods Sector and 18.5 percent for the Grocery Stores Sector.

Table 7A.4   Net direct losses given increased telecommunications and diversion of domestic travel

USC sectors	Activity	Amount ($ million)
36	Telecommunications	43,596.65
33, 35, 44, 45	Diversion to Domestic Travel	8,381.50
33, 35, 44, 45	Total Direct Loses	−110,145.09
	Net Direct Losses	−58,166.94

Note: We assume final demand for Telecommunications services increases by 25 percent during the one-year international travel ban using IMPLAN® Data Files 2001, Sector 422 (Minnesota IMPLAN Group, 2003).

Table 7A.5   Impacts of total air ticket sales losses ($ million), 47 USC sectors

	Sector code	Direct impact	Indirect impact	Total impact
Commodity	USC01	0.0	−57.1	−57.1
Sectors	USC02	0.0	−36.2	−36.2
	USC03	0.0	−12.2	−12.2
	USC04	0.0	−38.2	−38.2
	USC05	0.0	−80.8	−80.8
	USC06	0.0	−53.1	−53.1
	USC07	0.0	−0.1	−0.1
	USC08	0.0	−36.6	−36.6
	USC09	0.0	−12.5	−12.5
	USC10	0.0	−4,021.2	−4,021.2
	USC11	0.0	−93.9	−93.9
	USC12	0.0	−6.4	−6.4
	USC13	0.0	−16.2	−16.2
	USC14	0.0	−163.6	−163.6
	USC15	0.0	−380.4	−380.4
	USC16	0.0	−157.6	−157.6
	USC17	0.0	−248.4	−248.4
	USC18	0.0	−618.1	−618.1
	USC19	0.0	−67.0	−67.0
	USC20	0.0	−97.8	−97.8
	USC21	0.0	−174.9	−174.9
	USC22	0.0	−397.2	−397.2
	USC23	0.0	−488.4	−488.4
	USC24	0.0	−384.3	−384.3
	USC25	0.0	−826.6	−826.6
	USC26	0.0	−454.2	−454.2

Table 7A.5   (continued)

	Sector code	Direct impact	Indirect impact	Total impact
	USC27	0.0	−53.2	−53.2
	USC28	0.0	−29.4	−29.4
	USC29	0.0	−87.8	−87.8
Non-Commodity (Service) Sectors	USC30	0.0	−389.6	−389.6
	USC31	0.0	−264.2	−264.2
	USC32	0.0	−2,281.6	−2,281.6
	USC33	−45,327.8	−6,268.2	−51,596.0
	USC34	0.0	−850.0	−850.0
	USC35	0.0	−596.0	−596.0
	USC36	0.0	−1,710.7	−1,710.7
	USC37	0.0	−2,902.5	−2,902.5
	USC38	0.0	−2,889.2	−2,889.2
	USC39	0.0	−3,559.8	−3,559.8
	USC40	0.0	−647.2	−647.2
	USC41	0.0	−2,783.8	−2,783.8
	USC42	0.0	−48.9	−48.9
	USC43	0.0	−88.3	−88.3
	USC44	0.0	−103.8	−103.8
	USC45	0.0	−731.2	−731.2
	USC46	0.0	−645.7	−645.7
	USC47	0.0	−2,617.9	−2,617.9
Total		−45,327.8	−38,471.7	−83,799.5

Table 7A.6   *Impacts of a 25 percent increase in telecommunications expenditures ($ millions), 47 USC sectors*

	Sector code	Direct impact	Indirect impact	Total impact
Commodity Sectors	USC01	0.0	19.6	19.6
	USC02	0.0	12.9	12.9
	USC03	0.0	5.0	5.0
	USC04	0.0	12.1	12.1
	USC05	0.0	28.7	28.7
	USC06	0.0	21.0	21.0
	USC07	0.0	0.0	0.0
	USC08	0.0	12.7	12.7
	USC09	0.0	7.7	7.7
	USC10	0.0	213.2	213.2

Table 7A.6 (continued)

	Sector code	Direct impact	Indirect impact	Total impact
	USC11	0.0	40.1	40.1
	USC12	0.0	5.1	5.1
	USC13	0.0	7.6	7.6
	USC14	0.0	132.2	132.2
	USC15	0.0	227.3	227.3
	USC16	0.0	130.7	130.7
	USC17	0.0	282.1	282.1
	USC18	0.0	1,065.7	1,065.7
	USC19	0.0	38.4	38.4
	USC20	0.0	129.6	129.6
	USC21	0.0	150.0	150.0
	USC22	0.0	267.7	267.7
	USC23	0.0	219.8	219.8
	USC24	0.0	2,894.0	2,894.0
	USC25	0.0	111.8	111.8
	USC26	0.0	6.2	6.2
	USC27	0.0	26.6	26.6
	USC28	0.0	36.4	36.4
	USC29	0.0	55.9	55.9
Non-Commodity Sectors	USC30	0.0	261.2	261.2
	USC31	0.0	256.3	256.3
	USC32	0.0	832.9	832.9
	USC33	0.0	427.3	427.3
	USC34	0.0	400.7	400.7
	USC35	0.0	174.8	174.8
	USC36	43,596.7	8,205.4	51,802.0
	USC37	0.0	1,161.2	1,161.2
	USC38	0.0	2,195.2	2,195.2
	USC39	0.0	3,174.6	3,174.6
	USC40	0.0	257.6	257.6
	USC41	0.0	923.0	923.0
	USC42	0.0	51.1	51.1
	USC43	0.0	58.8	58.8
	USC44	0.0	706.1	706.1
	USC45	0.0	231.1	231.1
	USC46	0.0	177.4	177.4
	USC47	0.0	1,089.3	1,089.3
Total		43,596.7	26,744.0	70,340.7

Table 7A.7 State-by-state impacts of air ticket sales losses ($ million, with and without diversion)

State	Without diversion			With diversion		
	Direct impacts	Indirect impacts	Total impacts	Direct impacts	Indirect impacts	Total impacts
AL	-2.5	-235.4	-237.9	-2.3	-210.5	-212.8
AK	-89.6	-114.7	-204.2	-80.5	-101.9	-182.4
AZ	-1,129.9	-683.6	-1,813.5	-1,001.1	-604.5	-1,605.6
AR	-0.9	-182.1	-182.9	-0.8	-161.5	-162.3
CA	-10,795.8	-7,083.3	-17,879.0	-9,119.7	-6,064.2	-15,183.8
CO	-690.1	-551.1	-1,241.2	-574.0	-468.5	-1,042.5
CT	-80.4	-159.1	-239.5	-73.8	-141.8	-215.7
DE	0.0	-46.0	-46.0	0.0	-40.7	-40.7
DC	-4,336.7	-1,935.6	-6,272.3	-4,001.5	-1,779.3	-5,780.8
FL	-9,761.0	-5,759.9	-15,520.9	-9,258.1	-5,456.7	-14,714.8
GA	-1,918.5	-1,501.3	-3,419.8	-1,402.1	-1,187.7	-2,589.8
HI	-3,542.3	-1,969.3	-5,511.6	-3,242.3	-1,794.4	-5,036.7
ID	-0.3	-75.1	-75.4	-0.2	-65.9	-66.0
IL	-3,267.0	-2,420.6	-5,687.5	-2,847.9	-2,132.6	-4,980.5
IN	-57.6	-302.9	-360.5	-53.2	-268.5	-321.6
IA	-1.1	-259.5	-260.6	-0.8	-227.0	-227.8
KS	-1.1	-169.2	-170.3	-1.0	-148.8	-149.8
KY	-919.9	-722.6	-1,642.5	-840.9	-654.1	-1,495.0
LA	-63.2	-376.2	-439.4	-58.5	-335.1	-393.6
ME	-10.7	-70.9	-81.6	-9.9	-62.2	-72.1
MD	-456.5	-448.4	-904.9	-415.3	-407.1	-822.3
MA	-1,885.2	-1,158.7	-3,043.9	-1,633.8	-1,008.1	-2,641.9
MI	-979.8	-948.9	-1,928.7	-710.8	-754.9	-1,465.7
MN	-483.4	-630.6	-1,114.0	-298.1	-485.3	-783.4
MS	-1.2	-126.4	-127.6	-1.2	-110.9	-112.0
MO	-286.1	-375.8	-662.0	-262.9	-337.4	-600.3

MT	-0.1	-45.8	-45.9	-0.1	-40.2	-40.3
NE	-4.2	-220.1	-224.3	-4.0	-195.6	-199.6
NV	-1,435.4	-715.2	-2,150.6	-1,316.7	-652.7	-1,969.4
NH	-16.9	-44.5	-61.4	-15.5	-39.4	-54.9
NJ	-2,753.1	-1,856.2	-4,609.4	-2,334.1	-1,603.0	-3,937.1
NM	-0.5	-59.2	-59.7	-0.5	-52.2	-52.7
NY	-12,220.6	-6,447.9	-18,668.5	-10,460.7	-5,523.8	-15,984.5
NC	-710.2	-764.2	-1,474.4	-558.9	-643.8	-1,202.7
ND	-0.5	-62.9	-63.4	-0.2	-55.1	-55.3
OH	-296.0	-669.6	-965.6	-271.6	-594.3	-865.8
OK	-2.2	-192.3	-194.5	-1.6	-168.0	-169.6
OR	-343.2	-332.9	-676.1	-306.5	-294.7	-601.2
PA	-1,482.6	-1,431.8	-2,914.4	-1,231.2	-1,223.1	-2,454.3
RI	-30.2	-51.8	-82.0	-27.7	-46.6	-74.4
SC	-16.7	-150.3	-167.0	-15.3	-132.6	-147.9
SD	-1.2	-54.8	-56.0	-1.1	-48.0	-49.1
TN	-365.9	-421.7	-787.6	-336.2	-379.2	-715.4
TX	-3,038.0	-3,519.1	-6,557.1	-2,535.2	-3,062.9	-5,598.1
UT	-300.9	-255.9	-556.8	-273.5	-230.7	-504.2
VM	0.0	-32.5	-32.5	0.0	-28.6	-28.6
VA	-9.6	-217.5	-227.1	-8.8	-193.6	-202.5
WA	-866.2	-747.0	-1,613.3	-698.6	-624.3	-1,322.9
WV	-0.1	-72.9	-73.0	0.0	-63.2	-63.3
WI	-162.2	-493.9	-656.1	-148.4	-436.1	-584.5
WY	0.0	-54.6	-54.6	0.0	-49.4	-49.4
US subtotal	-64,817.3	-47,221.7	-112,039.0	-56,436.8	-41,390.7	-97,827.4
Foreign	0.0	-2,420.5	-2,420.5	0.0	-2,142.5	-2,142.5
Total	-64,817.3	-49,642.2	-114,459.5	-56,436.8	-43,533.2	-99,970.0

Table 7A.8 Impacts due to international trade losses ($ billion, with and without substitutions)

State	No substitution effects										Substitution effects		
	Imports (A)			Imports, except energy sector (USC 10) (B)			Exports (C)			Total (B) + (C)			
	Direct impacts	Indirect impacts	Total impacts	Direct impacts	Indirect impacts	Total impacts	Direct impacts	Indirect impacts	Total impacts	Total impacts	Direct impacts	Indirect impacts	Total impacts
AL	-19.4	-7.8	-27.2	-18.2	-6.5	-24.7	-10.8	-13.2	-24.0	-48.7	-22.4	-14.1	-36.5
AK	-3.2	-1.4	-4.7	-2.9	-1.3	-4.2	-0.7	-1.2	-1.9	-6.1	-2.6	-1.8	-4.4
AZ	-18.5	-8.7	-27.1	-17.5	-7.3	-24.7	-13.3	-8.6	-21.9	-46.6	-22.4	-11.4	-33.8
AR	-11.0	-4.7	-15.7	-10.4	-3.9	-14.3	-7.2	-8.9	-16.1	-30.4	-17.2	-11.0	-28.2
CA	-151.2	-57.3	-208.5	-130.6	-43.8	-174.5	-107.9	-83.9	-191.8	-366.2	-144.4	-76.2	-220.7
CO	-20.6	-9.9	-30.5	-19.6	-8.9	-28.5	-9.7	-8.9	-18.7	-47.2	-21.7	-13.0	-34.7
CT	-18.4	-7.7	-26.0	-17.4	-6.2	-23.6	-15.2	-11.4	-26.6	-50.2	-25.2	-13.2	-38.3
DE	-5.0	-2.2	-7.2	-4.2	-1.7	-6.0	-2.0	-2.2	-4.2	-10.2	-4.2	-2.8	-6.9
DC	-4.5	-2.2	-6.7	-4.0	-1.5	-5.5	-0.3	-0.3	-0.7	-6.1	-2.9	-1.3	-4.2
FL	-57.6	-29.0	-86.7	-55.0	-25.7	-80.7	-18.1	-15.9	-34.0	-114.7	-41.2	-25.3	-66.5
GA	-36.7	-16.6	-53.3	-34.3	-13.9	-48.2	-17.5	-18.0	-35.5	-83.7	-36.6	-21.3	-57.9
HI	-4.4	-2.6	-6.9	-3.5	-1.9	-5.4	-0.7	-0.8	-1.5	-7.0	-3.7	-2.2	-6.0
ID	-5.4	-2.4	-7.8	-5.2	-1.9	-7.1	-3.7	-3.0	-6.7	-13.8	-6.9	-3.7	-10.6
IL	-59.6	-28.2	-87.8	-53.4	-21.5	-74.9	-34.7	-36.8	-71.5	-146.4	-54.7	-35.8	-90.5
IN	-32.4	-13.5	-45.9	-29.9	-10.5	-40.4	-23.9	-28.4	-52.3	-92.6	-41.2	-26.7	-67.9
IA	-14.3	-6.5	-20.8	-13.3	-5.4	-18.7	-10.6	-11.5	-22.1	-40.8	-23.8	-14.9	-38.6
KS	-16.5	-7.7	-24.2	-15.5	-6.7	-22.3	-12.0	-11.9	-23.8	-46.1	-25.8	-16.3	-42.2
KY	-23.5	-8.7	-32.2	-22.3	-7.8	-30.2	-13.1	-15.4	-28.5	-58.7	-28.3	-15.6	-43.9
LA	-22.8	-10.3	-33.0	-15.4	-6.9	-22.3	-9.6	-13.8	-23.4	-45.7	-16.1	-13.1	-29.2
ME	-5.1	-2.3	-7.4	-4.8	-2.0	-6.9	-2.9	-3.0	-5.9	-12.8	-5.7	-3.5	-9.2
MD	-22.7	-10.7	-33.3	-21.5	-9.1	-30.6	-6.9	-6.6	-13.5	-44.1	-22.6	-11.5	-34.1
MA	-34.4	-14.0	-48.4	-32.6	-11.9	-44.5	-23.2	-17.4	-40.6	-85.1	-37.6	-19.5	-57.1

MI	-65.2	-25.6	-90.8	-62.9	-22.7	-85.6	-35.8	-37.7	-73.5	-159.1	-44.6	-29.4	-74.0
MN	-28.3	-12.5	-40.7	-26.0	-9.8	-35.7	-15.2	-15.9	-31.1	-66.8	-31.5	-18.9	-50.4
MS	-11.7	-4.9	-16.5	-10.2	-3.7	-13.9	-5.9	-7.4	-13.3	-27.2	-13.4	-8.5	-21.9
MO	-28.8	-12.8	-41.6	-27.1	-10.8	-37.8	-14.0	-14.7	-28.8	-66.6	-34.4	-18.8	-53.3
MT	-4.0	-2.2	-6.3	-3.1	-1.6	-4.7	-1.1	-1.9	-3.0	-7.7	-2.6	-2.2	-4.8
NE	-8.2	-4.6	-12.7	-7.3	-3.5	-10.8	-5.3	-6.1	-11.4	-22.2	-11.8	-8.3	-20.1
NV	-7.5	-4.2	-11.7	-7.1	-3.5	-10.6	-1.7	-1.6	-3.2	-13.8	-7.6	-4.2	-11.8
NH	-6.3	-2.5	-8.7	-6.0	-2.1	-8.1	-4.4	-3.9	-8.3	-16.4	-10.4	-5.2	-15.5
NJ	-38.0	-18.8	-56.7	-33.9	-14.1	-48.0	-19.7	-18.9	-38.5	-86.5	-35.9	-19.6	-55.5
NM	-8.1	-3.1	-11.3	-7.7	-2.8	-10.5	-2.7	-2.4	-5.2	-15.7	-8.4	-4.0	-12.4
NY	-75.5	-34.6	-110.1	-71.3	-29.0	-100.2	-34.9	-29.8	-64.7	-164.9	-51.4	-31.7	-83.0
NC	-35.6	-15.0	-50.5	-33.8	-12.5	-46.3	-26.2	-23.8	-50.0	-96.4	-47.3	-26.9	-74.2
ND	-3.6	-1.7	-5.3	-3.2	-1.3	-4.5	-2.2	-2.3	-4.5	-8.9	-3.6	-2.6	-6.2
OH	-63.4	-24.1	-87.5	-60.5	-20.6	-81.2	-39.3	-44.0	-83.4	-164.6	-52.3	-36.2	-88.5
OK	-15.7	-6.7	-22.4	-13.8	-5.8	-19.6	-7.7	-9.8	-17.6	-37.1	-21.1	-13.3	-34.4
OR	-15.9	-6.3	-22.2	-15.0	-5.0	-20.0	-12.4	-9.3	-21.7	-41.6	-19.3	-9.7	-29.0
PA	-53.6	-23.8	-77.4	-48.9	-19.1	-67.9	-32.1	-33.6	-65.7	-133.6	-50.1	-31.9	-81.9
RI	-4.8	-1.8	-6.7	-4.5	-1.5	-5.9	-3.1	-2.7	-5.9	-11.8	-7.5	-3.6	-11.2
SC	-16.9	-6.7	-23.6	-16.0	-5.5	-21.5	-11.6	-12.2	-23.8	-45.3	-18.4	-11.0	-29.4
SD	-3.5	-1.8	-5.2	-3.3	-1.5	-4.7	-2.1	-2.3	-4.4	-9.1	-4.3	-3.0	-7.3
TN	-29.3	-11.9	-41.2	-27.9	-10.2	-38.1	-16.3	-17.7	-34.0	-72.0	-32.7	-19.2	-52.0
TX	-96.1	-42.8	-139.0	-82.1	-35.3	-117.4	-59.8	-63.7	-123.5	-241.0	-87.3	-61.4	-148.7
UT	-8.7	-4.2	-12.9	-7.7	-3.3	-11.0	-5.0	-5.2	-10.2	-21.2	-10.8	-6.8	-17.5
VM	-2.8	-1.1	-3.9	-2.6	-0.9	-3.6	-2.5	-1.6	-4.2	-7.7	-3.0	-1.6	-4.6
VA	-34.2	-14.4	-48.6	-32.8	-12.6	-45.4	-13.1	-12.6	-25.7	-71.1	-32.8	-17.4	-50.3
WA	-33.1	-15.0	-48.1	-30.2	-11.3	-41.4	-23.9	-19.8	-43.7	-85.2	-39.3	-22.2	-61.6
WV	-6.7	-2.8	-9.5	-6.2	-2.4	-8.6	-4.7	-6.6	-11.3	-19.9	-10.9	-7.6	-18.4
WI	-30.6	-12.0	-42.6	-29.0	-10.1	-39.1	-18.9	-21.6	-40.5	-79.6	-38.9	-22.6	-61.6
WY	-2.4	-1.2	-3.6	-1.9	-1.0	-3.0	-0.8	-1.5	-2.2	-5.2	-2.7	-2.2	-4.8
US subtotal	-1,325.2	-573.5	-1,898.8	-1,213.3	-469.8	-1,683.2	-766.3	-751.9	-1,518.2	-3,201.4	-1,341.4	-804.0	-2,145.3
Foreign	0.0	-41.9	-41.9	0.0	-38.5	-38.5	0.0	-83.8	-83.8	-122.3	0.0	-77.7	-77.7
Total	-1,325.2	-615.5	-1,940.7	-1,213.3	-508.3	-1,721.7	-766.3	-835.8	-1,602.1	-3,323.7	-1,341.4	-881.7	-2,223.0

Table 7A.9 Impacts due to elimination of legal migration ($ million)

Classification	USC sector	Leontief price model				Demand-side USIO		
		Job losses (1000)	Increased wage	Increased price	Total industry output	Direct impact	Indirect impact	Total impact
Commodity Sectors	USC01	-17.506	0.0036%	0.0184%	173,097	-31.928	-53.292	-85.220
	USC02	-15.599	0.0032%	0.0135%	118,853	-16.100	-30.619	-46.720
	USC03	-4.087	0.0008%	0.0161%	44,785	-7.193	-15.563	-22.757
	USC04	-8.019	0.0017%	0.0137%	84,932	-11.594	-20.559	-32.153
	USC05	-17.407	0.0036%	0.0173%	286,070	-49.480	-71.343	-120.823
	USC06	-1.710	0.0004%	0.0109%	61,546	-6.715	-15.704	-22.420
	USC07	-0.773	0.0002%	0.0076%	52,637	-4.009	-0.186	-4.195
	USC08	-3.251	0.0007%	0.0077%	19,049	-1.459	-12.258	-13.718
	USC09	-0.968	0.0002%	0.0079%	9,129	-0.718	-3.894	-4.612
	USC10	-12.860	0.0027%	0.0135%	371,603	-50.313	-145.066	-195.379
	USC11	-3.033	0.0006%	0.0115%	76,034	-8.740	-25.064	-33.804
	USC12	-6.282	0.0013%	0.0098%	134,457	-13.218	-16.569	-29.787
	USC13	-0.831	0.0002%	0.0103%	16,209	-1.665	-5.881	-7.546

USC14	−6.736	0.0014%	0.0115%	142,133	−16.389	−42.933	−59.322
USC15	−19.663	0.0041%	0.0149%	203,666	−30.293	−90.718	−121.011
USC16	−12.398	0.0026%	0.0133%	101,676	−13.477	−73.066	−86.542
USC17	−10.040	0.0021%	0.0133%	142,353	−18.924	−61.830	−80.754
USC18	−22.982	0.0048%	0.0132%	203,883	−26.905	−87.329	−114.233
USC19	−23.036	0.0048%	0.0163%	172,998	−28.277	−29.044	−57.322
USC20	−10.892	0.0023%	0.0117%	97,801	−11.422	−67.565	−78.987
USC21	−8.249	0.0017%	0.0129%	121,498	−15.660	−50.146	−65.806
USC22	−24.032	0.0050%	0.0143%	184,519	−26.448	−88.621	−115.069
USC23	−32.231	0.0067%	0.0169%	331,350	−55.988	−65.114	−121.102
USC24	−42.166	0.0087%	0.0169%	601,195	−101.766	−96.724	−198.490
USC25	−24.500	0.0051%	0.0185%	447,184	−82.700	−65.058	−147.758
USC26	−9.550	0.0020%	0.0124%	118,010	−14.683	−4.403	−19.087
USC27	−11.311	0.0023%	0.0114%	114,130	−12.995	−13.696	−26.691
USC28	−13.267	0.0027%	0.0129%	73,637	−9.536	−16.183	−25.719
USC29	−13.410	0.0028%	0.0111%	282,474	−31.340	−23.446	−54.786
Non Commodity Sectors							
USC30	−10.323	0.0021%	0.0103%	296,699	−30.432	−75.830	−106.263
USC31	−386.254	0.0800%	0.0939%	1,013,114	−951.797	−43.806	−995.603
USC32	−90.127	0.0187%	0.0266%	875,258	−233.021	−260.171	−493.192
USC33	−50.485	0.0105%	0.0238%	502,771	−119.428	−141.814	−261.243
USC34	−23.662	0.0049%	0.0122%	162,269	−19.786	−85.979	−105.765
USC35	−238.062	0.0493%	0.0583%	942,803	−549.591	−129.268	−678.859
USC36	−28.886	0.0060%	0.0137%	586,269	−80.457	−185.599	−266.056
USC37	−68.963	0.0143%	0.0244%	1,287,273	−313.909	−338.570	−652.479

Table 7A.9   (continued)

Classification	Leontief price model			Total industry output	Demand-side USIO		
USC sector	Job losses (1000)	Increased wage	Increased price		Direct impact	Indirect impact	Total impact
USC38	−35.227	0.0073%	0.0146%	1,681,503	−246.257	−383.897	−630.153
USC39	−104.510	0.0216%	0.0276%	1,008,257	−278.631	−371.406	−650.037
USC40	−26.512	0.0055%	0.0114%	210,209	−23.881	−104.940	−128.821
USC41	−191.282	0.0396%	0.0478%	443,881	−212.121	−228.778	−440.899
USC42	−162.262	0.0336%	0.0485%	85,680	−41.535	−4.248	−45.782
USC43	−376.519	0.0780%	0.0896%	1,188,873	−1065.819	−24.860	−1090.679
USC44	−50.143	0.0104%	0.0201%	154,279	−30.940	−20.977	−51.917
USC45	−354.587	0.0734%	0.0837%	498,852	−417.576	−58.896	−476.472
USC46	−218.761	0.0453%	0.0471%	1,288,980	−607.182	−40.334	−647.516
USC47	−93.648	0.0194%	0.0302%	755,883	−228.573	−179.859	−408.432
Total	−2,887.000	0.5979%	1.0636%	17,769,757	−6,150.873	−3,971.107	−10,121.98

Note: We distributed the employment values to the USC sectors based on occupation-industry data sets available at the Bureau of Labor Survey web page, and a conversion bridge developed by the authors that maps 2-digit North American Industry Classification System (NAICS) sectors to USC sectors. The lower range labor supply elasticity estimate is −0.3 (Borjas, 2003). Total industry output values are available from the 2001 version of IMPLAN® (Minnesota IMPLAN Group, 2003); the authors aggregated the 509 IMPLAN sectors to the 47 USC sectors according to the process described in Park et al. (2007).

Source: Legal employment data are obtained from recent year of entry (2000 to 2004) in *US Census Bureau, Current Population Survey, Annual Social and Economics Supplement*, 2004, Table 2.8. Total employment (144,850 million) from the US Department of Labor (2006).

Table 7A.10 Impacts due to elimination of illegal migration ($ million, median estimate)

Classification	USC sector	Leontief price model			Total industry output	Demand-side USIO		
		Job losses (1000)	Increased wage	Increased price		Direct impact	Indirect impact	Total impact
Commodity Sectors	USC01	−24.477	0.0051%	0.0101%	173,097	−17.466	−10.141	−27.607
	USC02	−44.443	0.0092%	0.0112%	118,853	−13.284	−6.954	−20.239
	USC03	−9.338	0.0019%	0.0065%	44,785	−2.922	−4.512	−7.434
	USC04	0.000	0.0000%	0.0028%	84,932	−2.395	−1.547	−3.942
	USC05	−13.198	0.0027%	0.0064%	286,070	−18.267	−11.098	−29.365
	USC06	−0.727	0.0002%	0.0016%	61,546	−0.996	−2.270	−3.266
	USC07	−1.061	0.0002%	0.0011%	52,637	−0.591	−0.050	−0.640
	USC08	−1.029	0.0002%	0.0012%	19,049	−0.222	−4.747	−4.970
	USC09	−0.309	0.0001%	0.0010%	9,129	−0.095	−1.029	−1.124
	USC10	−4.307	0.0009%	0.0025%	371,603	−9.133	−33.883	−43.016
	USC11	−1.264	0.0003%	0.0017%	76,034	−1.278	−4.656	−5.933
	USC12	−2.635	0.0005%	0.0015%	134,457	−1.986	−0.845	−2.831
	USC13	−0.347	0.0001%	0.0012%	16,209	−0.196	−1.536	−1.732
	USC14	−2.809	0.0006%	0.0019%	142,133	−2.742	−11.310	−14.052
	USC15	−8.207	0.0017%	0.0032%	203,666	−6.563	−22.194	−28.757
	USC16	−10.137	0.0021%	0.0041%	101,676	−4.154	−28.239	−32.393
	USC17	−4.185	0.0009%	0.0025%	142,353	−3.516	−13.289	−16.804
	USC18	−11.972	0.0025%	0.0036%	203,883	−7.295	−17.423	−24.718
	USC19	−12.314	0.0026%	0.0044%	172,998	−7.559	−6.791	−14.350

Table 7A.10 (continued)

Classification	USC sector	Leontief price model			Total industry output	Demand-side USIO		
		Job losses (1000)	Increased wage	Increased price		Direct impact	Indirect impact	Total impact
	USC20	-4.546	0.0009%	0.0022%	97,801	-2.133	-26.967	-29.101
	USC21	-3.569	0.0007%	0.0020%	121,498	-2.489	-15.412	-17.901
	USC22	-10.399	0.0022%	0.0034%	184,519	-6.305	-31.243	-37.548
	USC23	-13.924	0.0029%	0.0044%	331,350	-14.579	-21.311	-35.890
	USC24	-20.422	0.0042%	0.0055%	601,195	-33.342	-26.007	-59.349
	USC26	-4.132	0.0009%	0.0025%	118,010	-2.922	-0.791	-3.712
	USC27	-4.894	0.0010%	0.0022%	114,130	-2.528	-2.327	-4.856
	USC28	-5.741	0.0012%	0.0027%	73,637	-2.022	-6.303	-8.325
	USC29	-8.413	0.0017%	0.0030%	282,474	-8.334	-5.380	-13.714
Non-Commodity Sectors	USC30	0.000	0.0000%	0.0014%	296,699	-4.226	-16.460	-20.686
	USC31	-207.570	0.0430%	0.0466%	1,013,114	-472.204	-7.098	-479.302
	USC32	0.000	0.0000%	0.0008%	875,258	-7.427	-62.525	-69.952
	USC33	0.000	0.0000%	0.0013%	502,771	-6.570	-32.776	-39.347
	USC34	0.000	0.0000%	0.0008%	162,269	-1.315	-17.880	-19.195
	USC35	-145.299	0.0301%	0.0313%	942,803	-295.085	-47.783	-342.868
	USC36	-0.397	0.0001%	0.0011%	586,269	-6.207	-38.087	-44.294
	USC37	-1.272	0.0003%	0.0008%	1,287,273	-10.640	-53.140	-63.780
	USC38	-0.930	0.0002%	0.0015%	1,681,503	-24.536	-71.522	-96.058
	USC39	-1.786	0.0004%	0.0009%	1,008,257	-8.747	-85.541	-94.288
	USC40	-0.282	0.0001%	0.0009%	210,209	-1.977	-28.798	-30.775

USC41	−1.547	0.0003%	0.0013%	443,881	−5.781	−38.806	−44.586
USC42	−0.325	0.0001%	0.0020%	85,680	−1.673	−0.638	−2.311
USC43	−2.556	0.0005%	0.0017%	1,188,873	−20.218	−2.653	−22.871
USC44	−0.529	0.0001%	0.0012%	154,279	−1.814	−3.391	−5.204
USC45	−1.861	0.0004%	0.0025%	498,852	−12.556	−9.015	−21.572
USC46	−3.695	0.0008%	0.0012%	1,288,980	−15.420	−7.491	−22.911
USC47	−20.937	0.0043%	0.0062%	755,883	−47.074	−42.712	−89.786
Total	−628.371	0.1301%	0.2044%	17,769,757	−1,138.696	−900.216	−2,038.91

Note: The lower range labor supply elasticity estimate is −0.3 (Borjas, 2003). Job proportions of unauthorized migrants in USC sectors estimated by combining employment shares from version 2001 of IMPLAN® Data Files (Minnesota IMPLAN Group, 2003) with tabular data available at the Wikipedia entry on the illegal immigrant population of the United States, http://en.wikipedia.org/wiki/Illegal_immigrant_population_of_the_United_States; summary calculations are available from the authors. Total industry output values are available from the 2001 version of IMPLAN® Data Files (Minnesota IMPLAN Group, 2003). The authors aggregated the 509 IMPLAN sectors to the 47 USC sectors according to the process described in Park et al. (2007).

Source: Total employment (144,850 million) from the US Department of Labor (2006).

Table 7A.11   State-by-state impacts of cross-border shopping losses
($ million)

State	Direct impacts	Indirect impacts	Total impacts
AL	0.0	−7.4	−7.4
AK	−9.2	−6.0	−15.2
AZ	−655.1	−330.9	−986.0
AR	0.0	−6.3	−6.3
CA	−1,685.7	−847.5	−2,533.2
CO	0.0	−5.4	−5.4
CT	0.0	−3.3	−3.3
DE	0.0	−0.8	−0.8
DC	0.0	−0.3	−0.3
FL	0.0	−7.3	−7.3
GA	0.0	−7.2	−7.2
HI	0.0	−0.8	−0.8
ID	−7.7	−5.6	−13.3
IL	0.0	−16.8	−16.8
IN	0.0	−10.8	−10.8
IA	0.0	−4.5	−4.5
KS	0.0	−3.9	−3.9
KY	0.0	−6.6	−6.6
LA	0.0	−16.7	−16.7
ME	−139.6	−80.4	−220.0
MD	0.0	−2.3	−2.3
MA	0.0	−7.2	−7.2
MI	−351.7	−195.8	−547.4
MN	−57.7	−38.4	−96.0
MS	0.0	−4.8	−4.8
MO	0.0	−7.1	−7.1
MT	−30.2	−19.9	−50.1
NE	0.0	−1.7	−1.7
NV	0.0	−1.9	−1.9
NH	0.0	−2.7	−2.7
NJ	0.0	−9.2	−9.2
NM	−42.7	−27.1	−69.8
NY	−456.1	−230.8	−686.9
NC	0.0	−7.5	−7.5
ND	−33.1	−20.7	−53.8
OH	0.0	−19.5	−19.5
OK	0.0	−13.5	−13.5
OR	0.0	−7.9	−7.9
PA	0.0	−14.3	−14.3
RI	0.0	−0.9	−0.9
SC	0.0	−4.9	−4.9

Table 7A.11   (continued)

State	Direct impacts	Indirect impacts	Total impacts
SD	0.0	−0.8	−0.8
TN	0.0	−7.4	−7.4
TX	−2,315.7	−1,237.5	−3,553.2
UT	0.0	−3.5	−3.5
VM	−45.3	−25.7	−71.1
VA	0.0	−4.8	−4.8
WA	−213.4	−119.4	−332.8
WV	0.0	−2.9	−2.9
WI	0.0	−13.1	−13.1
WY	0.0	−1.1	−1.1
US subtotal	−6,043.3	−3,422.8	−9,466.0
Foreign	0.0	−475.2	−475.2
Total	−6,043.3	−3,898.0	−9,941.2

Note: We assume expenditures of $100 in the retail trades (USC Sector 35) per arriving cross-border shopper. We assume 40 percent of arrivals crossing the border are US residents; these substitute domestic purchases for shopping abroad.

Source: Number of cross-border shoppers not arriving by air obtained from http://www.transtats.bts.gov/Fields.asp?Table_ID=1358. Data extracted from Table 3.2, 'Same-day travel between the United States and Canada and the United States and Mexico by transportation mode: 2000–2004 (thousands of visits)' (Research and Innovation Technology Administration and Bureau of Transportation Statistics, 2006).

8.   A foot-and-mouth epidemic

Bumsoo Lee, Peter Gordon, Harry W. Richardson, JiYoung Park, James E. Moore II and Qisheng Pan

8.1   INTRODUCTION

Agroterrorism presents an obvious and major terrorist threat to the USA and the world, with the potential for severe economic consequences and significant human health risks. Chalk (2001, p. 2) defines agroterrorism as 'the deliberate introduction of a disease agent, either against livestock or into the food chain, for purposes of undermining stability and/or generating fear.' An agroterrorism attack can be implemented at relatively low cost by an attacker. Terrorists can readily contaminate livestock, crops or any targets in the food supply chain, including farms, processing plants and distribution systems. Security levels have been significantly heightened for potential urban targets of terrorism and infrastructure since the attacks of 9/11. However, it remains almost impossible to identify and protect all potential targets of agroterrorism.

The agricultural sector is particularly vulnerable because biological attacks on agriculture require relatively little scientific expertise and technology, while a full-scale bioterrorist attack on human populations is more technically challenging (Wheelis et al., 2002). Many types of pathogens that can cause crop and animal disease are highly contagious and can be easily weaponized. Pathogens causing listed diseases classified by the Office International des Epizooties (OIE) are the greatest threats because they are highly transmittable and may potentially have serious socioeconomic and/or public health consequences, including international trade losses. The long list includes foot-and-mouth disease (FMD), avian influenza (AI) and exotic Newcastle disease (END).

Agriculture is a relatively vulnerable economic sector that can be easily disrupted by a bioterrorist attack, in part because of vertical integration in production (Cupp et al., 2004), although the poultry sector is much more integrated than the animal sector. During the natural outbreak of FMD in the UK in 2001, about 6.9 million animals had to be slaughtered, either for disease control or to mitigate losses to farmers because of an animal movement ban (Thompson et al., 2002). The economic losses to agriculture and the food chain were estimated to be about £3.1 billion, with tourism suffering losses of a similar amount (Thompson et al., 2002). Beyond these economic losses, there was also considerable institutional disruption. National elections had to be postponed and the Ministry of Agriculture, Fisheries and Food was replaced by the Department for Environment, Food and Rural Affairs after the FMD outbreak (Manning et al., 2005).

The costs of disruption in agricultural and related sectors are amplified where export markets are large. Non-FMD-endemic countries will normally prevent transmission of the virus by not permitting importation of livestock or animal products from countries subject to FMD, vaccinating herds after an outbreak is known to have occurred (strict protocols may govern vaccination practices; see OIE (2006, Chapter 2.1.1, Section D)) and interrupting transmission by destroying the host (Blackwell, 1980). It is likely that foreign importers would totally shut down the imports of related agricultural products when a highly contagious disease is identified. This is why impacts on export markets are much deeper and prolonged than the impacts on domestic demand. For instance, the discovery of bovine spongiform encephalopathy (BSE, also known as Mad Cow Disease) in a Canadian-born dairy cow in the state of Washington caused major beef importing countries to immediately impose a ban on US beef products, resulting in a 90 percent drop in exports (Park et al., 2006). Restrictions on access to international markets affect agriculture throughout the national economy, beyond the region where the outbreak occurred.

This chapter presents estimates of state-by-state economic impacts of a hypothetical bioterrorist attack using FMD pathogens. FMD is one of the highest priority animal diseases because it can be easily disseminated and has the potential for catastrophic economic disruption. FMD is a highly contagious viral disease that affects cloven-hoofed animals such as cattle, swine, sheep, goats and deer. It can be transmitted not only by direct contact but also via air and even inanimate objects such as animal byproducts, water and straw (Federal Inter-Agency Working Group, 2003, p. 3). Terrorists can easily disseminate the FMD virus by introducing a single piece of contaminated meat or sausage to a farm or feedlot (State of Minnesota, 2002).

The economic costs inflicted by intentional dissemination of FMD pathogens could be very high. Ekboir (1999) estimated the cost of an FMD epidemic in California to be $4.5 to $13.5 billion. We estimate the economic impacts across the US states by applying our National Interstate Economic Model (NIEMO), a Multiregional Input-Output

(MRIO) model. The next section includes a discussion of the analytical framework and NIEMO, followed by a description of a hypothetical FMD attack. Following this, we provide estimates of direct operational costs and predictions of potential demand changes in both domestic and export red meat markets, which we use as input data to estimate total economic impacts via NIEMO.

8.2   ANALYTICAL FRAMEWORK FOR ECONOMIC IMPACT ANALYSIS AND NIEMO

We conduct the economic impact analysis of a hypothetical FMD attack in four steps. First, we adopt a plausible scenario for a hypothetical FMD outbreak. This scenario includes the location of the attack, simulation of the epidemic and the emergency response. These determine the magnitude of direct damages.

Second, based on this scenario, direct operational costs are estimated. These include:

- the costs of killing and disposing of animals
- compensation payments to owners of slaughtered animals
- cleaning and disinfection costs
- the costs of quarantine enforcement.

While most previous studies stop at estimating these operational costs, we attempt to estimate the possible dual impacts of the resources directed at these hazard mitigation activities. On the one hand, these operational costs draw resources away from the US economy that could have been placed in other productive uses. Assuming that most of the expenditures on hazard mitigation services come from the federal government, we model the associated negative impact as reduced purchasing power by households (taxpayers). The resources employed in the hazard mitigation activities might have a stimulus effect on the corresponding economic sectors. Consequently, we estimate the net effects throughout the economy within the MRIO framework.

The third step looks at the disruption to domestic and export demands of US red meat-related products. Because there have been no domestic FMD incidents since 1929, we draw on other historical outbreaks of animal diseases to suggest plausible consumer behavior responses. We considered the aftermaths of the 2001 FMD outbreak in the UK and the 2003 BSE case in the USA.

Finally, we use NIEMO to estimate total economic impacts including indirect impacts. We have recently developed and applied NIEMO to esti-mate the impacts of various natural and man-made disasters. While many types of economic approaches, including benefit-cost analysis, single-region input-output (IO) modeling, social accounting models, partial equilibrium models and computable general equilibrium (CGE) models, are available for estimating economic impacts of animal diseases (Rich et al., 2005a; Rich et al., 2005b), none of these tools provides the national economic impacts at the level of individual states. We have chosen to use a MRIO model to highlight the fact that an FMD outbreak confined to a single state would have nationwide economic impacts, differentially dis-tributed across state borders.

Our economic impact study is based on a hypothetical FMD out-break scenario in which a terrorist group spreads the FMD virus into California's South San Joaquin Valley, which consists of key agricultural counties of Fresno, Kings, Tulare and Kern. Rather than conducting our own epidemic simulations, we have chosen to depend on the results of the FMD study by Ekboir (1999). We use his epidemiological scenario and estimates of direct operating costs, but we focus on estimating total eco-nomic impacts by state. We should point out that a simultaneous attack on several states is both feasible and likely, so that the impacts that we measure here could easily be magnified.

We use the results of Ekboir's Scenario 1 simulation in which he assumed:

● high dissemination rates
● no depopulation of latent infections
● 90 percent of infectious herds eliminated each week.

In this scenario, all herds in the South Valley are infected in four weeks and are destroyed by the end of the sixth week, although the FMD disease is successfully contained within the quarantine area. This scenario presents the most serious but probable outcome among his seven sug-gested simulations.

Even in the event that some proportion of the animals in the region are not infected, the animals could be slaughtered as a precaution in exchange for government compensation. Vaccination is normally only undertaken as a prophylactic step in countries where an outbreak has yet to occur (Bates et al., 2003); and sometimes as part of a coordinated, long-term eradication strategy (Leforban, 1999). In the aftermath of the 2001 FMD outbreak in the UK, about 2.6 million animals were slaughtered to minimize the economic losses of farmers because of movement restrictions on their live-stock, while about 4 million were killed for so-called 'humane slaughter,' a euphemism (Thompson et al., 2002). However, in our analysis the number of slaughtered animals is not the most critical factor in economic loss estimations because the major costs of an FMD outbreak are from reduced domestic and international demands for US meat products. These reductions are almost independent of the number of slaughtered animals.

Ekboir (1999) also provides an estimate of direct operating costs across three categories:

- compensation payments to producers for slaughtered animals
- cleaning and disinfection costs
- the costs of quarantine enforcement.

We use his estimates as direct impacts after adjusting to 2001 dollars (2001 was chosen because this is the year of our IO data using the consumer price index for all urban consumers (CPI-U). We use the urban consumer price index rather than a farm costs index because many of the indirect and induced impacts are related to urban consumption spending. In the current US FMD emergency response plan, farmers expect to be paid a fair market value for all slaughtered animals (Mathews and Janet, 2003). Table 8.1 shows compensation cost estimates by farm types. Table 8.2 contains cleaning and disinfection costs, including the costs of disinfect-

Table 8.1   Compensation payments for slaughtered animals

	Number of herds destroyed	Animals per herd	Number of animals killed	Compensation per herd ($ thousand)		Compensation costs ($ thousand)
				Destroyed feed	Destroyed animals	
Large dairies	175	2,000	350,000	619.6	2,648.2	571,872
Small dairies	441	500	220,500	151.1	662.1	358,618
Feedlots	15	15,000	225,000	1,002.7	14,896.3	238,484
Large pig operations	23	500	11,500	27.6	60.7	2,030
Backyard operations	1,001	1	1,001	–	0.1	121
Total			808,001			1,171,125

Note: All dollar values are adjusted to 2001 dollars using the consumer price index for all urban consumers (CPI-U). There are no significant cow-and-calf operations in California. Our research results include the costs of killing and disposing of animals. Ekboir (1999) does not estimate these costs.

Source: Ekboir (1999).

Table 8.2   Costs of cleaning and disinfection

	Number of herds	Cost per herd ($ thousand)	Cleaning and disinfection costs ($ thousand)
Large dairies	175	150.9	26,405
Small dairies	441	90.8	40,022
Feedlots	15	148.7	2,231
Large pig operations	23	102.5	2,358
Backyard operations	1,001	35.6	35,676
Processing plants	27	449.5	12,138
Total			118,830

Note: All dollar values are adjusted to 2001 dollars using the consumer price index for all urban consumers (CPI-U).

Source: Ekboir (1999).

ants and pesticides, and wages for the cleaning and disinfection crews. In addition, the cost of quarantine enforcement to maintain 300 checkpoints through 120 quarantine days after slaughtering the last exposed animal was estimated to be $286.9 million.

8.3   FINAL DEMAND CHANGES IN THE MARKET FOR RED MEAT

We expect that the major economic losses from agroterrorism events would result from consumers' responses, especially from abroad. Domestic demand for red meats will probably be affected first, though some proportion of the reduced domestic demand for red meats could be substituted by increasing consumption of poultry. Although FMD is known to not be harmful to human health, it is quite possible that people would choose to avoid or reduce red meat consumption. People tend to neglect the odds and are likely to show excessive risk aversion in cases of terrorism when intense emotions are involved (Sunstein, 2003). Further, US consumers were not able to distinguish FMD from BSE during the 2001 FMD outbreak in the UK (Paarlberg et al., 2002).

Second and more importantly, many countries importing US livestock and red meat products are likely to impose trade restrictions. While the impacts on domestic demand can perhaps be mitigated by government efforts, the demand shocks on exports are totally exogenous. The US red meat industries are likely to suffer an extended ban on foreign exports regardless of the size of the FMD outbreak.

While the direction of changes in consumer behavior and demands can easily be predicted, it is less simple to quantify the magnitudes of these changes. Given that there has been no historic FMD outbreak in the USA since 1929, the 2001 FMD outbreak in the UK and the 2003 BSE case in the USA provide the best set of comparisons.

8.4   UK FMD OUTBREAK IN 2001

In the UK, FMD cases continued from February 2001 to the end of September 2001. Disease-free status was declared in January 2002 (Thompson et al., 2002). The FMD outbreak resulted in killing about 6.6 million animals, but only modestly affected domestic consumption of red meats in 2001 or in the following years (Figure 8.1). Compared to the 1998–2000 average, total domestic consumption of red meats increased by 1.3 and 5.2 percent in 2001 and 2002, respectively. Public response to an intentional agroterrorist attack would likely be much more intense than the reaction to this natural event. Further, a significant drop in beef con-

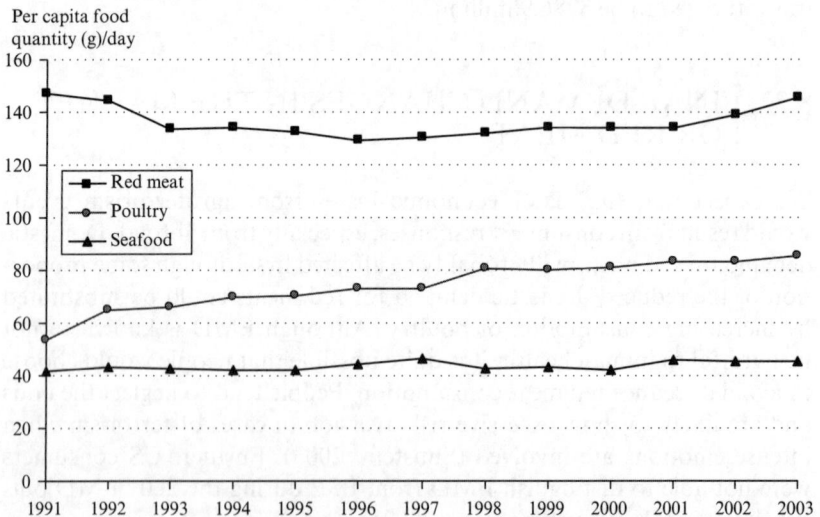

Source: Food and Agriculture Organization of the United Nations Statistical Database (UN FAOSTAT, http://www.faostat.fao.org/).

Figure 8.1   Per capita daily food consumptions in the UK, 1991–2003

Table 8.3   UK export of red meats, 1997–2002

Export ($ million)	1997–99			% change	
	average	2001	2002	2001	2002
Red meat	800.27	296.59	473.52	−62.9	−40.8
Bovine meat (including cattle and buffalo)	43.06	49.52	60.46	15.0	40.4
Pig meat	409.68	135.53	218.57	−66.9	−46.6
Sheep and goat meat	347.54	111.54	194.49	−67.9	−44.0

Source: Food and Agriculture Organization of the United Nations Statistical Database (UN FAOSTAT).

sumption and increased consumption of poultry, a substitution effect, can be identified during the period after the BSE outbreak in 1992.

The exports of pig meats and sheep and goat meats sharply declined in 2001, and did not recover to the previous levels until 2002 (Table 8.3 and Figure 8.2). Beef data are not relevant in this case because the export of bovine meat (beef) had dramatically declined since 1996, when the

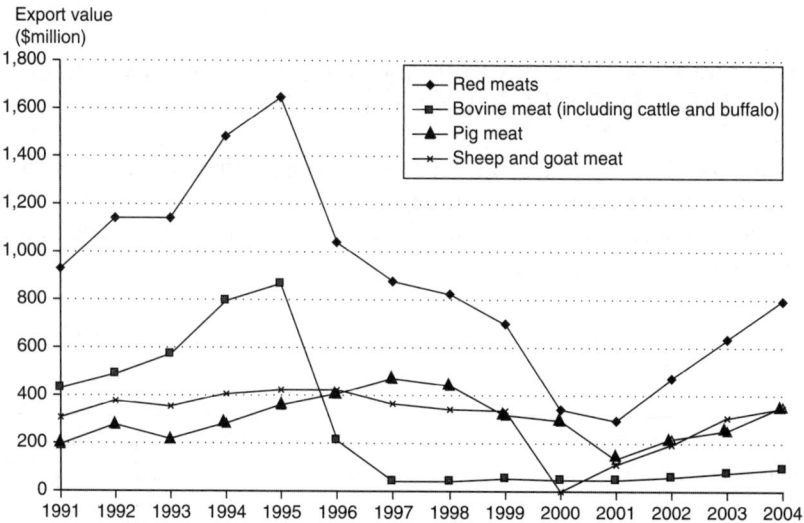

Source: Food and Agriculture Organization of the United Nations Statistical Database (UN FAOSTAT, http://www.faostat.fao.org/).

Figure 8.2   Trends in UK export of red meats, 1991–2004

Spongiform Encephalopathy Advisory Committee (SEAC) announced a possible link between a new variant of Creutzfeldt-Jakob Disease (nvCJD) and BSE-infected beef (Caskie et al., 1999). Despite the partial reduction of the export ban later, UK beef exports remained at levels between 4 and 11 percent of their 1995 peak ($863 million) until 2004.

8.5   US BSE OUTBREAK IN 2003

On 23 December 2003, it was made public that a Canada-born dairy cow in the state of Washington had tested positive for BSE. As in the UK FMD outbreak, beef exports collapsed while domestic consumption was barely impacted. The Food and Agriculture Organization Statistical Database of the United Nations (UN FAOSTAT, http://www.faostat.fao.org/) indicated that beef exports declined by 81 and 71 percent in 2004 and 2005, respectively, compared to the level of the early 2000s (Table 8.4). The BSE impact on beef exports was particularly large because high quality international beef markets account for the largest shares of US beef exports. Japan and Korea, which had imported 56 percent of US beef exports in 2003, completely ceased any imports of beef and related products immediately after the BSE discovery (Coffey et al., 2005).

8.6   ASSUMPTIONS FOR DOMESTIC AND FOREIGN DEMANDS FOR US RED MEATS

Given the difficulty of accurately predicting changes in domestic consumer behavior, we decided to adopt a range of estimates. We tested four scenarios combining assumptions about changes in foreign export and domestic demand for US red meats.

Table 8.4   Domestic consumption and export of red meats in the USA, 2001–2005

Meat, beef and veal (1,000 MT CWE)	2001–03	2004	2005	% change	
				2004	2005
Domestic consumption	12,476	12,667	12,666	1.5	1.5
Exports	1,094	209	313	−80.9	−71.4

Source: Food and Agriculture Organization of the United Nations Statistical Database (UN FAOSTAT, http://faostat.fao.org/).

Scenario 2 is our base scenario, in which we assume an 80 percent reduction in foreign export demand but no change in domestic demand. We have treated the 81 percent decline in beef exports in the 2003 US BSE case as our upper bound of foreign demand loss. This reflects our conservatism; a referee suggested that a 100 percent loss is more likely. It should be pointed out that although FMD, unlike BSE, is not a direct threat to human health, it is a far more contagious disease. Scenario 1 represents a lower bound of foreign export demand loss, 65 percent. In 2001 in the UK, FMD impacts on pig and sheep and goat meat were about 67 percent. We expect that the FMD impact in the USA would be larger because of the strict standards previously demonstrated by the major importers of US beef.

In Scenarios 3 and 4, we adopt the same assumptions as previous studies and assume a 10 percent reduction in domestic demand for red meats and a 10 percent increase of poultry demand as a substitute (Devadoss et al., 2006; Paarlberg et al., 2002) in addition to the export demand losses associated with Scenarios 1 and 2. Results from a CGE study of the 2003 BSE case (Devadoss et al., 2006) showed that a 10 percent reduction in beef consumption induced households to substitute consumption of 7.1 percent more pork and 5.5 percent more poultry, respectively. Paarlberg et al. (2002) is also an FMD study, while the Devadoss et al. (2006) study focuses on BSE, which affects only beef. In the case of FMD, the substitute effect toward poultry is higher because of reductions in demand for both beef and pork.

8.7   ESTIMATES OF TOTAL ECONOMIC IMPACTS

We estimated state-by-state economic impacts including indirect effects via a MRIO framework, implementing NIEMO. All the direct impacts that drive the model are summarized in Table 8.5. While we have four different scenarios for red meat demand changes, we treat operating costs in the same way for all four scenarios.

We attempt to capture both the positive and negative economic impacts of operating costs. First, California's expenditures on decontamination and quarantine activities enter the model as increased final demands for corresponding industrial sectors such as veterinary services (IMPLAN Sector 449) and environment and other technological consulting services (IMPLAN Sector 445). However, compensation costs for indemnity reflect a wealth loss to the economy. Second, federal spending on these activities and indemnity compensation will be paid for by taxpayers nationwide and will ultimately reduce household consumption. Thus, we

Table 8.5   Summary of direct impacts

	Scenario 1 (%)	Scenario 2 (%)	Scenario 3 (%)	Scenario 4 (%)
Meat demand changes				
Foreign exports of red meats	−65	−80	−65	−80
Domestic demand for red meats			−10	−10
Domestic demand for poultry			+10	+10
Operational costs				
Compensation costs	−$1,171.126 million * 1.05 reduction in overall household expenditures			
Cleaning and decontamination	−$118.829 million * 1.05 reduction in overall household expenditures + $118.829 million in environment consulting and in waste and disposal services in California			
Quarantine costs	−$286.9 million * 1.05 reduction in overall household expenditures +$286.9 million in veterinary services in California			

Note: The lower bound for the decrease in foreign exports (65%) is drawn from the 2001 FMD case in the UK. The upper bound for the decrease in foreign exports (80%) is based on the 2003 BSE case in the USA. Compensation payments are paid to farmers as are most of the quarantine cost reimbursements. Cleaning and decontamination costs are also shared, but primarily borne by the public sector. The decrease in domestic demand for red meats and the increase in poultry demand are based upon the results of a CGE study by Devadoss et al. (2006).

model all operating costs as reduced household spending. We used the expenditure pattern of households in the $35,000–$50,000 income bracket to which median household income belongs.

In modeling operating costs, it is important to consider the social costs of taxation that incur when transferring purchasing power from taxpayers to governments (Slemrod and Yitzhaki, 1996). In broad terms, the costs consist of administrative, compliance, and deadweight losses (Tran-Nam et al., 2000). In the interests of conservatism, we consider only the operating costs of taxation, including the administrative costs of collecting taxes and compliance costs incident to taxpayers. The magnitude of these costs is less controversial than the deadweight losses resulting from additional taxation.

A survey of empirical estimates (Evans, 2003) shows that compliance costs are typically a multiple of administration costs. The compliance costs of the US income tax in 1982 were estimated to range from 5 to 7 percent of the revenue (Slemrod and Sorum, 1984). The administrative and compliance costs of the UK income tax in the same year were estimated to be 2.3 and 3.6 percent, respectively (Sandford et al., 1989). The operating costs associated with the Canadian income tax amounted to about 7 percent of revenue in 1986 (Vaillancourt, 1989). We use an intermediate value of 5 percent to account for the operating costs of taxation. Thus, we reduce household consumption (final demand) by $1.05 for each dollar the government spends on FMD hazard mitigation activities.

The direct losses in the final demand for red meat and the associated substitution effects in each of the four scenarios are estimated using 2001 IMPLAN data. The impacted IMPLAN sectors are Sectors 11, 13, 67, 68 and 69 in the case of red meat and Sectors 12 and 70 in the case of poultry (that benefits from reduced red meat consumption). These industries are represented in NIEMO by two of the 47 USC sectors, Sector 1, Live animals and fish, meat, seafood, and their preparation, and Sector 5, Other prepared foodstuffs and fats and oils. Note that we attempt to eliminate any residual impacts of the 2003 BSE effects by using 2001 data.

All these direct impacts are distributed by state as shown in Figure 8.3 and in Table 8A.1 in the Appendix, and applied as inputs to the demand-side version of NIEMO to estimate indirect impacts resulting from

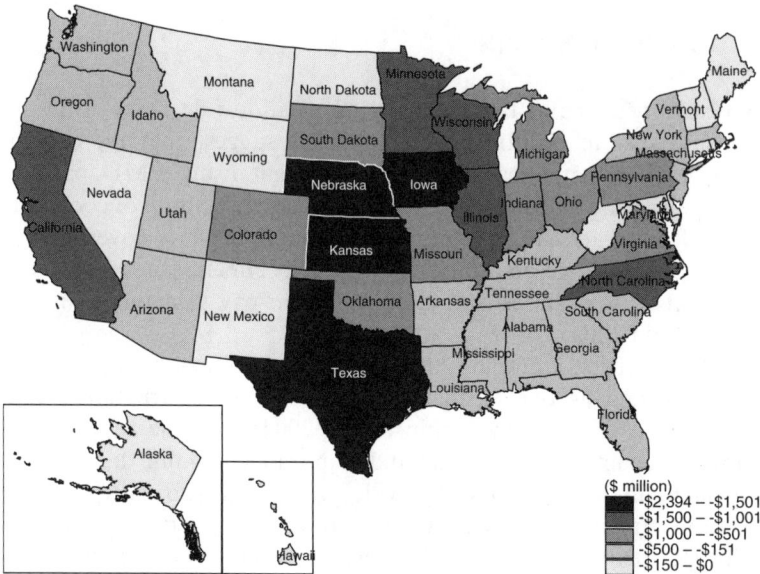

Figure 8.3   Total economic impacts by state (Scenario 2)

backward economic linkages. We believe that demand-side impacts would dominate supply-side impacts that might originate from any shortage of livestock due to animal slaughter.

We also assume that there is little demand-side impact in dairy markets. However, our estimation of total economic impacts may omit important supply-side impacts incident to dairy industries. As of 2002, California and the four-county South San Joaquin Valley area accounted for about 21 and 9 percent of total US milk production, respectively. Thus, the FMD outbreak in our scenario would disrupt about 10 percent of total US milk production for about one year. The loss in milk production would lead to supply constraints if other regions cannot increase milk production capacity quickly, and hence reduced production of other dairy products such as cheese and butter. These economic impacts resulting from forward economic linkages associated with milk production could be estimated using a supply-side IO model.

Our results for Scenario 2 are summarized in Figure 8.3 and in Tables 8A.2 and 8A.3 in the Appendix. Total economic impacts range from just under $23 billion to just over $34 billion. The overwhelming sources of the losses are due to domestic and international demand cuts. Although the scenario outbreak occurs in California, all of the major farm states are hit hard.

8.8   CONCLUSIONS

Our results describe at the state level the nationwide costs of an agro-terrorism event in California. These results suggest that the economic impacts of a hypothetical agroterrorism event using FMD pathogens could be large and nationwide. This implies the importance of cooperation between federal and state governments and among state governments to limit the possibility of an attack, or at least its effects. Our results benchmark what various states should be willing to pay to avoid a successful attack in California.

What might be done by the federal government? Agroterrorism is not classified as one of the weapons of mass destruction (WMD) under current federal law (Cupp et al., 2004), but the results of this economic impact study illustrate and elaborate the point that the losses from such an attack could be widespread and substantial. Federal legislation introduced by US Senators Burr (R – North Carolina) and Collins (R – Maine) (Burr and Collins, 2007) focuses on reinforcing the existing US Department of Agriculture Regional Emergency Animal Disease Eradication Organization (READEO) approach (Bowman and

Arnoldi, 1999) by clarifying lines of authority and improving coordination in the event of an agroterrorism attack, but falls short of Cupp et al.'s recommendation to classify weaponized pathogens as WMD. However, as in much of the research on the economic impacts of disasters, the results and their policy implications vary little regardless of whether the disaster is natural or man-made. We applied the terrorist example because of our association with counterterrorism research, although we have also applied this and related models to Hurricane Katrina and earthquakes.

Primarily because of the impact of a sizeable FMD attack/epidemic on US meat export revenues, the economic costs would be substantial. One argument against investing in prevention is that the public and private costs of preventing the full range of potential terrorist attacks would be impossible to cover. Preventive measures to avoid a man-made FMD attack would be especially difficult because of the large number of target locations, so a plausible strategy could be to focus more on mitigation and recovery.

Our approach provides an initial means of measuring the nationwide costs of state-specific attacks. However, state-level impacts are likely to be similar for any event that leads to a substantial loss of overall export demand for US red meat. An attack in Texas would produce a pattern of state-level impacts that is somewhat different from the pattern associated with the California scenario because trade flows between Texas and the rest of the USA are different from the trade flows between California and the rest of the USA, and NIEMO accounts for this. However, both scenarios would be similar in terms of state-level impacts because of large-scale export losses. Figure 8.3 shows that the main losses are in Texas, Kansas, Iowa and Nebraska even in the event of a distant attack (or epidemic) in California. The explanation, of course, is export losses, not direct epidemic costs. If there is a federal strategy that can reduce the likelihood of export losses, the benefits could be substantial. Transparent inspection and processing procedures might also limit the extent of any foreign boycott of US beef exports.

Linear models such as NIEMO do not capture many realistic market adjustments, and can overstate impacts. Prices are not present in these models, and the adjustments induced by equilibration of prices are unaccounted for. However, in an attempt to deal with price-substitution effects, there is a current model, which we call FlexNIEMO, that could address this issue. On the other hand, we have not attempted to model possible behavioral changes associated with the psychological impacts on the general population. This is outside our field of expertise, but these changes would certainly amplify the costs. We have also been conservative in other respects. For example, we ignore the impacts of supply-side constraints and the deadweight losses of additional taxation to fund government responses. These would also increase the cost estimates. The hope is that possible overestimates and underestimates associated with our approach roughly balance, and that the results provide a reasonable benchmark for total costs and their incidence with respect to geography and economic sectors.

REFERENCES

Bates, T.W., M.C. Thurmond and T.E. Carpenter (2003), 'Results of an epidemic simulation model to evaluate strategies to control the outbreak of foot-and-mouth disease'. *Journal of Veterinary Research*, **64**, 205–10.

Blackwell, J. (1980), 'Internationalism and survival of foot-and-mouth disease virus in cattle and food products', *Journal of Dairy Science*, **58**, 1019–30.

Bowman, Q.P. and J.M. Arnoldi (1999), 'Management of animal health in emergencies in North America: prevention, preparedness, response, and recovery', *Revue Scientifique et Technique – Office International des Epizooties*, **18**, 76–103.

Burr, R. and S. Collins (2007), National Agricultural and Food Defense Act of 2007, 110th Congress, 1st Session.

Caskie, P., J. Davis and J.E. Moss (1999), 'The economic impact of BSE: a regional perspective', *Applied Economics*, **31**, 1623–30.

Chalk, P. (2001), 'Testimony on terrorism, infrastructure protection, and the US food and agricultural sector', Hearings Before the Senate Subcommittee on Oversight of Government Management, Restructuring, and the District of Columbia, 107th Congress, 1st Session.

Coffey, B., J. Mintert, S. Fox, T. Schroeder and L. Valentin (2005), *Economic Impact of BSE on the US Beef Industry: Product Value Losses, Regulatory Costs, and Consumer Reactions*. Manhattan, KS: Agricultural Experiment Station and Cooperative Extension Service, Kansas State University.

Cupp, O.S., D.E.I. Walker and J. Hillison (2004), 'Agroterrorism in the US: key security challenge for the 21st century', *Biosecurity and Bioterrorism: Biodefense Strategy, Practice, and Science*, **2**, 97–105.

Devadoss, S., D.W. Holland, L. Stodick and J. Ghosh (2006), 'A general equilibrium analysis of foreign and domestic demand shocks arising from mad cow disease in the United States', *Journal of Agricultural and Resource Economics*, **31**, 441–53.

Ekboir, J.M. (1999), *Potential Impact of Foot-and-Mouth Disease in California*. Davis, CA: University of California, Davis, Agricultural Issues Center, Division of Agriculture and Natural Resources.

Evans, C. (2003), 'Studying the studies: an overview of recent research into taxation operating costs', *Journal of Tax Research*, **1**, 64–92.

Federal Inter-Agency Working Group, P (2003), *Animal Disease Risk Assessment, Prevention, and Control Act of 2001 – Final Report*. Washington, DC: US Department of Agriculture.

Leforban, Y. (1999), 'Prevention measures against foot-and-mouth disease in Europe in recent years', *Vaccine*, **17**, 1755–9.

Manning, L., R.N. Baines and S.A. Chadd (2005), 'Deliberate contamination of the food supply chain', *British Food Journal*, **107**, 225–45.

Mathews, K.H.J. and P. Janet (2003), *The Economic Consequences of Bovine Spongiform Encephalopathy and Foot-and-Mouth Disease Outbreaks in the United States*. Washington, DC: USDA Economic Research Services.

Office International des Epizooties (2006), *Manual of Diagnostic Tests and Vaccine for Terrestrial Animals*. Paris: Office International des Epizooties.

Paarlberg, P.L., J.G. Lee and A.H. Seitzinger (2002), 'Potential revenue impact of an outbreak of foot-and-mouth disease in the United States', *Journal of the American Veterinary Medical Association*, **220**, 988–92.

Park, J., C. Park and P. Gordon (2006), 'The state-by-state economic impacts of mad cow disease on the United States', Paper presented at the American Agricultural Economics Association (AAEA), Long Beach, California.

Rich, K.M., G.Y. Miller and A. Winter-Nelson (2005a), 'A review of economic tools for the assessment of animal disease outbreaks', *Revue Scientifique et Technique – Office International Des Epizooties*, **24**, 833–45.

Rich, K.M., A. Winter-Nelson and G.Y. Miller (2005b), 'Enhancing economic models for the analysis of animal disease'. *Revue Scientifique et Technique – Office International Des Epizooties*, **24**, 847–56.

Sandford, C., M. Godwin, P. Hardwick and D. Collard (1989), *Administrative and Compliance Costs of Taxation*. Bath, UK: Fiscal Publications.

Slemrod, J. and N. Sorum (1984), 'The compliance cost of the United States individual income-tax system', *National Tax Journal*, **37**, 461–74.

Slemrod, J. and S. Yitzhaki (1996), 'The costs of taxation and the marginal efficiency cost of funds', *International Monetary Fund Staff Papers*, **43**, 172–98.

State of Minnesota (2002), *Foot and Mouth Disease (FMD) Emergency Response Plan*. St Paul, MN: Minnesota Department of Agriculture.

Sunstein, C.R. (2003), 'Terrorism and probability neglect', *Journal of Risk and Uncertainty*, **26**, 121–36.

Thompson, D., P. Muriel, D. Russell et al. (2002), 'Economic costs of the foot and mouth disease outbreak in the United Kingdom in 2001', *Revue Scientifique et Technique – Office International Des Epizooties*, **21**, 675–87.

Tran-Nam, B., C. Evans, M. Walpole and K. Ritchie (2000), 'Tax compliance costs: research methodology and empirical evidence from Australia', *National Tax Journal*, **53**, 229–52.

Vaillancourt, F. (1989), *The Administrative and Compliance Costs of the Personal Income Tax and Payroll Tax System in Canada, 1986*. Toronto: Canadian Tax Foundation.

Wheelis, M., R. Casagrande and L.V. Madden (2002), 'Biological attack on agriculture: low-tech, high-impact bioterrorism', *BioScience*, **52**, 569–76.

APPENDIX

Table 8A.1 *Direct impacts by scenario and state ($ million)*

State	Changes in demands for meats by scenario				Operational costs[a]	
	Scenario 1	Scenario 2	Scenario 3	Scenario 4	Reduced household consumption	Federal expenditures
Alabama	-37.982	-46.747	-111.620	-120.385	-22.417	0
Alaska	-0.801	-0.986	-22.318	-22.503	-4.243	0
Arizona	-55.067	-67.775	-69.671	-82.379	-26.085	0
Arkansas	-58.372	-71.842	-133.829	-147.300	-12.680	0
California	-244.309	-300.687	-325.827	-382.206	-207.367	405.729
Colorado	-217.135	-267.243	-254.745	-304.853	-28.957	0
Connecticut	-8.299	-10.214	-18.004	-19.919	-23.438	0
Delaware	-1.280	-1.575	-20.443	-20.738	-4.541	0
DC	-0.079	-0.097	-0.877	-0.896	-11.200	0
Florida	-68.154	-83.882	-122.850	-138.578	-86.338	0
Georgia	-105.416	-129.743	-208.500	-232.827	-47.405	0
Hawaii	-7.189	-8.848	-10.164	-11.823	-6.505	0
Idaho	-67.490	-83.064	-81.247	-96.821	-6.574	0
Illinois	-450.576	-554.555	-537.471	-641.450	-73.210	0
Indiana	-121.322	-149.320	-173.656	-201.653	-32.766	0
Iowa	-796.413	-980.200	-890.423	-1,074.210	-16.146	0

Kansas	−561.595	−691.194	−618.586	−748.185	−16.122	0
Kentucky	−116.134	−142.934	−162.525	−189.325	−23.246	0
Louisiana	−39.762	−48.938	−69.827	−79.002	−22.034	0
Maine	−7.367	−9.067	−17.800	−19.500	−6.282	0
Maryland	−12.601	−15.509	−44.048	−46.956	−36.887	0
Massachusetts	−23.578	−29.019	−50.530	−55.971	−43.048	0
Michigan	−122.327	−150.556	−164.006	−192.235	−60.284	0
Minnesota	−233.695	−287.624	−301.507	−355.437	−30.726	0
Mississippi	−100.202	−123.325	−154.546	−177.670	−13.324	0
Missouri	−126.949	−156.245	−191.867	−221.163	−32.505	0
Montana	−14.357	−17.670	−19.928	−23.241	−4.530	0
Nebraska	−727.223	−895.044	−811.812	−979.633	−9.706	0
Nevada	−3.713	−4.570	−7.655	−8.512	−11.441	0
New Hampshire	−5.659	−6.965	−11.606	−12.912	−7.216	0
New Jersey	−45.959	−56.565	−76.504	−87.110	−51.309	0
New Mexico	−12.749	−15.692	−21.979	−24.921	−9.858	0
New York	−53.054	−65.298	−108.169	−120.412	−114.853	0
North Carolina	−356.602	−438.895	−482.628	−564.921	−45.490	0
North Dakota	−14.110	−17.366	−20.096	−23.353	−3.582	0
Ohio	−122.482	−150.747	−180.974	−209.239	−64.024	0
Oklahoma	−183.996	−226.457	−224.704	−267.164	−17.876	0
Oregon	−28.801	−35.448	−46.062	−52.708	−18.157	0
Pennsylvania	−233.088	−286.878	−309.539	−363.329	−68.795	0

Table 8A.1 (continued)

| State | Changes in demands for meats by scenario | | | | Operational costs[a] | |
	Scenario 1	Scenario 2	Scenario 3	Scenario 4	Reduced household consumption	Federal expenditures
Rhode Island	−1.518	−1.869	−5.098	−5.449	−5.340	0
South Carolina	−43.155	−53.113	−75.275	−85.234	−20.696	0
South Dakota	−148.458	−182.718	−169.116	−203.376	−4.157	0
Tennessee	−95.428	−117.450	−138.513	−160.535	−30.481	0
Texas	−616.751	−759.078	−786.729	−929.056	−124.702	0
Utah	−54.840	−67.496	−66.401	−79.056	−10.832	0
Vermont	−3.879	−4.775	−6.614	−7.510	−3.234	0
Virginia	−167.316	−205.928	−233.365	−271.976	−54.475	0
Washington	−119.733	−147.364	−169.644	−197.275	−38.363	0
West Virginia	−7.584	−9.334	−19.245	−20.995	−8.553	0
Wisconsin	−240.128	−295.542	−304.882	−360.296	−30.467	0
Wyoming	0.000	−14.062	−5.015	−19.077	−3.233	0
Foreign	0.000	0.000	−201.474	−201.474	0	0
Total	−6,884.7	−8,487.5	−9,259.9	−10,862.7	−1,655.7	405.7

Note: a. While our four scenarios include different assumptions about changes in the demand for meats, the same set of operating costs are applied to all scenarios.

New York	−216.540	−266.511	−348.042	−398.013	−179.266	1.046
North Carolina	−817.019	−1,005.561	−1,111.042	−1,299.585	−79.187	0.416
North Dakota	−108.950	−134.092	−140.231	−165.373	−6.836	0.045
Ohio	−456.016	−561.250	−633.686	−738.920	−116.001	0.790
Oklahoma	−545.669	−671.593	−674.841	−800.764	−34.633	0.298
Oregon	−104.255	−128.314	−151.587	−175.646	−31.401	0.521
Pennsylvania	−585.944	−721.161	−787.791	−923.009	−120.564	0.719
Rhode Island	−10.253	−12.619	−18.885	−21.251	−8.874	0.045
South Carolina	−133.169	−163.900	−211.460	−242.191	−36.693	0.174
South Dakota	−407.753	−501.850	−474.621	−568.718	−7.758	0.048
Tennessee	−284.531	−350.192	−402.137	−467.798	−53.805	0.323
Texas	−1,707.053	−2,100.988	−2,182.065	−2,576.000	−227.345	2.895
Utah	−141.137	−173.706	−173.186	−205.756	−19.063	0.321
Vermont	−15.198	−18.705	−23.450	−26.957	−5.641	0.032
Virginia	−385.859	−474.904	−538.542	−627.586	−88.173	0.195
Washington	−316.742	−389.836	−435.888	−508.982	−64.300	1.013
West Virginia	−35.572	−43.781	−64.216	−72.424	−16.432	0.081
Wisconsin	−787.797	−969.596	−1,001.170	−1,182.969	−58.774	0.599
Wyoming	−57.488	−70.755	−75.255	−88.522	−6.278	0.047
US subtotal	−19,726.7	−24,279.0	−25,726.3	−30,278.6	−2,839.9	542.4
Foreign	−795.8	−979.4	−1,246.7	−1,430.4	−76.7	5.2
Total	−20,522.5	−25,258.5	−26,973.0	−31,709.0	−2,916.6	547.6

Table 8A.3   Direct and total economic impacts by scenario and state ($ million)

State	Scenario 1		Scenario 2		Scenario 3		Scenario 4	
	Direct	Total	Direct	Total	Direct	Total	Direct	Total
Alabama	−60.40	−249.29	−69.16	−297.43	−134.04	−433.74	−142.80	−481.88
Alaska	−5.04	−32.87	−5.23	−38.74	−26.56	−81.22	−26.75	−87.09
Arizona	−81.15	−169.48	−93.86	−199.18	−95.76	−204.20	−108.46	−233.90
Arkansas	−71.05	−331.21	−84.52	−402.00	−146.51	−546.46	−159.98	−617.25
California	−45.95	−848.85	−102.33	−1,087.12	−127.47	−1,159.68	−183.84	−1,397.95
Colorado	−246.09	−583.43	−296.20	−707.14	−283.70	−685.40	−333.81	−809.11
Connecticut	−31.74	−67.89	−33.65	−74.92	−41.44	−89.07	−43.36	−96.09
Delaware	−5.82	−24.42	−6.12	−28.21	−24.98	−67.53	−25.28	−71.32
DC	−11.28	−18.94	−11.30	−19.53	−12.08	−20.90	−12.10	−21.49
Florida	−154.49	−339.48	−170.22	−386.60	−209.19	−464.47	−224.92	−511.59
Georgia	−152.82	−397.21	−177.15	−470.33	−255.90	−634.07	−280.23	−707.19
Hawaii	−13.69	−34.15	−15.35	−39.63	−16.67	−42.71	−18.33	−48.19
Idaho	−74.06	−206.54	−89.64	−251.52	−87.82	−252.28	−103.40	−297.26
Illinois	−523.79	−1,240.60	−627.76	−1,497.59	−610.68	−1,485.60	−714.66	−1,742.60
Indiana	−154.09	−428.08	−182.09	−512.77	−206.42	−569.81	−234.42	−654.49
Iowa	−812.56	−1,950.40	−996.35	−2,393.37	−906.57	−2,228.74	−1,090.36	−2,671.71
Kansas	−577.72	−1,473.76	−707.32	−1,806.88	−634.71	−1,667.79	−764.31	−2,000.91
Kentucky	−139.38	−349.29	−166.18	−420.17	−185.77	−466.14	−212.57	−537.02
Louisiana	−61.80	−206.82	−70.97	−244.70	−91.86	−295.59	−101.04	−333.47
Maine	−13.65	−38.80	−15.35	−45.19	−24.08	−62.13	−25.78	−68.52
Maryland	−49.49	−118.55	−52.40	−132.50	−80.93	−186.44	−83.84	−200.39
Massachusetts	−66.63	−142.22	−72.07	−159.24	−93.58	−198.65	−99.02	−215.67
Michigan	−182.61	−460.94	−210.84	−542.98	−224.29	−577.81	−252.52	−659.85
Minnesota	−264.42	−830.78	−318.35	−1,010.03	−332.23	−1,038.73	−386.16	−1,217.99
Mississippi	−113.53	−366.12	−136.65	−444.97	−167.87	−528.13	−190.99	−606.98
Missouri	−159.45	−538.56	−188.75	−649.85	−224.37	−730.36	−253.67	−841.64

Montana	−18.89	−85.58	−22.20	−103.42	−24.46	−108.68	−27.77	−126.52
Nebraska	−736.93	−1,836.61	−904.75	−2,256.10	−821.52	−2,085.59	−989.34	−2,505.07
Nevada	−15.15	−35.20	−16.01	−39.23	−19.10	−45.08	−19.95	−49.11
New Hampshire	−12.87	−29.56	−14.18	−33.61	−18.82	−42.60	−20.13	−46.64
New Jersey	−97.27	−238.64	−107.87	−274.35	−127.81	−313.91	−138.42	−349.62
New Mexico	−22.61	−81.60	−25.55	−96.55	−31.84	−110.85	−34.78	−125.80
New York	−167.91	−394.76	−180.15	−444.73	−223.02	−526.26	−235.27	−576.23
North Carolina	−402.09	−895.79	−484.39	−1,084.33	−528.12	−1,189.81	−610.41	−1,378.36
North Dakota	−17.69	−115.74	−20.95	−140.88	−23.68	−147.02	−26.93	−172.16
Ohio	−186.51	−571.23	−214.77	−676.46	−245.00	−748.90	−273.26	−854.13
Oklahoma	−201.87	−580.00	−244.33	−705.93	−242.58	−709.18	−285.04	−835.10
Oregon	−46.96	−135.14	−53.61	−159.19	−64.22	−182.47	−70.87	−206.53
Pennsylvania	−301.88	−705.79	−355.67	−841.01	−378.33	−907.64	−432.12	−1,042.85
Rhode Island	−6.86	−19.08	−7.21	−21.45	−10.44	−27.71	−10.79	−30.08
South Carolina	−63.85	−169.69	−73.81	−200.42	−95.97	−247.98	−105.93	−278.71
South Dakota	−152.61	−415.46	−186.87	−509.56	−173.27	−482.33	−207.53	−576.43
Tennessee	−125.91	−338.01	−147.93	−403.67	−168.99	−455.62	−191.02	−521.28
Texas	−741.45	−1,931.50	−883.78	−2,325.44	−911.43	−2,406.52	−1,053.76	−2,800.45
Utah	−65.67	−159.88	−78.33	−192.45	−77.23	−191.93	−89.89	−224.50
Vermont	−7.11	−20.81	−8.01	−24.31	−9.85	−29.06	−10.74	−32.57
Virginia	−221.79	−473.84	−260.40	−562.88	−287.84	−626.52	−326.45	−715.56
Washington	−158.10	−380.03	−185.73	−453.12	−208.01	−499.18	−235.64	−572.27
West Virginia	−16.14	−51.92	−17.89	−60.13	−27.80	−80.57	−29.55	−88.78
Wisconsin	−270.60	−845.97	−326.01	−1,027.77	−335.35	−1,059.34	−390.76	−1,241.14
Wyoming	−14.66	−63.72	−17.30	−76.99	−19.67	−81.49	22.31	−94.75
US subtotal	−8,146.1	−22,024.2	−9,737.5	−26,576.6	−10,319.8	−28,023.8	−11,911.2	−32,576.2
Foreign	0.0	−867.2	0.0	−1,050.9	−201.5	−1,318.2	−201.5	−1,501.8
Total	−8,146.1	−22,891.5	−9,737.5	−27,627.4	−10,521.3	−29,342.0	−12,112.7	−34,078.0
Total multipliers		2.810		2.837		2.789		2.813

9. The economic impacts of Hurricanes Katrina and Rita on the oil and port sectors*

JiYoung Park, Harry W. Richardson, Qisheng Pan, Peter Gordon and James E. Moore II

9.1 INTRODUCTION

Input-output models have been applied to the problem of economic impact estimation for many years. In recent years, our group has developed and applied IO models that include substantial spatial disaggregation. Most decision makers are interested in local effects and our models can estimate these.

The Southern California Planning Model (SCPM) applies to the greater Los Angeles area and is used to estimate impacts for a large number of traffic analysis zones (TAZs). The recently developed National Interstate Economic Model (NIEMO) is a multiregional IO model for the 50 states and the District of Columbia. Both models provide results for 47 industrial sectors (labeled USC Sectors).

NIEMO has a supply-side as well as a demand-side capability. In applications to hypothetical or actual port closures, for example, the loss of exports is best modeled via the demand-side NIEMO whereas the loss of imports is modeled via the supply-side NIEMO.

All of these models are most useful for short-term impact analysis because buyers and sellers can be expected to eventually make substitutions in light of the price changes that follow major disruptions. Missing these is a well-known limitation of the IO approach. In this chapter, we describe how to utilize post-event information on concurrent demand and value-added changes to identify the technological (production function) changes that actually occurred after a major disruption. We compare these results to the estimates from the baseline NIEMO to show the detailed impacts of the many substitutions and adaptations.

As seen in Table 9.1, Louisiana experienced economic decline (by

Table 9.1   Contributions to percent change in real GSP[a], 2004–2005

State and region	United States	Southeast[b]	Louisiana
Agriculture, forestry, fishing, and mining	−0.05	−0.01	−0.05
Utilities	0.01	0.00	−0.07
Construction	0.13	0.27	−0.07
Durable goods manufacturing	0.40	0.37	−0.04
Non-durable goods manufacturing	0.08	0.08	0.48
Wholesale trade	0.07	0.13	−0.04
Retail trade	0.20	0.32	0.03
Transportation and warehousing	0.11	0.11	0.02
Information	0.34	0.40	0.14
Finance and insurance	0.54	0.54	0.22
Real estate, rental and leasing	0.32	0.67	−0.41
Professional and technical services	0.48	0.47	−0.13
Management of companies	0.01	0.04	0.05
Administrative and waste services	0.21	0.32	0.19
Educational services	0.01	0.01	−0.02
Health care and social assistance	0.33	0.34	−0.08
Arts, entertainment and recreation	0.02	0.03	−0.05
Accommodations and food services	0.13	0.17	0.00
Other services	0.06	0.06	−0.06
Government	0.18	0.41	0.07
Total	3.60	4.60	−1.50

Notes:
a.   Real GSP is adjusted based on 2000 dollars.
b.   Southeast region includes AL, AR, FL, GA, LA, MS, NC, SC, TN, VA, WV.

Source: BEA data, http://bea.gov.regional/.

1.5 percent) in the years 2004 to 2005. According to the US Bureau of Economic Analysis (BEA) data (http://www.bea.gov/regional/), except for Louisiana and Alaska, all the other states had grown in terms of gross state product (GSP). Also, the mining sector including oil and gas production was the most negatively impacted component of gross domestic product (GDP).

Detailed examination of severe economic losses of oil refinery industries from Hurricanes Katrina and Rita need to be investigated to guide local and federal policy makers to prepare appropriate financial and mitigation support on the region. To analyse our economic impact results of the disasters, we introduce some of our previous research on the 2005 hurricanes. Then, a new approach, the expanded flexible NIEMO (FlexNIEMO) is described. Based on FlexNIEMO and our estimates of input data for FlexNIEMO, our simulated results are provided. Our conclusions finally address the implications of our research.

9.2   HURRICANES ON THE GULF OF MEXICO

A tropical depression formed over the southeastern Bahamas on 23 August 2005, moved toward the Gulf of Mexico and strengthened to Category 5 on the Saffir–Simpson Hurricane Scale over the central Gulf of Mexico (NCDC, 2005). When Hurricane Katrina made landfall on the Louisiana coast with Category 3 intensity on 29 August 2005, 130 mph of sustained winds breached the levees of New Orleans, and caused substantial inundation. A flood following the storm then devastated the Crescent City, and the disaster has been recorded as the costliest natural disaster ever in US history, resulting in 80 percent of the City of New Orleans being flooded and over 1,800 casualties (Kent, 2005).

Another hurricane, Rita, which had also strengthened to a Category 5 storm while at sea, hit the US coasts of the Gulf of Mexico on 24 September 2005. This was on the heels of the destruction caused by Katrina. Although Rita had weakened to Category 3 when it landed near the border of Texas and Louisiana, it produced a significant storm surge devastating southwestern coastal communities in Louisiana and was responsible for major wind and rain damage inflicted on eastern Texas. Because Louisiana had been severely devastated in the preceding days, the damage from Rita was considered far less than that of Katrina, with the total number of fatalities at 130 (Knabb et al., 2006).

Soon after these two catastrophic storms, several groups forecast the dollar-valued physical damages as well as economic impacts on the region and the entire country. Prior to the two hurricanes, the three costliest disasters in terms of dollar magnitude of damages recorded in the United States were the drought in 1988 with estimated losses of over $39 billion, Hurricane Andrew in 1992 that cost $30 billion and the Northridge Earthquake in 1994 that resulted in costs over $44 billion (National Research Council, 1999).

In the year since the Gulf disaster, several studies on the economic impacts of Hurricanes Katrina and Rita have been done. However, the majority of the research is from governmental reports mainly focusing on the magnitude of direct losses or on speculations about future impacts on the area. In terms of amounts for only Louisiana, it received federal reimbursements for losses reported from Katrina and Rita of about $105 billion and $10 billion respectively (Kent, 2006). More recently, Nordhaus (2006) utilized the economic impacts from the US hurricanes since 1950, and quoted $81 billion for Hurricane Katrina. The source Nordhaus referred to, Monthly Tropical Weather summary of the National Hurricane Center of the National Weather Service (2007), also released the damages from Hurricane Rita as $11.3 billion on 23 January 2007. Hence, it is plausible that the total economic damages from Hurricanes Katrina and Rita range between $92.3 billion to $115 billion.

However, total economic losses could well be beyond these estimates, considering the interrelations of economic industries and household consumption. On these points, Park et al. (2006a) estimated the direct and indirect economic losses due to New Orleans port inoperability during the immediate seven months after the hurricanes as $62.1 billion. This research was conducted because sectors that rely heavily on waterborne commerce are more severely affected, although all major economic sectors were partially inoperable during the storm and recovery period.

As port inoperability is only part of the story, it is useful to investigate other economic losses in the region. Several oil and gas refineries had been shut down for over a week. In the two hurricanes, 113 offshore oil and gas platforms were missing, sunk or had gone adrift (Energy Information Administration, 2006b). According to Katz et al. (2006), based on the assumption that half of 1.3 million evacuees from the New Orleans metropolitan area could not return within a month after the storm; a large portion of key workforces would have been out for a substantial time.

It is useful to analyse other industries beyond port activity to address the impacts of other economic losses. Recently, the Energy Information Administration (EIA, 2006a) released a report analysing historical impacts of tropical cyclones on Gulf of Mexico crude oil and natural gas production over the period 1960 through 2005, and refinery operations over the past 20 years. The analysis showed that tropical storms and hurricanes in the Gulf area typically cause seasonal disruption of shut-in production of 1.4 percent for crude oil and 1.3 percent for natural gas compared to normal annual production from wells on the Outer Continental Shelf (OCS). However, these averages are skewed upwards by the 19 percent of oil production and 18 percent of natural gas production that was shut in during 2005. Also, the Government Accountability Office (GAO, 2006) released a report addressing the factors causing natural gas price increases, influences on consumers according to the higher prices and the adequacy of roles the federal government agencies played in ensuring natural gas prices were competitive. In September 2005, natural gas spot prices increased to over $15 per million British thermal units (BTUs), which is roughly twice as high as the average price of $7.60 per million BTUs in July 2005. The skyrocketed price resulted from a substantial portion of domestic supply disruption and excessive demand due to the colder weather than expected in early December (GAO, 2006). In research of economic losses due to the employment changes, a report of the Bureau of Labor Statistics (BLS, 2006) presents the impacts of Katrina on employment in the Gulf Coast area by examining over-the-year changes. Employment in the most severely affected parish in Louisiana was down by nearly 40 percent in September 2005 compared to a year before. Colgan and Adkins (2006) discussed the proportion of employment and wages of the affected industries, defining them as ocean industries. Including oil and gas exploration as well as marine transportation and related goods and services, the ocean economy of the region encompassing Florida, Alabama, Mississippi, Louisiana and Texas employed 291,830 people in wage and salary jobs paying nearly $7.7 billion for the wages in 2004.

Figure 9.1 shows the severe impacts of the two hurricanes on oil and gas production platforms on the coast of the Gulf of Mexico where the

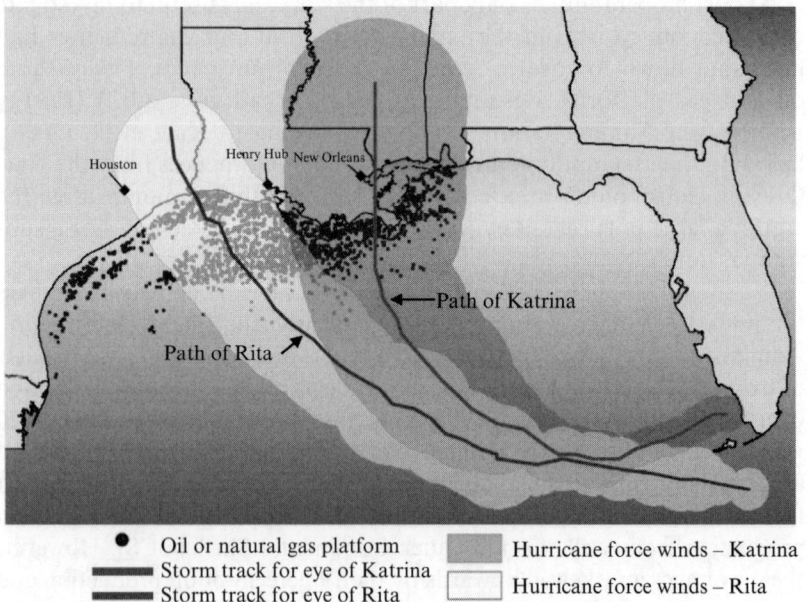

●	Oil or natural gas platform		Hurricane force winds – Katrina
▬	Storm track for eye of Katrina		
▬	Storm track for eye of Rita	☐	Hurricane force winds – Rita

Source: GAO (2006).

Figure 9.1   Storm tracks and winds of Hurricanes Katrina and Rita

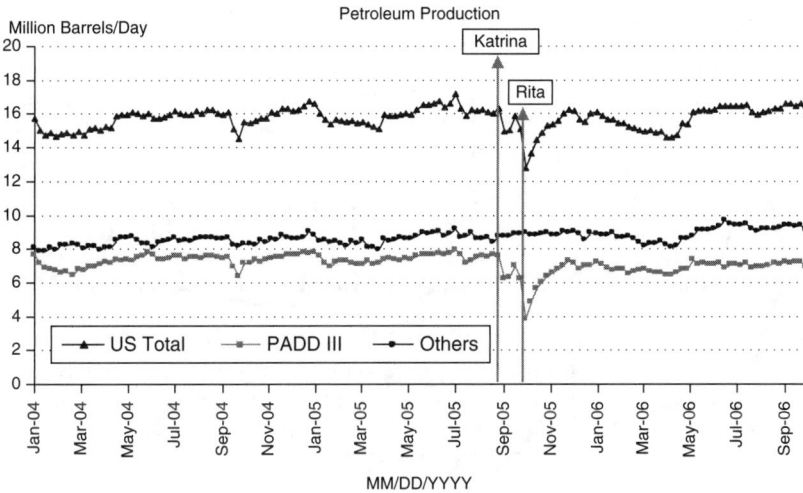

Source: Authors' calculations of raw data from EIA 2006 website (EIA, 2006a). The PADD III graph represents the local petroleum administrative district, http://tonto.eia.doe.gov/dnav/pet/pet_pnp_wiup_dcu_r30_w.htm.

Figure 9.2   Petroleum production pre- and post-Katrina and Rita

inoperability of gas and oil industries severely affected the US national market because crude oil production as well as petroleum products in the area accounted for nearly 60 percent of the total in the United States in 2004 (EIA, 2006b).

Not surprisingly, the Gulf of Mexico offshore installations have a significant place in the US oil and gas industries such that the domestic gasoline price escalated significantly right after the two storms. Figure 9.2 indicates the fact that the effects of the hurricanes were not constrained to the area. The total volume of production for the entire United States shows an abrupt drop in September 2005. The flow goes quite parallel to the Gulf Coast flow while the rest of the United States shows a relatively steady trend. In other words, the rapid decrease in petroleum production of the United States appearing in September 2005 mainly resulted from reduced production in the Gulf Coast.

Crude oil industries in the Gulf region are closely related to port activity. The analysis conducted by Park et al. (2006a) addressed disruptions of port activity, including oil industries. This study, however, focuses on just the oil refinery industries of the Gulf of Mexico by subtracting foreign and domestic exports from the total output of oil refineries.

Further, the Gulf of Mexico region is defined as PADD III (Texas

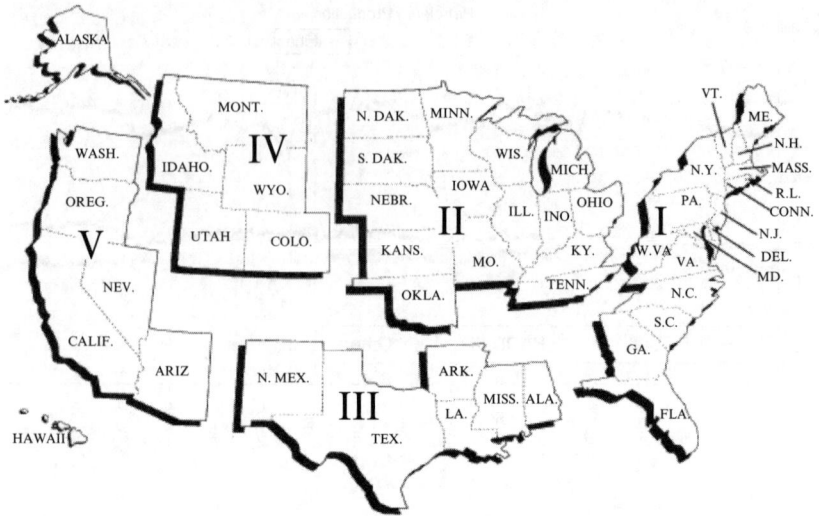

Figure 9.3 Petroleum administration for defense district maps

Inland, Texas Gulf Coast, Louisiana Gulf Coast, North Louisiana-Arkansas and New Mexico) shown in Figure 9.3. This requires spatial aggregation by modifying NIEMO, dropping to 47 regions from the original 52 (including the rest-of-the-world) regions. The next section describes our approach for estimating direct impacts required as input data for the 47-region NIEMO, and applying the newly developed Flexible National Interstate Economic Model (FlexNIEMO).

9.3 MODEL

This research utilized two methodologies. First, the Holt–Winters time-series approach was used to estimate normal economic trends if the two hurricanes had not occurred. These estimates provided the direct impacts necessary for input data into the supply-side NIEMO. Second, we utilized FlexNIEMO to construct month-to-month supply-side versions of NIEMO. The detailed methodological approach of FlexNIEMO is described in Chapter 2.

The Holt–Winters approach to estimating the normal economic status using times-series methodology is described in several recent articles (Gordon et al., 2007; Park et al., 2006a, 2006b; Richardson et al., 2007). The approach allows the estimated coefficients to change gradually over the periods, based on data for previous periods and exponentially declining weights. The estimated normal oil refinery products are obtained as follows in Equations (9.1) and (9.2).

$$ {}^tO_i = ({}^t\lambda_{1i} + {}^t\lambda_{2i})\,{}^t\zeta_i + {}^t\varepsilon_i, \tag{9.1} $$

where ${}^tO_i$ = the series oil refinery data for month t,

$\quad {}^t\lambda_{1i}$ = trend coefficient denoting smoothed average values of the trend for month t,

$\quad {}^t\lambda_{2i}$ = trend coefficient corresponding to the smoothed linear trend for month t,

$\quad {}^t\zeta_i$ = monthly seasonal adjustment parameters

i = USC sector

t = January 2002 through July 2005.

In Equation (9.1), parameters are updated via Equations (9.2-1, 9.2-2, 9.2-3)

$$ {}^t\lambda_{1i} = \omega_{1i}\frac{{}^tO_i}{{}^{t-1}\zeta_i} + (1 - \omega_{1i})({}^{t-1}\lambda_{1i} + {}^{t-1}\lambda_{2i}) \tag{9.2-1} $$

$$ {}^t\lambda_{2i} = \omega_{2i}({}^t\lambda_{1i} - {}^{t-1}\lambda_{1i}) + (1 - \omega_{2i})\,{}^{t-1}\lambda_{2i} \tag{9.2-2} $$

$$ {}^t\zeta_i = \omega_{3i}\frac{{}^tO_i}{{}^t\lambda_{1i}} + (1 - \omega_{3i}){}^{t-1}\zeta_i \tag{9.2-3} $$

where ω_{ki} (k = 1 to 3) is a smoothing weight. For the current study, the weights ω_{1i} and ω_{2i} are $(1 - 0.8^{1/\lambda})$, where $\lambda = 2$, and hence, ω_{1i} and ω_{2i} is fixed at 0.10557. The smoothing weight ω_{3i} is fixed at 0.25.

Based on the estimated coefficients, the forecast oil refinery industry values are obtained at the end of 2005 (August to December) and for the first three quarters of 2006. Direct impacts are calculated from the difference between the actual and predicted production of the oil refinery industry.

Second, we utilized FlexNIEMO to construct monthly versions of the supply-side NIEMO. The approach developed by Park et al. (2007b) allows the fixed coefficients in the IO world to be continuously modified, reflecting the previous economic events and interindustry relations. Because the oil refinery products are assumed to support the economy in the Gulf of Mexico and United States, it is useful to adopt the supply-side NIEMO. A problem with using the supply-side model is how to reflect demand-side adjustments during the recovery. With the supply-side FlexNIEMO, some of the major shortcomings inherent in the IO model can be overcome. Further, we aggregated 52 regions to 47 regions, because the Gulf of Mexico corresponds to six states, and treated the Gulf of Mexico as one region. Therefore, the newly defined NIEMO would have the (47 x 47) x (47 x 47) different coefficients for each month (August 2005 to September 2006) after Hurricane Katrina. Based on the NIEMO with 47 regions, the process of constructing the FlexNIEMO is as follows. As suggested in Equation (2.17) in Chapter 2, total impacts via the supply-driven model $\Delta_{t=i}\widetilde{X}^s$ for period i are estimated from Equation (9.3).

$$\Delta_{t=i}\widetilde{X}^s = \{\Delta_{t=i}^N V(I - {}^N B_0 C^s)^{-1}\} \tag{9.3}$$

The total sum of the impacts for each period $(\sum_i \Delta_{t=i}\widetilde{X}^s)$ can be obtained for 47 regions and 47 USC sectors. The total amount for the United States, therefore, would be $\sum_m \sum_n \sum_i \Delta_{t=i}\widetilde{X}^s$.

9.4   RESULTS

Figure 9.4 shows the 13 months of forecasts using the Holt–Winters method, which is adjusted monthly. The statistical results are reported in Table 9A.2 in the Appendix. The R-Square is 87 percent and Theil's U statistic, which summarizes the forecasting accuracy, is 0.071. Because the forecasts are near perfect, Theil's U is 0 and the U of no predictive power is 1 (Maddala, 1977, pp. 344–5; Theil, 1966). Therefore, our forecasts are statistically acceptable.

Table 9.2 compares the results from an application of NIEMO and an application of FlexNIEMO. The differences are dramatic. The original model estimates an overall multiplier of 1.83 when our results indicate that a multiplier effect of 1.07 was actually experienced. Approximately half of the adaptations occurred in the five states of the Gulf region and the rest were distributed over the other states. The relative impacts of the states (rankings), however, changed little.

Results in Table 9.3 underlie those of Table 9.2 and show the month-to-month output changes. The essence of the adjustments we are studying is that they involved considerable learning and adaptation. Our method is suitable for such analysis.

Our model includes 47 sectors. Table 9.4 reports total output effects for just one sector, USC Sector 10, oil and gas refineries. Tables 9.5 and 9.6 show results for all sectors for two of the regions covered, the Gulf of Mexico and California.

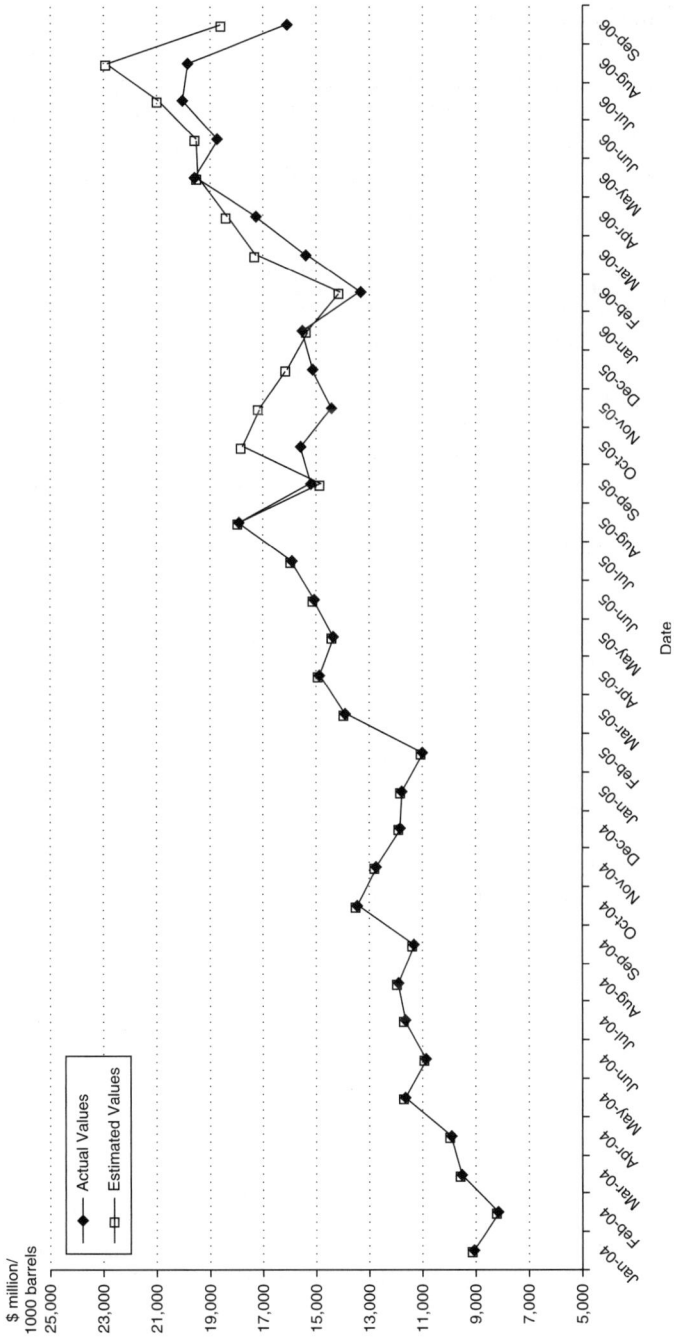

Sources: Authors' recalculated and estimated figures, based on Refiner Petroleum Product Prices by Sales Type (http://tonto.eia.doe.gov/dnav/pet/pet_pri_refoth_dcu_R30_m.htm) and Weekly Petroleum Production by Product (http://tonto.eia.doe.gov/dnav/pet/pet_pnp_wiup_dcu_r30_w.htm).

Figure 9.4   Changes of actual and estimated oil refinery values: PADD III (Gulf of Mexico)

Table 9.2   Total impacts of oil refinery losses from Hurricanes Katrina and Rita

State	FlexNIEMO			NIEMO		
	Total impacts	Percentage	Order	Total impacts	Percentage	Order
AK	−0.21	0.00%	45	−1.66	0.02%	44
AZ	−4.04	0.08%	16	−33.82	0.41%	17
CA	−28.81	0.59%	2	−324.30	3.90%	2
CO	−2.67	0.06%	20	−25.60	0.31%	20
CT	−0.74	0.02%	34	−5.69	0.07%	34
DE	−0.24	0.01%	44	−1.82	0.02%	41
DC	−0.40	0.01%	38	−2.43	0.03%	38
FL	−16.85	0.35%	3	−177.72	2.14%	3
GA	−11.78	0.24%	6	−124.39	1.50%	6
HI	−0.45	0.01%	36	−3.21	0.04%	36
ID	−0.27	0.01%	40	−1.85	0.02%	40
IL	−4.22	0.09%	15	−40.81	0.49%	15
IN	−1.59	0.03%	27	−14.09	0.17%	27
IA	−5.49	0.11%	13	−47.84	0.58%	14
KS	−0.83	0.02%	33	−6.73	0.08%	33
KY	−3.59	0.07%	17	−35.39	0.43%	16
ME	−0.42	0.01%	37	−2.72	0.03%	37
MD	−0.96	0.02%	32	−7.90	0.09%	32
MA	−7.29	0.15%	8	−69.09	0.83%	8
MI	−1.99	0.04%	24	−17.98	0.22%	25
MN	−6.30	0.13%	11	−66.62	0.80%	10
MO	−1.99	0.04%	25	−18.62	0.22%	23
MT	−0.25	0.01%	43	−1.80	0.02%	42
NE	−2.25	0.05%	22	−18.79	0.23%	22
NV	−1.53	0.03%	28	−11.91	0.14%	28
NH	−0.47	0.01%	35	−3.28	0.04%	35
NJ	−8.50	0.18%	7	−90.06	1.08%	7
NY	−5.46	0.11%	14	−51.62	0.62%	13
NC	−7.21	0.15%	9	−68.36	0.82%	9
ND	−0.26	0.01%	42	−1.50	0.02%	45
OH	−3.35	0.07%	19	−31.73	0.38%	18
OK	−1.85	0.04%	26	−18.10	0.22%	24
OR	−2.51	0.05%	21	−21.84	0.26%	21
PA	−12.00	0.25%	5	−127.88	1.54%	5
RI	−0.33	0.01%	39	−2.18	0.03%	39
SC	−3.38	0.07%	18	−31.57	0.38%	19
SD	−0.27	0.01%	41	−1.76	0.02%	43
TN	−6.42	0.13%	10	−62.98	0.76%	11
UT	−1.99	0.04%	23	−17.51	0.21%	26

Table 9.2   (continued)

State	FlexNIEMO			NIEMO		
	Total impacts	Percentage	Order	Total impacts	Percentage	Order
VM	−0.14	0.00%	47	−0.80	0.01%	47
VA	−1.34	0.03%	29	−10.85	0.13%	30
WA	−1.28	0.03%	30	−10.87	0.13%	29
WV	−1.07	0.02%	31	−9.21	0.11%	31
WI	−5.67	0.12%	12	−57.48	0.69%	12
WY	−0.16	0.00%	46	−1.01	0.01%	46
Gulf_MX	−4,668.06	96.26%	1	−6,506.51	78.22%	1
US total	−4,836.91	99.75%		−8,189.89	98.46%	
Rest of world	−12.30	0.25%	4	−128.40	1.54%	4
World total	−4,849.21	100.00%		−8,318.29	100.00%	
Direct impact on Gulf_MX	−4,543.47	–	–	−4,543.47	–	–

9.5   CONCLUSIONS

Impact modeling using widely available IO approaches routinely includes the caveat about the fixed technologies assumption and how that over-states the estimated results. We have adapted a new and operational multiregional IO model of the United States, NIEMO, to the study of adaptations and have considered their scale and scope for the case of oil and gas refinery losses in the Gulf of Mexico following Hurricanes Katrina and Rita in late 2005.

Our results show that the detailed study of adaptations is useful because overstated impacts from the application of conventional IO are substantial. NIEMO includes millions of multipliers and the detailed examination of selected individual adaptations is still before us.

We are now able to plot coefficient adaptations by month and by industry and by region. Questions about the effects of time, distance and industry linkage can be posed and studied. Those are in the tradition of IO structural decomposition analysis (see Rose and Casler, 1996) and will be taken up in our future research.

Table 9.3 Monthly changes of total impacts of oil refinery losses from Hurricanes Katrina and Rita

Oil refinery losses: ($million/1000barrels) State	FlexNIEMO													Summary
	Sep. 2005 Total impacts	Oct. 2005 Total impacts	Nov. 2005 Total impacts	Dec. 2005 Total impacts	Jan. 2006 Total impacts	Feb. 2006 Total impacts	Mar. 2006 Total impacts	Apr. 2006 Total impacts	May. 2006 Total impacts	Jun. 2006 Total impacts	Jul. 2006 Total impacts	Aug. 2006 Total impacts	Sep. 2006 Total impacts	Total impacts
AK	0.01	-0.04	-0.04	-0.01	0.00	-0.01	-0.03	-0.01	0.00	-0.01	-0.01	-0.04	-0.03	-0.21
AZ	0.21	-0.82	-0.79	-0.21	0.05	-0.13	-0.52	-0.25	0.04	-0.14	-0.25	-0.64	-0.58	-4.04
CA	0.54	-1.24	-4.75	-1.27	0.42	-1.02	-4.88	-2.10	0.41	-1.26	-2.40	-5.69	-5.58	-28.81
CO	0.11	-0.34	-0.45	-0.14	0.04	-0.10	-0.40	-0.19	0.03	-0.11	-0.19	-0.49	-0.44	-2.67
CT	0.06	-0.16	-0.15	-0.04	0.01	-0.03	-0.10	-0.05	0.01	-0.03	-0.05	-0.12	-0.11	-0.74
DE	0.04	-0.06	-0.06	-0.02	0.00	-0.01	-0.03	-0.02	0.00	-0.01	-0.01	-0.04	-0.03	-0.24
DC	0.00	-0.10	-0.08	-0.02	0.00	-0.01	-0.05	-0.02	0.00	-0.01	-0.02	-0.05	-0.04	-0.40
FL	0.99	-2.17	-2.87	-0.78	0.22	-0.58	-2.56	-1.17	0.22	-0.70	-1.28	-3.16	-3.00	-16.85
GA	0.86	-1.33	-2.16	-0.55	0.17	-0.41	-1.88	-0.83	0.16	-0.50	-0.93	-2.23	-2.16	-11.78
HI	0.01	-0.09	-0.08	-0.03	0.01	-0.02	-0.05	-0.03	0.00	-0.02	-0.02	-0.07	-0.06	-0.45
ID	0.02	-0.05	-0.07	-0.02	0.00	-0.01	-0.04	-0.02	0.00	-0.01	-0.02	-0.04	-0.04	-0.27
IL	0.16	-0.43	-0.71	-0.21	0.06	-0.15	-0.68	-0.30	0.06	-0.17	-0.32	-0.78	-0.74	-4.22
IN	0.10	-0.22	-0.30	-0.08	0.02	-0.06	-0.25	-0.11	0.02	-0.06	-0.12	-0.28	-0.27	-1.59
IA	0.54	-1.14	-1.16	-0.26	0.07	-0.17	-0.78	-0.34	0.06	-0.20	-0.37	-0.89	-0.86	-5.49
KS	0.08	-0.15	-0.18	-0.04	0.01	-0.03	-0.12	-0.05	0.01	-0.03	-0.06	-0.13	-0.13	-0.83
KY	0.11	-0.34	-0.62	-0.17	0.05	-0.13	-0.58	-0.25	0.05	-0.15	-0.28	-0.65	-0.63	-3.59
ME	0.03	-0.12	-0.09	-0.03	0.00	-0.01	-0.05	-0.02	0.00	-0.01	-0.02	-0.06	-0.05	-0.42
MD	0.08	-0.18	-0.19	-0.06	0.01	-0.04	-0.14	-0.07	0.01	-0.04	-0.06	-0.16	-0.15	-0.96
MA	0.42	-1.07	-1.38	-0.37	0.10	-0.25	-1.06	-0.49	0.09	-0.29	-0.51	-1.28	-1.19	-7.29
MI	0.14	-0.29	-0.37	-0.10	0.03	-0.07	-0.31	-0.13	0.03	-0.08	-0.15	-0.35	-0.34	-1.99
MN	0.84	-0.74	-1.26	-0.32	0.10	-0.23	-1.09	-0.46	0.09	-0.27	-0.52	-1.22	-1.21	-6.30

MO	0.12	-0.26	-0.36	-0.10	0.03	-0.07	-0.32	-0.14	0.03	-0.08	-0.15	-0.36	-0.34	-1.99
MT	0.03	-0.05	-0.07	-0.01	0.00	-0.01	-0.04	-0.01	0.00	-0.01	-0.02	-0.04	-0.04	-0.25
NE	0.21	-0.49	-0.45	-0.11	0.03	-0.07	-0.32	-0.14	0.03	-0.08	-0.15	-0.37	-0.35	-2.25
NV	0.10	-0.33	-0.33	-0.08	0.02	-0.05	-0.19	-0.09	0.02	-0.05	-0.09	-0.24	-0.21	-1.53
NH	0.04	-0.12	-0.10	-0.03	0.01	-0.02	-0.06	-0.03	0.00	-0.02	-0.03	-0.07	-0.06	-0.47
NJ	0.62	-0.85	-1.54	-0.42	0.12	-0.31	-1.39	-0.62	0.12	-0.37	-0.67	-1.63	-1.56	-8.50
NY	0.16	-0.64	-0.88	-0.28	0.08	-0.20	-0.84	-0.39	0.07	-0.22	-0.40	-0.99	-0.93	-5.46
NC	0.30	-0.92	-1.28	-0.35	0.10	-0.25	-1.11	-0.49	0.09	-0.29	-0.53	-1.28	-1.23	-7.21
ND	0.05	-0.11	-0.06	-0.01	0.00	-0.01	-0.03	-0.01	0.00	-0.01	-0.01	-0.03	-0.03	-0.26
OH	0.13	-0.37	-0.58	-0.16	0.05	-0.12	-0.54	-0.23	0.04	-0.13	-0.26	-0.60	-0.59	-3.35
OK	0.06	-0.17	-0.32	-0.09	0.03	-0.07	-0.30	-0.13	0.02	-0.08	-0.14	-0.34	-0.33	-1.85
OR	0.24	-0.51	-0.54	-0.12	0.03	-0.08	-0.36	-0.16	0.03	-0.09	-0.17	-0.41	-0.39	-2.51
PA	0.31	-0.90	-1.96	-0.56	0.17	-0.42	-1.96	-0.86	0.17	-0.51	-0.96	-2.30	-2.22	-12.00
RI	0.02	-0.08	-0.06	-0.02	0.00	-0.01	-0.04	-0.02	0.00	-0.01	-0.02	-0.05	-0.04	-0.33
SC	0.51	-0.74	-0.70	-0.16	0.05	-0.11	-0.50	-0.22	0.04	-0.13	-0.24	-0.59	-0.56	-3.38
SD	0.08	-0.12	-0.07	-0.02	0.00	-0.01	-0.03	-0.02	0.00	-0.01	-0.02	-0.04	-0.03	-0.27
TN	0.46	-0.86	-1.19	-0.32	0.09	-0.22	-1.00	-0.44	0.08	-0.26	-0.48	-1.16	-1.12	-6.42
UT	0.06	-0.22	-0.37	-0.10	0.03	-0.07	-0.31	-0.14	0.03	-0.08	-0.14	-0.35	-0.33	-1.99
VM	0.02	-0.04	-0.03	-0.01	0.00	0.00	-0.02	-0.01	0.00	0.00	-0.01	-0.02	-0.02	-0.14
VA	0.10	-0.24	-0.27	-0.07	0.02	-0.05	-0.20	-0.09	0.02	-0.05	-0.09	-0.22	-0.21	-1.34
WA	0.07	-0.16	-0.27	-0.07	0.02	-0.04	-0.20	-0.08	0.02	-0.05	-0.09	-0.22	-0.21	-1.28
WV	-0.03	-0.13	-0.18	-0.05	0.01	-0.03	-0.16	-0.07	0.01	-0.04	-0.07	-0.17	-0.17	-1.07
WI	0.66	-0.81	-1.04	-0.28	0.08	-0.20	-0.94	-0.41	0.08	-0.24	-0.45	-1.08	-1.04	-5.67
WY	0.02	-0.04	-0.04	-0.01	0.00	-0.01	-0.02	-0.01	0.00	-0.01	-0.01	-0.02	-0.02	-0.16
Gulf_MX	122.11	-625.06	-784.12	-282.18	57.84	-228.22	-556.89	-335.05	44.91	-214.25	-260.02	-877.47	-729.66	-4,668.06
US total	131.81	-645.27	-814.57	-290.35	60.21	-234.07	-583.36	-346.74	47.13	-221.17	-272.83	-908.38	-759.31	-4,836.91
Rest of wold	0.32	-1.69	-1.41	-0.75	0.12	-0.55	-1.43	-1.10	0.12	-0.65	-0.71	-2.92	-1.65	-12.30
World total	132.13	-646.96	-815.98	-291.10	60.34	-234.62	-584.79	-347.84	47.25	-221.83	-273.54	-911.30	-760.96	-4,849.21
Direct impact on Gulf_MX	120.42	-616.37	-767.52	-276.62	56.20	-224.00	-536.58	-325.40	43.15	-208.61	-249.79	-851.32	-707.04	-4,543.47

Note: Amounts of direct impacts of the USC Sector 10 losses are suggested in the last row of this table.

165

Table 9.4 Monthly changes of total impacts on USC Sector 10 in the various regions from Sector 10 losses from Hurricanes Katrina and Rita

Oil refinery losses: ($million/ 1000 barrels)	FlexNIEMO													Summary
State	Sep. 2005 Total impacts	Oct. 2005 Total impacts	Nov. 2005 Total impacts	Dec. 2005 Total impacts	Jan. 2006 Total impacts	Feb. 2006 Total impacts	Mar. 2006 Total impacts	Apr. 2006 Total impacts	May. 2006 Total impacts	Jun. 2006 Total impacts	Jul. 2006 Total impacts	Aug. 2006 Total impacts	Sep. 2006 Total impacts	Total impacts
AK	0.00	−0.01	−0.01	0.00	0.00	0.00	−0.01	−0.01	0.00	0.00	−0.01	−0.02	−0.01	−0.07
AZ	0.05	−0.24	−0.28	−0.08	0.02	−0.05	−0.23	−0.11	0.02	−0.06	−0.11	−0.28	−0.26	−1.61
CA	0.39	−0.63	−3.21	−0.84	0.28	−0.69	−3.26	−1.42	0.28	−0.86	−1.61	−3.86	−3.75	−19.19
CO	0.02	−0.10	−0.19	−0.06	0.02	−0.05	−0.20	−0.09	0.02	−0.06	−0.10	−0.25	−0.22	−1.25
CT	0.01	−0.01	−0.02	−0.01	0.00	0.00	−0.02	−0.01	0.00	0.00	−0.01	−0.02	−0.02	−0.12
DE	0.02	−0.01	−0.02	0.00	0.00	0.00	−0.01	−0.01	0.00	0.00	0.00	−0.01	−0.01	−0.06
DC	0.04	−0.02	−0.02	−0.01	0.00	0.00	−0.02	−0.01	0.00	0.00	−0.01	−0.02	−0.02	−0.08
FL	0.44	−0.76	−1.35	−0.35	0.11	−0.27	−1.25	−0.56	0.11	−0.34	−0.63	−1.54	−1.48	−7.88
GA	0.41	−0.51	−1.02	−0.25	0.08	−0.20	−0.92	−0.40	0.08	−0.24	−0.46	−1.10	−1.07	−5.61
HI	0.01	−0.03	−0.03	−0.01	0.00	−0.01	−0.03	−0.01	0.00	−0.01	−0.01	−0.04	−0.03	−0.19
ID	0.00	−0.01	−0.01	0.00	0.00	0.00	−0.01	0.00	0.00	0.00	0.00	−0.01	−0.01	−0.05
IL	0.02	−0.11	−0.28	−0.09	0.03	−0.07	−0.30	−0.14	0.03	−0.08	−0.15	−0.36	−0.34	−1.83
IN	0.01	−0.04	−0.08	−0.02	0.01	−0.02	−0.08	−0.04	0.01	−0.02	−0.04	−0.10	−0.09	−0.51
IA	0.16	−0.35	−0.46	−0.11	0.03	−0.08	−0.36	−0.16	0.03	−0.10	−0.18	−0.43	−0.42	−2.42

KS	0.00	−0.01	−0.02	−0.01	0.00	0.00	−0.02	−0.01	0.00	−0.01	−0.01	−0.02	−0.02	−0.12
KY	0.05	−0.17	−0.36	−0.10	0.03	−0.08	−0.37	−0.16	0.03	−0.09	−0.18	−0.42	−0.41	−2.23
ME	0.00	−0.01	−0.02	0.00	0.00	0.00	−0.01	−0.01	0.00	0.00	−0.01	−0.01	−0.01	−0.08
MD	0.01	−0.02	−0.03	−0.01	0.00	−0.01	−0.03	−0.01	0.00	−0.01	−0.01	−0.03	−0.03	−0.19
MA	0.17	−0.35	−0.58	−0.16	0.04	−0.11	−0.49	−0.23	0.04	−0.14	−0.24	−0.61	−0.57	−3.23
MI	0.01	−0.02	−0.04	−0.01	0.00	−0.01	−0.05	−0.02	0.00	−0.01	−0.02	−0.06	−0.05	−0.29
MN	0.51	−0.32	−0.65	−0.17	0.05	−0.13	−0.60	−0.26	0.05	−0.16	−0.29	−0.71	−0.68	−3.36
MO	0.02	−0.05	−0.10	−0.03	0.01	−0.02	−0.10	−0.05	0.01	−0.03	−0.05	−0.12	−0.12	−0.63
MT	0.00	0.00	−0.01	0.00	0.00	0.00	−0.01	0.00	0.00	0.00	−0.01	−0.01	−0.01	−0.07
NE	0.04	−0.12	−0.15	−0.04	0.01	−0.03	−0.13	−0.06	0.01	−0.03	−0.06	−0.15	−0.15	−0.86
NV	0.03	−0.08	−0.11	−0.03	0.01	−0.02	−0.08	−0.04	0.01	−0.02	−0.04	−0.10	−0.09	−0.54
NH	0.00	−0.02	−0.02	−0.01	0.00	0.00	−0.02	−0.01	0.00	0.00	−0.01	−0.02	−0.02	−0.12
NJ	0.39	−0.44	−0.89	−0.25	0.07	−0.18	−0.84	−0.37	0.07	−0.22	−0.41	−1.00	−0.96	−5.03
NY	0.04	−0.20	−0.31	−0.10	0.03	−0.08	−0.33	−0.15	0.03	−0.09	−0.16	−0.40	−0.37	−2.09
NC	0.10	−0.34	−0.54	−0.15	0.04	−0.11	−0.51	−0.23	0.04	−0.14	−0.25	−0.61	−0.58	−3.27
ND	0.00	0.00	0.00	0.00	0.00	0.00	0.00	0.00	0.00	0.00	0.00	0.00	0.00	−0.02
OH	0.02	−0.10	−0.20	−0.06	0.02	−0.04	−0.21	−0.09	0.02	−0.05	−0.10	−0.23	−0.23	−1.26
OK	0.01	−0.04	−0.14	−0.04	0.01	−0.03	−0.15	−0.07	0.01	−0.04	−0.07	−0.18	−0.17	−0.89
OR	0.07	−0.14	−0.21	−0.05	0.01	−0.03	−0.16	−0.07	0.01	−0.04	−0.08	−0.19	−0.18	−1.07
PA	0.18	−0.47	−1.15	−0.33	0.10	−0.25	−1.17	−0.52	0.10	−0.31	−0.58	−1.40	−1.35	−7.15
RI	0.00	−0.01	−0.01	−0.01	0.00	0.00	−0.01	−0.01	0.00	0.00	0.00	−0.01	−0.01	−0.07

Table 9.4 (continued)

Oil refinery losses: ($million/1000 barrels)	FlexNIEMO													
State	Sep. 2005	Oct. 2005	Nov. 2005	Dec. 2005	Jan. 2006	Feb. 2006	Mar. 2006	Apr. 2006	May. 2006	Jun. 2006	Jul. 2006	Aug. 2006	Sep. 2006	Summary
	Total impacts	Total impacts	Total impacts	Total impacts	Total impacts	Total impacts	Total impacts	Total impacts	Total impacts	Total impacts	Total impacts	Total impacts	Total impacts	Total impacts
SC	0.15	-0.21	-0.28	-0.07	0.02	-0.05	-0.22	-0.10	0.02	-0.06	-0.11	-0.27	-0.26	-1.43
SD	0.00	-0.01	-0.01	0.00	0.00	0.00	0.00	0.00	0.00	0.00	0.00	-0.01	-0.01	-0.03
TN	0.22	-0.35	-0.57	-0.15	0.04	-0.11	-0.50	-0.22	0.04	-0.13	-0.25	-0.59	-0.57	-3.13
UT	0.03	-0.08	-0.19	-0.05	0.02	-0.04	-0.17	-0.08	0.01	-0.05	-0.08	-0.20	-0.19	-1.09
VM	0.00	0.00	0.00	0.00	0.00	0.00	0.00	0.00	0.00	0.00	0.00	0.00	0.00	-0.01
VA	0.01	-0.03	-0.04	-0.01	0.00	-0.01	-0.03	-0.02	0.00	-0.01	-0.02	-0.04	-0.04	-0.22
WA	0.01	-0.01	-0.08	-0.02	0.01	-0.01	-0.07	-0.03	0.01	-0.02	-0.03	-0.08	-0.08	-0.41
WV	0.01	-0.04	-0.09	-0.03	0.01	-0.02	-0.10	-0.04	0.01	-0.02	-0.05	-0.11	-0.11	-0.57
WI	0.23	-0.28	-0.47	-0.13	0.04	-0.10	-0.46	-0.20	0.04	-0.12	-0.23	-0.55	-0.53	-2.77
WY	0.00	0.00	-0.01	0.00	0.00	0.00	-0.01	0.00	0.00	0.00	0.00	-0.01	-0.01	-0.04
Gulf_MX	121.03	-620.40	-772.04	-278.71	56.64	-225.31	-542.31	-328.85	43.65	-210.46	-252.64	-860.20	-712.47	-4,582.08
US total	124.92	-627.15	-786.32	-282.56	57.82	-228.25	-555.86	-334.87	44.80	-214.07	-259.32	-876.38	-728.01	-4,665.25
Rest of world	0.06	-0.52	-0.49	-0.28	0.05	-0.21	-0.55	-0.43	0.05	-0.26	-0.28	-1.15	-0.65	-4.67
World total	124.98	-627.67	-786.81	-282.84	57.86	-228.46	-556.41	-335.30	44.85	-214.32	-259.60	-877.53	-728.66	-4,669.92
Direct impact on Gulf_MX	120.42	-616.37	-767.52	-276.62	56.20	-224.00	-536.58	-325.40	43.15	-208.61	-249.79	-851.32	-707.04	-4,543.47

Table 9.5 Monthly changes of total impacts on all USC sectors in the Gulf of Mexico region

	FlexNIEMO													
Oil refinery losses ($million/1000 barrels)	Sep. 2005	Oct. 2005	Nov. 2005	Dec. 2005	Jan. 2006	Feb. 2006	Mar. 2006	Apr. 2006	May. 2006	Jun. 2006	Jul. 2006	Aug. 2006	Sep. 2006	Summary
USCsec.	Total impacts	Total impacts	Total impacts	Total impacts	Total impacts	Total impacts	Total impacts	Total impacts	Total impacts	Total impacts	Total impacts	Total impacts	Total impacts	Total impacts
USC01	0.01	−0.05	−0.15	−0.04	0.01	−0.03	−0.17	−0.07	0.01	−0.04	−0.08	−0.19	−0.19	−1.04
USC02	0.01	−0.04	−0.07	−0.02	0.01	−0.02	−0.08	−0.03	0.01	−0.02	−0.04	−0.09	−0.09	−0.51
USC03	0.01	−0.02	−0.04	−0.01	0.00	−0.01	−0.04	−0.02	0.00	−0.01	−0.02	−0.04	−0.04	−0.24
USC04	0.00	−0.02	−0.03	−0.01	0.01	−0.01	−0.03	−0.01	0.00	−0.01	−0.02	−0.04	−0.04	−0.22
USC05	0.01	−0.07	−0.13	−0.04	0.01	−0.03	−0.14	−0.06	0.01	−0.04	−0.07	−0.16	−0.16	−0.90
USC06	0.04	−0.13	−0.31	−0.08	0.03	−0.06	−0.30	−0.13	0.02	−0.08	−0.14	−0.34	−0.33	−1.94
USC07	0.00	0.00	0.00	0.00	0.00	0.00	0.00	0.00	0.00	0.00	0.00	0.00	0.00	−0.02
USC08	0.00	−0.02	−0.02	−0.01	0.00	−0.01	−0.02	−0.01	0.00	−0.01	−0.01	−0.03	−0.02	−0.15
USC09	0.00	−0.01	−0.01	0.00	0.00	0.00	−0.01	0.00	0.00	0.00	0.00	−0.01	−0.01	−0.07
USC10	121.03	−620.40	−772.04	−278.71	56.64	−225.31	−542.31	−328.85	43.65	−210.46	−252.64	−860.20	−712.47	−4,910.94
USC11	0.05	−0.16	−0.60	−0.15	0.05	−0.12	−0.58	−0.25	0.05	−0.15	−0.28	−0.67	−0.64	−3.69
USC12	0.00	−0.01	−0.01	0.00	0.00	0.00	−0.01	0.00	0.00	0.00	0.00	−0.01	−0.01	−0.06
USC13	0.01	−0.02	−0.05	−0.01	0.00	−0.01	−0.04	−0.02	0.00	−0.01	−0.02	−0.05	−0.05	−0.29
USC14	0.02	−0.10	−0.21	−0.06	0.02	−0.05	−0.22	−0.10	0.02	−0.06	−0.11	−0.26	−0.25	−1.44
USC15	0.03	−0.10	−0.28	−0.08	0.03	−0.06	−0.30	−0.13	0.03	−0.08	−0.15	−0.35	−0.34	−1.94

Table 9.5 (continued)

| | FlexNIEMO | | | | | | | | | | | | | |
Oil refinery losses: ($million/1000 barrels) USCsec.	Sep. 2005 Total impacts	Oct. 2005 Total impacts	Nov. 2005 Total impacts	Dec. 2005 Total impacts	Jan. 2006 Total impacts	Feb. 2006 Total impacts	Mar. 2006 Total impacts	Apr. 2006 Total impacts	May. 2006 Total impacts	Jun. 2006 Total impacts	Jul. 2006 Total impacts	Aug. 2006 Total impacts	Sep. 2006 Total impacts	Summary Total impacts
USC16	0.01	-0.02	-0.06	-0.02	0.01	-0.01	-0.07	-0.03	0.01	-0.02	-0.03	-0.08	-0.08	-0.44
USC17	0.01	-0.03	-0.09	-0.02	0.01	-0.02	-0.09	-0.04	0.01	-0.02	-0.04	-0.10	-0.10	-0.55
USC18	0.00	-0.01	-0.02	-0.01	0.00	-0.01	-0.03	-0.01	0.00	-0.01	-0.01	-0.03	-0.03	-0.18
USC19	0.01	-0.02	-0.05	-0.01	0.00	-0.01	-0.06	-0.02	0.00	-0.01	-0.03	-0.06	-0.06	-0.35
USC20	0.01	-0.05	-0.07	-0.03	0.01	-0.02	-0.09	-0.04	0.01	-0.02	-0.04	-0.11	-0.10	-0.61
USC21	0.01	-0.05	-0.09	-0.03	0.01	-0.02	-0.09	-0.04	0.01	-0.02	-0.05	-0.11	-0.10	-0.62
USC22	0.00	-0.02	-0.04	-0.01	0.00	-0.01	-0.04	-0.02	0.00	-0.01	-0.02	-0.05	-0.05	-0.28
USC23	0.00	-0.02	-0.04	-0.01	0.00	-0.01	-0.05	-0.02	0.00	-0.01	-0.02	-0.06	-0.05	-0.30
USC24	0.00	-0.01	-0.04	-0.01	0.00	-0.01	-0.06	-0.02	0.00	-0.01	-0.03	-0.07	-0.07	-0.35
USC25	0.00	-0.02	-0.04	-0.01	0.00	-0.01	-0.05	-0.02	0.00	-0.01	-0.03	-0.06	-0.06	-0.34
USC26	0.00	-0.01	-0.03	-0.01	0.00	-0.01	-0.03	-0.01	0.00	-0.01	-0.01	-0.03	-0.03	-0.19
USC27	0.00	0.00	-0.01	0.00	0.00	0.00	-0.01	0.00	0.00	0.00	0.00	-0.01	-0.01	-0.04
USC28	0.00	-0.01	-0.02	-0.01	0.00	-0.01	-0.02	-0.01	0.00	-0.01	-0.01	-0.03	-0.03	-0.15
USC29	0.00	-0.01	-0.01	0.00	0.00	0.00	-0.02	-0.01	0.00	-0.01	-0.01	-0.02	-0.02	-0.12
USC30	0.40	-1.38	-3.95	-1.05	0.38	-0.89	-4.53	-1.90	0.39	-1.17	-2.27	-5.31	-5.28	-28.45
USC31	0.04	-0.46	-0.87	-0.30	0.10	-0.25	-1.21	-0.52	0.11	-0.32	-0.63	-1.45	-1.47	-7.75

USC32	0.01	-0.04	-0.22	-0.06	0.02	-0.05	-0.29	-0.12	0.03	-0.08	-0.15	-0.35	-0.35	-1.77
USC33	0.18	-0.63	-2.11	-0.57	0.21	-0.50	-2.59	-1.08	0.22	-0.67	-1.32	-3.05	-3.07	-16.07
USC34	0.02	-0.14	-0.19	-0.06	0.02	-0.04	-0.23	-0.09	0.02	-0.06	-0.12	-0.26	-0.27	-1.49
USC35	0.02	-0.15	-0.29	-0.09	0.03	-0.08	-0.43	-0.18	0.04	-0.11	-0.23	-0.52	-0.54	-2.69
USC36	0.00	-0.01	-0.04	-0.01	0.00	-0.01	-0.06	-0.03	0.01	-0.02	-0.03	-0.08	-0.08	-0.40
USC37	0.00	-0.02	-0.06	-0.02	0.01	-0.02	-0.09	-0.04	0.01	-0.02	-0.05	-0.12	-0.12	-0.57
USC38	0.01	-0.04	-0.22	-0.06	0.03	-0.06	-0.33	-0.13	0.03	-0.08	-0.17	-0.39	-0.41	-1.95
USC39	0.00	-0.01	-0.05	-0.01	0.01	-0.01	-0.08	-0.03	0.01	-0.02	-0.04	-0.09	-0.10	-0.47
USC40	0.00	0.00	-0.01	0.00	0.00	0.00	-0.01	-0.01	0.00	0.00	-0.01	-0.02	-0.02	-0.09
USC41	0.02	-0.08	-0.18	-0.05	0.02	-0.04	-0.23	-0.09	0.02	-0.06	-0.12	-0.27	-0.28	-1.44
USC42	0.00	0.00	-0.01	0.00	0.00	0.00	-0.01	0.00	0.00	0.00	0.00	-0.01	-0.01	-0.05
USC43	0.01	-0.13	-0.26	-0.09	0.03	-0.07	-0.39	-0.16	0.03	-0.10	-0.21	-0.47	-0.49	-2.46
USC44	0.00	-0.01	-0.02	-0.01	0.00	-0.01	-0.03	-0.01	0.00	-0.01	-0.02	-0.04	-0.04	-0.20
USC45	0.01	-0.07	-0.15	-0.05	0.02	-0.04	-0.22	-0.09	0.02	-0.06	-0.11	-0.26	-0.27	-1.36
USC46	0.03	-0.29	-0.33	-0.15	0.03	-0.11	-0.43	-0.23	0.04	-0.14	-0.23	-0.61	-0.55	-3.19
USC47	0.03	-0.16	-0.60	-0.17	0.06	-0.15	-0.77	-0.32	0.07	-0.20	-0.39	-0.91	-0.91	-4.74
Total	122.11	-625.06	-784.12	-282.18	57.84	-228.22	-556.89	-335.05	44.91	-214.25	-260.02	-877.47	-729.66	-5,003.11
Direct impact on Gulf_MX	120.42	-616.37	-767.52	-276.62	56.20	-224.00	-536.58	-325.40	43.15	-208.61	-249.79	-851.32	-707.04	-4,543.47

Table 9.6 *Monthly changes of total impacts on all USC sectors in California*

Oil refinery losses: ($million/1000 barrels)	FlexNIEMO													
USCsec.	Sep. 2005	Oct. 2005	Nov. 2005	Dec. 2005	Jan. 2006	Feb. 2006	Mar. 2006	Apr. 2006	May. 2006	Jun. 2006	Jul. 2006	Aug. 2006	Sep. 2006	Summary
	Total impacts	Total impacts	Total impacts	Total impacts	Total impacts	Total impacts	Total impacts	Total impacts	Total impacts	Total impacts	Total impacts	Total impacts	Total impacts	Total impacts
USC01	0.01	−0.03	−0.04	−0.01	0.00	−0.01	−0.03	−0.01	0.00	−0.01	−0.01	−0.03	−0.03	−0.19
USC02	0.01	−0.02	−0.04	−0.01	0.00	−0.01	−0.03	−0.01	0.00	−0.01	−0.01	−0.03	−0.03	−0.19
USC03	0.01	−0.01	−0.01	0.00	0.00	0.00	−0.01	0.00	0.00	0.00	0.00	−0.01	−0.01	−0.05
USC04	0.00	−0.01	−0.01	0.00	0.00	0.00	−0.01	0.00	0.00	0.00	0.00	−0.01	−0.01	−0.05
USC05	0.01	−0.04	−0.05	−0.01	0.00	−0.01	−0.04	−0.02	0.00	−0.01	−0.02	−0.05	−0.04	−0.27
USC06	0.01	−0.02	−0.04	−0.01	0.00	−0.01	−0.04	−0.02	0.00	−0.01	−0.02	−0.04	−0.04	−0.24
USC07	0.00	0.00	0.00	0.00	0.00	0.00	0.00	0.00	0.00	0.00	0.00	0.00	0.00	−0.02
USC08	0.00	−0.01	−0.02	−0.01	0.00	−0.01	−0.02	−0.01	0.00	−0.01	−0.01	−0.03	−0.02	−0.14
USC09	0.00	0.00	0.00	0.00	0.00	0.00	0.00	0.00	0.00	0.00	0.00	0.00	0.00	−0.01
USC10	0.39	−0.63	−3.21	−0.84	0.28	−0.69	−3.26	−1.42	0.28	−0.86	−1.61	−3.86	−3.75	−19.19
USC11	0.01	−0.05	−0.10	−0.03	0.01	−0.02	−0.10	−0.04	0.01	−0.02	−0.05	−0.11	−0.10	−0.59
USC12	0.00	−0.01	−0.01	0.00	0.00	0.00	−0.01	0.00	0.00	0.00	0.00	−0.01	−0.01	−0.03
USC13	0.00	−0.01	−0.01	0.00	0.00	0.00	−0.01	0.00	0.00	0.00	0.00	−0.01	−0.01	−0.04
USC14	0.01	−0.03	−0.05	−0.02	0.00	−0.01	−0.05	−0.02	0.00	−0.01	−0.02	−0.06	−0.06	−0.32
USC15	0.01	−0.03	−0.06	−0.02	0.01	−0.01	−0.06	−0.03	0.01	−0.02	−0.03	−0.07	−0.07	−0.38

USC16	0.00	-0.01	-0.01	0.00	0.00	0.00	-0.01	0.00	0.00	0.00	0.00	-0.01	-0.01	-0.06
USC17	0.01	-0.03	-0.05	-0.01	0.00	-0.01	-0.05	-0.02	0.00	-0.01	-0.02	-0.05	-0.05	-0.29
USC18	0.00	-0.01	-0.01	0.00	0.00	0.00	-0.01	-0.01	0.00	0.00	-0.01	-0.02	-0.01	-0.09
USC19	0.01	-0.01	-0.02	-0.01	0.00	0.00	-0.02	-0.01	0.00	0.00	-0.01	-0.02	-0.02	-0.12
USC20	0.00	-0.03	-0.03	-0.01	0.00	-0.01	-0.03	-0.02	0.00	-0.01	-0.02	-0.04	-0.04	-0.23
USC21	0.00	-0.02	-0.02	-0.01	0.00	0.00	-0.02	-0.01	0.00	-0.01	-0.01	-0.02	-0.02	-0.14
USC22	0.00	-0.01	-0.02	0.00	0.00	0.00	-0.02	-0.01	0.00	0.00	-0.01	-0.02	-0.02	-0.12
USC23	0.00	-0.01	-0.02	0.00	0.00	0.00	-0.01	-0.01	0.00	-0.01	-0.01	-0.02	-0.02	-0.09
USC24	0.00	-0.01	-0.02	0.00	0.00	0.00	-0.02	-0.01	0.00	0.00	-0.01	-0.02	-0.02	-0.12
USC25	0.00	-0.01	-0.01	0.00	0.00	0.00	-0.01	-0.01	0.00	0.00	-0.01	-0.01	-0.01	-0.08
USC26	0.00	-0.01	-0.01	0.00	0.00	0.00	-0.01	-0.01	0.00	0.00	0.00	-0.01	-0.01	-0.06
USC27	0.00	0.00	0.00	0.00	0.00	0.00	0.00	0.00	0.00	0.00	0.00	0.00	0.00	-0.03
USC28	0.00	0.00	-0.01	0.00	0.00	0.00	-0.01	-0.01	0.00	0.00	-0.01	-0.01	-0.01	-0.04
USC29	0.00	0.00	-0.01	0.00	0.00	0.00	-0.01	-0.01	0.00	0.00	-0.01	-0.01	-0.01	-0.05
USC30	0.01	-0.06	-0.38	-0.09	0.04	-0.08	-0.41	-0.16	0.03	-0.10	-0.20	-0.45	-0.46	-2.31
USC31	0.00	-0.03	-0.08	-0.03	0.01	-0.02	-0.10	-0.04	0.01	-0.03	-0.05	-0.12	-0.12	-0.61
USC32	0.00	0.00	-0.02	-0.01	0.00	-0.01	-0.03	-0.01	0.00	-0.01	-0.01	-0.03	-0.03	-0.15
USC33	0.00	-0.01	-0.09	-0.02	0.01	-0.02	-0.11	-0.04	0.01	-0.03	-0.05	-0.12	-0.12	-0.59
USC34	0.00	-0.01	-0.02	-0.01	0.00	0.00	-0.02	-0.01	0.00	-0.01	-0.01	-0.03	-0.03	-0.14
USC35	0.00	-0.01	-0.03	-0.01	0.00	-0.01	-0.04	-0.02	0.00	-0.01	-0.02	-0.05	-0.05	-0.22
USC36	0.00	0.00	-0.01	0.00	0.00	0.00	-0.01	0.00	0.00	0.00	0.00	-0.01	-0.01	-0.05

Table 9.6 (continued)

Oil refinery losses: ($million/ 1000 barrels)	FlexNIEMO													
USCsec.	Sep. 2005 Total impacts	Oct. 2005 Total impacts	Nov. 2005 Total impacts	Dec. 2005 Total impacts	Jan. 2006 Total impacts	Feb. 2006 Total impacts	Mar. 2006 Total impacts	Apr. 2006 Total impacts	May. 2006 Total impacts	Jun. 2006 Total impacts	Jul. 2006 Total impacts	Aug. 2006 Total impacts	Sep. 2006 Total impacts	Summary Total impacts
USC37	0.00	0.00	-0.01	0.00	0.00	0.00	-0.01	0.00	0.00	0.00	-0.01	-0.01	-0.01	-0.06
USC38	0.00	0.00	-0.03	-0.01	0.00	-0.01	-0.04	-0.02	0.00	-0.01	-0.02	-0.05	-0.05	-0.24
USC39	0.00	0.00	-0.01	0.00	0.00	0.00	-0.01	-0.01	0.00	0.00	-0.01	-0.01	-0.02	-0.07
USC40	0.00	0.00	0.00	0.00	0.00	0.00	0.00	0.00	0.00	0.00	0.00	-0.01	-0.01	-0.03
USC41	0.00	0.00	-0.02	0.00	0.00	0.00	-0.02	-0.01	0.00	-0.01	-0.01	-0.03	-0.03	-0.13
USC42	0.00	0.00	0.00	0.00	0.00	0.00	0.00	0.00	0.00	0.00	0.00	0.00	0.00	-0.01
USC43	0.00	-0.01	-0.03	-0.01	0.00	-0.01	-0.04	-0.02	0.00	-0.01	-0.02	-0.05	-0.05	-0.24
USC44	0.00	0.00	0.00	0.00	0.00	0.00	-0.01	0.00	0.00	0.00	0.00	-0.01	-0.01	-0.03
USC45	0.00	-0.01	-0.02	-0.01	0.00	-0.01	-0.03	-0.01	0.00	-0.01	-0.01	-0.03	-0.03	-0.16
USC46	0.00	-0.02	-0.05	-0.02	0.00	-0.01	-0.06	-0.03	0.01	-0.02	-0.03	-0.08	-0.07	-0.37
USC47	0.00	-0.01	-0.03	-0.01	0.00	-0.01	-0.04	-0.02	0.00	-0.01	-0.02	-0.04	-0.04	-0.21
Total	0.54	-1.24	-4.75	-1.27	0.42	-1.02	-4.88	-2.10	0.41	-1.26	-2.40	-5.69	-5.58	-28.81
Direct impact on Gulf_MX	120.42	-616.37	-767.52	-276.62	56.20	-224.00	-536.58	-325.40	43.15	-208.61	-249.79	-851.32	-707.04	-4,543.47

NOTE

*   Acknowledgment: research contribution by Yunkyung Kim.

REFERENCES

BEA (Bureau of Economic Analysis) (annual), *Regional Economic Accounts*, available at http://www.bea.gov.regional/.
BLS (Bureau of Labor Statistics) (2006), 'The labor market impact of Hurricane Katrina: an overview', *Monthly Labor Review*, **129** (8), 3–10, available at http://www.bls.gov/opub/mlr/2006/08/art1abs.htm.
Colgan, C.S. and J. Adkins (2006), 'Hurricane damage to the ocean economy in the U.S. gulf region in 2005', *Monthly Labor Review*, **129** (8), 76–8, available at http://www.bls.gov/opub/mlr/2006/08/art7abs.htm.
EIA (Energy Information Administration) (2006a), *Weekly Petroleum Status Report*, available at http://www.eia.doe.gov/oil_gas/petroleum/data_publications/weekly_petroleum_status_report/wpsr.html.
EIA (Energy Information Administration) (2006b), *The Impact of Tropical Cyclones on Gulf of Mexico Crude Oil and Natural Gas Production*, available at http://tonto.eia.doe.gov/FTPROOT/features/hurricanes.pdf.
Gordon, P., H.W. Richardson, J.E. Moore II and J.Y. Park (2007), 'The economic impacts of a terrorist attack on the U.S. commercial aviation system', *Risk Analysis*, **27** (3), 505–12.
Government Accountability Office (2006), *Natural Gas: Factors Affecting Prices and Potential Impacts on Consumers (GAO-06-420T)*. Washington, DC: Government Accountability Office.
Katz, B., M. Fellowes and M. Mabanta (2006), *Katrina Index: Tracking Variables of Post-Katrina Reconstruction*. Washington, DC: The Brookings Institution.
Kent, J.D. (2005), *Louisiana Hurricane Impact Atlas*, Vol. 1, Louisiana Geographic Information Center, available at http://lagic.lsu.edu/lgisc/publications/2005/LGISC-PUB-20051116-00_2005_HURRICANE_ATLAS.pdf.
Knabb, R.D., D.P. Brown and J.R. Rhom (2006), *Tropical Cyclone Report Hurricane Rita: 18–26 September 2005*. National Hurricane Center, available at http://www.nhc.noaa.gov/pdf/TCR-AL182005_Rita.pdf.
Maddala, G.S. (1977), *Econometrics*. New York: McGraw-Hill.
National Hurricane Center of the National Weather Service (2007), *Tropical Weather Summary – 2005 Web Final*, available at http://www.nhc.noaa.gov/archive/2005/tws/MIATWSAT_nov_final.shtml.
National Research Council (1999), *The Impacts of Natural Disasters: A Framework for Loss Estimation*, available at http://www.nap.edu/catalog/6425.htmlb.
NCDC (National Climate Data Center) (2005), *Climate of 2005: Summary of Hurricane Katrina*, available at http://www.ncdc.noaa.gov/oa/climate/research/2005/katrina.html#top.
Nordhaus, W.D. (2006), 'The economics of hurricanes in the United States', National Bureau of Economic Research Working Paper 12813, Cambridge, Massachusetts.
Park, J.Y. (2006), 'The economic impacts of a dirty-bomb attack on the Los Angeles and Long Beach port: applying supply-driven NIEMO', Paper presented at the

17th Annual Meeting of the Association of Collegiate Schools of Planning, Fort Worth, Texas, 9–12 November.

Park, J.Y., P. Gordon, S.J. Kim, Y.K. Kim, J.E. Moore II and H.W. Richardson (2006a), 'Estimating the state-by-state economic impacts of Hurricane Katrina', Paper presented at the CREATE symposium, Economic and Risk Assessment of Hurricane Katrina, University of Southern California, California, 18–19 August.

Park, J.Y., C.K. Park and S.J. Nam (2006b), 'The state-by-state effects of mad cow disease using a new MRIO model', Paper presented at the 2006 American Agricultural Economic Association (AAEA) Annual Meeting, Long Beach, California, 23–26 July.

Park, J.Y., P. Gordon, J.E. Moore II and H.W. Richardson (2007a), 'Simulating the state-by-state effects of terrorist attacks on three major U.S. ports: applying NIEMO (National Interstate Economic Model)', in H.W. Richardson, P. Gordon and J.E. Moore II (eds), *The Economic Costs and Consequences of Terrorism*. Cheltenham, UK and Northampton, MA, USA: Edward Elgar, pp. 208–34.

Park, J.Y., P. Gordon, J.E. Moore II and H.W. Richardson (2007b), 'Constructing a new resilient National Interstate Economic Model', Paper presented at the 46th Annual Meeting of the Western Regional Science Association, Newport Beach, California, 21–24 February.

Richardson, H.W., P. Gordon, J.E. Moore II, S.J. Kim, J.Y. Park and Q. Pan (2007), 'Tourism and terrorism: the national and interregional economic impacts of attacks on major U.S. theme parks', in H.W. Richardson, P. Gordon and J.E. Moore II (eds), *The Economic Costs and Consequences of Terrorism*. Cheltenham, UK and Northampton, MA, USA: Edward Elgar, pp. 235–53.

Rose, A. and S. Casler (1996), 'Input-output structural decomposition analysis: a critical appraisal', *Economic Systems Research*, **8** (1), 33–62.

Theil, H. (1966), *Applied Economic Forecasting*, Amsterdam: North Holland.

APPENDIX

Table 9A.1   Definitions of USC sectors

Classification	USC	Description
Commodity Sectors	USC01	Live animals and live fish and meat, fish, seafood, and their preparations
	USC02	Cereal grains and other agricultural products except for animal feed
	USC03	Animal feed and products of animal origin, n.e.c.
	USC04	Milled grain products and preparations, and bakery products
	USC05	Other prepared foodstuffs and fats and oils
	USC06	Alcoholic beverages
	USC07	Tobacco products
	USC08	Nonmetallic minerals (monumental or building stone, natural sands, gravel and crushed stone, n.e.c.)
	USC09	Metallic ores and concentrates
	USC10	Coal and petroleum products (coal and fuel oils, n.e.c.)
	USC11	Basic chemicals
	USC12	Pharmaceutical products
	USC13	Fertilizers
	USC14	Chemical products and preparations, n.e.c.
	USC15	Plastics and rubber
	USC16	Logs and other wood in the rough and wood products
	USC17	Pulp, newsprint, paper, and paperboard and paper or paperboard articles
	USC18	Printed products
	USC19	Textiles, leather, and articles of textiles or leather
	USC20	Nonmetallic mineral products
	USC21	Base metal in primary or semi-finished forms and in finished basic shapes
	USC22	Articles of base metal
	USC23	Machinery
	USC24	Electronic and other electrical equipment and components, and office equipment
	USC25	Motorized and other vehicles (including parts)
	USC26	Transportation equipment, n.e.c.
	USC27	Precision instruments and apparatus
	USC28	Furniture, mattresses and mattress supports, lamps, lighting fittings, and illuminated signs
	USC29	Miscellaneous manufactured products, scrap, mixed freight, and commodity unknown

Table 9A.1   (continued)

Classification	USC	Description
Non-Commodity	USC30	Utility
(Service) Sectors	USC31	Construction
	USC32	Wholesale trade
	USC33	Transportation
	USC34	Postal and warehousing
	USC35	Retail trade
	USC36	Broadcasting and information services
	USC37	Finance and insurance
	USC38	Real estate and rental and leasing
	USC39	Professional, scientific, and technical services
	USC40	Management of companies and enterprises
	USC41	Administrative support and waste management
	USC42	Education services
	USC43	Health care and social assistances
	USC44	Arts, entertainment, and recreation
	USC45	Accommodation and food services
	USC46	Public administration
	USC47	Other services except public administration

Source: Park et al. (2007a).

Table 9A.2   *Statistical results for Holt–Winters approach*

Variables	Weights	Seasonal parameters
WEIGHT1	0.10557	
WEIGHT2	0.10557	
WEIGHT3	0.25000	
January		0.88949
February		0.80135
March		0.96353
April		1.00654
May		1.04548
June		1.02902
July		1.08578
August		1.16541
September		0.93095
October		1.09594

Table 9A.2   (continued)

Variables	Weights	Seasonal parameters
November		1.03316
December		0.95334
Total sum of squares (SST)	114,497,791	
Sum of the squared residuals (SSE)	15,729,114	
R-Square (= 1 − SSE/SST)	0.863	
Adj._R-Square	0.565	
Theil U	0.071	

10. The Gulf oil spill (FlexNIEMO)

JiYoung Park, Harry W. Richardson, Peter Gordon, James E. Moore II and Qisheng Pan

10.1 INTRODUCTION

Disasters, whether natural or man-made, often prompt responses that include compensation to victims. This can involve insurance companies, federal, state or local governments or industrial groups that share some of the culpability. All such compensation programs face the complex task of coming up with reasonable procedures to estimate the incidence of the losses.

In recent years, the September 11th Victim Compensation Fund was created by the US Congress via the Air Transportation Safety and System Stabilization Act. This was enacted shortly after the attacks to compensate victims or their families in exchange for their agreement not to take legal action against any of the airlines involved. Kenneth Feinberg was appointed to develop and administer the regulations and procedures governing the processing of claims. Feinberg was tasked with deciding and justifying how much compensation each family of a 9/11 victim could receive. His approach was to guestimate how much each victim would have earned in a full lifetime. If a family accepted his offer, it surrendered the right to appeal. This task was complicated by the fact that many of the World Trade Center victims were highly paid professionals. Families unhappy with the offer have been able to appeal in non-adversarial, informal hearings to present their case. Over 1,600 such hearings took place. At the end of the process approximately $7 billion had been awarded to almost all of the families involved; the average settlement was for $1.8 million. By February 2013 total British Petroleum settlements had reached about $42 billion; it is not the end because medical claims could be filed up to February 2015. There have been some estimates that the total economic impact might be $90 billion, but this cannot be verified.

Kenneth Feinberg has also assumed responsibility for distributing the $20 billion that British Petroleum has made available to victims of the April 2010 Gulf oil spill. However, the much larger economic losses involved make this problem even more complex. Supply chains that stretch all over the United States (and beyond) could have been impacted. On 24 October 2010, the *New York Times* included a long discussion of controversies over 'proximity claims' that remain to be sorted out (Segal, 2010).

In this study, we elaborate and apply our National Interstate Economic Model to estimate industry-level economic losses in each of the 50 states (and the District of Columbia, DC). We simulate the effects of three separate six-month direct loss scenarios of guestimates reported by several local sources. While the traditional NIEMO application only captured direct and indirect impacts, we developed a new module to estimate local induced impacts as well. The methodology could be applied to any similar scenario. Our approach is appropriate because the analysis is restricted to short-term impact phenomena such as the recent oil spill. Our model extension and application suggest a useful approach for when tasks such as the one assigned to Feinberg come along. The terror threat as well as the possibility of other mishaps and natural disasters suggests that there is always a serious possibility that these kinds of calculations will need to be made.

10.2 THE NATIONAL INTERSTATE ECONOMIC MODEL

To accomplish our research goals, we elaborated on the National Interstate Economic Model (NIEMO) to apply it to the task of estimating the losses from the recent Gulf oil spill. The basic model is summarized in Figure 10.1. It is a spatially disaggregated operational input-output (IO) model constructed from data reported in the Commodity Flow Survey (CFS) and IMPLAN's state-level IO accounts (Miller and Blair, 2009, pp. 371–2). While a detailed description of how NIEMO was constructed is in Park et al. (2007) and elaborated in Chapter 2 of this book, a brief introduction to NIEMO and recent applications is presented in this section.

The ideal spatially disaggregated IO model was first suggested by Isard (1951). Early efforts to apply the model were by Chenery (1953) and Moses (1955), who developed a Multiregional Input-Output (MRIO) model, a potentially operational approach of Isard's ideas but requiring a simpler data set. Our effort to construct the NIEMO update was based on the approach adopted in the late 1970s and early 1980s by Polenske (1980) and Jack Faucett Associates (1983), who developed a US version of a MRIO model.

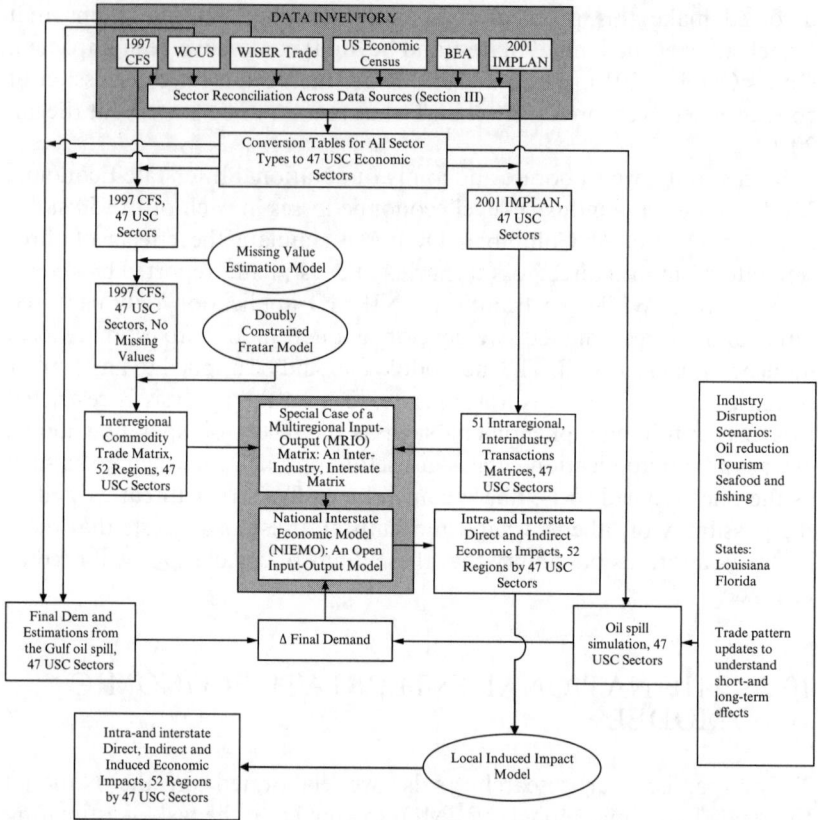

Note: BEA – US Bureau of Economic Analysis; WCUS – Waterborne Commerce of the United States.

Figure 10.1   NIEMO modeling and development process to add local induced impacts

To develop an operational state-level model of the United States, we combined state- (and DC data)-level intrastate coefficients from 51 IMPLAN state-level IO models with interstate freight trade flows data available from the CFS data source. Among the challenges in integrating these data sets, the first involved creating a bridge combining the IMPLAN and CFS sectors. To that end, NIEMO is based on a new sector system of 47 economic sectors (29 commodity sectors and 18 service sectors, the 'USC sectors'), which serves as a common denominator that easily converts to the domestic or internationally standardized sector codes systems. The Appendix reports the sector conversions required in this application.

NIEMO's technological and trade coefficients involve almost 6 million cells that facilitate the estimation of interindustry-interstate economic impacts. For example, when investigating the magnitude and policy implications of negative economic impacts resulting from disruptive events, including disruptions in infrastructure services because of natural or man-made disasters at different regional levels, standard single-region IO applications cannot measure regional interactions among industries.

Park (2008) included tests that showed NIEMO to be a reasonably accurate and low-cost method of developing disaggregated and plausible economic impact estimates. Empirical applications using NIEMO include a hypothetical temporary closure of three major US seaports (Park et al., 2007), a closure of US theme parks (Chapter 4 and Richardson et al., 2007), temporary US border closures (Chapter 7 and Gordon et al., 2009), the 2002 West Coast ports shutdown (Chapter 13 and Park et al., 2008) and an occurrence of foot-and-mouth disease in California (Chapter 8 and Lee et al., 2012).

Our extension of NIEMO in this research involved estimating induced effects for the states that were directly affected and accounting for the additional impacts of these induced effects in a full interregional trade system. We first obtained NIEMO results for the three scenarios. However, this was not presumed to be the final economic equilibrium. The induced effects in the directly affected states were calculated by applying IMPLAN's state-level models. These calculations yield the state's revised domestic imports and exports and were used to augment domestic imports and exports from the initial NIEMO application.

10.3 APPLICATION AND EXTENSION OF NIEMO

To illustrate our approach, we model the impacts of a scenario based on guestimates reported by several local sources for three key sectors (oil, seafood and tourism) in two states (Louisiana and Florida). The sources of 'guestimates' are noted at the bottom of each table in the Appendix. This underestimates the total impact because the seafood industry was affected to some degree in Mississippi and tourism also suffered in Louisiana and Mississippi. The difficulty in measuring the direct impact by each sector for a specific region still remains (Lindner, 2011). The guestimates include a $2.3133 billion loss of oil production in Louisiana, a $0.0972 billion loss by Louisiana's seafood industry and a $16.2467 billion loss by Florida's tourist industry. We estimated all these impacts only for the first six months after the oil spill; some of these impacts would continue, although at a diminished pace. Further detailed assumptions are explained in Table 10A.1 in the Appendix.

Table 10.1 summarizes the results of applying NIEMO to the three scenarios. Results like this are available for all USC sectors in all 50 states (plus DC). Recall that this step estimates the direct and indirect impacts only (Type I multipliers). In our previous applications, the effects of service sector trade across state lines were thought to be relatively small. In this application, however, we also modeled induced effects and estimated Type II multipliers. This step required an extension of NIEMO because we were interested in the latter multipliers for the states that were directly impacted. This prompted us to look for ways to estimate the interstate trade effects of induced effects in the directly impacted states and add them to the basic NIEMO trade effects.

Additional steps were required to capture total economic impacts including the induced effects and their full trade consequences. The first step involved the straightforward application of NIEMO for each of the three scenarios that provided direct and indirect impacts as shown in Table 10.1.

Table 10.1   Direct and indirect impacts of the first NIEMO run based on scenarios

(a) Scenario I: Oil production losses in Louisiana

Direct (USC Sector 10)	Indirect	Total
$2.3133 billion	$4.321 billion	$6.634 billion
Multiplier		2.8679

(b) Scenario II: Seafood production losses in Louisiana

Direct (USC Sector 1)	Indirect	Total
$0.0972 billion	$0.1714 billion	$0.2686 billion
Multiplier		2.7643

(c) Scenario III: Tourism and tourist-related activity losses in Florida

Direct	Indirect	Total
USC Sector 33 = $1.7622 billion		
USC Sector 35 = $8.0930 billion		
USC Sector 44 = $1.8525 billion		
USC Sector 45 = $4.5390 billion		
$16.2467 billion	$11.5428 billion	$27.7889 billion
Multiplier		1.7104

The next step involved estimating the induced effects that occurred in the target states (Florida and Louisiana) using the state-level IMPLAN (IMPLAN Group, 2009) models. This required that we also estimate additional interstate trade impacts. Ratios that related trade prompted by induced activity versus trade prompted by direct and indirect impacts were estimated. This step involved the following data manipulations:

$$D^{IMPLAN} = (INDU\_R^{IMPLAN}) \times (Dom\_Trade^{IMPLAN}), \quad (10.1)$$

where
D^{IMPLAN} = domestic trade effects ascribed to the induced effects that occurred in a state that experienced direct impacts; this is defined as the product of $INDU\_R^{IMPLAN}$ and Dom_Trade^{IMPLAN};
$INDU\_R^{IMPLAN}$ = ratio of induced effects to direct and indirect effects via IMPLAN in a state that experienced the impact; and
Dom_Trade^{IMPLAN} = total domestic trade effects for that state via IMPLAN.

Note that if $D^{IMPLAN} > Dom\_Trade^{IMPLAN}$, then we treat $D^{IMPLAN} = Dom\_Trade^{IMPLAN}$.
We translate the 509 IMPLAN sector system to the 47 USC sector system to be used as an input for the second NIEMO run, and redefine

$$EX^{NIEMO} = D^{IMPLAN} \text{ if the domestic trade is export;}$$

and

$$IM^{NIEMO} = D^{IMPLAN} \text{ if the domestic trade is import.}$$

Hence, the total impact prompted by local induced effects within the directly impacted state is defined as Tr_IP; Tr_IP^{exp} represents induced domestic export disruption and Tr_IP^{imp} represents induced domestic import disruption. These were calculated as

$$Tr\_IP^{exp} = DIVS \times DTC \times EX^{NIEMO}, \quad (10.2.1)$$

where
$DIVS = (I - DNIEMO)^{-1}$;
$DNIEMO$ = the technical and trade coefficients in the demand-driven NIEMO, that is, $(47 \times 52)^2$; and
DTC = the trade coefficients in the demand-driven NIEMO.

$$Tr\_IP^{imp} = IM^{NIEMO} \times STC \times SIVS, \quad (10.2.2)$$

where

$SIVS = (I - SNIEMO)^{-1}$;

SNIEMO = the technical and trade coefficients in the supply-driven NIEMO, that is, $(47 \times 52)^2$; and

STC = the trade coefficients in the supply-driven NIEMO.

In the next step, we estimated net induced impacts; which equal total induced impacts from the application of IMPLAN in the impacted Gulf States, but via subtracting the induced trade impacts. This is also a part of Type II's induced effects to be added to the original NIEMO results. The net induced impacts resulting from the IMPLAN sector system are again aggregated to the USC sector system.

Extending NIEMO to include local induced impacts and their interindustry and interstate effects leaves us with the following components of economic impact:

Total direct and indirect effects = Total impacts obtained from NIEMO run (Type I effects);

Total induced effects = Total induced trade impacts and net induced impacts determined in the steps previously outlined;

and

Total effects = Total direct and indirect effects + total induced effects (Type II effects).

The impacts are shown in Tables 10.2, 10.3 and 10.4. The latter two tables are a sample of the detailed impacts available – for all 50 states and DC and for all 47 sectors within each geographic unit.

Based on the direct impacts of Table 10.1, the tourism industry is the most impacted in the region; it accounts for 84 percent of total industrial

Table 10.2   Summary of aggregated results

Unit: $ million	Direct	Indirect	Type I	Induced			Type II
				Trade-oriented	Within state	Subtotal	
Oil	2,313	4,321	6,634	276	295	571	7,205
Seafood	97	171	269	18	17	36	304
Tourism	16,247	11,542	27,789	4,653	7,611	12,264	40,053

Table 10.3   Selected disaggregated results for top three states impacted by scenario

(a) Scenario I: Oil production losses in Louisiana

Top three states	$ million			
	Direct	Indirect	Induced	Total
LA	2,313.30	2,437.78	508.82	5,259.90
CA	0.00	515.76	7.62	523.38
TX	0.00	530.97	10.52	541.50
Foreign	0.00	598.10	10.15	608.25

(b) Scenario II: Seafood production losses in Louisiana

Top three states	$ million			
	Direct	Indirect	Induced	Total
LA	97.20	83.43	30.98	211.60
TX	0.00	8.64	0.84	9.48
MS	0.00	8.19	0.14	8.33
Foreign	0.00	12.18	0.80	12.98

(c) Scenario III: Tourism and tourist-related activity losses in Florida

Top three states	$ million			
	Direct	Indirect	Induced	Total
FL	16,246.70	8,422.92	11,616.69	36,286.30
TX	0.00	487.40	59.42	546.82
GA	0.00	297.83	62.49	360.31
Foreign	0.00	471.35	100.28	571.64

impact. However, the seafood industry shows relatively small disruptions when compared to the other two sectors.

Because Louisiana suffered sizable direct impacts from oil production losses, it is not surprising that it accounts for the largest total impact as well as largest indirect and induced impacts. The next two states in terms of impact are Texas and California, suffering $542 and $523 million in total losses, respectively. Induced impacts of Texas and California states account for about 2 percent of the total impacts. Louisiana experienced the largest seafood production losses; Texas and Missouri were the next two states in terms of losses in this sector. However, it should be noted that the induced impact in Texas accounted for 10 percent of the total impact. Further, in the case of tourism and tourist-related activity

Table 10.4   Selected disaggregated results for top three impacted industries by scenario

(a) Scenario I: Oil production losses in Louisiana

Top three industries	$ million			
	Direct	Indirect	Induced	Total
USC Sector 10	2,313.30	2,360.53	27.54	4,701.38
USC Sector 38	0.00	320.97	81.76	402.73
USC Sector 47	0.00	313.03	36.60	349.64

(b) Scenario II: Seafood production losses in Louisiana

Top three industries	$ million			
	Direct	Indirect	Induced	Total
USC Sector 1	97.20	43.13	0.64	140.97
USC Sector 32	0.00	14.14	1.47	15.60
USC Sector 5	0.00	12.82	0.54	13.36

(c) Scenario III: Tourism and tourist-related activity losses in Florida

Top three industries	$ million			
	Direct	Indirect	Induced	Total
USC Sector 45	8,093.00	228.84	1,121.60	9,443.44
USC Sector 35	4,539.00	178.10	710.53	5,427.63
USC Sector 44	0.00	1,432.71	1,779.51	3,212.23

losses in Florida, Texas and Georgia were the next two largest impacted states beyond Florida, of which induced impacts accounted for 10 to 20 percent of total impacts. It is not surprising that the third scenario shows a very high percentage of indirect and induced impacts to the total impacts.

Depending upon industry sectors, economic impacts varied. While each industry experiencing the largest economic loss makes the largest total economic impact, each scenario relates to different indirect and induced economic impacts. For example, Scenario I experienced the second largest loss in USC Sector 38, Real Estate and Rental and Leasing. Scenarios II and III show USC Sectors 32 (wholesale trade) and 35 (retail trade) accounting for the second largest loss among the indirect and induced impacts. Based on the results shown in Table 10.4, we should consider how additional damage of service sectors was seriously affected regardless of the direct impact that occurs in the commodity or service sectors.

10.4 DISCUSSION

There has been considerable controversy about the economic impacts of the federal Gulf deepwater oil drilling suspensions following the oil spill. A moratorium was proposed by President Obama in May 2010 and was later extended. Mason (2010) discusses the Administration's estimate of the economic consequences of such a moratorium. Mason based his critique on results he obtained via the application of the Regional Input-Output Modeling System II (RIMS II) models. His conclusions are not surprising and his results are in a similar range to our results, given that our direct guestimate is about twice Mason's estimated loss. Also, this was not very different from the results reported in the previous tables (Type I varies from 1.7 to 2.9; Type II varies from 2.5 to 3.1).

However, input-output caveats in the traditional IO models such as fixed coefficient characteristics and no technological substitution in the short run still exist even in our advanced approach (Park, 2008; Park et al., 2008). Further, Type II effects obtained by moving the household sectors endogenously into the traditional IO model are more appropriate to the established residents than newly in-migrated residents because the coefficients for the Type II effects, which refer to average relationships between final demand and industry sectors, may have different relationships for the new residents (Miller and Blair, 2009). Similarly, the Type II effects, because of the average characteristic, may be misleading if an aggregated final demand sector is endogenously added into the traditional model. By applying IMPLAN's nine disaggregated household sectors, we avoided the latter issue.

In spite of these caveats, our methodological innovation was to estimate the Type II effects in the impacted states and to trace their trade effects through the NIEMO system with only minor methodological elaborations. The advanced approach is not restricted only to NIEMO applications; it is a general approach to be applied to other traditional IO models. Our contribution exists in these merits.

REFERENCES

Chenery, H.B. (1953), 'Regional analysis', in H.B. Chenery, P.G. Clark and V.C. Pinna (eds), *The Structure and Growth of the Italian Economy*. Rome: US Mutual Security Agency, pp. 98–139.
Gordon, P., J.E. Moore II, J.Y. Park and H.W. Richardson (2009), 'The economic impacts of international border closure: a state-by-state analysis', in H.W. Richardson, P. Gordon and J.E. Moore II (eds), *Global Business and*

the Terrorist Threat. Cheltenham, UK and Northampton, MA, USA: Edward Elgar, pp. 341–74

IMPLAN Group (2009), *Supplemental Files 2001*. Huntersville, NC: IMPLAN.

Isard, W. (1951), 'Interregional and regional input-output analysis: a model of a space economy', *Review of Economics and Statistics*, **33**, 318–28.

Jack Faucett Associates, Inc. (1983), *The Multiregional Input-Output Accounts, 1977: Introduction and Summary*. Vol. I (Final Report). Washington, DC: US Department of Health and Human Services.

Lee, B., J.Y. Park, P. Gordon, J.E. Moore II and H.W. Richardson (2012), 'Estimating the state-by-state economic impacts of bio-terrors: the case study of FMD', *International Regional Science Review*, **35**, 26–47.

Lindner, R. (2011), 'Gulf of Mexico: between oil slicks and shrimp', *The Economist*, 16 April.

Mason, J.R. (2010), *The Economic Cost of a Moratorium on Offshore Oil and Gas Exploration to the Gulf Region*. Baton Rouge, LA: Louisiana State University.

Miller, R.E. and P.D. Blair (2009), *Input-Output Analysis: Foundations and Extensions*, 2nd edn, Englewood Cliffs, NJ: Prentice Hall.

Moses, L.N. (1955), 'The stability of interregional trading patterns and input-output analysis', *American Economic Review*, **45**, 803–32.

Park, J.Y. (2008), 'The economic impacts of dirty-bomb attacks on the Los Angeles and Long Beach ports: applying the supply-driven NIEMO (National Interstate Economic Model)', *Journal of Homeland Security and Emergency Management*, **5** (1), Article 21.

Park, J.Y., P. Gordon, J.E. Moore II, H.W. Richardson and L. Wang (2007), 'Simulating the state-by-state effects of terrorist attacks on three major U.S. ports: applying NIEMO (National Interstate Economic Model)', in H.W. Richardson, P. Gordon and J.E. Moore II (eds), *The Economic Costs and Consequences of Terrorism*. Cheltenham, UK and Northampton, MA, USA: Edward Elgar, pp. 208–34.

Park, J.Y., P. Gordon, J. E. Moore II and H.W. Richardson (2008), 'The state-by-state economic impacts of the 2002 shutdown of the Los Angeles-Long Beach ports', *Growth and Change*, **39** (4), 548–77.

Polenske, K.R. (1980), *The U.S. Multiregional Input-Output Accounts and Model*. Lexington, MA: DC Heath.

Richardson, H.W., P. Gordon, J.E. Moore II, S.J. Kim, J.Y. Park and Q. Pan (2007), 'Tourism and terrorism: the national and interregional economic impacts of attacks on major U.S. theme parks', in H.W. Richardson, P. Gordon and J.E. Moore II (eds), *The Economic Costs and Consequences of Terrorism*. Cheltenham, UK and Northampton, MA, USA: Edward Elgar, pp. 235–53.

Segal, D. (2010), 'Should BP's money go where oil didn't?', *New York Times*, 24 October.

APPENDIX

Table 10A.1   *IMPLAN to North American Industry Classification System (NAICS) to USC sector conversions using BEA's state gross domestic product (GDP) of 2008 for six-month period*

(a) Oil, Louisiana

USC Sector (IMPLAN Code)	IMPLAN Sector	NAICS 2002 Code	Direct
USC10 (19)	19, 142, 145, 146	211, 32411, 324191, 324199	$2.3133 billion

Note: Damage: 10 percent of oil extraction relating industries of Louisiana GDP.

Source: http://www.economy.com/dismal/article_free.asp?cid=199173&src=msnbc.

(b) Seafood, Louisiana (the closest we can get to shrimps and oysters)

USC Sector (IMPLAN Code)	IMPLAN Sector	NAICS 2002 Code	Direct
USC1 (16)	16, 71	1141, 3117	$0.0972 billion

Note: Damage: 10 percent of fishing relating industries of Louisiana GDP.

Source: http://www.economy.com/dismal/article_free.asp?cid=199173&src=msnbc.

(c) Tourism and tourist-related activities, Florida

Refer to the direct impact calculation procedure for tourism and related industries applied in Chapter 4 and in Richardson et al. (2007).

USC Sector (IMPLAN Code)	IMPLAN Sector	NAICS 2002 Code	Direct	Reference
USC33 (391)	391, 395, 397	481, 485, 487	$1.7622 billion	Richardson et al., 2007
USC35 (405)	405, 408–412	445, 448–454	$8.0930 billion	
USC44 (475)	475–478	712, 71394, 71395, 7131	$1.8525 billion	
USC45 (479)	479–481	72111, 72112, 72119, 7212, 7213, 722	$4.5390 billion	
Total			$16.2467 billion	

Note: Damage: 30 percent of tourism relating industries of Florida GDP.

Sources: http://www.americanthinker.com/2011/01/gulf_oil_spill_more_a_mancause.html; http://www.gulfoilspilllitigationgroup.com/blog/tag/gulf-coast-tourism/.

11. The Joplin tornado of 2011

Harry W. Richardson, JiYoung Park, Peter Gordon, Qisheng Pan and James E. Moore II

Despite the potential destruction that might result, tornadoes have not received much attention in natural disaster economic impact research, certainly compared with earthquakes, hurricanes and floods. There are several reasons for this. One is that there are more preventive and mitigating measures that can be adopted to deal with other types of natural disasters and one virtue of estimating the dollar value of economic impacts is that it offers some parameters of how much might be spent on prevention and mitigation using a cost-benefit approach. There is little that can be done to mitigate the effects of tornadoes other than construction improvements in terms of materials and incorporating basements in residential construction. It would be very difficult to do this within the framework of public policy; it could only be achieved by private sector (for example, individual or developer) actions. A second issue is that the geographical scope of most other natural disasters is much broader so that many more people are usually affected. Most disasters occur in urban areas whereas because of their limited spatial scale most tornadoes touch down in rural areas with sparse populations. Joplin is quite a small town but unusually large for a tornado-impacted area. Third, the location of a tornado is much less predictable. Of course, the existence of the 'Tornado Alley' is well known. However, its geographical boundaries are very vague not like the flood banks of the Mississippi, the hurricane zone on the Atlantic coast or the earthquake fault areas of California. Fourth, although tornadoes often have catastrophic effects, the fact that the impact areas are typically quite small and the number of people harmed is usually few helps explain why economic impact studies are rare. The Joplin tornado was more of an exception than the standard, and this helps to justify this study.

11.1   TORNADO FACTS

At 5:35 pm on Sunday, 22 May 2011 an EF4 (Enhanced Fujita Scale) tornado (later it became an EF5) related to a larger extratropical cyclone struck the city of Joplin, Missouri, which has a population of about 50,000. The winds were as high as 198 mph. The swath of the tornado was almost a mile wide. It killed 160 people and resulted in massive physical damage (as demonstrated later in this chapter). It was the deadliest tornado to hit the United States since 1947 and the first since 1953 to result in more than 100 deaths. The tornado first touched down at the Kansas–Missouri state line just southwest of Joplin and tracked east-northeast through major residential/commercial areas and intensified south of but close to downtown. The tornado destroyed several schools, downtown businesses and the St John's Regional Medical Center.

In March 2012, a series of tornados affected 12 states. The impact was serious but the number of deaths (34) was much lower than in Joplin. These occurred primarily in Kentucky and Indiana. About three-quarters of those killed lived in mobile homes, a recurrent phenomenon (one-third of the tornado-related deaths between 2006 and 2011), although not in Joplin.

11.2   APPROACH

Most of the studies on tornadoes focus solely on business interruption. Business interruption was important in Joplin too. Three major businesses were destroyed (St John's Hospital, Walmart and Home Depot) not to mention another 2,000 non-residential buildings, mainly small businesses but also public facilities such as schools and community centers. However, there were two other types of loss that are too large to be ignored: deaths (160 of them) and destroyed residential structures (about 7,000).

Hence, this study focuses on four economic impact components: business interruption; destruction and damage to houses; losses in housing services; and mortality costs. Residential structure losses and mortality costs are much easier to estimate, at least in approximate terms. Although it is difficult to find out a detailed breakdown of the housing types destroyed in the tornado a compromise is to multiply the number of dwelling units lost by the average price over all housing types. As for mortality costs, the key is the value attached to a human life. In earlier research, it was common to differentiate the numbers from one individual to another based on the discounted streams of future earnings, but in more recent years it has been more common on equity grounds to assign the same value of life to everyone. The consensus in recent research studies (for example, Dorman,

2009; Murphy and Topel, 2003; Viscusi, 2004) and by Federal agencies has been a range of $6 to $8 million. In this study we assign the average life value of $6 million at the low end of the scale to reflect the lower cost of living in Joplin compared, say, to Manhattan, New York City.

Estimating business interruptions for this study is much more difficult. Many of the case studies in this book deal with simulations rather than real world events so estimates of the direct effects are easy and errors barely matter. In the Joplin case, however, with 2,000 establishments affected it is very hard, without research in the field or detailed local knowledge, to come up with an accurate estimate of direct output and job losses and their sectoral allocation. It is relatively easy to measure the numbers for large enterprises such as Walmart, St John's Hospital and Home Depot, and for public sector activities such as schools and social services (eight schools were damaged, five so badly that they are being rebuilt; two fire stations were destroyed; and a large nursing home was wiped out with 11 deaths) but more complicated for small private sector businesses. Our best, although not perfect, approach is to allocate economic sector impacts according to the aggregate Joplin gross domestic product (GDP) proportions by sector (Table 11.1). A better allocation might require a degree of adjustment because the distribution of sectors in or near downtown (the area most impacted by the tornado) is not quite the same as in Joplin as a whole.

Although most of the business interruption effect measured via the National Interstate Economic Model (NIEMO) was because of non-residential buildings destroyed resulting in the loss of output and jobs, a modest component was associated with the loss of housing-related costs (for example, purchases of furniture, appliances and other household equipment, utility costs, property taxes) when houses are destroyed.

11.2.1   Items

Mortality costs
160 x $6 million = $960 million

Residential losses
(7,000 destroyed + 50% of 850 damaged) = 7,425 x $111,658 (average house prices in Joplin in 2009 from City-Data.com). This results in an estimate of residential losses of $829 million.

Housing services
The estimates are based on 2010 Consumer Expenditure Survey data for Missouri (US Department of Labor, Bureau of Labor Statistics, annual). There are five relevant USC sectors (Table 7.2). Annual average total

Table 11.1   Direct non-residential losses, Joplin City

Aggregate NAICS sector	Aggregate NAICS sector no.	Proportion of Joplin City output (%)	Direct estimates ($ million)
Agriculture, forestry, fishing, and hunting	11	2.71	53.43
Mining	21	0.20	3.97
Utilities	22	1.48	29.24
Construction	23	3.04	59.92
Durable goods manufacturing	33	11.94	235.36
Nondurable goods manufacturing	31–32	10.77	212.26
Wholesale trade	42	4.62	90.97
Retail trade	44–45	9.38	184.83
Transportation and warehousing	48–49	12.71	250.53
Information	51	1.90	37.54
Finance and insurance	52	3.32	65.34
Real estate and rental and leasing	53	4.32	85.19
Professional and technical services	54	2.18	42.96
Management of companies and enterprises	55	1.34	26.35
Administrative and waste services	56	3.06	60.29
Education, health and social services	61–62	11.85	233.56
Arts, entertainment, and recreation	71	0.33	6.50
Accommodation and food services	72	2.69	53.07
Other services, except government	81	2.78	54.87
Government	92	9.36	184.47
Total		100.00	1,971.00

Note: NAICS – North American Industry Classification System.

spending per household on housing services in Missouri was $8,591 and the total direct losses resulting from the 7,425 destroyed and severely damaged houses reaches $63.8 million, rising to $124.4 million including indirect and induced impacts.

Table 11.2   Direct housing services losses, 2010 data

Housing services components	USC sector	Annual adjusted average ($)	Direct losses ($ million)
Shelter-related costs	USC38	5,038	37.41
Utilities, fuel and public services	USC30	2,203	16.36
Household operating costs	USC43	811	6.02
Household spending on furniture	USC35	156	1.16
Household equipment spending	USC47	383	2.84
Total		8,591	63.79

Non-residential business interruption

The best estimate of total damages is $2.8 billion (ECECAT, 2011), not precisely verified but reasonable in light of estimated insurance payouts of $2.2 billion. The result of direct business interruption estimates is $2.8 billion – 829 million = $1.971 billion.

The impact analysis of non-residential business interruption involved three steps:

1. Constructing a proportional bridge that converts 2-digit NAICS sectors to the 47 USC sectors. The proportional bridge was built using the employment shares of Missouri available from IMPLAN data.
2. Allocating the total non-residential estimate of $1.971 billion according to the proportions of Joplin's 2008 GDP by NAICS sectors (Table 11.1).
3. Converting the NAICS sector-based estimates to the USC sectors using the bridge described above, and estimating the indirect effects (Table 11.3).

Interstate impacts were estimated via applying a supply-side version of NIEMO. Whereas the standard Multiregional Input-Output (MRIO) model is demand-based, a supply-side approach is more appropriate for estimating interregional trade effects. Unlike the standard model, it focuses on forward linkages rather than backward linkages. In this case, the decline in GDP in Joplin reduces imports from other states. However, this is offset to a degree by increased exports from other states substituting for unfulfilled demand in Joplin. The net effect in this type of analysis could vary from case to case. There is a debate whether the supply-driven model is appropriate for measuring forward linkages, but Park (2008) believes it is and this explains its use in this chapter.

Table 11.3 NIEMO results by USC sector ($ million)

USC sector	Description	Direct impacts	Indirect impacts	Total impacts
USC01	Live animals and live fish and meat, fish, seafood, and their preparations	34.47	32.68	67.15
USC02	Cereal grains and other agricultural products except for animal feed	28.08	8.93	37.01
USC03	Animal feed and products of animal origin, n.e.c.	9.25	13.07	22.31
USC04	Milled grain products and preparations, and bakery products	11.49	7.31	18.80
USC05	Other prepared foodstuffs and fats and oils	26.17	34.90	61.07
USC06	Alcoholic beverages	6.58	10.41	17.00
USC07	Tobacco products	0.03	0.08	0.10
USC08	Nonmetallic minerals (monumental or building stone, natural sands, gravel and crushed stone, n.e.c.)	2.14	1.16	3.30
USC09	Metallic ores and concentrates	0.80	0.68	1.48
USC10	Coal and petroleum products (coal and fuel oils, n.e.c.)	2.13	2.92	5.05
USC11	Basic chemicals	4.70	7.00	11.70
USC12	Pharmaceutical products	7.41	6.21	13.61
USC13	Fertilizers	0.81	0.70	1.51
USC14	Chemical products and preparations, n.e.c.	11.84	10.27	22.12
USC15	Plastics and rubber	28.55	16.04	44.59
USC16	Logs and other wood in the rough and wood products	16.47	9.75	26.22
USC17	Pulp, newsprint, paper, and paperboard and paper or paperboard articles	14.17	8.13	22.30

Table 11.3 (continued)

USC sector	Description	Direct impacts	Indirect impacts	Total impacts
USC18	Printed products	30.94	12.51	43.45
USC19	Textiles, leather, and articles of textiles or leather	19.26	7.57	26.84
USC20	Nonmetallic mineral products	15.68	7.68	23.36
USC21	Base metal in primary or semi-finished forms and in finished basic shapes	8.50	6.79	15.29
USC22	Articles of base metal	38.39	11.06	49.45
USC23	Machinery	50.18	22.78	72.95
USC24	Electronic and other electrical equipment and components, and office equipment	30.80	13.52	44.32
USC25	Motorized and other vehicles (including parts)	46.54	67.88	114.42
USC26	Transportation equipment, n.e.c.	20.15	14.86	35.01
USC27	Precision instruments and apparatus	7.47	2.70	10.17
USC28	Furniture, mattresses and mattress supports, lamps, lighting fittings, and illuminated signs	19.43	6.40	25.83
USC29	Miscellaneous manufactured products, scrap, mixed freight, and commodity unknown	14.70	4.78	19.47
USC30	Utility	29.25	10.90	40.15

USC31	Construction	59.94	73.55	133.48
USC32	Wholesale trade	90.99	35.13	126.11
USC33	Transportation	163.86	44.92	208.79
USC34	Postal and warehousing	86.71	6.70	93.41
USC35	Retail trade	184.86	42.18	227.04
USC36	Broadcasting and information services	28.29	26.87	55.16
USC37	Finance and insurance	65.35	39.97	105.32
USC38	Real estate and rental and leasing	85.21	34.42	119.63
USC39	Professional, scientific, and technical services	42.97	18.44	61.41
USC40	Management of companies and enterprises	26.36	8.58	34.94
USC41	Administrative support and waste management	60.30	12.63	72.92
USC42	Education services	28.09	4.53	32.61
USC43	Health care and social assistances	205.52	69.68	275.19
USC44	Arts, entertainment, and recreation	6.50	6.04	12.54
USC45	Accommodation and food services	53.08	32.40	85.47
USC46	Public administration	184.50	7.35	191.85
USC47	Other services except public administration	62.12	39.42	101.54
Total		1,971.00	862.45	2,833.45

In the context of the total direct economic impact of business interruption of $1.971 billion, the interregional trade impacts (excluding the intrastate effects in Missouri) associated with supply-side effects are relatively small, only $19.59 million. More than 50 percent of these impacts are concentrated in five states: Oklahoma (accounting for 32 percent of the total), Louisiana, Illinois, Kansas and Texas. Also, 70 percent of the nationwide impacts occurred in service sectors, especially in the retail trade.

Overall impacts

Most of the analysis in this chapter is based on Type 1 multipliers (that is, direct and indirect effects), but it is also necessary to estimate Type II multipliers (adding the induced (secondary consumption) impacts). However, because of the severe damage to the retail trade in Joplin, the induced effects were more significant at accessible locations outside the city, primarily in Newton and Jasper counties. In consequence, the analysis relies primarily on Missouri data (with minor modifications) and the induced effects are measured in the aggregate rather than relying on disaggregated sectoral data from Joplin.

The multipliers for Missouri are much lower than for the United States, largely because of low indirect effects. However, the indirect effects in Joplin are a little higher than in Missouri as a whole, 43.8 cents per direct dollar compared with 37.7 cents for Missouri. The Joplin Type II multiplier is 1.95 compared with the US estimate of 2.94. The overall business interruption impact including induced effects equals $1,971 × 1.95 = $3,843.5 million. The aggregate impact of the four main items (mortality costs, residential structure damage, housing services losses and business interruption) is estimated at $5,756.9 million (Table 11.4).

This estimate refers to the first year after the tornado. Some of the business interruption and housing services effects may have lingered on after May 2012; others may have recovered earlier. With more detailed information, adjustments could easily be made because NIEMO is linear. However, the numbers presented here are 'ballpark' estimates.

Table 11.4   Aggregate effects of the Joplin tornado in year 1

Main items	Estimated damages ($ million)
Mortality costs	960.0
Residential losses	829.0
Housing services	124.4
Business interruption	3,843.5
Total	5,756.9

11.2.2   Qualification

A common argument in natural disaster analysis is that the negative effects of business interruption after a major disaster are offset by the stimulus of subsequent recovery efforts. If the offset is complete, as is usually the case, the standard comment is that from an economic perspective the disaster is a 'wash.' This interpretation is completely misplaced. Leaving aside the social costs and the misery associated with a major disaster, the economic effects are far from neutral. The investments and other outlays needed to implement the recovery incur very high opportunity costs, the unavailability of resources that might have been used for other programs and/or other types of development. However, whatever the arguments that are marshaled, a disaster is a disaster not a worthy stimulus to the construction and social services industries.

11.3   MOORE, OKLAHOMA

A year after Joplin, there was another rash of tornadoes, the most serious in Moore, Oklahoma. Although the direct effects were of a similar order of magnitude (about $2 billion), the tornadoes were very different. The major distinction was that the Joplin hit was focused on downtown while the Moore tornado was spread out over a sprawling suburban area as shown in the image of Figure 11.1. This made a big difference to the death toll because many of the Joplin victims were concentrated in commercial and public buildings whereas the Moore victims were at home (although not too many of them because the tornado hit during afternoon working hours). The 24 deaths in Moore (a total cost of $144 million) contrasts with the 160 deaths in Joplin.

Reported figures for the Joplin tornado are that it destroyed 7,000 houses and damaged 850; in Moore, the numbers are 2,000 and 12,000, respectively. It is unclear whether the criteria were the same in both towns, but certainly the residential damages were significant. As usual, mobile homes figured prominently in both places.

The mobile home issue in particular raises the question of moral hazard. While it would be going too far to forbid mobile home construction in tornado-prone areas, an appropriate disincentive would be to stop Federal Emergency Management Agency (FEMA) compensation for damages (the same approach could be applied to the construction of standard homes without safe rooms or basements). As for shelters and safe rooms in schools, this is a problem that the public sector has to face.

Although we do not want to examine it in detail, another tornado

Source: Benjamin Krain, Getty Images.

Figure 11.1   Deadly storm strike that destroyed masses of houses and buildings in Moore, Oklahoma

worth mentioning is the one on 31 May 2013 that hit a southern suburb of Oklahoma City. It was the biggest tornado on record with a width of 2.6 miles; however, the death toll (23) was about the same as that in Moore. In addition, the 2014 tornado season has been quite dramatic. There have been more tornadoes, geographically very dispersed, extremely damaging to structures but fortunately not too many deaths.

11.4   CONCLUSIONS

The economic impacts of the Joplin tornado measured in this chapter are more of an approximate estimate than an accurate measure. There are two major reasons for this view. First, there is a degree of imprecision in identifying the details of the direct sectors (the authors are non-local and do not have the information about all the establishments destroyed or seriously damaged). Consequently, it was necessary in some cases to extrapolate from the sectoral distribution of output in the city as a whole. Second, the analysis here is based on the first year after the tornado while some of its adverse economic consequences lasted a little longer.

To put the scale of damage in some context, our estimate of the damages is about $5.757 billion. This is more than one year of Joplin's gross urban product. This implies that despite their short duration compared with some other natural disasters, such as hurricanes or floods, tornadoes may inflict massive damage. Earthquakes, also a short-term phenomenon except when there are severe aftershocks, rarely incur serious damage, at least in California. However, in both these types of disasters (tornadoes and earthquakes), the timing and location cannot be predicted (with the possible exception of very short tornado warnings). Hence, prevention and emergency preparedness are major problems, even more so with tornadoes than with earthquakes. As an example, as suggested, the prohibition of mobile homes in tornado-prone areas might have merit but its consequences for housing affordability would be serious.

REFERENCES

Dorman, P. (2009), *Markets and Mortality: Economics, Dangerous Work, and the Value of Human Life*. Cambridge: Cambridge University Press.

EQECAT (2011), *Devastating 2011 Tornado Season Continues: Joplin Tornado Could Cost $1–3 Billion*, available at http://www.eqecat.com.

Murphy, K.M. and R.H. Topel (2003), 'The value of health and longevity', *Journal of Political Economy*, **114**, 871–904.

Park, J. (2008), 'The economic impacts of dirty-bomb attacks on the Los Angeles and Long Beach ports: applying the supply-driven NIEMO (National Interstate Economic Model)', *Journal of Homeland Security and Emergency Management*, **5** (1). Article 21.

US Department of Labor, Bureau of Labor Statistics (annual), *Consumer Expenditure Survey*. Washington, DC: Bureau of Labor Statistics.

Viscusi, W.K. (2004), 'The value of life: estimates with risks by occupation and industry', *Economic Inquiry*, **42** (1), 29–48.

12. Hurricane Sandy

JiYoung Park, Harry W. Richardson, ChangKeun Park and Minsu Son

12.1 INTRODUCTION

Measuring economic impacts stemming from various natural disasters is an increasingly common interest in the United States. Even since the US economy experienced severe losses from the two hurricanes that consecutively hit the Gulf of Mexico coast in August 2005, we are still experiencing similar damage every year. The recent Hurricane Sandy is one of the greatest storms ever to hit the United States and clearly illustrates this problem, especially if a hurricane hits a mega metropolitan area located on the coast.

New York City (NYC) and Long Island have the most coast-concentrated population and economy in the United States. NYC and Long Island's geographical location exposes the region to a high level of vulnerability from the threat of storm surges. The recent physical disruptions and environmental damages caused by Hurricane Sandy demonstrate the fragility of NYC and Long Island in terms of built and natural environmental systems. Sandy and its profound impacts have prompted the discussion of constructing seawalls and other coastal barriers around the shorelines of the NYC and Long Island area to minimize the risk of destructive consequences from another such event in the future (Eshelman, 2012). New Jersey and Connecticut are two other states seriously affected.

Before Hurricane Sandy, the risk assessment studies for the city and its surrounding areas had been developed around the premise of a single or few flooding events. A recent study has begun analysing the flooding risk and its consequences more comprehensively (Aerts et al., 2013). So far, however, most of these studies have depended upon governmental reports, focusing on the magnitude of direct building losses or on speculations about future impacts on a damaged area. These economic impact readings have not accounted for indirect effects via economic and trade linkages, even though most direct economic losses lead to further economic losses via interindustrial and interregional economic relations. This research connects coastal hazards to economic impacts using the lost jobs during the first four days affected by Sandy available from a Census data source applied to the National Interstate Economic Model (NIEMO).

12.2 DATA

12.2.1 Input Data Process

Hurricane Sandy inflicted severe damage on several states. When Sandy hit, ten states had declared a state of emergency to report short-term economic losses mostly relating to job and building losses. The US Census Bureau provides the OnTheMap data for emergency management, which is an intuitive web-based interface; it allows us to access US population and workforce statistics in real time, especially for areas being affected by natural disasters.

We retrieved a report (MCEER, 2013) based on a study by the Federal Emergency Management Agency (FEMA) that calculated direct impacts, including the unemployed number of workers affected by Sandy from 26 October 2012 to 29 October 2012. The lost jobs by Sandy available from OnTheMap (onthemap.ces.census.gov) are classified only by state or by industry type (using the two-digit North American Industry Classification System, NAICS). With some minor adjustments to allocate job losses to each industry type per state using OnTheMap data, we applied average income data by industry sector available from the Bureau of Economic Analysis (BEA) to calculate income losses by industry and by the impacted state. The detailed steps and direct incomes losses follow.

First, we obtained two sets of day-by-day data of the affected workers from OnTheMap: the lost number of jobs for each state affected and the lost number of jobs by industry type for the entire region affected. Second, we calculated the day-by-day portion of each industry from the entire region dataset and multiplied the portion with the affected workers by state. We created new job losses affected by Sandy by each industry and by each state. Third, we prepared the average annual personal income by industry available from BEA. Fourth, we multiplied the new job losses with the average income in each industry from BEA. Finally, we transferred the two-digit NACIS code system to the USC sector system using the NAICS-USC bridge table developed by Park et al. (2007) and the weighted number of employment information at the national level available from IMPLAN. The final input data to the supply-side NIEMO application are presented in Table 12.1.

Table 12.1   Income losses of Hurricane Sandy by USC sector ($ million)

USC Sector	Income losses			
	26 October	27 October	28 October	29 October
USC01	−1.04	−0.64	−0.05	−183.53
USC02	−1.81	−1.14	−0.09	−322.24
USC03	−0.38	−0.24	−0.02	−68.26
USC04	−0.04	−0.01	0.00	−5.45
USC05	−0.60	−0.35	−0.03	−104.37
USC06	−0.01	0.00	0.00	−1.15
USC07	−0.03	−0.02	0.00	−5.07
USC08	−0.11	−0.35	0.00	−150.19
USC09	−0.03	−0.10	0.00	−43.76
USC10	−0.36	−1.15	−0.01	−486.48
USC11	−0.01	0.00	0.00	−2.01
USC12	−0.03	−0.01	0.00	−4.19
USC13	0.00	0.00	0.00	−0.55
USC14	−0.03	−0.01	0.00	−4.46
USC15	−0.09	−0.02	0.00	−13.04
USC16	−0.23	−0.12	−0.01	−39.02
USC17	−0.04	−0.01	0.00	−6.65
USC18	−0.27	−0.32	−0.02	−52.78
USC19	−0.19	−0.08	−0.01	−31.00
USC20	−0.05	−0.01	0.00	−7.22
USC21	−0.04	−0.01	0.00	−5.67
USC22	−0.11	−0.03	0.00	−16.53
USC23	−0.14	−0.03	0.00	−22.13
USC24	−0.35	−0.33	−0.02	−65.02
USC25	−0.11	−0.03	0.00	−16.82
USC26	−0.04	−0.01	0.00	−6.57
USC27	−0.05	−0.01	0.00	−7.78
USC28	−0.06	−0.01	0.00	−9.12
USC29	−0.15	−0.07	−0.01	−25.48
USC30	−1.50	−3.22	−0.18	−196.41
USC31	−2.32	−2.79	−0.18	−243.26
USC32	−3.55	−3.26	−0.21	−735.04
USC33	−0.66	−0.62	−0.04	−115.73
USC34	−0.37	−0.35	−0.02	−64.46
USC35	−0.90	−0.65	−0.08	−72.20
USC36	−0.68	−1.03	−0.06	−145.71
USC37	−1.24	−1.12	−0.11	−189.27
USC38	−0.03	−0.09	−0.02	−18.70
USC39	−7.07	−11.13	−0.62	−1,157.36
USC40	−0.18	−0.11	−0.01	−53.96

Table 12.1 (continued)

USC Sector	Income losses			
	26 October	27 October	28 October	29 October
USC41	−2.92	−2.58	−0.17	−303.85
USC42	−2.22	−4.38	−0.35	−342.37
USC43	−3.83	−3.89	−0.19	−403.39
USC44	−3.08	−6.01	−0.52	−358.55
USC45	−1.36	−2.68	−0.25	−155.04
USC46	−1.42	−0.94	−0.15	−243.39
USC47	−1.20	−1.60	−0.09	−413.75
Total	−40.92	−51.61	−3.53	−6,918.99

Note: Negative sign indicates economic losses.

The income losses of each day were highest on 29 October (−$6,919 million), followed by 27 October (−$52 million), 26 October (−$41 million), and 28 October (−$4 million). Furthermore, the losses were dominant in USC Sectors 32 (Wholesale Trade), 39 (Professional, Scientific, and Technical services), 42 (Education Services), 43 (Health Care and Social Assistances) and 44 (Arts, Entertainment, and Recreation), respectively.

The income losses of 26 October occurred in the state of Florida, and then the losses moved to the north to South Carolina and North Carolina. By 29 October, the losses occurred in Connecticut, Washington, DC, Maryland, New Hampshire, New Jersey, New York, North Carolina, Pennsylvania, Rhode Island and Virginia. The detailed income losses of each state by USC sector are shown in Table 12A.1 in the Appendix.

12.3 SUPPLY-SIDE NIEMO

Based on NIEMO constructed by Park et al. (2007), we applied the supply-side NIEMO to this part of the study. Park (2007, 2008) and Park et al. (2008) elaborated a supply-side NIEMO, including empirical tests. Equation (12.1) suggests the structure of the supply-side NIEMO in matrix form:

$$Q^I = V(I - GC)^{-1}, \tag{12.1}$$

where
Q^I = the total input row vector,

V = a row vector of region-specific value added factors,
G = $(\hat{Q}^d)^{-1}F$ and $\hat{Q}^d$ is the block diagonal matrix of vector Q^d, Q^d = the total output column vector,
F = the block diagonal matrix of direct technical flows between industries and
C = the block diagonal matrix of interregional trade flows.

12.4   RESULTS

We estimated income loss impacts of Hurricane Sandy on the US national economy using the supply-side NIEMO. In the result tables, 'Direct impact' refers to the initial economic impact experienced in each sector in each state relating to the income losses from Hurricane Sandy. These are the income losses of each day by USC sector. 'Indirect impact' indicates the economic impact from interindustry linkages, and these impacts are estimated via inverse coefficients in the supply-side NIEMO. A Type I multiplier describes the sum of direct and indirect impacts relative to direct impact. There are no Type II multipliers (measuring induced impacts in this chapter). The problem is that Hurricane Sandy resulted in the closure of retail stores and consumer facilities (although most of them were temporary). However, we did not have enough information about whether there are accessible substitutes to ensure no additional cutbacks in induced impacts.

We estimated the top three affected states' results of the income loss impacts by Hurricane Sandy (Table 12.2). The aggregated impacts of the days from 26 October through 29 October 2012 are displayed in the table. The full negative impacts are suggested in Table 12A.2 in the Appendix.

Table 12.2   Income loss impacts by Hurricane Sandy for the top three impacted states ($ million)

State	Direct impact	Indirect impact	Total impact
NY	−1,987.55	−808.45	−2,796.00
NJ	−1,084.01	−448.61	−1,532.62
NC	−790.65	−332.13	−1,122.78
US total	−7,015.04	−3,250.76	−10,265.80
Rest of world	0.00	−113.86	−113.86
World total	−7,015.04	−3,364.62	−10,379.66
Type I multiplier			1.48

Note: Negative sign indicates economic losses.

Because of the reduction of income during four days by $7 billion, the most affected state was New York ($-2.8 billion); New Jersey ($-1.5 billion) was second; and North Carolina ($-1.1 billion) third. The Type I multiplier was 1.48. The impacts of top three USC sectors for whole states are 39, 32 and 43, and the total economic losses are $1.3 billion, $0.9 billion and $0.7 billion, respectively.

A study of the impact of Sandy on New Jersey (Mantell et al., 2013) provides a useful comparison to our results. Although its results apply to the fourth quarter of 2012, most of the damages occurred in New Jersey on the fourth day of the hurricane (29 October 2012) so the comparability is quite reasonable. That study, using a very different model (R/ECON from the Bloustein School of Public Policy, Rutgers University), measured direct impacts at $1.2 billion compared with our estimate for a shorter time period using NIEMO of direct impacts at $1 billion (Mantell et al., 2013).

Recovery from Sandy still remains incomplete: there are beach areas where businesses remain closed; schemes from the government to buy up damaged/destroyed houses in flood-prone areas to permit residents to relocate rather than rebuild are on too small a scale to have much of an impact; denial of FEMA funds to coops; catering for residents who want to stay put that will delay a full recovery; insufficient funds from the federal government to the states for housing ($648 million on rebuilding houses and improving storm resistance out of $1.7 billion, part of a plan announced in 2013); expanding the number of potential evacuation zones in NYC to cover 3 million out of the 8 million resident population; a new Federal Flood Insurance law passed months before Sandy (in July 2012) that has dramatically increased both premiums and rebuilding costs; and the lag in offering mold treatments especially for low-income households.

Not all the reconstruction funds come from the public sector. Con Edison announced a not yet fully completed plan in late May 2013 to protect electricity substations in NYC and its northern suburbs by building a mile of concrete walls and steel plate glass to deal with future floods (Con Edison, 2013). The cost of the plan is estimated at $1 billion and would be recovered from utility customers. Certainly, the economic impact of Sandy is not yet at its maximum.

The recovery costs from Sandy will take at least until the end of 2014. To mention one example, the river tunnel subways (Lines G and R) from Brooklyn to Manhattan are closed from August 2013 for 14 months for repair. Mayor Bloomberg announced a plan in June 2013 to revise building ordinances to mitigate future flood problems. If implemented, the economic costs of Sandy might continue indefinitely (even though there would be compensating benefits). There have also been discussions about seagates to protect against future floods. Bae and Richardson (2008) analysed the Thames Barrier project that has protected Central London from flood surges since it was built in 1983. However, it took 17 years from 1966 to get it through and it took one man, Sir Hermann Bondi, a dominating scientific adviser to several prime ministers, not a politician, to achieve it. With only the Thames River Estuary flooding problem, London was relatively simple to resolve technically, if costly. The Port of London Authority grumbled that trade would shift east of the Barrier while the Transport Authority hated talk that the subways (Underground) might get flooded and were reluctant to pay for supplementary Barrier-related costs. However, Manhattan is much more complex, both technically and politically.

Probably the most detailed analysis of the economic impacts of Hurricane Sandy was published in September 2013 by the US Department of Commerce (2013). Its main component was construction costs in New York and New Jersey of $71.5 billion. It accounted for some Type 1 multiplier effects (measuring indirect effects, but rejected Type II multipliers because most of the construction workers came from outside the two states and spent much of their wages elsewhere (a similar process occurred in Florida after Hurricane Andrew in 1992)). Construction is still underway, but it is mixed between replacement and brand new construction (another example of the difficulty in separating out the effects of a natural disaster from standard changes in economic development). Calculating the total ultimate economic impact of Hurricane Sandy is very difficult with nothing better than a 'guestimate' of $130 billion, perhaps similar to the effects of Hurricane Katrina

12.5   HAZUS-NIEMO

12.5.1   Economic Loss Estimation Using HAZUS

To estimate total economic losses from potential disasters, it is essential to obtain or estimate direct losses from these disasters. HAZUS (Hazard US), software developed by FEMA, provides details for many scenarios and analyses on losses from potential disasters such as floods, hurricanes and earthquakes. Based on the Environmental Systems Research Institute's (ESRI) ArcGIS software, the HAZUS software provides data on most modern US historical experiences of natural disasters – as well as simulations and potential losses for similar disasters. These losses include physical damage, economic losses and social impacts. The economic loss in HAZUS only means directly impacted economic losses. However, due to the interrelations between industries, direct economic losses generally affect other industrial sectors. Still, input-output (IO) models are widely applied to capture the indirectly related economic impacts and provide total economic impacts stemming from the direct losses.

Currently, while HAZUS provides another tool for estimating indirect impacts based on the economic loss, its extension combining an IO model supported by IMPLAN software is not as easy to accept as the HAZUS results themselves directly. This is: (1) because of different sector classification systems by HAZUS and IMPLAN in spite of the fact that HAZUS provides a partial, but incomplete bridge; (2) a different concept of direct economic losses between the two softwares; and (3) IMPLAN's IO model only provides one region-specific information for the indirect impacts, while it is the most widely used IO model in the United States. However, there is no doubt that spatially interrelated, disaggregated information is important not only because political representatives have more interest in their own authority, but also because local economic losses can cancel each other when aggregated to the national level. The latter causes plausible measures at the national level to obscure key dimensions of events.

Therefore, the usefulness of an interstate Multiregional Input-Output (MRIO) model is clear. For the United States, the estimated subnational effects can provide proper mitigation and precautionary approaches to socioeconomic losses stemming from disasters. The recent development of NIEMO includes 47 industry sectors and 52 US states, District of Columbia and the rest of world (Park et al., 2007). As the first operational MRIO model of the United States, applying NIEMO to empirical studies of hypothetical terrorist attacks or natural disasters has already resulted in several publications (Park, 2008; Park et al., 2008; not to mention most of the chapters in this book). The most important merit in applying NIEMO is to provide interstate and interindustrial economic impacts, once direct economic losses are provided. Benefits combining NIEMO with HAZUS (NIEMO-HAZUS) are myriad in the sense that HAZUS provides historical and/or hypothetical scenarios plus direct economic losses from the natural disasters of the United States, and NIEMO can provide spatially distributed indirect and total economic losses occurring in the impacted region.

12.5.2 The Flood Information Tool

The flood loss estimation methodology consists of two basic analytical processes: flood hazard analysis and flood loss estimation analysis. Flood hazards in the Flood Information Tool (FIT) are divided into riverine and coastal. In the riverine hazard module, characteristics such as frequency, discharge and terrain elevation are used to model the spatial variation in flood elevation and flood depth. In the coastal hazard module, character-istics such as frequency, still water elevations, wave conditions and terrain information are used to model the spatial variation in flood-induced erosion, flood elevation and flood depth.

The FIT is an ArcGIS extension designed to process user-supplied flood hazard data into the format required by the HAZUS-MH (Multi-Hazard) Flood Model. The FIT, when given user supplied inputs (for example, ground elevations, flood elevations and floodplain boundary information), computes the extent, depth and elevation of flooding for riverine and coastal hazards. The overall FIT structure is provided in the upper panel of Figure 12.1, which also includes data input types and the FIT output (depth of flooding) to be used for the flood loss estimation.

12.5.3   Building HAZUS-NIEMO

Constructing HAZUS-NIEMO requires several steps.

1.   Generalizing recapture factors
One minor problem in the *economic loss* model of HAZUS is that the loss includes recapture amounts. Because the recapture factor is unitary at its maximum, the current economic loss might overestimate the direct economic losses available from HAZUS. Based on a new approach to gen-eralizing the recapture factors (Park et al., 2011) by region, industry and damage status from a disaster, HAZUS estimates of direct losses can be added to NIEMO. Recapture factors should be estimated along with every case study defined hypothetically or historically in the natural disaster of HAZUS.

2.   Constructing a conversion bridge
Constructing HAZUS-NIEMO requires building sector bridges between HAZUS and NIEMO. NIEMO sectors can easily be converted to other industrial sector schemes such as the North American Industry Classification System (NAICS), IMPLAN (Minnesota IMPLAN Group) sectors, BEA's industry sector system and so on. However, the HAZUS sector system is classified into occupational class types that are not directly converted to the industrial sector systems and requires a new conversion bridge so that HAZUS results can be plugged into NIEMO.

3.   Model testimony
Based on a new recapture function and newly developed sector bridges between HAZUS and NIEMO, there are six possible results:

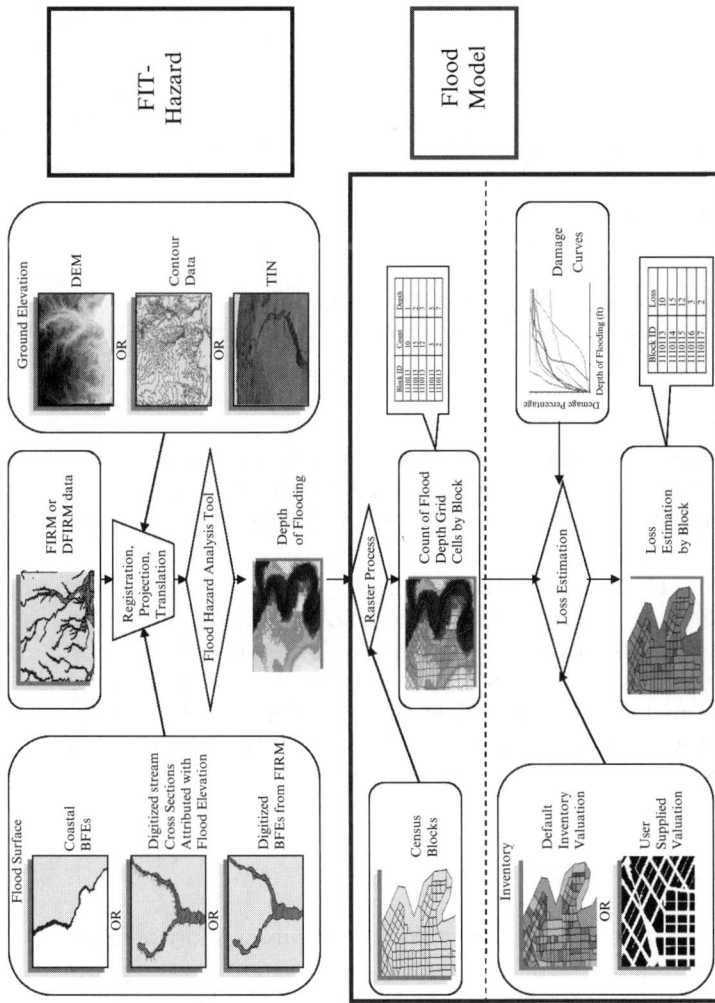

Note: BFE – Base Flood Elevations; FIRM – Flood Insurance Rate Map; DFIRM – Digital Flood Insurance Rate Map; TINs – Triangular Irregular Networks; DEM – Digital Elevation Model; FIT – Flood Information Tool.

Source: Multi-hazard Loss Estimation Methodology, Flood Model Technical Manual, available on the FEMA Hazus website at http://www.fema.gov/plan/prevent/hazus.

Figure 12.1   Overview of the integration of the FIT and the HAZUS Flood Model

Table 12.3   Comparison of Hurricane Andrew damage estimates for Florida

Effects	Without RF	With RF		Other results without RF
		Unitary RF	Adjusted RF	
Direct	HAZUS0	OHAZUS	HAZUS	$22.649 billion (West and Lenze, 1994)
Indirect	HAZUS0-NIEMO	OHAZUS-NIEMO	HAZUS-NIEMO	

Note: RF = Recapture Factor.

1. HAZUS0 (excluding unitary recapture factors)
2. OHAZUS (original HAZUS result without adjustment of economic loss)
3. HAZUS (with adjustments of economic losses with general recapture factor functions)
4. HAZUS0-NIEMO (adding indirect impacts to HAZUS0)
5. OHAZUS-NIEMO (adding indirect impacts to OHAZUS)
6. HAZUS-NIEMO (adding indirect impacts to HAZUS).

Table 12.3 shows all possible models explained above. A case study of Hurricane Andrew is selected to compare HAZUS-NIEMO with other HAZUS-related results. Because Hurricane Andrew is one of the most expensive natural disasters in US history (Liu et. al., 1997), of which the cost was estimated from $20 billion to $25 billion (Reinhold, 1995; Willoughby and Black, 1995), another benefit would be to compare the six results with the previous studies of Hurricane Andrew.

12.6   CONCLUSIONS

In this chapter, we have analysed economic impacts using short-term job losses associated with Hurricane Sandy. We traced Sandy's moving path from Florida to New Hampshire. Since Hurricanes Katrina and Rita, Sandy brought another tragedy mainly to the NYC and Long Island areas, reaching $2.8 billion in four days with 99 percent of the loss occurring in the last day of Sandy. Furthermore, the national impacts attained $10 billion losses as shown by the NIEMO interindustrial and interregional economic model.

While Sandy resulted in physical disruptions and environmental damages, this study does not include the losses associated with these. These consequences need to be analysed in a different way. We introduced a conceptual approach to combining HAZUS with NIEMO. The HAZUS-NIEMO approach will contribute to: (1) a disaster policy simulation model that combines with a state-by-state economic model; (2) resilient paths of the lost business production; and (3) the economic effects of mitigation and prevention policies that have been already implemented, to be modified or to be newly introduced for a future disaster. It is another virtue that the NIEMO-HAZUS approach can supply most historical and/or hypothetical scenarios plus direct economic losses from the natural disasters of the United States.

The results measured by HAZUS-NIEMO will advance our understanding on how Hurricane Sandy could affect the state economies and how various adaptation and resilience efforts have been and can be effective in reducing the economic losses after a disaster. It would be an important benefit for HAZUS-NIEMO to provide long-term strategies on the effectiveness of disaster policies against coastal hazards in this and other regions for local, state and federal planners and policy makers.

REFERENCES

Aerts, J.C.J.H., K. Emanuel, N. Lin, H. De Moel and W.J. Botzen (2013), 'Low-probability flood risk modeling for New York City', *Risk Analysis*, **33** (5), 772–88.

Bae C.-H.C. Bae and H.W. Richardson (2008), 'Not Katrina: the Thames barrier decision', in H.W. Richardson, P. Gordon and J.E. Moore II (eds), *Natural Disaster Analysis After Hurricane Katrina*. Cheltenham, UK and Northampton, MA, USA: Edward Elgar, pp. 120–33.

Con Edison (2013a), *Fortifying the Future*, available at http://www.coned.com/newsroom/news/pr20130528.asp.

Con Edison (2013b), *Post-Sandy Enhancement Plan*, available at http://www.coned.com/public_issues/pdf/post_sandy_enhancement_plan.

Eshelman, R.S. (2012), 'Adaptation: political support for a sea wall in New York Harbor begins to form', available at http://www.eenews.net/stories/ 1059972561.

Liu, Y., D. Zhang and M.K. Yau (1997), 'A multiscale numerical study of Hurricane Andrew (1992). Part I: explicit simulation and verification', *Monthly Weather Review*, **125** (12), 3073–93.

Mantell, N.H., J.J. Seneca, M. Lahr and W. Irving (2013), 'The economic and fiscal impacts of Hurricane Sandy in New Jersey', Rutgers Regional Report, Issue Paper Number 34. The State University of New Jersey, New Brunswick, NJ.

MCEER (2012), *Post-tropical Cyclone Sandy 2012 – Statistics and News*. Buffalo, NY: MCEER.

Park, J.Y. (2007), 'The supply-driven input-output model: a reinterpretation and extension', Paper presented at the 46th Annual Meeting of the Western Regional Science Association, Newport Beach, California, 21–24 February.

Park, J.Y. (2008), 'The economic impacts of dirty-bomb attacks on the Los Angeles and Long Beach ports: applying the supply-driven NIEMO (National Interstate Economic Model)', *Journal of Homeland Security and Emergency Management*, 5 (1), Article 21.

Park, J.Y., P. Gordon, J.E. Moore II, H.W. Richardson and L. Wang (2007), 'Simulating the state-by-state effects of terrorist attacks on three major U.S. ports: applying NIEMO (National Interstate Economic Model)', in H.W. Richardson, P. Gordon and J.E. Moore II (eds), *The Economic Costs and Consequences of Terrorism*. Cheltenham, UK and Northampton, MA, USA: Edward Elgar, pp. 208–34.

Park, J.Y., P. Gordon, S.J. Kim, Y.K. Kim, J.E. Moore II and H.W. Richardson (2008), 'Estimating the state-by-state economic impacts of Hurricane Katrina', in H.W. Richardson, P. Gordon and J.E. Moore II (eds), *Natural Disaster Analysis After Hurricane Katrina*. Cheltenham, UK and Northampton, MA, USA: Edward Elgar, pp. 147–86.

Park, J.Y., J.K. Cho and A. Rose (2011), 'Modeling a major source of economic resilience to disasters: recapturing lost production', *Natural Hazards*, 58 (1), 163–82.

Park, J.Y., J.E. Moore II and H. Richardson (2013), 'The interregional and inter-industry impacts of the Gulf oil spill: applying the National Interstate Economic Model (NIEMO)', *Journal of Homeland Security and Emergency Management*, 10 (1), 231–44.

Reinhold, P. (1995), 'An exposure-based analysis of property-liability insurer stock values around Hurricane Andrew', *Journal of Risk and Insurance*, 62 (1), 111–23.

US Department of Commerce (2013), *Economic Impact of Hurricane Sandy*. Washington, DC: US Department of Commerce.

West, C.T. and D.G. Lenze (1994), 'Modeling the regional impact of natural disaster and recovery: a general framework and an application to Hurricane Andrew', *International Regional Science Review*, 17, 121–50.

Willoughby, H.E. and P.G. Black (1995), 'Hurricane Andrew in Florida: dynamics of a disaster', *Bulletin of the American Meteorological Society*, 77 (3), 543–9.

APPENDIX

Table 12A.1 Income losses in each state by USC sector ($ million)

USC sectors	Oct. 26	Oct. 27		Oct. 28	Oct. 29									
	FL	NC	SC	NC	CT	DC	MD	NC	NH	NJ	NY	PA	RI	VA
USC 1	-1.039	-0.574	-0.064	-0.049	-16.696	-2.384	-13.532	-5.052	-2.367	-27.994	-89.583	-10.660	-5.015	-10.250
USC 2	-1.815	-1.026	-0.115	-0.087	-29.912	-0.338	-23.651	-8.844	-4.183	-50.156	-159.634	-18.485	-8.969	-18.063
USC 3	-0.385	-0.216	-0.024	-0.018	-6.305	-0.271	-5.015	-1.875	-0.885	-10.572	-33.693	-3.928	-1.891	-3.823
USC 4	-0.036	-0.008	-0.001	-0.001	-0.200	-1.978	-0.455	-0.163	-0.056	-0.333	-1.497	-0.431	-0.068	-0.271
USC 5	-0.596	-0.317	-0.035	-0.027	-9.201	-3.251	-7.748	-2.886	-1.332	-15.425	-49.790	-6.175	-2.772	-5.796
USC 6	-0.008	-0.002	-0.000	-0.000	-0.042	-0.419	-0.096	-0.035	-0.012	-0.071	-0.317	-0.091	-0.014	-0.057
USC 7	-0.029	-0.015	-0.002	-0.001	-0.449	-0.139	-0.376	-0.140	-0.065	-0.754	-2.428	-0.299	-0.135	-0.282
USC 8	-0.107	-0.321	-0.034	-0.003	-14.960	-0.007	-18.501	-9.555	-1.770	-41.297	-51.241	-2.413	-2.283	-8.168
USC 9	-0.031	-0.094	-0.010	-0.001	-4.358	-0.007	-5.390	-2.784	-0.516	-12.029	-14.928	-0.704	-0.665	-2.380
USC 10	-0.355	-1.039	-0.109	-0.011	-48.356	-0.591	-59.863	-30.897	-5.730	-133.428	-165.867	-7.913	-7.389	-26.449
USC 11	-0.013	-0.003	-0.000	-0.000	-0.074	-0.729	-0.168	-0.060	-0.021	-0.123	-0.552	-0.159	-0.025	-0.100
USC 12	-0.027	-0.006	-0.000	-0.000	-0.153	-1.519	-0.349	-0.125	-0.043	-0.256	-1.150	-0.331	-0.052	-0.208
USC 13	-0.004	-0.001	-0.000	-0.000	-0.020	-0.200	-0.046	-0.016	-0.006	-0.034	-0.151	-0.043	-0.007	-0.027
USC 14	-0.029	-0.006	-0.000	-0.000	-0.163	-1.619	-0.372	-0.133	-0.046	-0.273	-1.226	-0.353	-0.056	-0.222
USC 15	-0.085	-0.018	-0.001	-0.001	-0.477	-4.731	-1.088	-0.390	-0.135	-0.797	-3.582	-1.030	-0.163	-0.648
USC 16	-0.226	-0.112	-0.012	-0.009	-3.218	-2.641	-2.936	-1.088	-0.488	-5.393	-17.741	-2.394	-0.975	-2.141
USC 17	-0.044	-0.009	-0.001	-0.001	-0.243	-2.413	-0.555	-0.199	-0.069	-0.406	-1.826	-0.525	-0.083	-0.331
USC 18	-0.265	-0.280	-0.041	-0.020	-3.055	-6.158	-5.656	-5.955	-1.174	-5.938	-10.545	-7.496	-0.676	-6.126
USC 19	-0.188	-0.072	-0.007	-0.006	-2.027	-5.502	-2.427	-0.888	-0.363	-3.395	-12.017	-2.105	-0.630	-1.642
USC 20	-0.047	-0.010	-0.001	-0.001	-0.264	-2.621	-0.603	-0.216	-0.075	-0.441	-1.984	-0.571	-0.090	-0.359
USC 21	-0.037	-0.008	-0.001	-0.001	-0.208	-2.058	-0.473	-0.170	-0.059	-0.347	-1.558	-0.448	-0.071	-0.282
USC 22	-0.108	-0.023	-0.002	-0.002	-0.605	-5.995	-1.379	-0.494	-0.171	-1.010	-4.538	-1.305	-0.206	-0.822
USC 23	-0.145	-0.031	-0.002	-0.002	-0.810	-8.027	-1.847	-0.662	-0.229	-1.352	-6.077	-1.748	-0.276	-1.100

Table 12A.1 (continued)

USC sectors	Oct. 26	Oct. 27		Oct. 28	Oct. 29									
	FL	NC	SC	NC	CT	DC	MD	NC	NH	NJ	NY	PA	RI	VA
USC 24	-0.348	-0.290	-0.041	-0.021	-3.464	-11.056	-6.633	-6.168	-1.279	-6.591	-14.046	-8.347	-0.828	-6.612
USC 25	-0.110	-0.024	-0.002	-0.002	-0.616	-6.102	-1.404	-0.503	-0.174	-1.028	-4.619	-1.328	-0.210	-0.836
USC 26	-0.043	-0.009	-0.001	-0.001	-0.240	-2.382	-0.548	-0.196	-0.068	-0.401	-1.803	-0.519	-0.082	-0.326
USC 27	-0.051	-0.011	-0.001	-0.001	-0.285	-2.822	-0.649	-0.233	-0.081	-0.475	-2.136	-0.614	-0.097	-0.387
USC 28	-0.060	-0.013	-0.001	-0.001	-0.334	-3.310	-0.761	-0.273	-0.095	-0.558	-2.505	-0.721	-0.114	-0.454
USC 29	-0.151	-0.066	-0.007	-0.005	-1.879	-3.157	-1.957	-0.721	-0.308	-3.148	-10.714	-1.649	-0.576	-1.374
USC 30	-1.502	-3.176	-0.048	-0.184	-14.043	-1.931	-9.703	-31.655	-2.361	-32.452	-46.095	-28.233	-5.730	-24.207
USC 31	-2.320	-2.411	-0.383	-0.180	-18.007	-18.577	-16.158	-24.787	-5.659	-46.005	-64.216	-25.311	-3.489	-21.049
USC 32	-3.547	-2.864	-0.396	-0.208	-48.171	-70.484	-72.917	-58.093	-14.398	-68.855	-193.506	-110.391	-14.701	-83.521
USC 33	-0.659	-0.537	-0.088	-0.041	-8.030	-11.716	-11.240	-14.607	-3.622	-11.424	-27.956	-10.276	-2.791	-14.071
USC 34	-0.367	-0.299	-0.049	-0.023	-4.473	-6.526	-6.261	-8.136	-2.018	-6.363	-15.572	-5.724	-1.554	-7.838
USC 35	-0.895	-0.599	-0.048	-0.085	-2.906	-5.387	-5.220	-5.787	-0.728	-7.754	-30.498	-8.394	-0.855	-4.670
USC 36	-0.684	-0.898	-0.136	-0.064	-9.119	-9.084	-16.376	-19.109	-3.624	-18.045	-26.706	-22.723	-1.879	-19.048
USC 37	-1.240	-1.000	-0.123	-0.109	-6.667	-3.452	-20.334	-34.847	-4.231	-23.662	-36.349	-25.298	-2.825	-31.600
USC 38	-0.034	-0.084	-0.009	-0.019	-0.474	-0.011	-0.468	-0.658	-0.167	-0.656	-1.241	-11.618	-0.000	-3.403
USC 39	-7.070	-9.727	-1.407	-0.617	-72.759	-43.206	-116.136	-205.572	-23.042	-134.338	-281.711	-128.663	-25.780	-126.152
USC 40	-0.176	-0.072	-0.040	-0.008	-2.971	-3.384	-11.637	-3.783	-1.483	-6.334	-15.073	-5.409	-0.368	-3.521
USC 41	-2.924	-2.340	-0.242	-0.173	-22.102	-2.773	-35.647	-30.466	-8.842	-40.014	-75.870	-47.968	-4.787	-35.384
USC 42	-2.220	-3.865	-0.519	-0.345	-33.234	-0.379	-19.368	-62.685	-10.646	-52.261	-55.035	-69.229	-5.453	-34.076
USC 43	-3.833	-3.469	-0.420	-0.191	-29.317	-3.026	-31.027	-54.837	-10.609	-84.520	-82.293	-57.784	-5.093	-44.887
USC 44	-3.082	-5.339	-0.671	-0.523	-13.341	-2.627	-38.818	-46.876	-11.180	-66.752	-80.121	-53.026	-4.671	-41.134
USC 45	-1.362	-2.443	-0.242	-0.248	-9.132	-1.033	-12.847	-14.415	-1.893	-32.790	-37.214	-27.173	-1.310	-17.234
USC 46	-1.424	-0.864	-0.077	-0.149	-18.885	-1.753	-10.407	-15.185	-4.434	-35.615	-91.751	-35.225	-4.094	-26.044
USC 47	-1.203	-1.476	-0.123	-0.091	-38.592	-1.140	-42.728	-28.840	-4.884	-92.145	-158.588	-15.968	-7.762	-23.105
Total	-40.923	-46.070	-5.535	-3.528	-500.84	-268.92	-641.771	-741.055	-135.62	-1084.01	-1987.55	-771.196	-127.56	-660.480

Note: Negative sign indicates economic losses.

218

Table 12A.2   Income loss impacts from Hurricane Sandy ($ million)

State	Direct impact	Indirect impact	Total impact
AL	0.0000	−7.6019	−7.6019
AK	0.0000	−1.2517	−1.2517
AZ	0.0000	−5.5135	−5.5135
AR	0.0000	−3.6420	−3.6420
CA	0.0000	−49.1253	−49.1253
CO	0.0000	−7.0589	−7.0589
CT	−500.8351	−199.5441	−700.3792
DE	0.0000	−5.1775	−5.1775
DC	−268.9149	−87.5501	−356.4650
FL	−40.9229	−43.6025	−84.5254
GA	0.0000	−16.1538	−16.1538
HI	0.0000	−2.0611	−2.0611
ID	0.0000	−1.4826	−1.4826
IL	0.0000	−23.7699	−23.7699
IN	0.0000	−10.3701	−10.3701
IA	0.0000	−5.8395	−5.8395
KS	0.0000	−4.6823	−4.6823
KY	0.0000	−6.2082	−6.2082
LA	0.0000	−5.9758	−5.9758
ME	0.0000	−4.6431	−4.6431
MD	−641.7710	−280.8488	−922.6198
MA	0.0000	−30.8259	−30.8259
MI	0.0000	−18.8088	−18.8088
MN	0.0000	−7.5224	−7.5224
MS	0.0000	−3.7559	−3.7559
MO	0.0000	−8.3069	−8.3069
MT	0.0000	−1.2149	−1.2149
NE	0.0000	−3.0994	−3.0994
NV	0.0000	−2.1973	−2.1973
NH	−135.6202	−53.9827	−189.6029
NJ	−1,084.0073	−448.6113	−1,532.6186
NM	0.0000	−2.0005	−2.0005
NY	−1,987.5464	−808.4490	−2,795.9954
NC	−790.6532	−332.1289	−1,122.7822
ND	0.0000	−1.1363	−1.1363
OH	0.0000	−28.6345	−28.6345
OK	0.0000	−4.8809	−4.8809
OR	0.0000	−3.9606	−3.9606
PA	−771.1960	−336.8265	−1,108.0225
RI	−127.5603	−49.7850	−177.3453
SC	−5.5351	−13.8146	−19.3498
SD	0.0000	−1.3279	−1.3279

Table 12A.2   (continued)

State	Direct impact	Indirect impact	Total impact
TN	0.0000	−10.6721	−10.6721
TX	0.0000	−34.5049	−34.5049
UT	0.0000	−2.3815	−2.3815
VM	0.0000	−3.6914	−3.6914
VA	−660.4797	−240.9923	−901.4720
WA	0.0000	−8.3913	−8.3913
WV	0.0000	−5.5352	−5.5352
WI	0.0000	−10.3925	−10.3925
WY	0.0000	−0.8241	−0.8241
US total	−7,015.04	−3,250.76	−10,265.80
Rest of world	0.00	−113.8617	−113.8617
World total	−7,015.04	−3,364.62	−10,379.66

Note: Negative sign indicates economic losses.

13. West Coast ports shutdown

JiYoung Park, Peter Gordon, James E. Moore II and Harry W. Richardson

13.1 INTRODUCTION

The terrorist attack of 2001 prompted renewed interest in port security. The 11-day shutdown of the West Coast ports in 2002 as a result of the lock-out of potentially striking port workers was a natural experiment leading to considerable economic losses. It is not accurate to treat an economic impact analysis of the ports shutdown case as if it was the same as a terrorist attack because the predictable nature of a labor action makes it different. However, it remains possible to study the extent to which substitutions were made because the experience may have informed important contingency planning by shippers. The purpose of this study is to examine the extent to which the event's impacts were mitigated via substitutions over time, by mode and by port.

Attacks on key operational ports such as the Los Angeles and Long Beach twin ports, for example, by dirty bombs, may have profound non-economic as well as economic consequences from direct losses of lives and commodities. Also, during the time that any leaked radiation is cleaned up, the ports and areas around the ports would be shut down resulting in substantial indirect economic losses (Gordon et al., 2005). Because the Los Angeles and Long Beach twin ports account for 17 percent of all US exports and 32 percent of all US imports, the economic losses would spread nationally (Park, 2008). Bouchard's (2005, pp. 5–6) Department of Homeland Security report on port disruptions is interesting in this respect.

> Various estimates have been made of the impact that a terrorist attack on a seaport would have, particularly if the federal response were to shut down all shipping. On September 11, all air, land and sea ports of entry were closed. This caused some factories to shut down and stores to run low on some goods. The 2002 dock worker lockout at the ports of Los Angeles and Long Beach is estimated to have cost between $6.3 billion to $19.4 billion in loss to the U.S. economy, with the lower figure being most credible. A 2002 port security war

game, which simulated a nine-day shutdown of all U.S. ports, resulted in an estimated $58 billion loss. The Brookings Institution estimated that a successful terrorist attack with a weapon of mass destruction smuggled into the country in a shipping container could amount to $1 trillion if subsequent draconian security measures were adopted that impeded trade. A Center for Homeland Security and Defense (CHSD) estimate of the impact of a terrorist attack on U.S. ports begins with an immediate impact of between $1.5 and $2.7 billion dollars a day loss; rising to $5 billion a day after 3–5 days; and exponentially within 10–15 days. After about 45 days, perhaps even sooner, the U.S. economy would collapse into an unprecedented depression due to a severe energy crisis, widespread shortages and rampant price gouging by the energy industry.

Apparently, the Department of Homeland Security regards the consequences of terrorist attacks as comparable to a port shutdown from a labor dispute. A study by Cohen (2002) reports the total losses from the shutdown were $1.96 billion per day.

However, while the times and places of labor actions are generally anticipated, terrorist attacks are not. Further, because the Los Angeles and Long Beach ports are in densely settled areas of Southern California with close links to many industrial activities, the anticipated lock-out case should be differentiated from any unexpected disaster. For the latter, it is unclear how quickly and how adequately alternative shipping options such as to ports in San Diego or Oakland might be discovered. The Congressional Budget Office (CBO, 2006) and Hall (2004) suggest that more sophisticated models with additional data are required to better understand such impacts. Therefore, a study of the West Coast ports shutdown that can account for possible substitution effects that might have occurred from choosing other ports or other modes, or adjusting trade behavior for the periods before or after the shutdown makes sense.

For this study, we consider three types of possible substitution effects: between modes; between periods; and between ports. To address these substitutions, we used monthly Customs District shipments data by mode for the West Coast regions for the period January 2000 to December 2003. Without considering industrial sectors, we can verify some intuitions via Figures 13.1 through 13.4. These monthly data suggest that trade by air and other modes were up modestly for imports and exports during October 2002. However, Figures 13.3 and 13.4 show that trade activities differed by Customs District. As also seen in the figures, because the sea vessel mode and Los Angeles Customs District had the largest trade volume, our research focus should be on this mode and this district. Also instead of only analysing economic impacts for the shutdown period, we examined the 'before' and 'after' periods of four months each, respectively. We sought to identify pre-event effects as shippers may have planned for

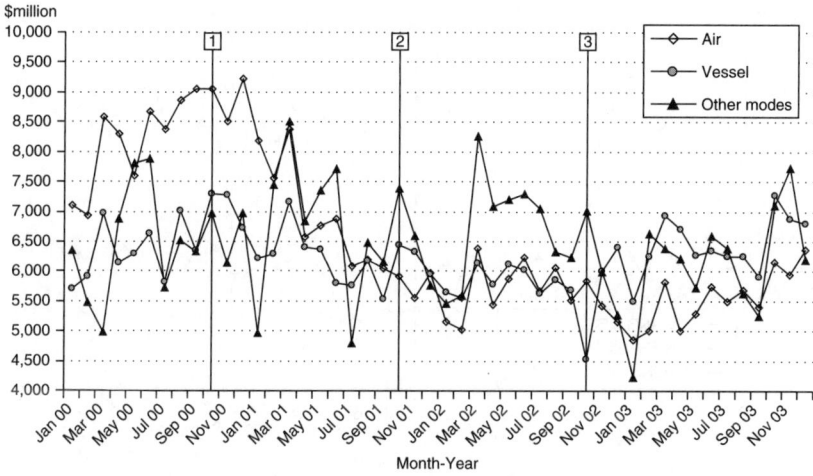

Note: Line 3 indicates the month the ports shutdown occurred.

Figure 13.1   Total exports of West Coast area by mode

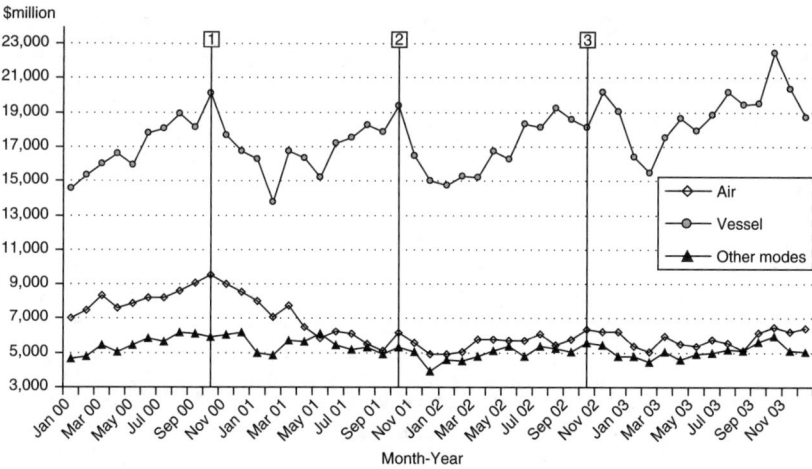

Note: Line 3 indicates the month the ports shutdown occurred.

Figure 13.2   Total imports of West Coast area by mode

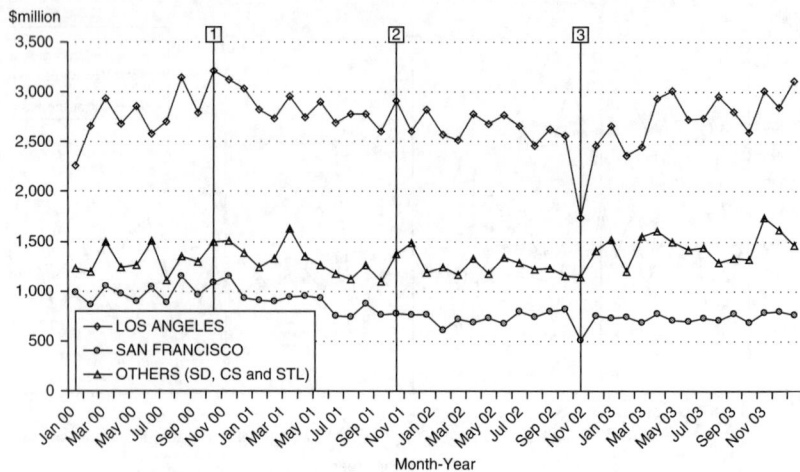

Note: Other Customs Districts include San Diego, Columbia-Snake and Seattle. Line 3 indicates the month the ports shutdown occurred.

Figure 13.3   Foreign exports for vessel mode by Customs District

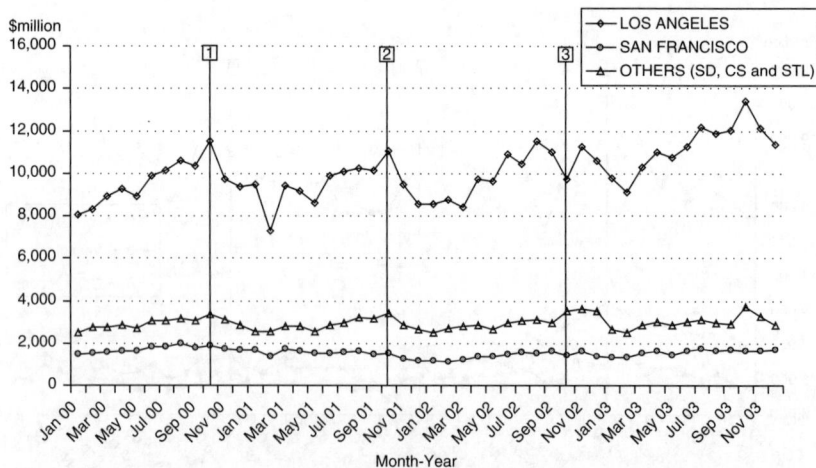

Note: Other Customs Districts include San Diego, Columbia-Snake and Seattle. Line 3 indicates the month the ports shutdown occurred.

Figure 13.4   Foreign imports for vessel mode by Customs District

the shutdown. We also looked at post-event effects that may have included catch-up and recovery efforts.

To control for industry sector differences, we used a multilevel model instead of using dummy variables. Using the multilevel model, we tested various substitutions: (1) periodic changes, (2) regional (ports) changes and (3) modal changes. Based on our tests and estimated coefficients, we estimated the expected normal status of trade. With the help of direct impacts obtained from the difference between the actual and estimated trades, we calculated total economic impacts using the National Interstate Economic Model (NIEMO).

The next section provides background on NIEMO-type models and their applications. The third section describes methodology and data necessary to test our hypotheses. The results of multilevel estimations and the application of NIEMO, and policy implications of the results are addressed in the fourth section. The chapter concludes with a brief summary and caveats.

13.2 BACKGROUND

13.2.1 The National Interstate Economic Model

The detailed steps involved in constructing NIEMO are described in Park et al. (2007) and in Chapter 2, so only a brief introduction is included here. Following the suggestion of an ideal Interregional Input-Output model (IRIO) by Isard (1951), a Chenery–Moses-type Multiregional Input-Output (MRIO) model was developed as an alternative and potentially operational approach requiring a simpler data set than an IRIO (Chenery, 1953; Moses, 1955). NIEMO revives an approach adopted in the late 1970s and early 1980s (Jack Faucett Associates, 1983; Polenske, 1980), the development of a MRIO model. NIEMO is an operational state-level model of the United States; it combines state (and District of Columbia data) from 51 IMPLAN input-output models with interregional trade flows based on the Commodity Flow Survey (CFS). Data from both are aggregated to 47 economic sectors (we call them the USC sectors, 29 commodity sectors and 18 service sectors). They are easily converted to other US industry codes, including the North American Industry Classification System (NAICS). The model simulates production and trade between 52 regions (50 states, Washington, DC and the 'Rest of the World'). This results in a MRIO matrix with almost 6 million cells.

Among NIEMO's many strengths, the most important is the ability to estimate spatially detailed indirect economic impacts. Direct economic impacts by place are often estimated in the aftermath of an event. If, for example, plausible scenarios for the time-profile of reduced shipping facilities are available, spatially detailed indirect and induced economic effects can be estimated with a NIEMO-type model. Standard applications of input-output (IO) approaches that determine indirect and induced impacts typically do not include interactions between industries across various regions.

Preliminary results to test NIEMO's accuracy showed that approximately 6 million multipliers within NIEMO can be estimated at low cost. We have also shown that NIEMO's estimates are plausible (Park, 2008). A book chapter by Park et al. (2007) reports the estimates of the state-by-state impacts of hypothetical terrorist attacks on three major US ports, applying the demand-side version of NIEMO. Also using NIEMO, Richardson et al. (2007) examined the national and interstate economic impacts of terrorist attacks on major US theme parks (see Chapter 4).

Park et al. (2006) reported the economic impacts from foreign export closures resulting from Bovine Spongiform Encephalopathy (BSE) in the State of Washington. The development and application of a supply-driven NIEMO can be found in Park (2008). Recently, demand- and supply-driven versions of NIEMO were applied to address the economic impacts of Hurricane Katrina (Park et al., 2008).

13.2.2 West Coast Ports Shutdown

A widely cited report by Cohen (2002) put the ports' shutdown impacts on the US economy at $1.96 billion per day. However, Anderson and Geckil (2002) reported the total economic losses were approximately $1.67 billion for 12 days, that is, $140 million per day, but only considering the actual reduction in US earnings. This was also noted by CBO (2006) and Hall (2004). According to recent CBO estimates that included some adjustments, the estimated impacts declined to $6 million per day in a one-week port shutdown (CBO, 2006, p. 17). Furthermore, another CBO approach using willingness-to-pay information suggested that the economic losses would be $65 million per day on average for a one-week shut own (CBO, 2006, p. 18). In other words, the estimates are all over the place.

We first set up econometric models to estimate the potential substitution effects, and then modeled these via NIEMO. The next section examines these two methodologies.

13.3   DATA AND MODELS

Our approach required two procedures. The first was to estimate direct economic impacts necessary to implement NIEMO. The second was to exercise NIEMO to estimate indirect and total economic impacts on the basis of the estimated direct impacts.

13.3.1   Data

To estimate direct impacts, we required an approach to identify several plausible substitution effects because of the ports shutdown. Because we hypothesize possible periodic, regional (port) and modal substitutions, it is important to assemble a robust econometric model from which the estimated values can be used to estimate direct economic impacts of the shutdown. We used WISERTrade data (a widely used source of proprietary data from http://www.wisertrade.org/home/index.jsp) at the Customs District level for the period January 2000 to December 2003. The WISERTrade data for the West Coast areas are available for five Customs Districts: San Diego, Los Angeles, San Francisco, Columbia-Snake and Seattle, consisting of 98 seaports and airports.[1] Also, because the data are provided for the four-digit Harmonized System (HS) code, we converted these data to the 29 USC Commodity Sector system to be used for the NIEMO runs. This was based on a conversion technique reported in Park et al. (2007). The total available observations were 6,960 by each mode for imports and exports, respectively, and we constructed separate econometric models for each mode and trade type.[2] This is because the trade patterns by mode (vessel, air and other modes[3]) and by trade type (imports and exports) are different from each other. Therefore, we modified the raw data from WISERTrade into six pairs, which commonly have the same number of 6,960 observations.

13.3.2   Multilevel Linear Model and Variables

For the first procedure, we used a multilevel model. Multilevel models are widely used when observations in the sample data are nested in a higher-level group. If we use the traditional ordinary least squares (OLS) approach for the estimation of parameters, we cannot consider the different effects of each sector on each observation because OLS assumes that each observation behaves independently irrespective of its sector. Also, the statistical problems associated with OLS are reduced when using the random coefficients method (Bryk and Raudenbush, 1988; Duncan et al., 1993; Lee and Bryk, 1989; Lee and Myers, 2003; Longford,

1993; Raudenbush and Bryk, 1986, 1988). Instead of using the multilevel approach, an alternative approach might be to use dummy variables for the USC sectors in OLS. However, a good rule of thumb is that it is better to use the multilevel approach if the number of upper-level observations is larger than ten (Snijders and Bosker, 1999). Furthermore, it is interesting to verify whether or not the trade patterns are diverse across industry sectors. Although we can estimate relative effects of each sector with respect to a reference sector by identifying explanatory dummy variables, we cannot verify the significance of unobserved diversity among sectors from the coefficients estimated for dummy variables: the multilevel approach provides upper-level variances with standard errors, and hence we can judge the significance of the unobserved diversity of trade patterns among industry sectors. These variances are so-called 'unobserved effects' (Wooldridge, 2002). Finally, because the USC sector system is somewhat aggregated from the detailed sector code system and redefined by us, it is reasonable to allow the means of industry sectors to be distributed randomly about the grand mean rather than being constrained to be constantly adjacent to the reference industry sector in the form of fixed effects.

Variables are defined in Table 13.1. For our research, we used four types of independent variables at the first level: Time, Events, Customs District and Cross-effect variables. Time-type variables included lagged variables (LAG1, LAG3 and LAG12), a monthly smoothing variable (SMOOTH) and time trend variables (T and T_SQ). We classified Events-type using four variables. One is a dummy variable for the 9/11 terrorist attack (T911). Our test was to find whether the 9/11 event that occurred mainly in New York could affect national freight trade. Air passenger numbers were dramatically decreased by that event, resulting in economic losses in the range of $214 to $420 billion (Gordon et al., 2007).

The possible effects of behavior during three key periods – before, during and after the shutdown – are tested via the use of dummy variables. We hypothesized that economic actions might anticipate the port shutdowns as much as four months prior to October 2002 and prompt adjusted trade patterns in advance to reduce economic losses (specified as BIMPACT). Also, because we expected some economic losses would occur during the harbor shutdown, we tested the effects of October (specified as DIMPACT). It is also possible that the 11-day shutdown was too short to prompt significant economic losses for the US economy. Based on the shutdown period, we assumed economic behavior that anticipated the shutdown might last a long time, and thus prompt a speedy recovery from the strike. Therefore, after reopening the ports, shippers might have tried to recapture some economic losses. To test for these recapture effects, we also examined the impacts for four months after October 2002 (specified

Table 13.1 Variables

Variables		Description	Mode*
Dependent	TRADE	Foreign imports or exports of Tth month ($ million)	V, A, O
	LAG1	Foreign imports or exports of (T-1)th month	V, A, O
	LAG3	Foreign imports or exports of (T-3)th month; quarterly seasonal effects	V, A, O
	LAG12	Foreign imports or exports of (T-12)th month; yearly seasonal effects	V, A, O
Time	SMOOTH	Monthly Smoothing factor $\left(= \sum_{j=Jan.,2000}^{j} TRADE_{j} / \sum_{j=Jan.,2000}^{j} j \right)$ where J is each month	V, A, O
	T	Time trend factor (t =1 to 48)	V, A, O
	T_SQ	T*T	V, A, O
	T911	Dummy of 9/11 events; if date < Sep. 2001 then T911 = 0, otherwise T911 = 1	V, A, O
Events	BIMPACT	BIMPACT = 1 if 4 months before harbor shutdown, or Jun. 2002 = < date = < Sep. 2002; otherwise BIMPACT = 0	V
	AIMPACT	AIMPACT = 1 if 4 months after harbor shutdown, or Nov. 2002 = < date = < Feb. 2003; otherwise AIMPACT = 0	V
	DIMPACT	DIMPACT = 1 if date is in harbor shutdown, or date = Oct. 2002; otherwise DIMPACT = 0	V, A, O

Table 13.1 (continued)

Variables			Description	Mode*
Independent		CD1	Los Angeles Customs District (LACD); Reference	V, A, O
		CD2	San Diego Customs District (SDCD)	V, A, O
	Customs	CD3	San Francisco Customs District (SFCD)	V, A, O
	District	CD4	Snake-Columbia Customs District (SCCD)	V, A, O
		CD5	Seattle Customs District (STCD)	V, A, O
		CD2_BIMP	BIMPACT*CD2	V
		CD3_BIMP	BIMPACT*CD3	V
		CD4_BIMP	BIMPACT*CD4	V
		CD5_BIMP	BIMPACT*CD5	V
	Cross effects	CD2_AIMP	AIMPACT*CD2	V
	variables	CD3_AIMP	AIMPACT*CD3	V
		CD4_AIMP	AIMPACT*CD4	V
		CD5_AIMP	AIMPACT*CD5	V
		CD2_DIMP	DIMPACT*CD2	V, A, O
		CD3_DIMP	DIMPACT*CD3	V, A, O
		CD4_DIMP	DIMPACT*CD4	V, A, O
		CD5_DIMP	DIMPACT*CD5	V, A, O

Note: V = Vessel mode, A = Air mode and O = Other modes. Multilevel models are regressed by mode.

as AIMPACT).[4] Also, to understand whether there were substitutions between ports, we tested five West Coast Customs District (CD) dummy variables, treating the Los Angeles Customs District (LACD) as the reference group. Finally, we created cross-effect dummy variables, which could provide information on 'before,' 'during' and 'after' impacts interacting with each Customs District. The basic statistics on means and standard deviations for each variable are provided in Table 13.2.

The multilevel linear model used to estimate parameters is shown in Equations (13.1-1) and (13.1-2).

$$Y = \beta_0 + X^t\rho + X^{imp}\beta_{imp} + X^{CD}\beta_{CD} + X^{cross}\beta_{cross} + Zu + \varepsilon \tag{13.1-1}$$

$$= X\beta + Zu + \varepsilon, \text{ where } \varepsilon \sim N(0, \sigma^2) \text{ and } u \sim N(0, \zeta^2), \tag{13.1-2}$$

where
Y indicates monthly foreign imports or exports;
β_0 = the coefficient of the constant unit vector;
X^t = the matrix of time variables;
X^{imp} = the matrix of impact variables;
X^{CD} = the matrix of Customs District variables;
X^{cross} = the matrix of cross-effects variables;
ρ = the coefficient vector of autoregressive parameters;
β^k = the coefficient vector of parameters, including coefficients for each independent variables group k (where k = imp, CD and cross);
>Z = the design matrix in terms of the USC sectors;
u = the random effects parameters for Z;
ε = the error term;
$X = [E, X^t, X^{imp}, X^{CD}, X^{cross}]$, where E is a unit vector; and
$\beta = [\beta_0, \rho, \beta^{imp}, \beta^{CD}, \beta^{cross}]$.
Equation (13.1-2) can be simplified to

$$Y = W\Gamma + \varepsilon, \tag{13.2}$$

where
W = [X, Z] and
Γ = [β, u].

From Equation (13.2), β and u in Γ are estimated as

$$\hat{\beta} = (W'\hat{V}^{-1}W)^{-1}W'\hat{V}^{-1}Y \text{ and} \tag{13.3–1}$$

$$\hat{u} = \hat{\zeta}^2 Z'\hat{V}^{-1}(Y - W\hat{\Gamma}), \tag{13.3–2}$$

Table 13.2 Basic statistics: means and standard deviations of variables

		Dependent variable	Continuous independent variables					
		TRADE	LAG1	LAG3	LAG12	SMOOTH	T	T_SQ
IMPORTS								
VESSEL	MEAN	100.51	98.23	93.09	73.27	95.89	24.50	792.17
	S.D.	316.86	312.73	301.56	265.47	290.16	13.85	700.21
AIR	MEAN	41.22	40.35	38.66	32.03	46.09	24.50	792.17
	S.D.	238.85	236.63	232.36	217.34	270.30	13.85	700.21
OTHER	MEAN	18.21	17.85	17.04	13.80	18.48	24.50	792.17
	S.D.	72.11	71.42	69.66	63.95	70.82	13.85	700.21
EXPORTS								
VESSEL	MEAN	33.76	33.00	31.45	25.16	34.21	24.50	792.17
	S.D.	60.84	60.17	58.86	54.13	58.68	13.85	700.21
AIR	MEAN	42.17	41.33	39.73	33.31	47.64	24.50	792.17
	S.D.	215.84	214.15	211.02	199.91	243.50	13.85	700.21
OTHER	MEAN	22.83	22.38	21.28	17.38	22.92	24.50	792.17
	S.D.	139.01	138.01	134.02	124.70	135.41	13.85	700.21

Note: S.D. indicates standard deviation.

where

V is the variance of Y, defined as $Z\zeta^2 Z' + \sigma^2$.

We used Equation (13.1) for the sea vessel mode. Seagoing shipments are typically very large and more likely to be substituted over time periods than between modes. However, we excluded the BIMPACT and AIMPACT variables from X^{imp} and hence only used DIMPACT for air and other modes. The regressed results are shown in Tables 13.3 and 13.4 in the Results section.

Based on the estimated coefficients and random effects for each USC sector, we obtained the estimated values Y, denoted $\hat{Y}$, by assuming impact variables are zero, meaning no period-specific. Therefore, the final demand losses from the *ex post* incidents were calculated as $\hat{Y} - Y$, because $\hat{Y}$ denotes the normal international trade that would have occurred had the ports not shut down. Note that we obtained two types of estimates $\hat{Y}$, focusing on the BIMPACT variable for the vessel mode. In the first case, $\hat{Y}$ is obtained based on the extreme assumption that economic behavior would not change as a result of knowledge of the ports shutdown. In this case, the BIMPACT values are set to zero. However, the second assumption is that the trade-related activities might adapt to the changed situation regardless of the ports shutdown, because prior shipping would not make any difference to the shippers involved. In the second case, we do not assume (test) that the BIMPACT variable is zero. We use superscript e to identify the extreme case of no anticipatory adjustments prior to the ports shutdown, making the notion for the first case $\hat{Y}^{e,V}$. We use the superscript r to identify the more realistic case of allowing anticipation of the ports shutdown prior to the event, making the notation for the second case as $\hat{Y}^{r,V}$. The estimated values $\hat{Y}$ for air and other modes are denoted as $\hat{Y}^A$ and $\hat{Y}^O$. Therefore, we have two classes of estimated column vectors $\hat{Y}$,

$$\hat{Y}^e = [\hat{Y}^{e,V}, \hat{Y}^A, \hat{Y}^O]' \text{ and} \tag{13.4–1}$$

$$\hat{Y}^r = [\hat{Y}^{r,V}, \hat{Y}^A, \hat{Y}^O]'. \tag{13.4–2}$$

The direct impacts vector necessary for applying NIEMO will also be of two classes, imports and exports,

$$^{Imports}D^e = \hat{Y}^e - Y, \tag{13.5–1}$$

$$^{Imports}D^r = \hat{Y}^r - Y, \tag{13.5–2}$$

$$^{Exports}D^e = \hat{Y}^e - Y \text{ and} \tag{13.5–3}$$

$$^{Exports}D^r = \hat{Y}^r - Y. \tag{13.5–4}$$

With direct impacts obtained from Equations (13.5), we use NIEMO to estimate state-to-state economic impacts. The estimated results are shown in Table 13.5 in the Results section.

13.3.3   Demand- and Supply-driven NIEMOs

We depart from the traditional interindustry IO approach that focuses on a single region, and that is still widely used to estimate the economic impacts in cases of certain sectoral disruptions. We applied NIEMO, a spatially disaggregated IO model, to estimate different direct impacts on California, Oregon and Washington, and to address their cross-regional and cross-sectoral impacts simultaneously.[5] The application of the demand-side version of NIEMO to an analysis addressing economic impacts is useful for tracing backward linkages, that is, in the case of export disturbances. However, for the case of economic activity that is devoted to imports, a supply-driven model should be used to analyse the economic impacts (Cai et al., 2005; Park, 2007, 2008; Park et al., 2008). Although there have been debates about the plausibility of supply-side IO models (Dietzenbacher, 1997), Park (2007, 2008b) shows that a supply-driven IO model can be reasonably used in the case of constraints on economic activity. We use the supply-driven NIEMO in the case of imports disturbances (Park, 2008; Park et al., 2008), and apply the demand-driven NIEMO to treat export disturbances (Park et al., 2006, 2007; Richardson et al., 2007). Park and Gordon (2005) tested for NIEMO's accuracy and showed that NIEMO's estimates are plausible while available at low computational cost. Using the supply-driven version of NIEMO to account for demand-side adjustments during the recovery period presents a challenge, but we tried to avoid the problem by assuming relatively short-term impacts as well as trying to consider possible substitutions when estimating direct impacts.

Because the demand-driven version and supply-driven version of NIEMO are described in detail in Park et al. (2007) and Park (2008), respectively, we only briefly introduce these models here.

$$X^I = (I - C^O A)^{-1 export} D^e \tag{13.6a}$$

$$X^I = (I - C^O A)^{-1 export} D^r, \tag{13.6b}$$

where
X^I is the total input row vector for the various commodity and service sectors $m(= 1, \ldots, 47)$ and $n(= 1, \ldots, 52)$ regions;
$A = Z(\hat{X}^I)^{-1}$ and $\hat{X}^I$ is a $nm \times nm$ block diagonal matrix of vector X^I in which the elements in all blocks off the regional diagonal are zero;

Z = a $nm \times nm$ block diagonal matrix of direct technical flows between industries within each region;

$C^O = C(\hat{C}_j^m)^{-1}$ and $\hat{C}_j^m$ is a $nm \times nm$ diagonal matrix of $1 \times nm$ row vectors;

$C_j^m = \sum_i c_{ij}^m$ in which the off-diagonals for a each region's block are zero and c_{ij}^m is an element of matrix C describing the trade flows for USC sector m between regions i and j;

C = a $nm \times nm$ diagonal block matrix of interregional trade flows; and

$^{export}D$ = a column vector of final demand losses incident to West Coast states in the demand-driven version of NIEMO.

Based on the same definitions as in Equations (13.6), the final equation of the supply-side NIEMO with 52 regions is shown in Equations (13.7).

$$X^O = {}^{import}D^e(I - BC^I)^{-1} \tag{13.7a}$$

$$X^O = {}^{import}D^r(I - BC^I)^{-1} \tag{13.7b}$$

where

X^O = Total output column vector for $m(= 1, \ldots, 47)$ USC sectors and $n(= 1, \ldots, 52)$ regions;

$B = (\hat{X}^O)^{-1}Z$ and $\hat{X}^O$ is a $nm \times nm$ block diagonal matrix of vector X^O in which the elements in all blocks off the regional diagonal are zero;

$C^I = (\hat{C}_i^m)^{-1}C$ and $\hat{C}_i^m$ is a $nm \times nm$ diagonal matrix of $nm \times 1$ column vectors;

$C_i^m = \sum_j c_{ij}^m$, in which the off-diagonals for each region's block are zero and c_{ij}^m is an element of matrix C describing the trade flows for USC sector m between regions i and j; and

$^{import}D$ = a row vector of regional specific losses of value added factors incident to West Coast states in the supply-driven version of NIEMO.

The next section shows the results of using multilevel estimation along with estimates provided by NIEMO.

13.4 RESULTS

The multilevel results for January 2000 to December 2003 by each mode for foreign imports and exports are shown in Tables 13.3 and 13.4, respectively.

For the case of foreign imports shown in Table 13.3, we observe results for three modes. Because port activity stopped during the lock-out period, our main focus is on the sea vessel model. The null model, which is not

Table 13.3 *Multilevel results for foreign imports for vessel, air and other modes*

Modes	Vessel Model 1		Air Model 2		Other Model 3	
	Coeff.	S.E.	Coeff.	S.E.	Coeff.	S.E.
Fixed effect						
Intercept	7.1910***	2.5493	9.1906***	1.5437	1.0441	0.7470
Time						
LAG1_M	0.4745***	0.0093	0.2833***	0.0083	0.4919***	0.0101
LAG3_M	-0.1312***	0.0077	0.0164***	0.0058	0.0195***	0.0088
LAG12_M	0.0456***	0.0044	-0.2532***	0.0033	-0.1123***	0.0051
SIMP_M	0.6765***	0.0097	0.7665***	0.0069	0.5749***	0.0107
T	-1.2370***	0.2119	-0.1900	0.1295	-0.1199*	0.0650
T_SQ	0.0252***	0.0035	0.0050**	0.0021	0.0024**	0.0011
Events						
T911	-0.6750	2.3100	0.1159	1.4252	0.0468	0.7114
BIMPACT	16.5102***	4.4985				
AIMPACT	-3.3692	4.4697				
DIMPACT	-32.6758***	8.5531	20.3505***	5.3413	0.5762	2.6652
Customs District						
CD2	2.3845	2.0412	-8.4298***	1.1005	1.0724*	0.5582
CD3	-0.6070	2.0060	-8.8079***	1.0914	-0.0512	0.5429
CD4	1.8927	2.0283	-8.2966***	1.0995	-0.1127	0.5429
CD5	0.6125	2.0050	-7.9584***	1.0977	-1.1549**	0.5535

Cross-effects

CD2_BIMP	−12.4258**	6.2582				
CD3_BIMP	−11.7709*	6.2537				
CD4_BIMP	−12.2937**	6.2563				
CD5_BIMP	−10.4047*	6.2519				
CD2_AIMP	6.7315	6.2506				
CD3_AIMP	3.3119	6.2487				
CD4_AIMP	3.4945	6.2499				
CD5_AIMP	4.2458	6.2468				
CD2_DIMP	39.0777***	12.0499	−20.175***	7.5389	9.0201**	3.7627
CD3_DIMP	30.4416**	12.0475	−24.422***	7.539	0.1260	3.7615
CD4_DIMP	39.1505***	12.0493	−19.777***	7.5388	−0.7605	3.7615
CD5_DIMP	47.1345***	12.0454	−18.26**	7.5387	0.2149	3.7616
Random effect						
Level 1						
Intercept (σ^2)	2,047.6***	34.8	806.8***	13.7	200.9***	3.4
Level 2						
Intercept (ζ^2)	13.9**	6.0	12.9***	4.4	2.1***	0.8
−2RLL	72,773.5		66,381.8		56,709.7	
AIC	72,777.5		66,385.8		56,713.7	
Pseudo R_SQ	0.9797		0.9919		0.9612	
Obs. of Level 1	6,960		6,960		6,960	
Obs. of Level 2	29		29		29	

Note: Dependent variable is foreign imports (\$ million). The Pseudo R-squares are calculated using the method proposed by Snijders and Bosker (1999, pp. 102–3). All models reject the null hypothesis that each null model with only the fixed effects equal or better than the fitted multilevel model at the 1 percent significant level. * significant at the 10 percent level, ** significant at the 5 percent level, *** significant at the 1 percent level.

237

Table 13.4 Multilevel results for foreign exports for vessel, air and other modes

Modes	Vessel		Air		Other	
	Model 4		Model 5		Model 6	
	Coeff.	S.E.	Coeff.	S.E.	Coeff.	S.E.
Fixed effect						
Intercept	2.0340**	0.8228	7.5225***	1.3024	0.8154	1.7584
Time						
LAG1_M	0.2687***	0.0104	0.3206***	0.0090	0.0825***	0.0105
LAG3_M	−0.0304***	0.0088	0.0260***	0.0065	0.0018	0.0094
LAG12_M	−0.0556***	0.0055	−0.2407***	0.0034	−0.0082	0.0067
SIMP_M	0.8157***	0.0121	0.7333***	0.0073	0.9158***	0.0136
T	−0.1970***	0.0607	−0.1093	0.1178	−0.0689	0.1639
T_SQ	0.0048***	0.0010	0.0021	0.0019	0.0009	0.0027
Events						
T911	−0.6611	0.6363	−0.607	1.293	−0.5972	1.8041
BIMPACT	−5.2925***	1.2227				
AIMPACT	−5.2661***	1.2254				
DIMPACT	−32.5635***	2.3285	5.0445	4.8397	9.4293	6.7744
Customs District						
CD2	−0.8122	0.6224	−6.2154***	0.9997	1.5504	1.3835
CD3	−3.2055***	0.5673	−8.0476***	0.989	0.6393	1.3801
CD4	−0.8321	0.5957	−6.7994***	0.9989	0.5311	1.3801
CD5	−0.2195	0.5695	−4.9371***	0.9968	0.191	1.3990

Cross-effects

	M1		M2		M3	
CD2_BIMP	5.7290***	1.7052				
CD3_BIMP	6.4829***	1.7022				
CD4_BIMP	4.8106***	1.7037				
CD5_BIMP	4.5416***	1.7027				
CD2_AIMP	5.1793***	1.7089				
CD3_AIMP	4.7998***	1.7055				
CD4_AIMP	6.4868***	1.7096				
CD5_AIMP	8.0015***	1.7047				
CD2_DIMP	32.8233***	3.2818	-4.6182	6.8309	-3.4800	9.5617
CD3_DIMP	23.5285***	3.2799	-11.282*	6.8307	-8.9362	9.5612
CD4_DIMP	36.0843***	3.2797	-3.925	6.8308	-8.8624	9.5612
CD5_DIMP	26.3654***	3.2791	-2.7742	6.8309	-10.9950	9.5632

Random effects

	M1		M2		M3	
Level 1						
Intercept	151.7***	2.6	662.4***	11.3	200.9***	3.4
Level 2						
Intercept	3.1***	1.0	2.5**	1.4	2.1***	0.8
-2RLL	54,739.0		64,985.8		56,709.7	
AIC	54,743.0		64,989.8		56,713.7	
Pseudo R_SQ	0.9586		0.8220		0.8436	
Obs. of Level 1	6,960		6,960		6,960	
Obs. of Level 2	29		29		29	

Note: Dependent variable is foreign exports ($ million). The Pseudo R-squares are calculated using the method proposed by Snijders and Bosker (1999, Chapter 7). All models reject the null hypothesis that each null model with only the fixed effects equal or better than the fitted multilevel model at the 1 percent significant level. * significant at the 10 percent level, ** significant at the 5 percent level, *** significant at the 1 percent level.

239

reported here, provides information on the trade variances (δ^2) and between-sector variances (ξ^2), and thus provides a basis for understanding the structure of total variances (Raudenbush and Bryk, 2002). From Table 13.2, we see that the mean of foreign imports is $100.5 million for the vessel mode. This can also be determined from the intercept in the null model, which showed that the proportion of trade variance to total variance is 70 percent and the proportion of variance between sectors to total variance is 30 percent.

We did not include any independent variables explaining the characteristics of the USC sectors. Also, the estimated coefficients for the Time variables are consistent even if we add dummy variables via the Events variables. We use the -2 Restricted Log Likelihood (-2RLL) values to select the best model from the several competing alternatives we estimated. We identify Model 1 as the final model to estimate $\hat{Y}^c$, because the decreased value of -2RLL from the other models along with the increases in the number of variables using the chi-square tests is statistically significant.[6] Models 2 and 3 test specifications for air freight and other modes.

None of our models for foreign imports show that there were significant effects from the 9/11 attacks for any mode. The air travel story after 9/11 primarily involved personal travel rather than freight (Gordon et al., 2007). Leinbach and Bowen (2004) have written about the growth in air freight, especially in high-value to weight goods such as electronics. Hummel (1999) has compared ocean and air freight shipping rates over almost half a century. Sea freight costs have increased whereas air freight costs have declined. So, the trend is from sea-going vessels to air transport, at least for goods with high values per unit weight. However, over the nine months before and after the shutdown, the decline in sea-borne imports ($586.4 million) was close to the increase in air-borne imports ($455.0 million). However, it is unlikely that this was because of a mode substitution effect. The length of the shutdown was too short for shippers to make significant new arrangements. Also, air freight exports declined modestly, by $29.3 million. However, Figure 13.2 does not indicate much of a trend in either air or sea vessel imports, so it is probable that the import changes were more a matter of random noise than either substitutions or trends.

Another interesting result relating to the sea vessel mode in Model 1 concerns the 'before' and 'during' impacts, BIMPACT and DIMPACT, respectively. The coefficient of BIMPACT shows positive effects of about $16.5 million for ports in Los Angeles Customs District even before the ports lock-out. Other ports also showed positive impacts that were in the range of $4–$6 million, on average.[7] However, the DIMPACT estimates for Los Angeles Customs District show losses of $32.7 million. The San

Francisco Customs District incurred losses of \$2.2 million (= (–32.67) + 30.44), while the other Customs Districts show positive impacts in the range of \$6 million to \$14.5 million, on average. Although the ports lock-out occurred on the entire West Coast, severe economic losses are only found in the Los Angeles and San Francisco Customs Districts. The other Customs Districts studied did not experience any negative impacts from the lock-out. The latter finding might be due to weaker actions in these ports, faster recapture activity or alternative roles taking over trade from the Los Angeles and San Francisco Customs Districts ports. This is reasonable because shippers importing goods would not keep their goods on the ship. Rather they would try to find other docks or otherwise make up for the effects of delays to minimize cost. It is also interesting that there were some modest positive impacts except for the San Francisco Customs District for the air mode, and only positive impacts for other modes for the San Diego Customs District during the lock-out. Therefore, in the case of foreign imports, the two estimated impact variables show that there was considerable economic adjustment behavior before the lock-out, but that only Los Angeles and San Francisco Customs Districts experienced negative impacts due to the lock-out. Also, only slightly positive impacts occurred as a result of mode substitutions.

The results obtained for foreign exports show a different pattern, although it is still difficult to find a strong indication of 9/11 effects. All foreign export impact variables for the Los Angeles Customs District using sea-going vessels show statistically significant, modest negative impacts (Model 4 in Table 13.4). However, the impacts for the other Customs Districts varied according to the variable type. Exporters normally using San Diego and San Francisco Customs Districts had planned ahead moderately; but, on average, they had not recovered entirely after the lock-out. In contrast, the exporters in the Snake-Columbia Customs District and Seattle Customs District experienced negative impacts before the event, but recovered after the lock-out. It is hard to find evidence of modal substitutions involving exports in our results (Models 5 and 6).

Based on the estimated coefficients, we simulated two cases to obtain baseline estimates for imports and exports. As shown in Equations (13.4) and (13.5), we simulated: (1) an extreme case that assumes no adjustment before the ports shutdown; and (2) a more realistic case allowing behavior that anticipates the ports shutdown. As shown in Table 13.5, the negative or positive direction of aggregate direct impacts on USC sectors by substitution type for each Customs District and for imports and exports are consistent overall with the expectations from the multilevel results. By anticipating the ports shutdown with respect to imports, the economy of the West Coast ports obtained positive gains of \$3,758 million in the

Table 13.5 Aggregate direct impacts on USC sectors by substitution type for each Customs District and for imports and exports ($ million)

Customs District	Substitution	Imports		Exports	
		importD^e	importD^r	exportD^e	exportD^r
Los Angeles	BIMPACT	1,915.19	0.00	-610.10	0.00
	DIMPACT	-960.67		-891.51	
	AIMPACT	-462.44		-606.86	
	Air	590.16		146.29	
	Other	11.13		273.45	
	Subtotal	1,093.38	-821.81	-1,688.73	-1,078.63
San Diego	BIMPACT	269.44	0.00	-38.54	0.00
	DIMPACT	185.65		-10.28	
	AIMPACT	329.03		-70.73	
	Air	-20.27		-10.39	
	Other	278.29		192.98	
	Subtotal	1,042.14	772.71	63.04	101.58
San Francisco	BIMPACT	422.25	0.00	113.75	0.00
	DIMPACT	-100.33		-261.57	
	AIMPACT	-124.68		-83.69	
	Air	-173.50		-239.81	
	Other	14.31		2.07	
	Subtotal	38.06	-384.19	-469.23	-582.99

Snake-Columbia	BIMPACT	442.90	-102.46	0.00	0.00
	DIMPACT	187.77	97.39		
	AIMPACT	-88.82	124.22		
	Air	-1.99	8.78		
	Other	-16.56	0.00		
	Subtotal	523.30	127.93	80.40	230.39
Seattle	BIMPACT	708.24	-88.09	0.00	0.00
	DIMPACT	419.30	-181.63		
	AIMPACT	28.81	317.31		
	Air	60.62	65.84		
	Other	18.66	-305.01		
	Subtotal	1,235.63	-191.58	527.39	-103.49
Total	BIMPACT	3,758.01	-725.43	0.00	0.00
	DIMPACT	-268.27	-1,247.60		
	AIMPACT	-318.10	-319.75		
	Air	455.03	-29.29		
	Other	305.84	163.50		
	Subtotal	3,932.51	-2,158.57	174.50	-1,433.14

Note: Direct impacts for IMPACT variables are calculated as (Actual imports or exports) – (Estimated imports or exports if the ports shutdown had not occurred during six months between September 2002 and February 2003). Direct impacts for mode variables are calculated as (Actual imports or exports) – (Estimated imports or exports if the ports shutdown had not occurred during the month of October 2002). $^{trade}D^e = \hat{Y}^e - Y$, extreme case assuming no adjustment before the ports shutdown. $^{trade}D^r = \hat{Y}^r - Y$, realistic case allowing the behaviors to anticipate the ports shutdown before it occurred. 'Trade' denotes imports or exports.

aggregate. The avoided costs, therefore, can be seen as the benefit of prior information for shippers of foreign imports.

For the case of exports, however, all the ports except San Francisco showed negative impacts as a result of anticipation. Port handling capacities, especially union labor, is limited in the short run. It makes sense that as imports increase substantially, exports may have been crowded out. This shift can explain losses of $725 million before the shutdown.

Even though we can simulate possible anticipatory impacts, the US economy had already adjusted to new economic conditions before the shutdown. Any increase or decrease in trade before the shutdown involved a gamble. Therefore, it is also plausible that economic impacts might have occurred solely from the ports shutdown, as other impact studies have assumed. We excluded the 'before' impacts to reflect the realistic case. For this case, the economic impacts of foreign imports had changed dramatically, as seen in Table 13.5. Total economic impacts of Los Angeles and San Francisco Customs Districts are negative, showing $821.8 and $384.2 million losses, respectively, but the other Customs Districts experienced positive economic impacts. Hence, total impacts show positive net gains of about $174.5 million. Also, the realistic case for foreign exports generated a $1,433 million loss.

Finally, the state-by-state NIEMO results for the four cases were estimated based on the estimated direct impacts. The total impact of reducing foreign imports for the extreme (myopic) case over nine months reached about $6 billion. The total impact for the realistic (anticipatory) case over five months shows $579 million in gains, though the total impact of California is negative. This is because Washington and Oregon experienced positive impacts during and after the ports shutdown. The latter case shows that the indirect impacts spread regionally are limited, not amounting to over $1 million in the Eastern states. These findings are different from the generally held belief that the labor shutdown in the West Coast ports resulted in serious losses throughout the US economy.

However, the economic impacts for the case of exports are clear. Total economic losses were about $3 billion during five months, that is, $20 million per day on average. Only Oregon had positive impacts, partially offsetting the direct economic losses in California. The national economic losses were substantial, reaching the Eastern states such as Pennsylvania ($22.1 million), New York ($21.7 million) and New Jersey ($14.8 million). Therefore, more severe impacts resulted from the disruption of exports during the lock-out than of imports. This suggests that it is easier to prepare for and mitigate the consequences of disruption to import flows than disruptions to export flows. Figure 13.5 summarizes these findings.

13.5 CONCLUSIONS

Giuliano and her colleagues (2005) studied the freight truck traffic effects of the 2002 ports lock-out and referred to it as a 'natural experiment' on which we could test our models and methods. We took this approach in analysing the various economic impacts of the ports shutdown. Although it was pointed out that substitution effects are likely, it had previously been reported that the economic impacts of the ports shutdown were in the range of $1 billion to $2 billion per day. Some of this was recognized in a newspaper report on 18 October 2002.

> For example, truckers who are unable to return containers to port terminals by a specified date have to pay penalty fees. But that money doesn't disappear from the economy. It goes to terminal operators as income. Similarly, some revenue lost by shipping companies ends up in the hands of air freight lines. Burlington Northern and Santa Fe Railway lost its business shipping containers to the ports, a volume that normally runs 4,000 to 7,000 units per day. But much of that traffic was shipped before or after the lockout, resulting in relatively little loss. Meanwhile, the company said it suffered little disruption to its operations. (Zuckerman, 2002)

We tried to model some of these regional, periodic and modal substitutions based on actual month-to-month trade data. In the results, we found there were positive and negative impacts by mode, region and period for foreign imports and foreign exports. Our finding, based on realistic assumptions, is that the positive total economic impacts were estimated as equal to $579 million for foreign imports, for which effects by region were diverse. In contrast, the economic losses were $3 billion for foreign exports for the total of five months during and after the shutdown. The spillover effects with respect to the various states were also complex. While the economic impacts due to foreign imports disruption were limited to the near West Coast regions, the economic impacts of foreign exports were national (Park, 2008). Considering that a third of total foreign trade is foreign exports, it is clear that the ports shutdown of 2002 seriously affected the delivery of domestically produced items to other countries.

Our approach requires some caveats. We selected the periods of analysis, four months before and after shutdown, based on judgment. Also, the demand- and supply-driven versions of NIEMO can be criticized for the same limitations as the traditional IO models, that is, fixed coefficients characteristics and no scope for short-run technological substitutions in production. Our approach was to look for substitutions of direct effects over time and space: we tried to estimate reasonable direct impacts

$$^{export}D^e$$

$$^{import}D^e$$

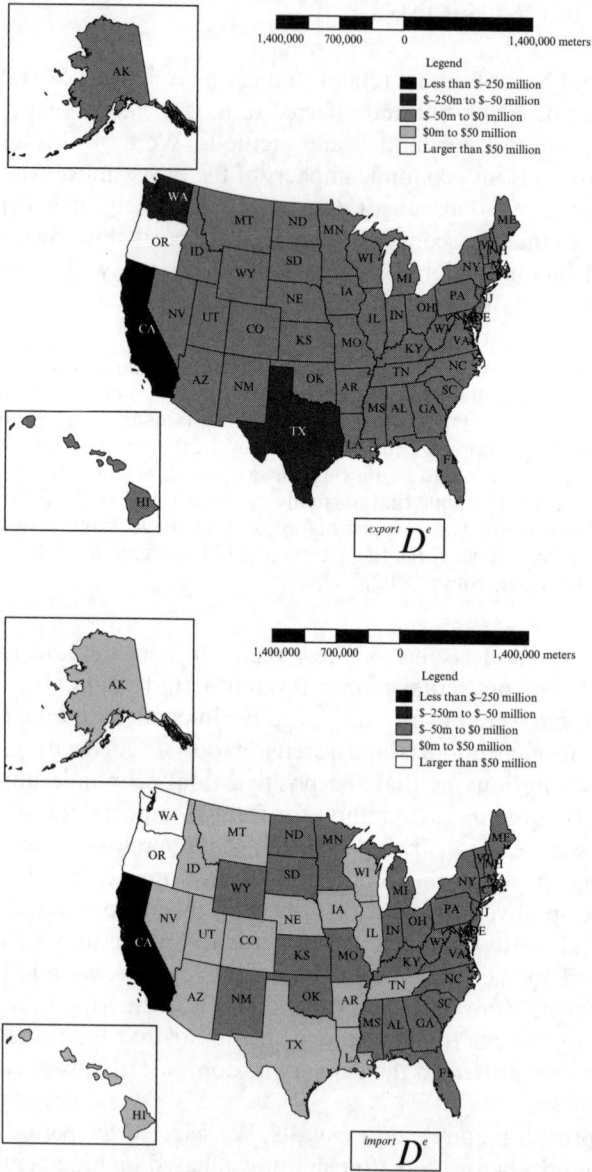

Note: $^{trade}D^e = \hat{Y}^e - Y$, extreme case assuming no adjustment before the ports shutdown. $^{trade}D^r = \hat{Y}^r - Y$, realistic case allowing the behaviors to anticipate the ports shutdown before it occurred. 'Trade' denotes imports or exports.

Figure 13.5   The state-by-state total economic impacts

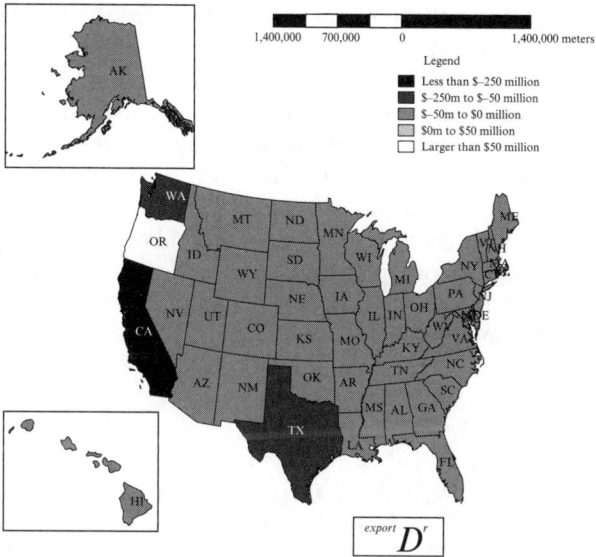

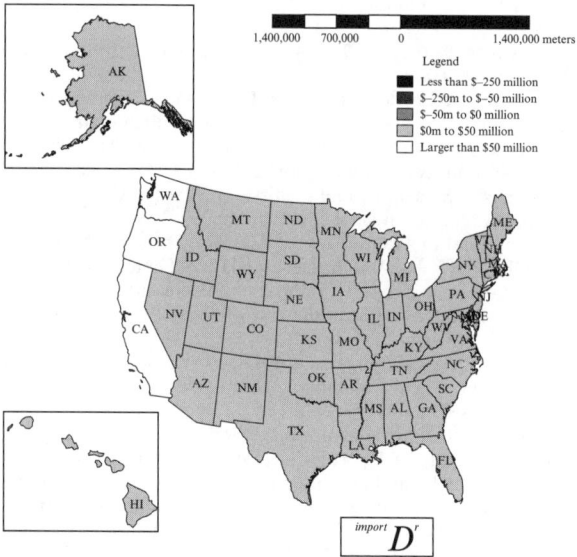

Figure 13.5 (continued)

considering several substitution effects and then used the spatially disaggregate, demand- and supply-driven versions of NIEMO to assess the impacts of backward and forward linkages to the US economy.

Much of our research in recent years with the model has been in the terrorism area. Terrorist events are unanticipated in time and location, and their impacts are difficult to measure *ex ante*. In contrast, the 2002 West Coast ports shutdown was a widely anticipated event. This is what distinguishes it. Nevertheless, it was a real event, like 9/11, and it has some relevance to the analysis of terrorism because all our studies were simulations. In particular, the exercise sheds some light on the economic importance of recapture and resilience.

NOTES

1. There are three ports, Reno (NV), Las Vegas (NV) and Boise (ID), which are in three West Coast states, California, Oregon and Washington. However, the first two ports belong to the Los Angeles District, and the third belongs to the Columbia-Snake Customs District. As they are all located near the borders of West Coast states and as data for these ports were not available before 2003, we analysed the Customs District-level data under the assumption that these three have close economic ties to the West Coast states.
2. 6,960 = 5 (Customs District) * 29 (USC commodity sector) * 48 (months from January 2000 to December 2003).
3. WISERTrade uses the US Census Foreign Trade Statistics terminology (see http://www. census.gov/foreign-trade/guide/sec2.html), which highlights air and vessel modes and includes all of the rest in an 'other' category. The latter refers to rail and truck when these modes are involved in seaport and airport access.
4. The last two days of September and the first nine days of October mark the ports shutdowns, which resulted in direct economic impacts. Because trade data are only available monthly, we had to assume that only October is the impacted period. We selected October for DIMPACT because the last two days of September are not expected to contribute much direct impact relative to the rest of the month. For this reason, DIMPACT might be underestimated, because the rest of October might include some recapture impacts.
5. California includes the Los Angeles, San Diego and San Francisco Custom Districts. Oregon includes the Snake-Columbia Customs District and Washington includes the Seattle Customs District.
6. The chi-square values with 12 degrees of freedom reject the null hypothesis that the two models are the same at the 1 percent level if it is larger than 26.217. Because the difference between Model 1 and another model that does not include cross-effects is 94.4 (= 72773.5 − 72867.9), the null hypothesis is rejected at the 1 percent level.
7. If we focus on Seattle Customs District, we can calculate the impacts from the coefficients in BIMPACT and CD5_BIMP as 16.5 + (−10.4) = 6.1. The impacts for other Customs Districts are calculated similarly.

REFERENCES

Anderson, P.L. and I.K. Geckil (2002), *Flash Estimate: Impact of West Coast Shutdown*. Lansing, MI: Anderson Economic Consulting Group.

Bouchard, J.F. (2005), 'New strategies to protect America: safer ports for a more secure economy', Center for American Progress, available at http://www.americanprogress.org/atf/cf/%7BE9245FE4-9A2B-43C7-A521-5D6FF2E06E03%7D/port_security.pdf.

Bryk, A.S. and S.W. Raudenbush (1988), 'Toward a more appropriate conceptualization of research on school effects; a three level hierarchical linear model', *American Journal of Education*, **97** (1), 65–108.

Cai, J., P. Leung, M. Pan and S. Pooley (2005), *Linkage of Fisheries Sectors to Hawaii's Economy and Economic Impacts of Longline Fishing Regulations*. Honolulu, HI: University of Hawaii – NOAA, Joint Institute for Marine and Atmospheric Research.

Chenery, H.B. (1953), 'Regional analysis', in H.B. Chenery, P.G. Clark and V.C. Pinna (eds), *The Structure and Growth of the Italian Economy*. Rome: US Mutual Security Agency, pp. 98–139.

Cohen, S.S. (2002), *Economic Impacts of a West Coast Dock Shutdown*, Report for the Pacific Maritime Association, Berkeley Roundtable on the International Economy, University of California at Berkeley, available at http://brie.berkeley.edu/~briewww/publications/ships%202002%20final.pdf.

Congressional Budget Office (2006), *The Economic Costs of Disruptions in Container Shipments*, available at http://www.cbo.gov/ftpdocs/71xx/doc7106/03-29-Container_Shipments.pdf.

Dietzenbacher, E. (1997), 'In vindication of the Ghosh model: a reinterpretation as a price model', *Journal of Regional Science*, **37**, 629–51.

Duncan, C., K. Jones and G. Moon (1993), 'Do places matter? A multi-level analysis of regional variations in health-related behaviour in Britain', *Social Science and Medicine*, **37**, 725–33.

Giuliano, G., A. Agarwal, C. Li and A. Linder (2005), *CalTrans/MTA/METRANS Port Impact Study*, Final report. Los Angeles, CA: University of Southern California, METRANS Transportation Center.

Gordon, P., J.E. Moore II, H.W. Richardson and Q. Pan (2005), 'The economic impact of a terrorist attack on the twin ports of Los Angeles-Long Beach', in H.W. Richardson, P. Gordon and J.E. Moore II (eds), *The Economic Impacts of Terrorist Attacks*. Cheltenham, UK and Northampton, MA, USA: Edward Elgar, pp. 262–86.

Gordon, P., J.E. Moore II, J.Y. Park and H.W. Richardson (2007), 'The economic impacts of a terrorist attack on the U.S. commercial aviation system', *Risk Analysis*, **27** (3), 505–12.

Hall, P. (2004), '"We'd have to sink the ships": impact studies and the 2002 West Coast port lockout', *Economic Development Quarterly*, **18** (4), 354–67.

Hummel, D. (1999), 'Have international transportation costs declined?', GTAP Applications, available at https://www.gtap.agecon.purdue.edu/resources/download/1238.pdf.

Isard, W. (1951), 'Interregional and regional input-output analysis: a model of a space economy', *Review of Economics and Statistics*, **33**, 318–28.

Jack Faucett Associates, Inc. (1983), *The Multiregional Input-Output Accounts,*

1977: Introduction and Summary, Vol. I (Final report). Washington, DC: US Department of Health and Human Services.

Lee, S.W. and D. Myers (2003), 'Local housing-market effects on tenure choice', *Journal of Housing and the Built Environment*, **18** (2), 129–57.

Lee, V.E. and A.S. Bryk (1989), 'A multilevel model of the social distribution of high-school achievement', *Sociology of Education*, **62** (3), 172–92.

Leinbach, T.R. and J.T. Bowen, Jr (2004), 'Air cargo services and the electronics industry in Southeast Asia', *Journal of Economic Geography*, **4** (3), 299–321.

Longford, N.T. (1993), *Random Coefficient Models*. Oxford: Oxford University Press.

Moses, L.N. (1955), 'The stability of interregional trading patterns and input-output analysis', *American Economic Review*, **45**, 803–32.

Park, J.Y. (2007), 'Supply-driven input-output model: a reinterpretation and extension', Paper presented at the 46th Annual Meeting of the Western Regional Science Association, Newport Beach, California, 21–24 February.

Park, J.Y. (2008), 'The economic impacts of a dirty-bomb attack on the Los Angeles and Long Beach port: applying supply-driven NIEMO', *Journal of Homeland Security and Emergency Management*, **5** (1), Article 21.

Park, J.Y. and P. Gordon (2005), 'An evaluation of input-output aggregation error using a new MRIO model', Paper presented at the North American Meetings of the Regional Science Association International 52nd Annual Conference, Riviera Hotel & Casino, Las Vegas, Nevada, 10–12 November.

Park, J.Y., C.K. Park and S.J. Nam (2006), 'The state-by-state effects of mad cow disease using a new MRIO model', Paper presented at the 2006 American Agricultural Economic Association (AAEA) Annual Meeting, Long Beach, California, 23–26 July.

Park, J.Y., P. Gordon, J.E. Moore II, H.W. Richardson and L. Wang (2007), 'Simulating the state-by-state effects of terrorist attacks on three major U.S. ports: applying NIEMO (National Interstate Economic Model)', in H.W. Richardson, P. Gordon and J.E. Moore II (eds), *The Economic Costs and Consequences of Terrorism*. Cheltenham, UK and Northampton, MA, USA: Edward Elgar, pp. 208–34.

Park, J.Y., P. Gordon, J.E. Moore II, H.W. Richardson, S. Kim and Y. Kim (2008), 'Estimating the state-by-state economic impacts of Hurricane Katrina', in H.W. Richardson, P. Gordon and J.E. Moore II (eds), *Natural Disaster Analysis After Hurricane Katrina*. Cheltenham, UK and Northampton, MA, USA: Edward Elgar, pp. 147–86.

Polenske, K.R. (1980), *The U.S. Multiregional Input-Output Accounts and Model*. Lexington, MA: DC Heath.

Raudenbush, S.W. and A.S. Bryk (1986), 'A hierarchical model for studying school effects', *Sociology of Education*, **59** (1), 1–17.

Raudenbush, S.W. and A.S. Bryk (1988), 'Methodological advances in analyzing the effects of schools and classrooms on student learning', *Review of Research in Education*, **15**, 423–75.

Raudenbush, S.W. and A.S. Bryk (2002), *Hierarchical Linear Models: Applications and Analysis Methods*, 2nd edn. Thousand Oaks, CA: Sage.

Richardson, H.W., P. Gordon, J.E. Moore II, S.J. Kim, J.Y. Park and Q. Pan (2007), 'Tourism and terrorism: the national and interregional economic impacts of attacks on major U.S. theme parks', in H.W. Richardson, P. Gordon and J.E. Moore II (eds), *The Economic Costs and Consequences of Terrorism*. Cheltenham, UK and Northampton, MA, USA: Edward Elgar, pp. 235–53.

Snijders, T. and R. Bosker (1999), *Multilevel Analysis: An Introduction to Basic and Advanced Multilevel Modelling*. London: Sage.

Wooldridge, J.M. (2002), *Econometric Analysis of Cross Section and Panel Data*. Cambridge, MA: MIT Press.

Zuckerman, S. (2002), 'Shutdown not so bad after all', *San Francisco Chronicle*, 18 October, available at http://www.sfgate.com/cgi-bin/article.cgi?f=/c/a/2002/10/18/BU197898.DTL.

14. Extension of the Panama Canal

JiYoung Park, ChangKeun Park and Harry W. Richardson

14.1 INTRODUCTION

The simplest way to approach the difficult problem of estimating the economic effects of the Panama Canal expansion is via the use of input-output models. The National Interstate Economic Model (NIEMO) is useful because it models all interstate trade among the US states. In addition, NIEMO has a demand-side as well as a supply-side impact estimation capability. Larger ships traversing the canal will prompt a redirection of some seaborne trade among US (and other) ports that will involve secondary effects in terms of the use of the other freight modes.

This chapter provides first-cut estimates by describing how available data can be used to estimate the effects of *one* of these dimensions, reduced seaborne imports to the West Coast Customs Districts (WCCD: Los Angeles Customs District, San Francisco Customs District, Columbia-Snake Customs District and Seattle Customs District). Reduced port activities into California, Oregon and Washington have negative effects on transportation and warehousing industries in the states that receive foreign imports; however, there are simultaneous positive effects in the various states from increased imports into the other port states because of the modal shift.

14.2 MODEL AND DATA

As input data for application of the supply-side NIEMO to estimate the effects of trade diversion from the WCCD, we used foreign imports data provided by WISERTrade, available at http://www.wisertrade.org, which is collected from the US Census Bureau's Foreign Trade Division. We selected foreign imports from 15 Pacific Rim countries[1] to the WCCD ports. We used a three-year average of total imports data, from 2010 through 2012, and show the resulting imports data in Table 14.1 by each Customs District.

Table 14.1   Selected foreign seaborne imports to the West Coast Customs Districts ($ million)

Customs District	Total imports	Transportation cost		Warehousing cost
		Rail	Truck	
Los Angeles	169,518.14	4,059.60	10,954.29	4,109.48
San Francisco	23,733.60	568.37	1,533.67	575.35
Columbia-Snake	9,452.28	226.36	610.81	229.14
Seattle	28,831.68	690.46	1,863.11	698.94
Total	231,535.70	5,544.79	14,961.88	5,612.91

Note: Imports values are averaged from 2010 through 2012.

We derived transportation (each truck and rail mode) and warehousing margins to total foreign imports available from the Bureau of Economic Analysis (BEA). Multiplying these margins to total imports of each Customs District in Table 14.1, we can calculate the transportation- and warehousing-related activity values for foreign imports of California, Oregon and Washington as displayed in Table 14.1.

To distribute transportation and warehousing values now headed to each state, we applied the modal proportions of the Freight Analysis Framework version 3 (FAF³), of which the Origin-Destination State Database for 2007 is available from the US Department of Transportation, Federal Highway Administration (USDOT-FHWA, 2009). The Freight Analysis Framework (FAF) provides a comprehensive picture of freight movements among states and major metropolitan areas by every major mode of freight transportation, while there are still some discussions on the accuracy of the data (Park et al., 2011).

Based on the studies of Rodrigue (2010) and Knight (2008), we chose 12 states (Alabama, Delaware, Florida, Georgia, Maryland, Massachusetts, New Jersey, New York, Pennsylvania, South Carolina, Texas and Virginia) in which ports potentially impacted by the Panama Canal expansion are located. From the FAF³ database for 2007, we calculated the portion of foreign imports distributed to those destination states from the WCCD ports by both truck and rail modes. Along with the portion going to each state, we estimated transportation and warehousing activity values of foreign imports distributed to each state by truck and rail modes; these estimated transportation and warehousing activity values of foreign imports to each state are presented in Table 14.2.

In determining the change of transportation activity values in destination

Table 14.2   Decreased transportation and warehousing activity values of foreign imports distributed from each West Coast Customs District to various states ($ million)

State	Los Angeles		San Francisco		Columbia-Snake		Seattle	
	TP value	WH value	TP value	WH value	TP value	WH value	TP value	WH value
AL	85.34	23.36	0.73	0.20	0.01	0.00	2.05	0.56
DE	2.05	0.56	0.13	0.04	0.00	0.00	0.84	0.23
FL	106.83	29.24	4.57	1.25	0.23	0.06	1.92	0.53
GA	193.28	52.90	5.82	1.59	0.41	0.11	9.14	2.50
MD	27.58	7.55	1.41	0.39	0.01	0.00	6.62	1.81
MA	40.68	11.13	6.88	1.88	0.03	0.01	3.24	0.89
NJ	468.05	128.11	7.25	1.99	5.49	1.50	19.67	5.38
NY	435.13	119.10	74.89	20.50	2.98	0.82	59.56	16.30
PA	120.97	33.11	6.77	1.85	0.82	0.23	20.01	5.48
SC	30.64	8.39	2.32	0.64	0.06	0.02	1.99	0.54
TX	909.63	248.98	32.57	8.91	92.09	25.20	9.28	2.54
VA	36.19	9.90	4.43	1.21	0.96	0.26	4.47	1.22
Total	2,456.36	672.33	147.78	40.45	103.09	28.22	138.77	37.98

Note: TP – Transportation; WH –Warehousing.

states by modal shift, we assumed that the transportation distance by ship from each Customs District to destination states is identical to the geographical distance between origin and destination states. We also assumed the freight arriving at destination states would additionally travel to nearby areas within 100 miles only using truck mode. Using Google maps we obtained the approximated highway distance from the core city of each WCCD to the principal cities of destination states. Note we also used weight data of foreign imports from WISERTrade to calculate the transportation values because we adopted freight transport costs per ton-mile from Ballou (2004): water mode is $0.0074/ton-mile, truck mode $0.2619/ton-mile and rail mode $0.0228/ton-mile. These data are shown in Table 14.3.

Based on NIEMO constructed by Park et al. (2008), we applied the supply-side NIEMO for this part of the study. Park (2008) and Park et al. (2008) elaborated a supply-side NIEMO, including empirical tests. Equation (14.1) suggests the structure of the supply-side NIEMO in a matrix form:

$$X^I = V(I - BC)^{-1}, \qquad (14.1)$$

Table 14.3   Weight and transportation activity values of foreign imports distributed from each Customs District to various states

State	Los Angeles			San Francisco		
	Distance (mile)	Weight (ton)	TP_delta ($ million)	Distance (mile)	Weight (ton)	TP_delta ($ million)
AL	2,200	152,231	81.25	2,400	2,119	0.84
DE	2,800	3,663	2.51	3,000	378	0.28
FL	2,700	190,575	125.64	3,000	13,325	9.82
GA	2,500	344,791	203.94	2,800	16,977	11.65
MD	2,700	49,196	31.94	2,900	4,109	2.89
MA	3,000	72,568	50.98	3,200	20,061	15.81
NJ	2,900	834,941	587.25	3,000	21,139	14.24
NY	2,900	776,213	539.51	3,000	218,287	160.89
PA	2,900	215,800	152.37	3,000	19,746	14.52
SC	2,600	54,659	34.74	2,800	6,767	4.64
TX	1,600	1,622,673	586.49	1,900	94,917	42.91
VA	2,800	64,552	43.23	3,000	12,898	6.73
Average	2,633	312,990	203.32	2,833	30,766	23.77
Total	31,600	4,381,862	2439.84	34,000	430,722	285.22

State	Columbia-Snake			Seattle		
	Distance (mile)	Weight (ton)	TP_delta ($ million)	Distance (mile)	Weight (ton)	TP_delta ($ million)
AL	2,600	35	0.022	2,700	3,911	1.66
DE	2,900	4	0.003	2,900	1,602	1.14
FL	3,300	833	0.678	3,400	3,671	3.08
GA	2,900	1,458	1.038	3,000	17,441	12.86
MD	2,800	49	0.033	2,800	12,635	8.67
MA	3,100	113	0.071	3,000	6,174	4.28
NJ	2,900	19,683	13.615	2,900	37,534	26.67
NY	2,900	10,676	7.541	2,900	113,663	80.78
PA	2,900	2,949	2.085	2,900	38,184	27.05
SC	2,900	217	0.154	3,000	3,796	2.80
TX	2,300	330,151	183.960	2,300	17,702	9.34
VA	3,000	3,446	2.358	3,000	8,526	6.29
Average	2,875	26,401	17.630	2,900	18,917	15.38
Total	34,500	369,614	211.559	34,800	264,840	184.61

Note: TP_delta = baseline transportation activity values (via truck and rail modes) – alternative transportation activity values (via water and truck modes).

where

X^I = the total input row vector,

V = a row vector of region-specific value added factors,

$B = (\hat{X}^d)^{-1}Z$ and $\hat{X}^d$ is the block diagonal matrix of vector X^d,

X^d = the total output column vector,

Z = the block diagonal matrix of direct technical flows between industries and

C = the block diagonal matrix of interregional trade flows.

14.3   RESULTS

For this part of the impact analysis of Panama Canal expansion, we assumed that foreign imports that currently arrive in the WCCD ports and are transported to the other US South and East Coast states by truck and rail modes, would be directly shipped to these states through the deepened Panama Canal. Therefore, transportation and warehousing activity values of foreign imports presented in Table 14.2 are assumed to decrease in California, Oregon and Washington. However, new transportation and warehousing activities occur in each state designated. We measured the difference between baseline transportation and alternative transportation modes to address transportation activity benefit. We did not account for any other transportation mode cost changes. Also, we allocate the decreased warehousing activity values to other destination states to be increased, assuming the warehousing margin is identical in the nation.

Based on this assumption, we estimated reduced impacts of transportation and warehousing activities for foreign imports in California, Oregon and Washington and increased impacts in other states separately, using the supply-side NIEMO. 'Direct impact' refers to the initial economic impact experienced in each sector in each state relating to the Panama Canal expansion. These are the change of foreign imports in California and the other 12 states in Table 14.2. 'Indirect impact' indicates the economic impact arising due to interindustry linkages, and are estimated via inverse coefficients in NIEMO. A Type I multiplier describes the sum of direct and indirect impacts relative to direct impact.

The main summary results of the reduced impacts into California, Oregon and Washington are shown in Tables 14.4 and 14.5. Tables 14.6 and 14.7 summarize the simultaneous positive impacts in the selected states stemming from the increased diverted transportation and warehousing values of imports relating to their augmented seaport activities. The full negative impacts are shown in Tables 14A.1 and 14A.2, while the positive impacts are shown in Tables 14A.3 and 14A.4 in the Appendix.

Table 14.4   Impacts of reduced transportation and warehousing activities in California, Oregon and Washington for the top three negatively impacted states ($ million)

Top three states	Direct impact	Indirect impact	Total impact
CA	−3,316.92	−1,608.90	−4,925.82
WA	−176.75	−119.21	−295.96
OR	−131.31	−80.65	−211.96
US total	−3,624.98	−2,092.81	−5,717.79
Rest of world	0.00	−76.93	−76.93
World total	−3,624.98	−2,169.74	−5,794.72

Note: Negative sign indicates economic losses.

Table 14.5   Impacts of reduced transportation and warehousing activities in California, Oregon and Washington for the top three impacted USC sectors ($ million)

USC Sector	Description	Direct impact	Indirect impact	Total impact
USC33	Transportation	−2,846.00	−263.09	−3,109.08
USC34	Postal and Warehousing	−778.98	−38.82	−817.80
USC30	Utility	0.00	−144.05	−144.05
Total		−3,624.98	−2,169.74	−5,794.72
Type I multiplier				1.599

Note: Negative sign indicates economic losses.

The reduced impacts of transportation and warehousing values for foreign imports in California, Oregon and Washington negatively affected the US national economy. Table 14.4 summarizes effects in the top three negatively impacted states.

Due to the reduction of transportation and warehousing values for foreign imports in the three West Coast states by $3, $0.2 and $0.1 billion, respectively, the most affected state was California ($–4,926 million); Washington ($–296 million) would be second and Oregon ($–212 million) third. Because the imports distributed to Texas by truck and rail modes were relatively large among the 12 port states, the total loss to Texas was relatively sizable (–$33 million).

In Table 14.5, the impacts of the top three USC sectors are shown. In USC Sectors 33, 34 and 30, the total economic losses are $3,109, $818 and $144 million, respectively. The Type I multiplier of this case was 1.599.

Table 14.6   Positive impacts of transportation mode change and
warehousing activity increase in other states for the top three
alternative destination states ($ million)

Top three states	Direct impact	Indirect impact	Total impact
TX	1,108.33	608.46	1,716.79
NY	945.44	467.39	1,412.83
NJ	778.75	361.44	1,140.19
US total	3,900.20	2,329.33	6,229.53
Rest of world	0.00	74.3042	74.30
World total	3,900.20	2,403.63	6,303.83

Note: Positive values indicate economic gains.

Table 14.7   Positive impacts of transportation modes change and
warehousing activity increase in other states for the top three
USC sectors ($ million)

USC Sector	Description	Direct impact	Indirect impact	Total impact
USC33	Transportation	3,121.22	345.36	3,466.58
USC34	Postal and Warehousing	778.98	41.74	820.72
USC43	Health Care and Social Assistances	0.00	163.11	163.11
Total		3,900.20	2,403.63	6,303.83
Type I multiplier				1.616

The economic impacts for all states and USC sectors are presented in Tables 14A.1 and 14A.2 in the Appendix.

Total positive gains due to the shift of transportation modes and new warehousing activities for foreign imports in the other states were $6,304 million. The impacts in the top three states and USC sectors are presented in Tables 14.6 and 14.7, respectively. Individual economic gain from the shift of transportation modes and increase of warehousing value was greatest in Texas at $1,717 million, and New York ($1,413 million) and New Jersey ($1,140 million) were ranked the second and third benefited states among the 12 states.

As transportation modes changed and warehousing activity of foreign imports to the 12 states increased, the gain to USC Sector 33 ($3,467 million) is the highest as expected, and USC Sectors 34 ($821 million) and 43 ($163 million) follow. The Type I multiplier in this increased activity case was 1.616. The impacts in all states and USC sectors are shown in Tables 14A.3 and 14A.4 in the Appendix.

14.4   CONCLUSIONS AND DISCUSSION

There are many analytical difficulties in attempting to estimate the US economic effects of the Panama Canal expansion. Among these are: (1) the problem of selecting an appropriate economic model; and (2) the problem of adapting plausible scenarios. The discussion in this chapter is a first attempt to face these challenges.

Modeling can only address short-term effects. In the longer term, an uncountable number of prices adjust and modeling is inconceivable. In the short term, there are demand-side as well as supply-side impacts – both as well as imports to various US ports are affected. The approach taken here only addresses imports because total foreign imports in the West Coast region account for total trade in the United States more than five times that of total foreign exports (Park, 2008). To do so, it applies NIEMO's supply-side interstate input-output model; Pacific Rim imports not destined for California, Oregon or Washington are subtracted from the Customs Districts of Los Angeles, San Francisco, Columbia-Snake and Seattle and added (diverted) to various competing US seaports. The results presented are the net multiplier effects of both phenomena.

However, the economic modeling approach adopted in this study has limits. First, we only focused on the change of transportation and warehousing activity values for foreign imports and did not account for any other transportation activity changes associated with importing weight. Also, we did not consider the entry point change for foreign trade of the states located in the US Midwest region[2] and the Mountain Division of the West region.[3] This was because these states' choice of ports for foreign trade depends on the decision process to minimize the multimodal delivery costs, a game theory type of decision process could be combined with the current NIEMO approach.

Indeed, a parallel demand-side analysis is the next analytical step to be taken. For example, as Los Angeles-Long Beach exports fewer shipments because Pacific Rim exports from other states can avoid land route shipping to Southern California, how will business at other ports grow and how will it fall in the Los Angeles-Long Beach area? This will involve demand-side modeling and the demand-side NIEMO will be applied. Also, we did not consider the US port investment strategy in this research. We assumed only the 100-mile distance, which is speculative in each destination state. For example, Savannah as a major recipient port in the

United States is undertaking port facility improvement and may offer lower delivery costs to destination cities from East and Gulf ports within the state or in adjacent states; or the same relative proportions of destination cities in the original baseline. This may be possible with the delivery via rail mode.

The other obvious elaborations will involve various smaller diversions. The discussion in this chapter assumes a 100 percent diversion of foreign imports arriving at the West Coast region, but being delivered to other regions outside the West Coast region. Yet, scaling down is easily done because NIEMO is linear. Furthermore, it will be valuable to model and address to what extent changes in shippers' (and to a lesser extent truckers') behavior will undermine the logistics and their activity cost. Modeling and forecasting are necessarily heroic, but they are useful conversation starters as policy makers develop plans for coping with the new realities of the Panama Canal. The original opening date of the Panama Canal has slipped from the 100th anniversary date of August 2014 to the current forecast of January 2016.

NOTES

1. China, Japan, Republic of Korea, Hong Kong, Singapore, Australia, Taiwan, Malaysia, Philippines, Indonesia, New Zealand, Macao, Papua New Guinea, Brunei and Thailand.
2. Indiana, Illinois, Michigan, Ohio, Wisconsin, Iowa, Kansas, Minnesota, Missouri, Nebraska, North Dakota and South Dakota.
3. Arizona, Colorado, Idaho, New Mexico, Montana, Utah, Nevada and Wyoming.

REFERENCES

Ballou, R.H. (2004), *Business Logistics/Supply Chain Management*, 5th edn. Upper Saddle River, NJ: Pearson Education.
Knight, K. (2008), *The Implications of Panama Canal Expansion to U.S. Ports and Coastal Navigation Economic Analysis*, US Army Corps of Engineers, Institute for Water Resources, White Paper.
Park, J.Y. (2007), 'The supply-driven input-output model: a reinterpretation and extension', Paper presented at the 46th Annual Meeting of the Western Regional Science Association, Newport Beach, California, 21–24 February.
Park, J.Y. (2008), 'The economic impacts of dirty-bomb attacks on the Los Angeles and Long Beach ports: applying the supply-driven NIEMO (National Interstate Economic Model)', *Journal of Homeland Security and Emergency Management*, **5** (1), Article 21.
Park, J.Y., P. Gordon, S.J. Kim, Y.K. Kim, J.E. Moore II and H.W. Richardson (2008), 'Estimating the state-by-state economic impacts of Hurricane Katrina', in H.W. Richardson, P. Gordon and J.E. Moore II (eds), *Natural Disaster*

Analysis After Hurricane Katrina. Cheltenham, UK and Northampton, MA, USA: Edward Elgar, pp. 147–86.

Park, J.Y., J. Cho, P. Gordon, J.E. Moore II, H.W. Richardson and S. Yoon (2011), 'Adding a freight network to a National Interstate Input-Output Model: a TransNIEMO application for California', *Journal of Transport Geography*, **19** (6), 1410–22.

Rodrigue, J.P. (2010), *Factors Impacting North American Freight Distribution in View of the Panama Canal Expansion*. Calgary: The Van Horne Institute.

USDOT-FHWA (2009), *Freight Analysis Framework State Database*. Washington, DC: FHWA.

APPENDIX

Table 14A.1   *The impacts of transportation and warehousing costs decreasing in California, Oregon and Washington for whole states ($ million)*

State	Direct impact	Indirect impact	Total impact
AL	0.00	−3.63	−3.63
AK	0.00	−1.60	−1.60
AZ	0.00	−21.16	−21.16
AR	0.00	−4.71	−4.71
CA	−3,316.92	−1,608.90	−4,925.82
CO	0.00	−11.75	−11.75
CT	0.00	−2.96	−2.96
DE	0.00	−0.97	−0.97
DC	0.00	−1.08	−1.08
FL	0.00	−12.77	−12.77
GA	0.00	−5.92	−5.92
HI	0.00	−4.80	−4.80
ID	0.00	−4.58	−4.58
IL	0.00	−12.65	−12.65
IN	0.00	−5.08	−5.08
IA	0.00	−2.88	−2.88
KS	0.00	−3.80	−3.80
KY	0.00	−3.30	−3.30
LA	0.00	−8.88	−8.88
ME	0.00	−1.33	−1.33
MD	0.00	−4.48	−4.48
MA	0.00	−7.30	−7.30
MI	0.00	−10.65	−10.65
MN	0.00	−6.34	−6.34
MS	0.00	−1.88	−1.88
MO	0.00	−5.38	−5.38
MT	0.00	−2.89	−2.89
NE	0.00	−6.50	−6.50
NV	0.00	−11.26	−11.26
NH	0.00	−1.61	−1.61
NJ	0.00	−6.20	−6.20
NM	0.00	−2.42	−2.42
NY	0.00	−14.42	−14.42
NC	0.00	−6.41	−6.41
ND	0.00	−0.59	−0.59
OH	0.00	−8.36	−8.36
OK	0.00	−3.35	−3.35

Table 14A.1   (continued)

State	Direct impact	Indirect impact	Total impact
OR	−131.31	−80.65	−211.96
PA	0.00	−8.52	−8.52
RI	0.00	−0.98	−0.98
SC	0.00	−2.37	−2.37
SD	0.00	−1.05	−1.05
TN	0.00	−3.79	−3.79
TX	0.00	−33.12	−33.12
UT	0.00	−6.18	−6.18
VM	0.00	−0.53	−0.53
VA	0.00	−4.89	−4.89
WA	−176.75	−119.21	−295. 96
WV	0.00	−1.58	−1.58
WI	0.00	−6.46	−6.46
WY	0.00	−0.71	0.71
US total	−3,624.98	−2,092.81	−5,717.79
Rest of world	0.00	−76.93	−76.93
World total	−3,624.98	−2,169.74	−5,794.72

Table 14A.2   *The impacts of transportation and warehousing costs decreasing in California, Oregon and Washington for whole USC sectors ($ million)*

USC Sector	Direct impact	Indirect impact	Total impact
USC01	0.00	−19.79	−19.79
USC02	0.00	−28.74	−28.74
USC03	0.00	−11.21	−11.21
USC04	0.00	−18.09	−18.09
USC05	0.00	−62.20	−62.20
USC06	0.00	−12.87	−12.87
USC07	0.00	−0.24	−0.24
USC08	0.00	−2.17	−2.17
USC09	0.00	−0.55	−0.55
USC10	0.00	−70.75	−70.75
USC11	0.00	−5.92	−5.92
USC12	0.00	−15.63	−15.63
USC13	0.00	−2.55	−2.55
USC14	0.00	−17.60	17.60
USC15	0.00	−32.26	−32.26
USC16	0.00	−20.08	−20.08
USC17	0.00	−17.46	−17.46

Table 14A.2   (continued)

USC Sector	Direct impact	Indirect impact	Total impact
USC18	0.00	−28.69	−28.69
USC19	0.00	−27.90	−27.90
USC20	0.00	−26.36	−26.36
USC21	0.00	−13.25	−13.25
USC22	0.00	−21.44	−21.44
USC23	0.00	−25.29	−25.29
USC24	0.00	−70.66	−70.66
USC25	0.00	−22.41	−22.41
USC26	0.00	−28.50	−28.50
USC27	0.00	−17.02	−17.02
USC28	0.00	−12.48	−12.48
USC29	0.00	−13.76	−13.76
USC30	0.00	−144.05	−144.05
USC31	0.00	−142.75	−142.75
USC32	0.00	−116.21	−116.21
USC33	−2,846.00	−263.09	−3,109.08
USC34	−778.98	−38.82	−817.80
USC35	0.00	−129.92	−129.92
USC36	0.00	−41.69	−41.69
USC37	0.00	−90.07	−90.07
USC38	0.00	−95.33	−95.33
USC39	0.00	−83.77	−83.77
USC40	0.00	−7.12	−7.12
USC41	0.00	−42.85	−42.85
USC42	0.00	−4.41	−4.41
USC43	0.00	−123.62	−123.62
USC44	0.00	−15.02	−15.02
USC45	0.00	−59.73	−59.73
USC46	0.00	−39.06	−39.06
USC47	0.00	−86.37	−86.37
Total	−3,624.98	−2,169.74	−5,794.72

Table 14A.3   *The impacts of transportation modes changing and*
warehousing cost increasing in other states for whole states
($ million)

State	Direct impact	Indirect impact	Total impact
AL	107.89	62.58	170.47
AK	0.00	0.75	0.75
AZ	0.00	6.10	6.10
AR	0.00	4.49	4.49
CA	0.00	50.58	50.58
CO	0.00	6.40	6.40
CT	0.00	8.39	8.39
DE	4.76	4.47	9.24
DC	0.00	1.64	1.64
FL	170.30	115.76	286.06
GA	286.60	134.91	421.50
HI	0.00	1.11	1.11
ID	0.00	1.09	1.09
IL	0.00	15.05	15.05
IN	0.00	6.83	6.83
IA	0.00	6.76	6.76
KS	0.00	4.21	4.21
KY	0.00	6.06	6.06
LA	0.00	9.83	9.83
ME	0.00	2.21	2.21
MD	53.27	34.94	88.21
MA	85.06	58.95	144.01
MI	0.00	13.17	13.17
MN	0.00	7.80	7.80
MS	0.00	5.11	5.11
MO	0.00	6.69	6.69
MT	0.00	1.06	1.06
NE	0.00	3.26	3.26
NV	0.00	2.25	2.25
NH	0.00	2.56	2.56
NJ	778.75	361.44	1,140.19
NM	0.00	3.44	3.44
NY	945.44	467.39	1,412.83
NC	0.00	15.15	15.15
ND	0.00	0.82	0.82
OH	0.00	18.03	18.03
OK	0.00	5.78	5.78
OR	0.00	3.34	3.34
PA	236.68	147.02	383.70

Table 14A.3   (continued)

State	Direct impact	Indirect impact	Total impact
RI	0.00	2.01	2.01
SC	51.92	33.49	85.41
SD	0.00	0.99	0.99
TN	0.00	11.23	11.23
TX	1,108.33	608.46	1,716.79
UT	0.00	2.97	2.97
VM	0.00	1.41	1.41
VA	71.21	43.58	114.78
WA	0.00	5.85	5.85
WV	0.00	2.22	2.22
WI	0.00	9.08	9.08
WY	0.00	0.66	0.66
US total	3,900.20	2,329.33	6,229.53
Rest of world	0.00	74.3042	74.30
World total	3,900.20	2,403.63	6,303.83

Table 14A.4   *The impacts of transportation modes changing and warehousing cost increasing in other states for whole USC sectors ($ million)*

USC Sector	Direct impact	Indirect impact	Total impact
USC01	0.00	27.66	27.66
USC02	0.00	10.50	10.50
USC03	0.00	10.68	10.68
USC04	0.00	16.40	16.40
USC05	0.00	46.44	46.44
USC06	0.00	15.78	15.78
USC07	0.00	4.84	4.84
USC08	0.00	3.09	3.09
USC09	0.00	0.44	0.44
USC10	0.00	88.67	88.67
USC11	0.00	23.67	23.67
USC12	0.00	19.73	19.73
USC13	0.00	4.09	4.09
USC14	0.00	38.51	38.51
USC15	0.00	49.17	49.17
USC16	0.00	15.50	15.50
USC17	0.00	33.81	33.81
USC18	0.00	41.37	41.37
USC19	0.00	39.73	39.73

Table 14A.4 (continued)

USC Sector	Direct impact	Indirect impact	Total impact
USC20	0.00	33.82	33.82
USC21	0.00	25.85	25.85
USC22	0.00	23.13	23.13
USC23	0.00	31.48	31.48
USC24	0.00	42.70	42.70
USC25	0.00	31.38	31.38
USC26	0.00	12.92	12.92
USC27	0.00	9.17	9.17
USC28	0.00	9.59	9.59
USC29	0.00	13.54	13.54
USC30	0.00	134.79	134.79
USC31	0.00	145.97	145.97
USC32	0.00	142.89	142.89
USC33	3,121.22	345.35	3,466.57
USC34	778.98	41.74	820.72
USC35	0.00	132.28	132.28
USC36	0.00	49.14	49.14
USC37	0.00	119.29	119.29
USC38	0.00	90.59	90.59
USC39	0.00	78.74	78.74
USC40	0.00	4.83	4.83
USC41	0.00	43.03	43.03
USC42	0.00	6.42	6.42
USC43	0.00	163.11	163.11
USC44	0.00	9.95	9.95
USC45	0.00	58.13	58.13
USC46	0.00	28.32	28.32
USC47	0.00	85.39	85.39
Total	3,900.20	2,403.63	6,303.83

Table 14A.5   Definition of USC sector system

USC Sector	Description
USC01	Live animals and live fish and meat, fish, seafood, and their preparations
USC02	Cereal grains and other agricultural products except for animal feed
USC03	Animal feed and products of animal origin, n.e.c.
USC04	Milled grain products and preparations, and bakery products
USC05	Other prepared foodstuffs and fats and oils
USC06	Alcoholic beverages
USC07	Tobacco products
USC08	Nonmetallic minerals (monumental or building stone, natural sands, gravel and crushed stone, n.e.c.)
USC09	Metallic ores and concentrates
USC10	Coal and petroleum products (coal and fuel oils, n.e.c.)
USC11	Basic chemicals
USC12	Pharmaceutical products
USC13	Fertilizers
USC14	Chemical products and preparations, n.e.c.
USC15	Plastics and rubber
USC16	Logs and other wood in the rough and wood products
USC17	Pulp, newsprint, paper, and paperboard and paper or paperboard articles
USC18	Printed products
USC19	Textiles, leather, and articles of textiles or leather
USC20	Nonmetallic mineral products
USC21	Base metal in primary or semi-finished forms and in finished basic shapes
USC22	Articles of base metal
USC23	Machinery
USC24	Electronic and other electrical equipment and components, and office equipment
USC25	Motorized and other vehicles (including parts)
USC26	Transportation equipment, n.e.c.
USC27	Precision instruments and apparatus
USC28	Furniture, mattresses and mattress supports, lamps, lighting fittings, and illuminated signs
USC29	Miscellaneous manufactured products, scrap, mixed freight, and Commodity unknown
USC30	Utility
USC31	Construction
USC32	Wholesale trade
USC33	Transportation
USC34	Postal and warehousing

Table 14A.5   (continued)

USC Sector	Description
USC35	Retail trade
USC36	Broadcasting and information services
USC37	Finance and insurance
USC38	Real estate and rental and leasing
USC39	Professional, scientific, and technical services
USC40	Management of companies and enterprises
USC41	Administrative support and waste management
USC42	Education services
USC43	Health care and social assistances
USC44	Arts, entertainment, and recreation
USC45	Accommodation and food services
USC46	Public administration
USC47	Other services except public administration

15. Conclusions
Harry W. Richardson and JiYoung Park

The primary purpose of this book has been to develop a version of a multiregional input-output (MRIO) model for the US economy as a whole. The model has a moderate degree of sectoral aggregation (47 sectors aggregated from more than 500). The key focus has been on spatial disaggregation with each of the 50 states featured plus Washington, DC and the 'Rest of the world'. The model (National Interstate Economic Model – NIEMO) was built quite recently, beginning about nine years ago.

The extensive geographical disaggregation permitted us to develop a highway network for the model that made it possible to investigate transportation issues. We placed the conceptual and methodological components of the model in Chapter 2. This permits regional scientists and economists to evaluate how the model was built, and to spare the practicing planners (if they so desire) from having to deal with complex model details, enabling them to focus on the applications of the model and their policy implications.

An interesting feature of the model is that it did not require primary data collection, except from the perspective of estimating direct (final demand) inputs for each case study application. However, the model required complex construction of connections and bridges between multiple and different data sets. However, once developed, the model is very adaptable to a wide range of applications, in this book primarily in terms of terrorist attacks and natural disasters.

The examination of bridge and tunnel closures on the National Interstate Highway System (we focused on terrorist attacks, but a single event could be a natural disaster) enabled an assessment of how truckers might adjust their routes (Chapter 3). A somewhat surprising finding was that travel costs and times did not increase substantially, primarily because of route redundancies and the possibility of route planning on very long freight hauls. Eventually, we plan to develop a multimodal system (taking account of rail and air freight) that should exhibit even greater flexibility in the national transportation system.

We wrote a paper on how the 9/11 attack affected the New York region, but it was excluded from this book because it relied more on econometric time series than on the economic impact model. If we had used NIEMO or even FlexNIEMO, we would have been restricted to state-wide impacts (New York, New Jersey and Connecticut) and the level of spatial disaggregation would have been much too limited for analysis of a local (nevertheless shattering) event.

A conceptual question of interest is whether we could spatially disaggregate the national model (NIEMO) even more. Currently, it is an interstate model. Would it be possible to disaggregate to the county level with 3,000+ zones? Conceptually, yes. In practice, it would be very difficult. For example, in theory one could outline a model with 3,000 zones and 500 sectors, the maximum degree of spatial and sectoral disaggregation. However, there is inadequate computer capacity to invert a matrix with 2.25 trillion cells. Moreover, data availability is problematic because although we have developed interstate trade flow data (with a heavy emphasis on data obtained from the Commodity Flow Survey) there are no parallel sources for inter-county trade flows. In Chapter 11, we have made an attempt to descend below the state level because most of the damages associated with the Joplin, Missouri tornado of May 2011 were confined to two counties (Newton and Jasper). However, the sub-state analysis is not very sophisticated, and relies on proportions. Another possible route to more spatial disaggregation might be to develop a nationwide inter-metropolitan model. The number of zones would be more manageable, and except for agricultural products, it might be possible to re-estimate state trade flows down to the metropolitan level.

Many of the chapters in the book deal with direct output or employment impacts that are simulations based on exogenous shocks (for example, terrorist attacks). Only a few (for example, Hurricane Katrina, the Gulf oil spill, the Joplin tornado, Hurricane Sandy and the West Coast ports shutdown) deal with real world events. A generic problem in dealing with regional policies and/or exogenous shocks is how to 'unscramble the eggs,' that is, to separate out the 'no policy' or 'zero shock' situation. For example, consider the case of 9/11. It happened in a period of mild recession so it was very difficult to isolate the economic disruption resulting from the 9/11 incident from the normal course of economic events. When a policy or shock is inextricably intertwined with other changes in economic activity, accurately separating out the direct final demand inputs is a major challenge.

A major criticism of input-output models is their reliance on fixed production coefficients, and neglect of the relative price-substitution effects beloved by economists. This can be contrasted with computable general equilibrium (CGE) models, all of which deal with the combined demand-supply price effects of markets. The major difference is that none of the CGE models have a significant degree of spatial disaggregation, not surprising given that data on small area price changes are very difficult to obtain. In our research, because of our focus on spatial changes we believe that the payoff in terms of geographical disaggregation compensates for the limited attention to market adjustments.

However, we have made some modest modifications of the models to allow for relaxation in the constant production coefficients assumptions. Some years ago (1992), we introduced price-substitutions into a version of the model dealing with Hurricane Andrew. The key idea was to measure the supply inelasticities associated with the construction recovery costs. The results are not reported in this book. Much more recently, we developed a version of NIEMO that we call FlexNIEMO, which complemented the typical demand-side model with a supply-driven model.

FlexNIEMO has a supply-side as well as a demand-side capability. For example, in applications to hypothetical or actual port closures (such as the impact of Hurricane Katrina on the Port of New Orleans), the loss of exports is best modeled via the demand-side NIEMO whereas the loss of imports is modeled via the supply-side NIEMO.

All of these models are most useful for short-term impact analysis because buyers and sellers can be expected to eventually make substitutions in light of the price changes that follow major disruptions. Missing these is a well-known limitation of the input-output approach. In Chapter 10 we described how to use post-event information on concurrent demand and value-added changes to identify the technological (production function) changes that occurred after a major disruption. We compared these results to the estimates from the baseline NIEMO to show the detailed impacts of the many substitutions and adaptations.

We used FlexNIEMO to construct a supply-side model of NIEMO that generates month-by-month changes (see Chapter 9). The approach allows the fixed coefficients in the input-output world to be continuously modified, reflecting previous economic events and changes in interindustry relationships. The analysis was restricted to USC Sector 10 (petroleum refining) to model the disruptions to the oil industry resulting from the closure of the Port of New Orleans. The major result in comparing the standard NIEMO results with FlexNIEMO was a dramatic reduction in the multiplier from 1.83 to 1.07, indicating that allowing for adjustments substantially moderates the multiplier impacts.

Another major modification to standard input-output analysis is introduced in the Gulf oil spill analysis (Chapter 10). The traditional approach in MRIO models is to estimate only Type I multipliers (direct and indirect; see Miller and Blair, 2009). The main reason was that services were assumed to be non-tradable, and hence induced impacts do not occur across state boundaries. This is not accurate. The induced effects in the directly affected states were calculated by applying IMPLAN's state-level models. These calculations yielded the state's domestic imports and exports and these were used to augment domestic imports and exports from the initial NIEMO application. Another requirement was to estimate the additional interstate trade impacts, using ratios that relate trade prompted by induced activity versus trade prompted by direct and indirect impacts. An important rationale for this extension is that the consequences of the oil spill had major ripple effects in other states that included induced impacts, especially in large states such as California and Texas.

Although there are more case studies in a companion book using the Southern California Planning Model (SCPM) than in this book (Richardson et al., 2015), it could be argued that NIEMO is more significant. This is in spite of the fact that SCPM was much longer in development and that it closely conforms to the concept of a regional economic model. One of the reasons is that SCPM applications are restricted to Southern California. Although, as that book reveals, there is a wide range of feasible problems that the model can handle going beyond terrorist attacks and natural disasters, the limitation in the model's geographical scope is a drawback. While it is possible to develop a version for other metropolitan areas it has never been attempted. Hence, NIEMO has many more applications, with very few limits.

The other main reason for the attraction of NIEMO is its role in the historical development of MRIO models. The key ideas were developed by Leontief, Isard and their followers but full implementation was held back by incomplete data and computer capacity constraints. We were able to overcome these former obstacles and build a fully-fledged operational model capable of tackling almost any economic impact problem. Furthermore, we have refined the analysis in directions not predicted by the founders of this approach: TransNIEMO (adding the national highway network), FlexNIEMO (combining demand and supply models and introducing price-substitution effects) and accommodating interstate trade in services via Type II multiplier effects.

REFERENCES

Miller, R.E. and P.D. Blair (2009), *Input-Output Analysis: Foundations and Extensions*, 2nd edn. Englewood Cliffs, NJ: Prentice Hall.

Richardson, H.W., Q. Pan, J.Y. Park and J.E. Moore II (eds) (2015), *Regional Economic Impacts of Terrorist Attacks, Natural Disasters and Metropolitan Policies*. Heidelberg: Springer.

Index

ports shutdown 227–8, 231–5, 241–2
re-routings/diversions 39, 56, 257–9, 263–7
US Department of Commerce results of Sandy 210
USDOT (US Department of Transportation) 4, 6, 25, 26

vaccination measures 98, 129, 131
value transfer approach 82
VAR (vector autoregressive model) 92
Vatn, A. 82
vessel trade mode 222–4, 232, 233, 235, 236, 238, 240
victim compensation 180
VSL (value of statistical life) 80, 193–4

Wang, Z. 7
warehousing, and trade diversion 252–9, 262–6
Washington (State), impact of trade diversion 253, 256–7, 262–4
waterborne commerce *see* seaborne trade
WCCD (West Coast Custom Districts) Panama Canal expansion 252–60
welfare costs 81

West Coast 256–60
Customs Districts 224, 244, 247, 253, 272
impact on import-exports 223–4, 226, 235–44, 245
Los Angeles-Long Beach ports 221–2
multilevel model 227–34
NIEMO 225–6
ports shutdown 221–2
sectoral impacts 242–3, 244
State impacts 246–7
Wheelis, M. 128
Willoughby, H.E. 214
Winston, C. 40
WISER trade 101, 227, 252, 254
WMD (weapons of mass destruction) 140, 141
Wolfe, P. 40
Woodridge, J.M. 251

Xie, F. 25

Yoon, S. 42

zero sum game in tourism 47
Zuckerman, S. 245